BEST PRACTICES in COMMUNITY MENTAL HEALTH

Also available from Lyceum Books, Inc.

A Pocket Guide

BEST PRACTICES in COMMUNITY MENTAL HEALTH

Edited by

VIKKI L. VANDIVER

*Portland State University and Oregon Health &
Science University, Portland, Oregon*

LYCEUM
BOOKS, INC.

Chicago, IL 60637

Published by

LYCEUM BOOKS, INC.
5758 S. Blackstone Ave.
Chicago, Illinois 60637
773+643-1903 fax
773+643-1902 phone
lyceum@lyceumbooks.com
www.lyceumbooks.com

6 5 4 3 2   13 14 15 16

ISBN 978-1-935871-04-0

Cover credit: © Teresa Levite | Dreamstime.com.

Printed in the United States of America.

Library of Congress Cataloging-in-Publication Data

Best practices in community mental health : a pocket guide / edited by Vikki L. Vandiver.
    pages cm
  Includes bibliographical references.
  ISBN 978-1-935871-04-0 (pbk. : alk. paper)
  1. Community mental health services—Handbooks, manuals, etc. 2. Mental health services—Handbooks, manuals, etc. I. Vandiver, Vikki, 1956–
  RA790.5.B47   2013
  362.19689—dc23
                                                          2012028610

To Kevin, man of myth, magic, mirth, and mischief and my eternal muse. And to the memories of my parents, who taught me that kindness would always be the gold standard of best practices.

To Kevin, man of myth, magic, mirth, and mischief and my eternal muse. And to the memories of my parents, who taught me that kindness would always be the gold standard of best practices.

Contents

Tables

Figures

Preface

Whether you work in a community mental health agency, manage a behavioral health organization, or see individuals and families privately, you have probably asked yourself, "What are the best practices I can offer my clients, and where do I go to get them?" The answers to these questions start with this book, *Best Practices in Community Mental Health: A Pocket Guide.* In twenty short chapters, readers will walk away with a useful reference guide to some of the most commonly applied best-practice interventions, approaches, and programs used in community mental health, behavioral health, and educational settings for individuals with mental health conditions and their family members.

The purpose of this book is to help busy mental health practitioners, administrators, and students from a variety of disciplines—social work, counseling, psychiatric nursing, public psychiatry, psychiatric rehabilitation—rapidly identify and select from a variety of mental health approaches using a single source that provides a portable summary of clinical resources. Although this book is not meant to replace the need for practitioners to cull through academic and web-based resources to locate specific best practices for their unique settings and clientele, it can help fast-track that effort by providing readers with a ready list of practices considered the foundation of a well-rounded mental health system.

Although many of the best practices described in this book are linked with widely established evidence-based practices, such as those found at sites like the Substance Abuse and Mental Health Services Administration, the Robert Wood Johnson Foundation, and the Hazelden and Dartmouth Psychiatric Research Center, other topics are considered promising or emerging best practices that have strong clinical or cultural consensus (e.g., supported education, tribal best practices). Some approaches emphasize an empowerment focus (e.g., recovery), and others focus on children- and youth-oriented best practices (e.g., early intervention for youth psychosis). For administrators, a final section describes the implementation of an organizational best practice, the Sanctuary Model, which promotes a trauma-free, healthy, and safe environment for staff and clients. Ultimately, the best practices described in this book were selected on the basis of a combination of expert knowledge (e.g., clinical consensus) and science (e.g., empirical evidence), not personal practice styles or methodology.

What Do We Mean by "Best Practice"?

For the purposes of this book, best practices are considered in the context of the following definitions:

• Research evidence proving that a practice "works" (evidence based) (Hayes, 2005)

• Practitioners' opinions about what works in practice (clinical consensus) (Pliszka et al., 2007)

• Cultural and local context that determines whether and how a practice works here and now (practice-based evidence), along with a scientific framework that incorporates culture-based interventions (practice-based evidence) (Walker, Singer, & Bigelow, 2012)

• Guidelines or a general plan of action that requires specification to fit particular circumstances in which the system of care is being implemented (Public Health Agency of Canada, 2002)

Methodology
How Topics Were Chosen

The list of best practices selected for this book was developed through reviewing bibliographies of book chapters, journal articles, and governmental and foundation reports, and asking mental health professionals and chief executive officers for descriptions of practices used in their settings. The literature searches covered the period 2000–2010. Recent authoritative reviews of literature and professional and governmental reports that were in press or presented at scientific meetings in the past five years were given priority for inclusion. In addition, a comprehensive search of eight primary online mental health and behavioral sites was conducted: the Substance Abuse and Mental Health Services Administration (http://www.samhsa.gov), the National Association of State Mental Health Program Directors (http://nasmhpd.org), One Sky Center—American Indian/ Alaska Native National Resource Center (http://www.oneskycenter.org/mhsa/ best-practices.cfm), the Cochrane Collaboration (http://www.cochrane.org), the Campbell Collaboration (http://www.campbellcollaboration.org), the American Academy of Child and Adolescent Psychiatry (http://www.aacap.org), the Robert Wood Johnson Foundation (http://www.rwjf.org), and the Hazelden and Dartmouth Psychiatric Research Center (http://geiselmed.dartmouth.edu).

Description of Online Sites

This section describes the sites searched for readers interested in more detail about these sources.

Clinicians often look to the Substance Abuse and Mental Health Services Administration (SAMHSA) for the most currently approved best practices in mental health. Specifically, two resources in the SAMHSA website that were particularly useful for this book are the National Registry of Evidence-Based Practices and Programs (NREPP) (http://www.nrepp.samhsa.gov/AboutNREPP.aspx) and the Center for Substance Abuse Treatment's Treatment Improvement Protocols (TIPS) (http://www.ncbi.nlm.nih.gov/books/NBK82999/).

The NREPP is a searchable online registry of mental health and substance abuse interventions that have been reviewed and rated by independent reviewers. The purpose of the registry is to provide the public with a summary of scientifically based intervention approaches that provide general information about the intervention, research outcomes, quality of research and dissemination readiness, materials reviewed, and developer contact information. The caveat regarding the interventions listed in the registry is that not all report effective outcomes, and they should be screened closely for efficacy and practicality to your particular organization and setting.

The TIPS are best-practices guidelines developed by expert consensus guideline processes and/or a search of the literature. Clinicians can select from fifty-four different guidelines that range from substance abuse treatment for persons with co-occurring disorders to pharmacotherapies.

The National Association of State Mental Health Program Directors is a nonprofit organization dedicated to serving the needs of the nation's public mental health systems, which are responsible for serving nearly seven million people annually on a budget of nearly $31 billion. The organization serves as the national representative and advocate for state mental health agencies and their directors. Along with its research institute, it is the only membership organization that works to keep its members current on emerging policy issues, research findings, best practices, and the latest on human and technical network development and management. In other words, the organization helps put the glue to the pieces of how best practices are integrated into and institutionalized in public mental health agencies and organizations in all states.

One Sky Center is a national resource center and leader among American Indian and Alaska Native communities for developing literature, conducting research, and influencing policy as it affects tribes' health, mental health, and well-being. A goal of the center has been to lead a national and state effort to introduce more culturally competent best practices in Indian country. Readers will appreciate the expanding list of culturally endorsed best practices that One Sky Center has been responsible for developing and disseminating.

The Cochrane and Campbell collaborations are online, web-based resources that represent the gold standard in terms of providing a resource for practitioners seeking the highest level of evidence-based reviews. In particular, practitioners use the sites to determine whether their services or interventions have the evidence to support their (continued) use. Specifically, the Cochrane Collaboration provides readers with a list of systematic reviews of primary research in human health care (e.g., prevention, treatment, rehabilitation), whereas the Campbell Collaboration produces systematic reviews of the effects of social interventions.

The American Academy of Child and Adolescent Psychiatry is a professional association for physicians specializing in child psychiatry. The goal of the organization is to promote healthy development of children, adolescents, and families through research and training. The organization specializes in developing evidence-based guidelines and best-practices parameters for specific childhood disorders. What makes this site so useful to readers is the emphasis on practice parameters that include patient-oriented and clinician-oriented parameters. Patient-oriented parameters provide recommendations to guide clinicians toward best practices for clients, whereas clinician-oriented parameters guide clinicians with information (i.e., principles) needed to develop their practice-based skills (Pliszka et al., 2007).

The Robert Wood Johnson Foundation is a private, philanthropic foundation that supports a variety of projects related to health and mental health. For this pocket guide, we included the results from a multiyear evidence-based practices project with the foundation and the New Hampshire–Dartmouth Psychiatric Research Center. This collaborative project identified six core mental health best practices and established the tool kits to implement them. These practices include medication management, illness management and recovery, assertive community treatment, (family) psychoeducation, supported employment, and integrated dual-disorders treatment. This site includes many other references to best practices that will be useful to readers.

The Hazelden and Dartmouth Psychiatric Research Center is a new collaboration between Hazelden, a nonprofit organization, and the Dartmouth Psychiatric Research Center, both of which are leaders in the research and development of evidence-based practices. A hallmark of this collaboration is the publication of the Co-Occurring Disorder Program, which is the first comprehensive, evidence-based program for the treatment of nonsevere co-occurring disorders. Readers interested in more in-depth reviews of the best practices described in this book are referred to these larger sites.

Selecting the Topics

As a result of the literature search, interviews, and website reviews, approximately twenty best practices in mental health were identified for the review process. Using a combination of empirical evidence and clinical consensus, four criteria were used to determine the strength of the underlying empirical and/or clinical support of each best practice topic. Using a slightly modified version of the four-level rating criteria established by the American Academy of Child and Adolescent Psychiatry for patient- and clinician-oriented best-practice parameters (Pliszka et al., 2007), each topic had to meet at least one of the top three categories (e.g., levels 1–3) to be included in this guide:

Level 1: MS = *Minimal Standard* refers to recommendations or practices based on rigorous empirical evidence (e.g., randomized, controlled trials) and/or overwhelming clinical consensus. Minimal standards apply more than 95 percent of the time (i.e., in almost all cases).

Level 2: CG = *Clinical Guideline* refers to recommendations or practices that are based on strong empirical evidence (e.g., nonrandomized, controlled trials) and/or strong clinical consensus. Clinical guidelines apply approximately 75 percent of the time (i.e., most cases).

Level 3: OP = *Option* refers to recommendations or practices that are acceptable based on emerging empirical evidence (e.g., uncontrolled trials or case series/reports) or clinical opinion, but lack strong empirical evidence and/or strong clinical consensus.

Level 4: NE = *Not Endorsed* refers to practices that are known to be ineffective or contraindicated. (Pliszka et al., 2007, p. 898)

The initial review of all topics was conducted by the editor and cross-checked with research colleagues and community providers. Through a consensus process, it was determined that each of the topics met the criteria for level 1, 2, or 3 evidence or consensus. There are no level 4 (not endorsed) topics included in the book. Key authors associated with these literature reviews were then contacted and solicited to write a brief chapter for the pocket guide. Because of the overlap of some categories, the chapters do not list the assigned ratings (e.g., level 1) used in the screening process. Instead, authors were asked to describe the supporting evidence for their topic. We believe that this process allows readers to determine the relevance and practicality of each of the best practices for their particular setting.

Limitations

Although this pocket guide offers an excellent introduction to some of the most meaningful mental health best practices available to clients and their families, let's talk briefly about what it does not offer.

If readers are looking for a textbook that is an exhaustive overview of all evidence-based practices in mental health, is discipline specific (e.g., social work, psychology), is diagnostic specific (e.g., major depression, schizophrenia), provides a workbook with forms, or is a guide for accreditation purposes (e.g., social work's emphasis on retooling academic textbooks to meet new accreditation competencies), our book may disappoint.

As noted earlier, we do not make the claim that every practice, program, or intervention described in this book meets the conventional criteria of evidence, such as having one to two random, controlled trials—although many practices listed in the book certainly have met the research standards for qualifying as a level 1 minimal standard (e.g., supported employment, supported housing, illness management and recovery, assertive community treatment). Nor do we suggest that each of the interventions or approaches described, such as tribal best practices, recovery-oriented services, or spirituality, consistently meets strong clinical consensus (level 2) or is broadly endorsed by all community mental health programs.

Although each chapter is grouped into a particular part, this does not preclude each chapter from overlapping with other sections. Just because integrated treatment (chapter 1) is listed under behavioral health care (part 1) does not imply that it cannot have community features (part 2) as well. The choice to place each chapter under a specific subtitle was an editorial decision. Readers are encouraged to think of all the chapters as overlapping in multiple categories. For example, psychiatric rehabilitation (chapter 15) operates as both a field of practice and an intervention based on an educational approach (part 4) to delivery. However, as a best practice, it is also very empowering (part 3), can be delivered in the community (part 2), and has a curriculum that emphasizes an orientation toward behavioral health care (e.g., mental health, wellness) (part 1). But mostly it has an educational orientation. So clinicians who are interested in offering best practices with an educational or curriculum-based design will enjoy the three chapters in the part "Education-Oriented Best Practices." Last, the book is not intended to be comprehensive or exhaustive; it is intended more as a handy resource for busy practitioners who want a succinct and easily accessible, desktop overview of client- and community-directed interventions and approaches.

Unique Features

This book has several unique features. First, when referring to individuals with mental health conditions, the language used in this book adheres as closely as possible to the use of person-centered language, or person-first language, as endorsed by the psychiatric rehabilitation literature. This means that the reader will see phrases like "person with schizophrenia," "consumer," "client," "student," and "family member who has a relative with a mental health condition." The choice of term is determined more by the context of discussion rather than any allegiance to a particular diagnosis (e.g., major depression) or diagnostic category (e.g., mood disorders). For example, in the chapter on supported education, Unger refers to participants with mental health conditions enrolled in an educational program as "students."

Second, each chapter begins with a personal story of an individual, family member, or provider who has experience with the best practice described. The idea for a case description for each best practice was to illustrate how the practices or programs described were experienced from the ground up. In other words, how do participants experience the practice, service, or intervention? By providing a first-person account of how services are experienced from the user side, readers can have a better idea of what the practice or service looks like from an insider's viewpoint.

Third, each chapter is written using the following outline: introduction, case study, background or history of practice, theoretical perspective, principles, implementation steps, evidence, assessment and evaluation, provider competencies, and future challenges. This format is borrowed from the work of Hayes

(2005), who developed a best-practice protocol that follows scientific methodology and can be used as a model for training agency staff.

The introduction is designed to provide readers with an overview of each chapter topic and objectives. In some cases, the topic is a specific best practice, like supported employment (chapter 10). Other topics provide an overview of best practices used to work with people with co-occurring health and mental health conditions (e.g., chapter 4).

The case study provides readers with a personal account of how each best practice described is experienced through the eyes of the user, client, family member, and/ or clinician.

The section on background or history of each chapter is designed to introduce readers to the foundation or history of the practice described.

The theoretical perspective is a brief reference to the larger theory, lens, or perspective that shapes the best practice described. Readers are provided a short reference section on related theories and are encouraged to explore these theories more in depth separate from the pocket guide.

Principles are used throughout each chapter to provide a conceptual anchor to the methods and strategies described in each chapter. Although empirical evidence may be available to support these principles, they are primarily based on expert opinion and clinical experience. It is the editor's belief that principles help practitioners connect their practices to overarching goals rather than personal ideology and serve as valuable road maps for professional behavior.

The step-by-step implementation guidelines are practical, specific strategies that clinicians can use to implement or demonstrate their best practice. As in most how-to guidelines, clinician training will influence how much fidelity (i.e., adherence to original model) is maintained with the delivery of each best practice.

The "evidence" listed for each practice is meant to inform readers of the various levels of empirical and nonempirical evidence that supports the best practice described. In some cases, the practice described would be considered a promising practice with research under way (level 2 or 3) (e.g., chapter 16, on supported education; chapter 18, on early intervention for youth psychosis), or a culturally sanctioned best practice (e.g., chapter 6, on tribal best practices). Other best practices described meet the more rigorous criteria for evidence-based practices—two or more random, controlled trials (level 1; e.g., chapter 7, on assertive community treatment; chapter 10, on supported employment). Whereas other best practices described (e.g., chapter 11, on spirituality; chapter 12, on recovery-oriented services) reflect practice philosophies that are strongly woven into existing research protocols and emerge as positive outcomes (levels 2 and 3).

The point of having each chapter describe the evidence that supports the described practice is to illustrate to readers that not all best practices meet the rigorous criteria of having undergone a random, controlled trial. Yet there can still be value and meaning for an agency or community mental health program in having a broad menu of best practices for clients, families, and clinicians to select from. The benefit of using the "best practice" label for selected services is that the term opens the door for a wider balance of offerings that balance scientific rigor (e.g., evidence-based practices), practicality, and adaptation to local context and culture (e.g., best practices).

Assessment and evaluation are described in each chapter as a means for clinicians to understand the responsibility we have to provide comprehensive assessments, define our outcomes, and measure those outcomes. Each chapter provides readers with references to commonly used assessment and evaluation measures for the best practices described. For example, Anthony, Forbess, and Furlong-Norman (chapter 15, on psychiatric rehabilitation) list three core psychiatric rehabilitation outcome measures to assess and evaluate residential stability, social functioning, vocational functioning, and social support.

Provider competencies have been recognized as a key goal in workforce development strategies for mental health programs that are implementing best practices. Staff development trainings are commonly included in many practice manuals and tool kits (e.g., see the website of the Hazelden and Dartmouth Psychiatric Research Center). Each chapter identifies specific competencies that clinicians can strive toward as they move forward in offering specific best practices. For example, Unger (chapter 16, on supported education) describes four critical provider competencies necessary for implementing supported-education practices: familiarity with the postsecondary environment, understanding requirements for financial aid, skills for setting educational goals, and linking students to resources on campus and the community. Other chapters have equally practical recommendations.

All chapters conclude with a brief listing of relevant websites and glossary of terms.

Finally, most figures and tables were created specifically for each chapter and thus are self-contained illustrations of the practices described. The figures are designed to provide a heuristic overview of the organization and concepts described in each chapter. For example, Bloom (chapter 20, on the Sanctuary Model) provides a five-stage figure illustrating the steps for reducing organizational trauma through the implementation of the Sanctuary Model of Organizational Change.

Structure and Content

The book is structured as follows: introduction, six parts, twenty chapters, and concluding remarks.

The book begins with the introduction "What Are Best Practices and Why Should We Care?" The overview is designed to introduce readers to the core definitions of best practices, application toward practice, and research challenges inherent in practice.

The book is divided into six parts: part 1, "Behavioral-Health-Care-Oriented Best Practices"; part 2, "Community-Oriented Best Practices; part 3, "Empowerment-Oriented Best Practices"; part 4, "Education-Oriented Best Practices"; part 5, "Children- and Youth-Oriented Best Practices"; and part 6, "Organization-Oriented Best Practices: Pulling It All Together."

Part 1: Behavioral-Health-Care-Oriented Best Practices

Part 1 begins with an overview of best practices that address behavioral health issues increasingly seen in community mental health settings, such as high rates of comorbid medical and psychiatric conditions, co-occurring mental health and substance use issues, role ambiguity between medical and nonmedical providers involved in psychopharmacotherapy, medication and treatment self-management, and challenges regarding providing psychotherapeutic treatment for clients who choose not to be abstinent. The chapters selected for this section emphasize best practices that illustrate integrated care models, wellness- and health-promotion philosophies, and person-directed care strategies.

Chapter 1, "Integrated Treatment for People with Co-occurring Mental Illness and Substance Use Disorders," provides readers with a solid understanding of the need for practitioners to expand their skills and for systems to integrate their services to better treat clients who present with co-occurring disorders and are in need of multiple treatment approaches, or what is referred to as integrated treatment. The authors emphasize that a steady stream of research over the past two decades has yielded promising results, suggesting that integrated treatment is effective and that certain components contribute to its success.

Chapter 2, "Nonmedical Roles in Psychopharmacotherapy," describes different roles that a nonmedical mental health provider would assume when working with clients who are prescribed psychiatric medications. These roles are counselor, consultant, educator, advocate, researcher, and monitor—much of what resembles a psychoeducational model of practice but with a medical focus. The authors stress a collaborative approach between provider and client, as well as recognition of potential ethical conflicts and power differentials related to coercion and medication use.

Chapter 3, "Illness Management and Recovery," picks up on the provider roles described in chapter 2 for managing medications and expands it to the larger perspective of helping clients manage all aspects of their psychiatric disorder. The authors describe the main goals of illness management and recovery as an intervention designed to help clients set their own goals and personal strategies for managing their illness.

Chapter 4, "Best Practices for Improving the Health of Persons with Serious Mental Illness and Comorbid Physical Health Conditions," provides a broad overview of best-practice strategies and implementation approaches for individuals with severe mental illness complicated by physical health conditions, such as diabetes, cardiovascular disease, and hypertension. The authors emphasize best practices that incorporate access to continuous, coordinated, and comprehensive health services for clients and their families.

Chapter 5, "Harm Reduction in Mental Health Practice," describes individual harm-reduction psychotherapy for individuals who are engaging in problem behavior and want to minimize the hazards of that behavior, without abstinence.

Despite the lack of randomized clinical trials, the authors make a solid case for incorporating this practice into mainstream mental health practice settings.

Part 2: Community-Oriented Best Practices

Part 2 overviews five best practices in which the primary point of provider and client engagement occurs in community settings or environments rather than in-office clinics. These settings include barns, neighborhoods, and businesses.

Chapter 6, "Tribal Best Practices: A Native American Horsemanship Program for Indian Youth," describes a unique equine-assisted intervention program for at-risk Indian youth that is recognized by state and tribal authorities as a tribal best practice and is endorsed by nine confederated tribes and state government. In a different twist of what constitutes evidence, readers will gain an understanding of different ways of knowing what works for culturally diverse communities and the efforts to describe, document, disseminate, and measure culturally specific programs.

Chapter 7, "Assertive Community Treatment and Recovery," overviews a model of community treatment for persons in the early stages of developing a mental illness and in need of a community and team approach to care. The authors emphasize the flexibility of ACT, integration of multiple disciplines, and the importance of practitioners conveying a message of recovery, hope, and compassion.

Chapter 8, "Supported Housing," describes the importance of housing as an essential component of mental health services and a critical factor affecting community integration of persons with psychiatric disabilities. The authors describe in clear detail how supported housing is the housing approach most conducive to the goals of consumer empowerment and community integration and is based on the belief that individuals with psychiatric disabilities can assume roles and lifestyles as community members in a normal, integrated housing setting.

Chapter 9, "Housing First: Homelessness, Recovery, and Community Integration," expands the previous chapter on supported housing by examining the evidence for combining housing, intensive community-based treatment, and a consumer-driven philosophy for people with psychiatric disabilities and co-occurring addiction disorders. The authors effectively debunk myths surrounding the treatment-first model of housing by illustrating solid empirical data for housing first, especially as it pertains to individuals with profound socioeconomic and dual diagnostic issues.

Chapter 10, "Supported Employment," describes an individualized psychiatric rehabilitation approach designed to help people with mental health conditions obtain and maintain competitive employment in the community. The authors provide crisp detail describing the practical aspects of implementing the step-by-step process for helping clients access employment.

Part 3: Empowerment-Oriented Best Practices

Part 3 provides an overview of best practices most often associated with the overarching goal of (personal) empowerment, or activities that involve taking action to help oneself. Collectively and individually, the authors make the case for incorporating empowerment-oriented practices such as spirituality, recovery, motivational interviewing, and family involvement in all aspects of mental health practice. The chapters selected for this section emphasize best practices that illustrate the powerful duo of hopefulness and choice as both goals and treatment strategies.

Chapter 11, "Spirituality and Mental Health," examines the broad role of spirituality as a best practice and its applicability in mental health assessments, interventions, and evaluations. The author provides a detailed overview of the eco-bio-psycho-social-spiritual assessment framework and how it can be used to assist clients through their own spiritual transformation strategies and understanding of levels of consciousness.

Chapter 12, "Recovery-Oriented Services," explores the philosophical and practice principles underlying recovery, a best practice emphasizing empowerment, choice, and hopefulness that is delivered in a person-centered or person-directed format. The authors provide an extensive history of the recovery movement, review practice principles, and provide numerous examples of recovery-oriented models of care in traditional and nontraditional mental health settings.

Chapter 13, "Motivational Interviewing," describes a client-centered best practice for helping individuals identify health-related problem behaviors and their internal motivation for change. The authors provide a comprehensive overview of practice principles, the role of self-efficacy, resistance, empathy, ambivalence and discrepancy in clinical work, client support for the practice, and limitations of research.

Chapter 14, "Best Practices for Family Caregivers of People with Severe Mental Illness," is a chapter that shifts the focus from practices benefiting the individual client and moves the discussion to the needs of family members. Using a case study to create a story frame, the author guides readers through the complicated maze of issues that families face when trying to access care for a family member who is ill. Recommended best practices include the use of a to-do list to enhance the family's sense of involvement, empowerment, and control.

Part 4: Education-Oriented Best Practices

Part 4 provides an overview of three best practices whose unifying theme is centered on education. Addressing an often-overlooked component of mental health services, yet a critical social gap in the lives of many clients we work with, the authors describe approaches that any agency or practitioner can use or incorporate into their practice setting to help clients, students, and participants gain more personal coping skills and knowledge, educational attainment, and employment opportunities.

Chapter 15, "Psychiatric Rehabilitation," describes how the philosophy and practice of psychiatric rehabilitation has merged into mainstream mental health practices primarily because of its approach to rehabilitation oriented toward strengths, behavior, education, and skills. The authors highlight the unique features of psychiatric rehabilitation practices, which include an integrated emphasis on people's vocational, residential, educational, and social outcomes.

Chapter 16, "Supported Education," describes the rationale and practice strategies behind helping people with mental illness complete or continue their education as a means to preparing for gainful employment, training programs, colleges, and universities. Many times, the education of clients with mental health conditions has been interrupted by the development of symptoms during key developmental years. To take advantage of some of the employment opportunities offered through other best practices (e.g., supported employment), clients may benefit from educational support. The author overviews the core elements of supported education, including personal support, coaching, and accessing mental health services; supporting evidence; and specific strategies that mental health workers and educational personnel can provide to clients and students.

Chapter 17, "Psychoeducation," provides a broad based review of mental health interventions that focus on enhancing participants' education, support, and coping skills development through the use of individual, family, and group modalities. The author provides an extensive review of different psychoeducation applications and describes a specific model program, Coping with Depression, as an example of a structured psychoeducational course.

Part 5: Children- and Youth-Oriented Best Practices

Within the mental health population, there is a co-population—children—that requires even closer scrutiny in the application of best practices. This part takes a different twist on previous sections and offers two broad, sweeping approaches to discussing which best practices work for children and youth—one influenced by a system of universal health care (Australia) and one influenced by a pluralistic, multipayer system of care (United States). First is a specialized program in Australia that emphasizes early intervention with a team of specialists and community services. A second chapter provides an even broader overview of children's mental health, describing evidence-based interventions for child trauma, maltreated children, and co-occurring disorders. The authors of both chapters acknowledge the complexity of trying to describe such critical information in a short, pocket-guide version of best practices, but they have nonetheless assembled core content that can encourage readers to dig deeper on their own using the resources provided.

Chapter 18, "Early Intervention for Youth Psychosis: The Australian Model," describes a widely recognized youth mental health organization and program, the Early Psychosis Prevention and Intervention Center (EPPIC). The center is known for providing comprehensive, early intervention care for at-risk youth; it is also a model that has been replicated worldwide. The authors provide an overview of the complex structure of EPPIC, describing such features as specialist interventions (e.g., peer support, social and vocational recovery program, family support, prolonged recovery), triage, continuing care, and acute care. Readers will find a variety of best practices embedded in this unique system of care.

Chapter 19, "Best Practices in Children's Mental Health," is a comprehensive examination of children's mental health issues and practices. The chapter starts with a review of epidemiological evidence supporting the need for providing services to children with untreated mental health conditions. Additional information is provided on core treatment principles (e.g., life-span development, community resources, cultural diversity). Readers will be interested in a substantial review of evidence-based practice treatment interventions, core components, related outcomes, and population-specific categories

Part 6: Organization-Oriented Best Practices: Pulling It All Together

Our final chapter begins with a nod to the previous chapters—each highlighting at some level the importance of clinical goals incorporating the values of well-being, empowerment, choice, wellness, support, recovery, personal motivation, safety, social justice, growth, and change. This chapter takes these core values and reminds administrators that part of their jobs is to ensure that these values are also part of the workplace environment. The success of any best practice for clients and their family also relies on the success of the staff and organization offering the service. One way to ensure staff success is by creating work environments that also reflect best practices, free of institutional trauma, full of healthy people, and managed through healthy policies. The Sanctuary Model is one such best practice designed to create this environment.

Chapter 20, "The Sanctuary Model: A Best-Practices Approach to Organizational Change," is our final chapter and concludes with a call for administrators to incorporate trauma-recovery-oriented best practices and principles into agency life and practice. The author's assumption is that staff reexperience their own trauma through work with clients and troubled agency environments. Administrators can interrupt this process by recognizing the issues and making an organizational commitment to change. Examples include a commitment to nonviolence, emotional intelligence, social learning, open communication, democracy, social responsibility, and growth and change. The author provides several strategies for organizations to begin this journey, such as the Safety, Emotional Management, Loss, and Future model and the Sanctuary Toolkit.

The concluding chapter, "Are We There Yet? Ensuring Quality Best Practices," uses the framework for reform of mental health offered by the Institute of Medicine. The closing section offers readers five guidelines for how organizations can use criteria to benchmark and evaluate their organization's choice of best practices.

About the Authors

The book hosts twenty-six authors. As evident in their biographies, readers will observe a mixture of established leaders in the field and rising new talent. Many of the chapters are authored by the most prominent and experienced mental health professionals in the United States and Australia, several of whom are the original founders of particular models and approaches described in this book. Other authors are new and emerging scholars in their respective areas, and their contributions and fresh insights greatly enhanced the quality of this book.

References

Hayes, R. (2005). Build your own best practice protocols. In C. Stout & R. Hayes (Eds.), *The evidence-based practice: Methods, models, and tools for mental health professionals* (pp. 306–331). Hoboken, NJ: Wiley.

Pliszka, S., Bernet, W., Bukstein, O., Walter, H., Arnold, V., Beitchman, J., et al. (2007). Practice parameter for the assessment and treatment of children and adolescents with attention-deficit/hyperactivity disorder. *Journal of the American Academy of Child & Adolescent Psychiatry, 46*(7), 894–921.

Public Health Agency of Canada. (2002). *Executive summary: Review of best practices in mental health reform.* Retrieved from http://www.phac-aspc.gc.ca/mh-sm/pubs/bp_review/reves-eng.php.

Walker, R. D., Singer, M., & Bigelow, D. (2012). *Meeting the evidence standard.* Portland, OR: One Sky Center—American Indian/Alaska Native National Resource Center. Retrieved from http://www.oneskycenter.org/mhsa/best-practices.cfm.

Introduction: What Are Best Practices and Why Should We Care?

Vikki L. Vandiver

Anyone who works in the field of behavioral health, which includes mental, physical, and substance use, has heard of the term *best practices*. This book attempts to group a variety of best practices that illustrate the range of meaningful and varying levels of empirically supported interventions available to clinicians. Before we describe actual interventions, let's review what we mean by "best practices."

What Are Best Practices?

Sometimes the phrase "best practices" is used as the subject of a verb (e.g., "we only *do* best practices"), and other times as a measure of organizational compliance (e.g., "our accrediting body says we must use only evidence-based best practices to get paid"). The phrase has also found its way into human resource departments as a means to measure employee productivity (e.g., "we are measured and evaluated on the number of best practices we use with our clients on a weekly basis"). However it is used, it is seldom without controversy or challenge. The controversy is usually around issues involving clinician autonomy and lack of training, both of which are influenced by organizational culture and policy. The challenge is whether organizations can or will support staff in their efforts to continually upgrade their skills and knowledge of evolving best practices while also determining risks, benefits, and cost estimates that certain best practices generate (Guyatt & Rennie, 2002). For example, can an agency fiscally afford the personnel costs of an intensive assertive community treatment program even though best-practice research identifies the intervention as a vital service for individuals at risk of hospitalization? Such decisions often influence whether best-practice interventions are part of the treatment package of services.

Definitions

Let's look at four terms often used to describe differing kinds of mental health best practices: *best practices* (BP), *evidence-based practices* (EBPs), *practice-based evidence* (PBE), and *emerging and promising practices*.

Best practices is a term with a wide range of definitions that have numerous applications. Its focus ranges from the micro-application of a single practice intervention, such as psychoeducation, to macro-applications such as accreditation standards. Let's look at two core definitions and applications of best practices as seen in the literature: organizational and clinical.

First, organizational best practices is a top-down approach defined as the measurement, benchmarking, and identification of processes that result in better outcomes (Kramer & Glazer, 2001). Generally speaking, best practices involve an organizational approach to assessing variations in practice from the individual level up through hospital and provider agencies and regions (Glazer, 1998). Organizations such as the Joint Commission on Accreditation of Healthcare Organizations have created quality indicators that are driving health-care-provider systems toward the acquisition of better-quality clinical data for their performance-improvement initiatives. Best-practice guidelines are one result of these initiatives (Vandiver, 2009). Best practices are often considered activities and programs that are in keeping with the best possible evidence about what works (Public Health Agency of Canada, 2002).

Clinical best practices, also referred to as practice guidelines, are a set of client-care strategies and methods to aid practitioners in making clinical decisions. They involve assessment, intervention, or evaluation practices identified by authoritative review groups, such as committees set up by professional organizations, as being most appropriate for routine use in service systems. These review groups examine available scientific evidence as well as professional consensus (Levine, 2004). One example of an authoritative review group is the Robert Wood Johnson Foundation's (2008) project in collaboration with the New Hampshire–Dartmouth Psychiatric Research Center, which used a consensus panel to develop six areas of intervention in which the research evidence strongly supports the effectiveness of one or more approaches. These interventions include medication management, illness management and recovery, supported employment, assertive community treatment, family psychoeducation, and integrated dual-disorders treatment, all of which are described in this book. Another source of governmental endorsement of best practices is the Ontario Centre for Addiction and Mental Health, which has an extensive listing of recognized best practices on its website (http://www.camh.ca). Examples of best practices included at this site are the Mood and Anxiety Program and the Schizophrenia Program.

The US Substance Abuse and Mental Health Services Administration defines best practices as "a method or technique that has consistently shown results superior to those achieved with other means, and is often used as a benchmark for others to base their practices on; best practice guidelines are determined through a thorough process that includes research findings, clinical experience and implementation guidelines that are then debated and discussed by panels of specialists including clinicians, researchers, program administrators and client advocates" (SAMHSA, 2012, n.p.). Australia's Victorian Government Department of Human Services (2008) defines best practices as "a set of guidelines that have been created based on careful identification and synthesis of the best available evidences in a particular field" (n.p.).

More briefly, evidence-based practices are those interventions for which there is consistent scientific evidence showing that they improve client outcomes, meaning one or more replications of the original studies (Drake et al., 2001; Howard, McMillen, & Pollio, 2003; Mills, Montori, & Guyatt, 2004). For example, assertive community treatment (see chapter 7) has more than thirty years of empirically supported evidence to substantiate its effectiveness with individuals who have serious mental illness and are at risk for rehospitalization. Whereas EBPs are based more on scientific evidence, practice-based evidence (PBE) is a sample of routine practices that can still have high external validity but have little inferential generalizability (Barkham & Mellor-Clark, 2003). Practice-based evidence is best defined as evidence of real-world data collection, and it focuses heavily on improving practice. There are two components of PBE: effectiveness and practice. An example of a PBE is equine-assisted therapy for Native American youth (see chapter 6). Despite being recognized as a tribal best practice among a consensus of Oregon tribes, the program does not yet have the conventional empirical evidence to support its generalizability outside of a specific cultural group.

Emerging practices are defined as treatments and services that are promising, are less thoroughly documented than EBPs, and have a strong research foundation but fewer than five published scientifically rigorous studies (Substance Abuse and Mental Health Services Administration, 2012; Vandiver, 2009). One example of an emerging practice is the Early Interventions for Youth Psychosis program (chapter 18). Promising practices are those administrative or clinical practices that have proved effective at achieving a specific aim, hold promise for other organizations, and show effectiveness in small-scale projects but whose research designs are less rigorous or use self-report measures (Network for the Improvement of Addiction Treatment, 2012; Substance Abuse and Mental Health Services Administration, 2012; Vandiver, 2009). One example of a promising practice recognized by the Substance Abuse and Mental Health Services Administration is supported education (chapter 16).

Components of Best Practices

Rosenthal (2004) has noted that the components necessary to establish best practices are data collection systems, systemic quality-improvement processes, and systems of health-care providers. He describes the following steps for how best practices may be developed:

1. Agencies set benchmarks.

2. Organizations pool provider data, which include low-resolution clinical information from hospital-encounter data and billing records.

3. Pooled data are given to agencies such as the Agency for Healthcare Research and Quality and the Joint Commission on Accreditation of Healthcare Organizations, which create quality indicators driving health-care-provider systems toward the acquisition of better-quality clinical data for their performance improvement initiatives.

4. The provider organization receives feedback against benchmarks, which tend to drive the quality process—which also occurs as a macro-level and micro-level process.

Goals of Best Practices

There are two main goals for the inclusion of best practices in organizations: (1) to assure clients, families, and insurers that the organization provides services that are of high quality and worthy of being considered on the forefront of practice knowledge and (2) for them to become institutionalized in organizations so that organizations not only recognize the utility of evidence-based practices but also consider them best practices in their agencies.

Limitations of Best Practices

What constitutes best practice in behavioral health organizations may vary from one setting to the next. Critics of best practices argue that there is no standard format for determining, establishing, or describing best practices in behavioral health (Munson, 2004). Nor is their consensus about what is a best practice, much less about how to measure it, the most valid metrics, dosage, or evaluation procedures for client change (Rosenthal, 2004).

Best practices can be based on research evidence, expert testimonials, lobbying, marketing, or other efforts to promote their acceptance (Manela & Moxley, 2002). Munson (2004) has recommended that before the concept of best practices can be considered evidence based, there must be clarification of the criteria and procedures for determining what constitutes a best practice in clinical settings.

Other limitations include limited time and resources for organizations and providers to develop, implement, and measure best practices; insufficient equipment and funding for database access; too much information and not enough guidance on overcoming cultural, organizational, and communication dynamics crucial to point-of-service delivery; costly training manuals; and lack of evidence in certain clinical practice areas (Barry, 2007; Newnham & Page, 2010; Shlonsky & Gibbs, 2004).

When Best Practices Become Worst Practices

Practices with the best intentions can sometimes go sour. For example, best practices can be experienced as the worst kind of practice when staff feel that intervention models (e.g., evidence-based practices) have been imposed on them without an understanding of why, when training is not supported, and when sanctions (e.g., letters of warning) are punitively applied to "underperforming" staff who do not use the agency's standard treatment model (e.g., group therapy) or measure up to organizationally established performance measures. In one preeminent behavioral health-care organization in the Northwest United States, clinicians have complained that a "corporate structure of performance measurement" has "hijacked" their work life, with examples such as posting therapists' client show and no-show rates on a public board in hopes of incentivizing and motivating staff through competition to keep up billable hours (personal communication, May 3, 2011). The result is that to keep numbers up, individual best-practice options are abandoned, and group therapies are created whether or not clients want them. So even though group-therapy work can be considered a best practice for some conditions and some clients, not all clients or disorders benefit from this approach.

What Makes Best Practices Become Even Better Practices?

Let's pose the question of what makes best practices even better practices to three stakeholders: clients, staff, and the organization. The responses are as follows:

- *Clients*—When consumers and families feel respected and heard, and when their perspectives are honored and the interventions offered promote recovery, empowerment, and change

- *Staff*—When there is opportunity and autonomy to generate a variety of approaches that are more generic, have greater external validity, and lead to good clinical outcomes

- *Organization*—When there is strong leadership that supports institutional commitment to principles of best practices and invests in workforce development training in the area of continuing education

Munson (2004) has made the argument that evidence-based practice must be balanced with a relationship model. Best practices cannot be grounded only in evidence, and they are more than compiling supportive research evidence and cataloging outcomes. Implementing best practices without a relationship-based structure can lead to staff resistance and outcome errors, as described earlier.

Best practices can also reflect agency values. For example, the choice of one organization to embrace tribal best practices over state-endorsed evidence-based practices makes a statement about what the organization stands for.

Why Should We Care?

Best practices matter. They matter to clients who want a respectful and helpful relationship with their clinician. They matter to staff who want the best for their clients and require the resources and training to offer the best. They matter to organizations that are in the business of helping vulnerable populations and thus want to deliver a product that meets that need.

Rosenthal (2004) reminds us that agencies will always need to weigh the risk and benefits of particular best practices for their organization and clinicians, regardless of the evidence base supporting an intervention, because patients and staff have characteristics related to compliance, culture, age, and comorbidity that affect the estimates of benefits and risks that come from critical appraisal of the literature. This rationale becomes one's motivation to discover the best practices, which are really about effectiveness, or how well a treatment works when given to heterogeneous community samples or persons with a particular disorder. Using best practices is really about practicing our best.

References

Barkham, M., & Mellor-Clark, J. (2003) Bridging evidence-based practice and practice-based evidence: Developing a rigorous and relevant knowledge for the psychological therapies. *Clinical Psychology and Psychotherapy, 10,* 319–327.

Barry, K. (2007). Collective inquiry: Understanding the essence of best practice construction in mental health. *Journal of Psychiatric and Mental Health Nursing, 14,* 558–565.

Drake, R. E., Goldman, H. H., Leff, H. S., Lehman, A. F., Dixon, L., Mueser, K. T., et al. (2001). Implementing evidence-based practices in routine mental health service settings. *Psychiatric Services, 52,* 179–182.

Glazer, W. (1998). Defining best practices: A prescription for greater autonomy. *Psychiatric Services, 49,* 1013–1016.

Guyatt, G. H., & Rennie, D. (2002) *Users' guides to the medical literature: A manual for evidence-based practice.* Chicago: American Medical Association.

Howard, M., McMillen, C., & Pollio, D. (2003). Teaching evidence-based practice: Toward a new paradigm for social work education. *Research on Social Work Practice, 13*(2), 234–259.

Kramer, T., & Glazer, W. (2001). Our quest for excellence in behavioral health care. *Psychiatric Services, 52,* 157–159.

Levine, E. R. (2004). Glossary. In A. Roberts & K. Yeager (Eds.), *Evidence-based practice manual: Research and outcome measures in health and human services* (p. 973). New York: Oxford University Press.

Manela, R. W., & Moxley, D. P. (2002). Best practices as agency-based knowledge in social welfare. *Administration in Social Work, 26*(4), 1–24.

Mills, E. J., Montori, V. M., & Guyatt, G. H. (2004). Evidence-based clinical practice. *Brief Treatment and Crisis Intervention, 4*(2), 187–194.

Munson, C. E. (2004). Evidence-based treatment for traumatized and abused children. In A. Roberts & K. Yeager (Eds.), *Evidence-based practice manual: Research and outcome measures in health and human services* (pp. 252–263). New York: Oxford University Press.

Network for the Improvement of Addiction Treatment. (2012). *Promising practices.* Center for Health Enhancement Systems Studies, University of Wisconsin, Madison. Retrieved from http://www.niatx.net/PromisingPractices/Search.aspx.

Newnham, E., & Page, A. C. (2010). Bridging the gap between best evidence and best practice in mental health. *Clinical Psychology Review, 30*(1), 127–142.

Public Health Agency of Canada. (2002). *Review of best practices in mental health reform.* Retrieved from http://www.phac-aspc.gc.ca/index-eng.php.

Robert Wood Johnson Foundation. (2008). *Project identifies mental health best practices, creates tool kits to help implement them: Mental Health Best Practices Project.* Retrieved from http://www.rwjf.org/reports/grr/044030.htm.

Rosenthal, R. (2004). Overview of evidence-based practice. In A. Roberts & K. Yeager (Eds.), *Evidence-based practice manual: Research and outcome measures in health and human services* (pp. 21–29). New York: Oxford University Press.

Shlonsky, A., & Gibbs, L. (2004). Will the real evidence-based practice please step forward? Teaching evidence-based practice in the helping professions. *Journal of Brief Therapy and Crisis Intervention, 4*(2), 137–153.

Substance Abuse and Mental Health Services Administration. (2012). *Welcome to the National Center for Trauma Informed Care: Substance Abuse and Mental Health Services Administration.* Retrieved from http://www.samhsa.gov/nctic/.

Vandiver, V. (2009). *Integrating health promotion and mental health: An introduction to policies, principles, and practices.* New York: Oxford University Press.

Victorian Government Department of Human Services. (2008). *Protocol between mental health branch and community corrections: Best practices.* Melbourne, Australia: Author. Retrieved from www.health.vic.gov.au/mentalhealth.

PART I
Behavioral-Health-Care-Oriented Best Practices

Best practices oriented toward behavioral health care are those interventions and strategies that combine the fields of health care, mental health, and substance use with the public health approaches of prevention and health maintenance, using an array of individual- and group-initiated activities.

Part 1 introduces the reader to five core best practices commonly found in the field of behavioral health, namely integrated treatment approaches for mental health and substance use conditions, psychopharmacotherapy, illness management and recovery, health-care management of individuals with comorbid health and mental health conditions, and harm reduction. The chapters selected for this section emphasize best practices that illustrate integrated care models, wellness and health promotion philosophies, and person-directed strategies.

In chapter 1, "Integrated Treatment for People with Co-occurring Mental Illness and Substance Use Disorders," Rafferty and Drake introduce the reader to the notion of concurrent treatment of all disorders rather than single strategies of intervention. In chapter 2, "Nonmedical Roles in Psychopharmacotherapy," Bentley and Walsh review the multiple roles of nonmedical providers when working with clients who receive psychotropic medications. In chapter 3, "Illness Management and Recovery," Mueser and Gingerich describe a set of recovery-oriented strategies designed to help people take charge of managing their mental illness. In chapter 4, "Best Practices for Improving the Health of Persons with Serious Mental Illness and Comorbid Physical Health Conditions," Bressi Nath overviews the intersection of behavioral and medical services, health promotion, and shared decision making as strategies for helping clients and families manage health and mental health issues. In chapter 5, "Harm Reduction in Mental Health Practice," Witkiewitz, Walthers, and Marlatt describe the history and practice of harm reduction as a means to help individuals with problem behaviors (e.g., substance use) use pragmatic strategies that are not driven by abstinence policies.

1

Integrated Treatment for People with Co-occurring Mental Illness and Substance Use Disorders

Madeleine S. Rafferty and Robert E. Drake

This chapter reviews traditional, current, and future best-practice approaches to treatment of people with co-occurring mental illness and substance use disorders. Concurrent treatment of all disorders, called integrated treatment, has replaced traditional approaches in theory and in research but not in practice. Current implementation efforts will require leadership, financing, training, and health information technology. Let's begin this chapter with a case review of Lindy Fox (see box 1.1), whose first-person account describes her journey through various health-care systems and how her co-occurring conditions affected her and her family.

> **Box 1.1. Case Study: Lindy Fox**
>
> "At the age of seventeen I began having mood swings, and depression was prominent in my life by the time I went away to college. I had started using alcohol, which only exacerbated the problem. At age nineteen, I married a guy I met in a bar, thinking that would ease my situation, but the depression only worsened. I managed to finish college and find a job but felt empty inside. I decided that having a baby would be the answer. I had four children in five years. The postpartum depressions were very severe, and I never rebounded after my third child before I was pregnant again. At that point my functioning really began to decline. I was having a hard time getting to work and caring for my three little girls. I finally got into treatment for depression, which helped me get through my fourth pregnancy. After my fourth daughter was born, however, I fell into a deep depression and was hospitalized for the first time. I went home still very depressed, made a suicide attempt, was rehospitalized, and received the diagnosis of bipolar disorder. My husband sought a divorce and got custody of our children.

I started drinking again. I had stayed sober during my pregnancies, but now alcohol soothed my nerves and eased the depressions. This started a roller coaster ride of over thirty hospitalizations in a four-year period of time, [in which I was] only seeing my children on the weekends. I was suffering from a dual disorder but was not getting integrated treatment. When my mental health treatment providers recognized my alcoholism, they didn't know what to do about it.

Finally I was sent to Dartmouth Hitchcock Hospital for shock treatments. A young doctor there who understood co-occurring disorders sent me to a drug and alcohol treatment program. When my ex-husband visited with my children, it was the turning point. I decided to be a well person instead of a sick person—I didn't want my children visiting their mother in hospitals and alcohol treatment programs, so I decided to get sober. That was more than twenty years ago.

Once I stopped drinking, my bipolar illness stabilized, and I stopped going into the hospital. I went back to graduate school, got a degree in counseling psychology, and began working as a drug and alcohol counselor. For the past twenty years, I have worked for Dartmouth developing treatment protocols for people with dual diagnosis. I do training, supervision, and consultation. I love my job! I also have a wonderful relationship with my four daughters and a chance to be a grandmother without the stigma of my co-occurring disorders. I can't get back the time I missed with my daughters, but I am grateful to be present for all the things that are happening in their lives now."

Background

Beginning in the 1950s, deinstitutionalization shifted the locus of care for people with serious mental illnesses from hospitals to the community. Poverty forced most people with mental illness to move into poor living environments replete with physical danger, antisocial gangs, and drugs. The lack of protection conferred by safe housing, jobs, families, social networks, and other responsibilities rendered them extremely vulnerable to substances of abuse. Indeed, epidemiologic studies show that about 50 percent of individuals with severe mental illness also experience lifetime substance use disorders, a phenomenon referred to as dual diagnosis (Regier et al., 1990). Since the early 1980s, research has consistently shown negative outcomes associated with co-occurring mental health and substance use disorders. Clients with dual diagnosis suffer from higher rates of relapse, hospitalization, victimization, violence, legal problems, incarceration, homelessness, and serious medical conditions (e.g., HIV, hepatitis) (Drake & Brunette, 1998).

Co-occurring disorders pose a significant challenge to traditional treatment systems, which have historically addressed patients' psychiatric needs separate from their substance abuse issues. Clinicians working in separate and parallel mental health and substance abuse treatment systems have difficulty coordinating care, and clients experience difficulty navigating the labyrinthine system or deciphering disparate messages regarding treatment and recovery. Both the substance abuse and mental health systems, by viewing client needs through their own particular lenses, have routinely failed to serve people with dual disorders.

In 1987, the National Institutes of Health issued a national call for integrated treatment, defined as simultaneous treatment of both mental illness and substance use disorder by the same clinician or team of clinicians (Ridgely, Osher, & Talbott, 1987). Within an integrated treatment model, the responsibility of coordinating care for the two disorders shifts from the client to the treatment system. After twenty-five years of clinical research, integrated treatment for clients with severe mental illness is emerging as an evidence-based practice (Drake, O'Neal, & Wallach, 2008). This chapter summarizes current knowledge about integrated treatment.

Theoretical Perspective

Integrated treatment evolved from practical rather than theoretical considerations. Clients with dual disorders could not make sense of disparate messages from parallel treatment systems and dropped out of treatment. Parallel treatment meant no treatment. Although not an emphasis of this chapter, we refer readers to the literature on systems, empowerment, and cognitive-behavioral theories for a review of theories associated with integrated treatment for co-occurring disorders.

Principles

There are five guiding principles for applying the integrated treatment model with individuals experiencing co-occurring disorders: integration, individualization, stagewise recovery, harm reduction, and comprehensiveness (Fox et al., 2010).

• *Integration*—Integrated care involves much more than counseling for two disorders. All programs need to be modified to ensure that they are optimally tailored for clients with dual disorders. For example, medication management avoids medications that involve dangerous interactions with alcohol and other drugs, and use of addictive medications such as benzodiazepines. Supported employment (see chapter 10) focuses on jobs that enhance abstinence. Skills training addresses strategies for avoiding drug purveyors as well as for making friends. Family interventions include education on substance use and co-occurring disorders as well as serious mental illness (see chapter 14).

• *Individualization*—Dual diagnosis typically affects many areas of a person's life, and research shows that recovery encompasses different pathways, styles, preferences, outcomes, and timing from one individual to the next. To address these complex idiosyncrasies, clinicians work with clients in a process of shared decision making to individualize intervention packages.

• *Stagewise recovery*—People with co-occurring disorders vary in their levels of awareness and motivation to work on problems related to substance use. Interventions must be motivation-based, that is, adapted to clients' readiness for change and corresponding to individual goals (see chapter 13). Different interventions are effective at different stages of recovery. Long-term studies on dual diagnosis show that most people recover from these disorders gradually, over months and years, as they become more hopeful and more motivated to change their substance use behavior.

• *Harm reduction*—Harm reduction refers to a set of pragmatic strategies designed to minimize the most negative and costly consequences of substance use, such as death and HIV infection. In the initial stages of treatment, most people with co-occurring disorders are not ready to endorse abstinence as a goal even if they recognize that they have a problem. The traditional approach of waiting for negative consequences to motivate change is ineffective for people with serious mental illness. Furthermore, research shows that gradual change strategies work best for individuals with co-occurring disorders. Some examples of harm reduction include providing safe housing for active alcohol users, clean needles for injection drug users, and supported employment for active users. Harm reduction can save lives, prevent serious diseases, increase therapeutic relationships, and create hope for recovery.

- *Comprehensiveness*—One goal of integrated treatment is to help people decrease or eliminate substance use, but achieving this goal necessarily involves more than addressing substance use behaviors. People need to experience hope for a more satisfying life without drugs. They often need help with other priorities before they are ready for abstinence: for example, managing psychiatric symptoms, finding safe housing, increasing social support, pursuing medical health, finding employment, or adopting leisure activities that do not involve drugs.

Steps for Implementing Stagewise Recovery as an Integrated Treatment Approach

In the stagewise recovery approach, different models of the change process and of treatment stages are used to design and monitor treatment. Goals and specific treatments correspond to stages, with multiple options possible at each stage, including engagement, persuasion, active treatment, and relapse prevention. Table 1.1 summarizes the definitions and goals of each stage.

As mentioned already, the integrated dual-diagnosis treatment approach is founded on a core principle of comprehensiveness. Assessing each client in a comprehensive way, through an understanding of both psychiatric and substance use issues, is key to achieving treatment goals. Figure 1.1 illustrates the steps of this model.

Table 1.1. Stages of Treatment, Definitions, and Goals

Stage	Definition	Goal
Engagement Stage	Client does not have regular contact with dual-diagnosis clinician	To establish a working relationship with the client.
Persuasion Stage	Client has regular contact with clinician, but does not want to work on reducing substance abuse.	To develop the client's awareness that substance use is a problem, and increase motivation to change.
Active Stage of Treatment	Client is motivated to reduce substance use, as indicated by reduction for at least 1 month but less than 6 months.	To help the client further reduce substance use and, if possible, attain abstinence. *Based on what?*
Relapse Prevention Stage	Client has not experienced problems related to substance use for at least 6 months (or is abstinent).	To maintain awareness that relapse can happen, and to extend recovery to other areas (e.g., social relationships, work).

Figure 1.1. Steps of Integrated Dual-Diagnosis Treatment

1. Screen all mental health clients for substance use

Does this happen

2. Assess in detail clients who show positive or possible signs of substance use disorder (e.g., frequent emergencies or relapses).

3. Using shared decision making, develop an individualized treatment plan with each client who has a positive assessment based on the client's severity, resources, personal recovery goals, and stage of treatment and recovery.

4. Monitor timeline and specific treatment goals using ratings by client, clinician, and third party (if possible).

5. Reevaluate and revise treatment plan every three months if client is not making progress toward recovery.

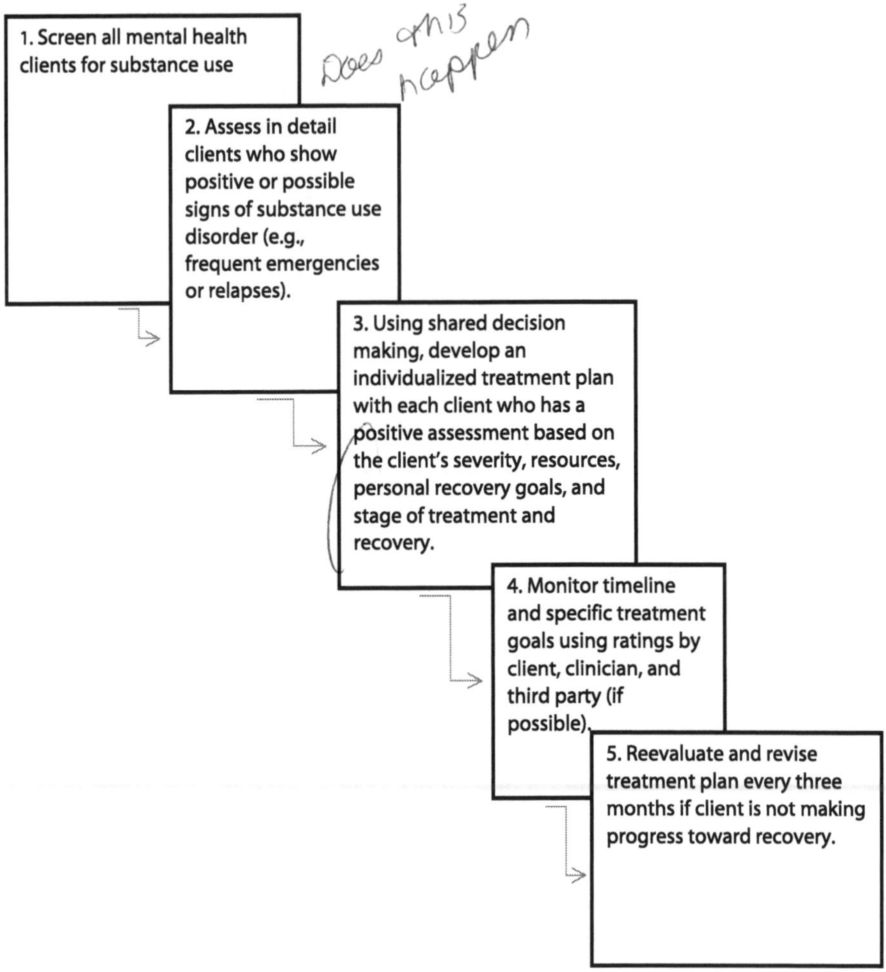

What's the Evidence?

Numerous studies have addressed treatment of people with co-occurring mental illness and substance use disorder. Current controlled research indicates that three types of integrated interventions—group counseling, contingency management, and residential dual-diagnosis treatment—are effective in helping dual-diagnosis clients reduce their substance use (Drake & Bond, 2010; Drake et al., 2008). Intensive case management (see chapter 7), supported employment (see chapter 10), legal interventions, and supported housing (see chapter 8) have been shown to

Do you know of more needs?

improve other areas of adjustment, such as community tenure, employment, treatment participation, and stable housing, respectively. Involvement in twelve-step peer-support groups is strongly correlated with positive peer relationships and other recovery outcomes (see chapter 12).

These results are promising, but the heterogeneity of interventions, participants, methods, outcomes, and measures significantly limits strong conclusions. Researchers must standardize interventions and outcome measures to facilitate greater comparability of studies, the potential for meta-analysis, and stronger inferential validity.

Assessment and Evaluation

Effective treatment needs to be guided by systematic and thorough assessments. Several validated instruments have been developed to address different aspects of mental illness and addiction. The Substance Abuse Treatment Scale (McHugo, Drake, Burton, & Ackerson, 1995) is used to assess a person's stage of substance abuse treatment and recovery. Assessment of psychosocial functioning can also inform treatment planning. Assessments should cover a broad range of domains of functioning, including social relationships (e.g., relationships with nonusing peers), role functioning (e.g., work, school, parenting), housing, medical health (see chapter 4), and quality of life.

In addition, evaluation efforts that include process and outcome data are needed to reinforce good clinical care and recovery. Outcome measurement allows clinical supervisors to assess program functioning and to identify areas for improvement. Fidelity instruments, such as the Dual Diagnosis Capability in Addiction Treatment (DDCAT) Index, the Dual Diagnosis Capability in Mental Health Treatment (DDCMT) Index, and the Integrated Dual Disorders Treatment (IDDT) fidelity scales, have been developed to identify whether evidence-based elements of dual-diagnosis services are being accurately implemented (Fox et al., 2010).

Implementation Issues

Although integrated dual-diagnosis services are widely advocated, they are rarely offered in routine mental health treatment settings. In fact, fewer than 5 percent of clients in the United States receive evidence-based services for co-occurring disorders (Substance Abuse and Mental Health Services Administration, 2007). Although barriers are legion, three areas are noteworthy: policy, program, and clinical.

With respect to policy, the US public mental health and substance abuse treatment systems developed independently and in parallel. As a result, federal, state, county, and city mental health authorities often encounter policies related to organizational structure, financing, regulations, and licensing that militate against integration. Policy makers confront fiscal incentives, guild issues, and strong advocates, wanting to maintain the status quo (Drake et al., 2001).

At the local (program) level, administrators of clinics, centers, and programs often lack the resources needed to offer dual diagnosis services, including clear service models, administrative guidelines, contractual incentives, training capacity, quality assurance procedures, and outcome measures. When clinical needs nevertheless compel changes, administrators have difficulty hiring a skilled workforce with experience in providing dual diagnosis interventions.

Finally, although the clinical philosophy and practical guidelines to integrated dual-diagnosis treatment have been delineated for more than two decades, educational institutions rarely teach the approach. Consequently, mental health clinicians typically lack training in effective interventions and have to rely on other mechanisms for learning current interventions. Further, the strongest evidence supports interventions that clinicians often consider secondary: group treatments, residential treatments, and supported employment. Clinicians typically prefer pharmacotherapy and psychotherapy—the core of their training experiences—rather than these more effective interventions.

As guidelines and algorithms for dual-diagnosis treatment develop, the field also needs evidence-based approaches to changing systems of care and implementing integrated treatments. Many demonstration projects as well as the recent National Evidence-Based Practices Project (McHugo et al., 2007) have identified successful strategies. These include clear guidelines regarding active leadership, financing, longitudinal training and supervision, record keeping, and quality improvement.

Leaders must bring all stakeholders together, articulate a vision, and modify all services in an orderly manner. Financing must align with evidence-based interventions and reward programs and clinicians for helping clients with more complications. All clinicians need training and ongoing supervision regarding co-occurring disorders. Further, clinicians who provide specialty services could benefit from additional expertise in specific therapeutic modalities. The flow of clinical care, reinforced by complementary medical records, needs to guide clinicians in providing evidence-based assessments and treatments.

Provider Competencies

To provide evidence-based services for clients with co-occurring disorders, all clinicians need basic skills. These include the ability to screen and assess clients for co-occurring disorders, to plan for effective interventions, to guide clients toward dual recovery, to monitor progress, and to help clients sustain their recoveries. In addition, clinicians who work in specialty areas need more refined skills. For example, prescribers need to address multiple disorders and avoid dangerous medication interactions, addictive medications, and inadvertent overdoses. Clinicians who direct group interventions need specific training in providing such services. Similarly, those who provide supported employment, housing supports, family interventions, skills training, and other interventions need specialty skills for working with dual-diagnosis clients. Manuals and guidelines are available for all of these skills, but clinicians need appropriate training and ongoing supervision to master them.

Training in specific psychotherapy approaches is controversial. Many dual-diagnosis programs invest in teaching clinicians motivational interviewing and/or cognitive-behavioral treatment. Although these interventions probably enhance working alliances, evidence for the effectiveness of these approaches is minimal (Barrowclough et al., 2010). Facilitating twelve-step affiliations might be just as successful. In any case, clinicians need to know how to help clients develop and pursue their own recovery plans, including family and peer group supports, jobs, safe housing, and friends who do not use alcohol and other drugs.

Future Directions

Two decades of research on interventions for individuals with co-occurring disorders has yielded promising results: integrated treatment has been shown to be effective, and significant progress has been made in determining the critical components that contribute to its success. Current research focuses on refining specific components, bundling services, using information technology, and increasing client-centeredness.

Specific approaches need refinement and specification. For example, the field needs clear guidelines regarding family interventions and how to incorporate contingency management. Health-care reform calls for bundling services for people with long-term illnesses, and co-occurring disorders should be a primary target for specialized behavioral health contracts. Increasing the use of information technology, another central goal of health-care reform, will enhance the efficiency of assessments, self-treatments, shared decision making, monitoring progress, and quality improvement. All of these changes need to empower clients to play active roles in their own recovery processes.

Evidence-based medicine requires that both clients and practitioners have access to up-to-date information on treatments, effectiveness, side effects, and individualized risks. Electronic decision-support systems, which use two or more items of patient data to generate case-specific advice, can disseminate this information directly, providing unbiased data on illnesses and treatments, and can help with values clarification as well as guidance or coaching for deliberation and communication with providers (Drake et al., 2010). Research in many areas of medicine shows that decision aids improve individuals' information base and the quality of their decision making—that is, decisions are more in line with the evidence and with personal values (O'Connor et al., 1999). Decision supports for clinicians typically encompass diagnostic systems, reminder systems, disease management systems, and medication-prescribing systems.

Co-occurring serious mental illness and substance use disorder, often called dual diagnosis, has become a central focus of community-based treatment. Clinical research has evolved rapidly, producing several evidence-based approaches, based on a philosophy of dual recovery, to integrating mental health and substance abuse services for these clients. As in the rest of the US health-care system, uptake of effective care has been slow. Health-care reform should encourage the use of evidence-based practices, focusing on client-centeredness, bundled services, and information technology.

Web Resources

Behavioral Health Evolution—http://www.cooccurring.org/public/index.page

Dartmouth Psychiatric Research Center (Dartmouth Dual Diagnosis Center)— http://www.dartmouth.edu/~prc/page0/page0.html

Substance Abuse Mental Health Services Administration, Co-occurring Disorders—http://www.coce.samhsa.gov/co-occurring/

Glossary

Co-occurring disorders: The presence of two or more disorders at the same time. This term usually describes the disorders of people who have one or more substance-related disorder as well as one or more mental health disorder, but it can also refer to mental health as well as physical health disorders or other co-occurrences.

Dual diagnosis: The co-occurrence of a substance use disorder and a severe mental illness, such as schizophrenia or bipolar disorder. The term is also used for other co-occurring conditions, such as mental illness and developmental disability.

Harm reduction: A range of pragmatic and evidence-based public health policies designed to reduce the harmful consequences associated with substance use and other high-risk activities. Harm reduction programs include syringe exchange, drug-substitution therapy using substances such as methadone, safe housing for active users, and HIV screening.

Integrated treatment: The simultaneous treatment of both mental illness and substance use disorder by the same clinician or team of clinicians. In this approach, clinicians combine and tailor interventions to best address the individual's needs. This approach is emerging as an evidence-based practice to replace traditionally separate treatment of substance use disorder and severe mental illness, which has been shown to be ineffective for individuals with dual diagnoses.

References

Barrowclough, C., Haddock, G., Wykes, T., Beardmore, R., Conrod, P., Craig, T, et al. (2010). Integrated motivational interviewing and cognitive behavioural therapy for people with psychosis and comorbid substance misuse: Randomized controlled trial. *British Medical Journal, 341*, c6325. Retrieved from http://www.bmj.com/content/341/bmj.c6325.

Drake, R. E., & Bond, G. R. (2010). Implementing integrated mental health and substance abuse services. *Journal of Dual Diagnosis, 6*, 251–262.

Drake, R. E., & Brunette, M. F. (1998). Complications of severe mental illness related to alcohol and other drug use disorders. In M. Galanter (Ed.), *Recent developments in alcoholism: Vol. 14. Consequences of alcoholism* (pp. 285–299). New York: Plenum.

Drake, R. E., Deegan, P., Woltmann, E., Haslett, W., Drake, T., & Rapp, C. (2010). Comprehensive electronic decision support systems. *Psychiatric Services, 61*, 714–717.

Drake, R. E., Essock, S. M., Shaner, A., Carey, K. B., Minkoff, K., Kola, L., et al. (2001). Implementing dual diagnosis services for clients with severe mental illness. *Psychiatric Services, 52,* 469–476.

Drake, R. E., O'Neal, E. L., & Wallach, M. A. (2008). A systematic review of psychosocial research on psychosocial interventions for people with co-occurring severe mental and substance use disorders. *Journal of Substance Abuse Treatment, 34,* 123–138.

Fox, L., Drake, R. E., Mueser, K. T., Brunette, M. F., Becker, D. R., McGovern, M. R., et al. (2010). *Integrated dual disorders treatment: Best practices, skills, and resources for successful client care.* Center City, MN: Hazelden.

McHugo, G. J., Drake, R. E., Burton, H. L., & Ackerson, T. H. (1995). A scale for assessing the stage of substance abuse treatment in persons with severe mental illness. *Journal of Nervous and Mental Disease, 183,* 762–767.

McHugo, G. J., Drake, R. E., Whitley, R., Bond, G. R., Campbell, K., Rapp, C. A., et al. (2007). Fidelity outcomes in the National Implementing Evidence-Based Practices Project. *Psychiatric Services, 58,* 1279–1284.

O'Connor, A. M., Rostom, A., Fiset, V., Tetroe, J., Entwistle, V., Llewellyn-Thomas, H., et al. (1999). Decision aids for patients facing health treatment or screening decisions: Systematic review. *British Medical Journal, 319,* 731–734.

Regier, D. A., Farmer, M. E., Rae, D. S., Locke, B. Z., Keith, S. J., Judd, L. L., et al. (1990). Comorbidity of mental disorders with alcohol and other drug abuse: Results from the Epidemiologic Catchment Area (ECA) Study. *Journal of the American Medical Association, 264,* 2511–2518.

Ridgely, M. S., Osher, F. C., & Talbott, J. A. (1987). *Chronic mentally ill young adults with substance abuse problems: Treatment and training issues.* Rockville, MD: Alcohol, Drug Abuse, and Mental Health Administration.

Substance Abuse and Mental Health Services Administration. (2007). *National and state substance abuse treatment services (NSSATS).* Rockville, MD: Author.

2

Nonmedical Roles in Psychopharmacotherapy
Kia J. Bentley and Joseph Walsh

Psychotropic medications are increasingly used by and with clients who have a variety of mental, emotional, and behavioral challenges and/or "disorders" and who are served by health, mental health, and human service agencies. Nonmedical providers, such as social workers and counselors, are increasingly called on to be resources for, and collaborators with, clients with respect to complex psychosocial issues related to medication use. This chapter presents a brief overview of those medications, overarching practice goals, and specific roles and competencies that mental health and human service providers should embrace in their practice with these clients. We begin with a case review of Rebecca (see box 2.1), which highlights the goals and roles of the mental health provider as illustrated in this chapter.

Box 2.1. Case Study: Rebecca

We introduce to you Rebecca, a forty-year-old divorced attorney with no children, living alone, and recently diagnosed during a brief psychiatric hospitalization with schizoaffective disorder, characterized by delusions of persecution and agitated behavior. The goals and roles of the mental health provider are highlighted in the chapter as Rebecca's story unfolds: Rebecca's problems worsened while she represented her law firm overseas. She confronted her associates about their inappropriate "spying" on her and began threatening lawsuits in retaliation. Her agitation became so severe that she was hospitalized against her will by her parents and sister. Although she partly stabilized with medication in the hospital, she vehemently declined to take it as an outpatient. Her family was especially concerned about how Rebecca's symptoms and problematic behaviors could ruin her already-damaged legal career. They helped locate a social worker in private practice who could see her almost immediately.

Source: Chapter reprinted with permission from Roberts, A. (2008). *Social work desk reference* (2nd ed.). New York: Oxford University Press. Portions of the original chapter were revised and updated for this volume.

The social worker learned during his assessment that Rebecca perceived medication use as prima facie evidence that she was "crazy," and taking it would have a devastating effect on her self-image as an independent woman succeeding in a primarily male profession. Further, Rebecca believed that the medication represented efforts of others to "control her mind" and "sabotage" her important legal work. In light of this, rather than refer her directly to a prescribing physician, the social worker spent several weeks getting to know her more deeply, empathizing with the meaning of medication for her, and not pushing her use of medications (counselor role). Rebecca gradually developed trust in the worker, who eventually began to teach her about theories of medication's "cause of action" and to provide her with data on its effectiveness with others. He shared his own experiences with clients who use medication and, when appropriate, talked in general about its potential role in helping her remain calm and stay active professionally (educator). She agreed to be evaluated for a trial of minimal-dose medications that might help her "relax and deal with the stress" of her situation. The social worker met with the prescribing physician before Rebecca's first session to let him know of her history and her attitudes about medication (consultant). The social worker arranged for Rebecca to receive free medications for three months from the agency's funding pool, as she had lost her job and most of her assets (advocacy). With the social worker's encouragement, the physician also validated Rebecca's understandable concerns about the medications and agreed to be available to her and to the social worker should her ambivalence became more pronounced (monitor). The social worker also maintained contact with the client's family, with Rebecca's permission, to respond to their questions about the medication's typical effects and side effects, to provide advice on how to be supportive to Rebecca, and of course to keep them generally and appropriately informed about and involved with the complex situation (multiple roles as collaborative resource).

Background

The introduction of chlorpromazine (Thorazine) in the 1950s is often cited as a key factor in stimulating the modern era in psychopharmacology. The explosion of brain research in the past decades, and the renewed emphasis on etiological models of mental illness emphasizing genetics and neurotransmission, has and continues to have a defining influence on pharmacological research and mental health care. Today, psychiatric medications are routinely prescribed for, or used by, people receiving services in a wide variety of mental health, health, and human service settings. Importantly, psychiatric medications, similar to other medical interventions, are considered effective for most consumers who use them (Sands & Gellis, 2012). However, the case of Rebecca illustrates that clinical drug trials and effectiveness studies are only part of the story in working with clients with mental health challenges. There are a vast set of psychosocial issues and dilemmas that interface with the prescribing and monitoring of psychiatric medications, and with the managing of mental health care and treatment more broadly. Today, almost all nonmedical mental health providers work with clients like Rebecca who use psychotropic medications as part of their intervention plans. In many service settings, mental health providers assess the client's mental status and inquire about psychiatric (and other) medication use as a part of the biopsychosocial assessment. However, we argue that mental health clinicians and nonmedical providers should continue to elaborate a more complete range of professional roles with regard to psychiatric medication. Toward this end, they are more frequently expected by clients and other professionals to possess sound knowledge of medications and their consequences for clients' lives, not merely to complement the physician's role but because they bring important insights, techniques, and a special appreciation of client self-determination and the client's lived experience.

Both the scholarly literature and anecdotal accounts suggest that nonmedical providers such as those to whom this book is directed—social workers, psychologists, and psychiatric rehabilitation counselors (to name a few)—have always played some role in helping clients make decisions about medication use, addressing its meaning and impact on client's lives, addressing adherence challenges, problem solving relevant issues about access, and in general helping to monitor and support their clients' psychiatric medication choices (Sands & Gellis, 2012). However in hopes of providing more comprehensive and compassionate care for clients and families, our view is that there must be a greater urgency for the nonmedical provider to be available and assertive in offering help for the medication-related dilemmas that arise for clients and families.

Before reviewing the roles developed for nonmedical providers, we list the five classes of medications for which providers are likely to interface with people taking these medications, and then we list examples of each. We are cognizant that many people take more than one kind of medication:

1. *Antipsychotics*—Nonmedical providers most often encounter people taking antipsychotic medication in public inpatient settings and in outpatient and community-based programs such as clubhouses. Conventional medications include fluphenazine (Prolixin), haloperidol (Haldol), and thioridazine (Mellaril). Atypical medications include risperidone (Risperdal), olanzapine (Zyprexa), aripiprazole (Abilify), and ziprasidone (Geodon).

2. *Antidepressants*—Nonmedical providers can encounter adults and children taking antidepressant medication in all mental health and human service settings. Data suggests women are by far the greatest consumers of antidepressants. Three different types of antidepressant medications include the monoamine oxidase inhibitors, such as phenelzine (Nardil) and tranylcypromine (Parnate); cyclic drugs such as amitriptyline (Elavil), nortriptyline (Pamelor), doxepin (Sinequan), and imipramine (Tofranil); and the selective serotonin reuptake inhibitors (SSRIs), including fluoxetine (Prozac), citalopram (Celexa), paroxetine (Paxil), sertraline (Zoloft), and fluvoxamine (Luvox). Other antidepressants include bupropion (Wellbutrin) and duloxetine (Cymbalta).

3. *Mood stabilizers*—Nonmedical providers encounter people taking mood stabilizers in any health or mental health setting. Lithium has been the most widely prescribed medication for the treatment of bipolar disorder, but anticonvulsant drugs including valproate (Depakote), lamotrigine (Lamictal), and others have emerged since the late 1970s as alternatives.

4. *Antianxiety medications*—Benzodiazepines, the largest category of antianxiety drugs, are widely prescribed in the United States and seem to have relatively little stigma associated with them; thus, nonmedical providers encounter clients who use these medications on both a short-term and a long-term basis. Exemplar medications in this category include diazepam (Valium), alprazolam (Xanax), and triazolam (Halcion), but these drugs are not used as much today because of their abuse potential. Increasingly, the SSRI medications have been used to effectively treat anxiety disorders. Buspirone (Buspar) represents another type of antianxiety drug.

5. *Stimulants*—Nonmedical health and mental health providers regularly encounter children and adolescents (and some adults) who have been diagnosed with attention deficit/hyperactivity disorder (ADHD) and who have been prescribed stimulants, or a nonstimulant medication like atomoxetine (Straterra), to treat the same symptoms. The stimulants and other medications

for attention difficulties include amphetamine (Adderall), pemoline (Cylert), and methylphenidate (Ritalin, Concerta) (Bentley & Walsh, 2006).

Theoretical Perspectives

Six core theories and perspectives underlie the vision for the nature of helping in psychopharmacotherapy:

1. *Neurotransmission theory*—This theory proposes that influencing the complex electric and chemical processes, especially those between brain cells (the synapse of neurons) along certain pathways in the brain, can influence dimensions of behavior, mood, and cognition (Andreasen & Black, 2006).

2. *Stress-diathesis model of mental illness*—This model posits that although genetics and biology play a significant role in the "causes" of mental illnesses, the course of disorders is in part related to stresses and life events. It sets up a clear role for nonmedical providers in helping clients cope with stress and effectively deal with life events by articulating their unique sets of risk and protective factors (MacKain, Liberman, & Corrigan, 1994).

3. *Empowerment theory*—Clients respond best to help when they are active in their own life changes and have decision-making power and a sense of control. Client insight into any blocks to this power can help reduce them, including an awareness of the impact of stigma and discrimination (Browne & Mills, 2001).

4. *Strengths perspective*—Rejecting a lens of pathology and weakness, in this perspective clients are viewed as capable and resourceful, full of assets, gifts, capacities, and positive characteristics that can be used and built on when responding to challenges and striving to reach goals (Saleebey, 2006).

5. *Partnership model*—Providers who embrace this model are comfortable with reconceptualizing the helping relationship as one of shared power, shared expertise, negotiation, and collaborative problem solving. Mutuality, genuineness, and authenticity characterize the helping endeavor (Solomon, 2004).

6. *Recovery and rehabilitation*—Consistent with other chapters in this book, we note that helping people with medication-related issues and dilemmas is not about "reducing psychopathology" or "achieving compliance" but, importantly, about helping them "get back to where they were," "be normal again," or "be better than before." It is about being fully human and seeking high quality of life (Onken, Craig, Ridgway, Ralph, & Cook, 2007).

Goal-Directed Principles

Contemporary practice requires that the nonmedical provider strive for two related overarching goals with respect to psychiatric medication. The following bullet points describe research-based and theoretically grounded practice principles that emerge from each goal:

Goal 1: Be an Effective Collaborator with Clients, Families, and Prescribing Physicians

- Embrace a client-centered "partnership" perspective around the range of medication-related dilemmas and issues that emerge in practice. As noted earlier, this suggests working toward a nonthreatening alliance, a demystification of the helping process, and a mutual sharing of respective expertise.

- Maintain a balanced perspective about psychiatric medication in the face of admittedly complex issues related to human rights and professional roles, and the "costs" and "benefits" of medication use.

- Work toward the successful integration of psychosocial interventions and psychopharmacology, and recognize the intrinsic power of combined treatments.

- Work toward interdisciplinary relationships characterized by equality, flexibility, decreased professional control, and mutual understanding and shared goals, and appreciate the challenges that emerge in managing parallel treatment.

- Appreciate both the strengths and the limits of clients and their families. Interventions should center on clients and families' unique strengths and aspirations and away from symptoms or weaknesses. Barriers to progress, such as a lack of skills or inadequate resources, must be appreciated.

Goal 2: Be a Meaningful Resource to Participants around Medication-Related Issues and Dilemmas

- Be a valuable source of whatever information, support, or "supplies" are called for in reaching specific wants and goals of clients with respect to their medication.

- Focus first on assessing and clarifying medication-related issues, which can occur on psychological, social, strategic, practical, and informational levels.

- Be creative in applying skills and techniques drawn from evidence-based practice theories and models to medication-related issues, and in emphasizing the use of both individual and environmental supports and resources.

- Encourage the client and family to share their own experiences and emotions about medication use, provide input to the helping process, generate and weigh options, negotiate, and offer feedback as decisions are made.

Steps for Implementing Medication Management Referral

Bentley, Walsh, and Farmer (2005a) reported that referring clients for psychiatric medication is one of the two most frequently performed practice roles related to medication management but that little information existed on how to best do so. On the basis of a literature review, Bentley, Walsh, and Farmer (2005a) concluded that a good referral for psychiatric medication requires attention to six dimensions:

1. Establishing and maintaining collaborative relationships with prescribers

2. Sharing up-to-date information about psychiatric medications with clients and families

3. Helping clients and families manage the meaning of medication

4. Preparing clients and families for the actual medication evaluation and anticipating issues that might emerge

5. Following up the results of the referral

6. Managing legal and ethical concerns about the referral process

The management of meaning is an especially key role of mental health providers. Recent research has highlighted the fact that clients may consider medication a necessary fact of life, a godsend, mind control, and a reminder of their illness, but also a source of recovery and hope (Bentley, 2010).

What's the Evidence?

Implicit in what has been written about the roles of nonmedical providers in psychopharmacotherapy are what might be called best practices in this area. We review here the results of two of our own studies that have implications toward best practices. One survey of National Association of Social Workers members regarding their practice roles and activities with psychiatric medication found considerable variability, but perceptions of competence and appropriateness in those roles was positively associated with frequency of roles performed (Bentley, Walsh, & Farmer, 2005b). Social workers frequently carried out some familiar roles, such as talking about client feelings and problems related to medication, discussing treatment effects, and making referrals to prescribers. These were also considered appropriate activities, and social workers perceived adequate levels of competence in carrying them out. Some roles and activities were not performed as frequently as might be expected or desired. A majority of respondents said that it is appropriate for social workers to assist clients with decision making around medication, but only half reported that they often do so. Other roles that seemed to be underperformed given their centrality to social work practice include talking to clients' families about medication and communicating with treatment team members. Similarly, although a majority of respondents reported that preparing a client for an interview with a physician is appropriate, a minority did so often.

In a second article using the same sample, the authors studied ethical dilemmas that social workers face in their roles of physician's assistant, educator, monitor, advocate, consultant, and counselor (Walsh, Farmer, Taylor, & Bentley, 2003). Providing these services to clients produced ethical dilemmas for social workers in the following areas:

- Client self-determination versus external pressures to take medication

- The lack of knowledge about potential long-term adverse effects of medications

- The short-term cost (adverse physical and psychological effects) versus benefit (symptom reduction) profile of a medication

- The use of medications with children and adolescents

- The relative effectiveness of medical versus psychosocial interventions

- The extent to which clients' rights are respected by their treating professionals to be educated, ask questions, and express opinions about medication

Assessment and Evaluation

There are varied approaches for assessing and evaluating medication management. As discussed in more detail here, the nonmedical provider often assumes the role of researcher. Documentation of medication management approaches often takes the form of case reports, single-subject designs, or more elaborate designs.

Implementation Issues and Provider Competencies

We have already made reference to the many roles of nonmedical providers with clients around their psychiatric medication. Figure 2.1 summarizes the six often-overlapping roles, with notations about their relevance for psychopharmacotherapy.

Figure 2.1. Roles of the Mental Health Provider

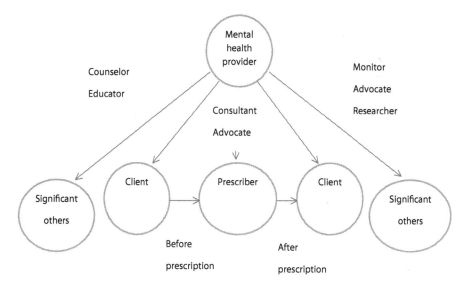

Roles
Consultant

The mental health provider performs preliminary screenings to determine clients' possible need for medication, makes referrals to physicians, assists in information sharing and decision making, and consults with clients and providers as needed. The provider prepares clients for active participation in the psychiatric assessment. Related responsibilities include articulating the rationale for the referral, addressing the client's attitude toward psychiatrists, discussing the client's expectations and concerns about medications, assessing the client's ability to pay for medication, and addressing issues of adherence. The provider monitors the client's subjective experience as well, particularly the meaning and impact of the referral to the client.

Counselor

The mental health provider helps clients articulate goals, weigh alternatives, and take action to solve problems and reach personal goals related to medication. Counseling can also involve giving accurate information about medication and offering advice. The counselor recognizes the importance of empathy, especially around the client's experience of side effects or impatience with therapeutic effect. Toward this end, listening to the life stories of clients, including how medication and self-definitions of mental illness or emotional distress are intertwined, is essential.

Advocate

Mental health providers may advocate directly for clients and families or empower and facilitate their self-advocacy. Examples of such advocacy include trying to increase client access to newer types of medication, obtaining free medication when needed, discussing potential overmedication with a client's physician, challenging the termination of a clinical trial, and appealing to an insurance company that declines coverage of a drug.

Monitor

The mental health provider helps the client keep track of both positive and negative effects of medication so that prompt physician action can be summoned when indicated. This requires that providers have an understanding of basic pharmacokinetics (effects of the body on a drug) and pharmacodynamics (effects of a drug on the body). Monitoring adverse psychological effects involves watching for any changes in the client's self-image and identity that emerge as a result of using medications. Adverse social effects include any potentially negative consequences that go beyond the individual to how medication use affects one's employment or standing with certain social institutions. Finally, providers can be creative in using existing measures or devising systematic procedures to evaluate a medication's effectiveness over time.

Educator

The mental health provider performs as a teacher for clients, families, and perhaps other providers regarding issues including drug actions, benefits, risks, common side effects, dosing regimens, routes of administration, withdrawal, toxicity, and adherence. In addition, social workers, in collaboration with nurses, pharmacists, and others, offer practical suggestions to help clients take medication appropriately. Teaching clients skills in assertiveness and negotiation can help clients maximize their relationship to the prescribing physicians.

Researcher

Using case reports, single-case designs, or more elaborate designs, the mental health provider documents how medications affect the lives of clients and families, how medications interact with other interventions, and how interdisciplinary relationships can be best coordinated.

Future Directions

As Bentley and Kogut (2008) have noted, mental health providers work with clients and families "right in the midst of exploding knowledge about neurotransmission, increasing research into the specificity of drug action and new modes of administration, differing views of scientific certainty about effectiveness, controversy about medication use with children and others, social injustices related to access, and, perhaps most importantly, vastly different experiences of people with psychiatric medication" (n.p.). Issues of importance to mental health care with respect to psychopharmacology and psychopharmacotherapy in the coming years will include the following:

- The appearance of new drug treatments with a more precise action on specific neurotransmitters (or their subtypes) so that drugs produce fewer unwanted side effects

- New delivery routes, such as brain implants, skin patches, and under-the-tongue medications

- New information about the differential physical and psychological effects of medications on people of different ages, genders, races, and ethnicities

- Findings about the placebo effect and how to harness it

- Findings about the additive or interactive effects of combining traditional (e.g., psychotherapy, brief treatment) and innovative psychosocial (e.g., meditation, exercise) or other (e.g., acupuncture, magnetic brain stimulation) interventions

- The popularity and acceptability of herbs and vitamins and holistic alternatives

- The political and practical aspects of expanding prescription privileges among nonphysician mental health-care providers
- Increased public scrutiny and criticisms of psychiatric medications, clinical drug trials, drug companies, and advertising agencies
- New models of health-care delivery and financing that will influence drug availability, use, and personal data and information exchange

Ideal practices for nonmedical mental health providers around psychopharmacotherapy will always feature a collaborative helping environment in which the work is comfortably paced but action oriented and relationships are characterized by honesty, genuineness, and warmth. More attention should be paid to the ethical dimensions of medication management, such as avoiding subtle coercion of clients, respecting clients' decisions not to take medication, being vocal about concerns related to over- or undermedication, and waiting lists for medication evaluation. Finally, providers should maintain a critical perspective on medication use in society while appreciating the power of integrated treatment to improve the quality of lives of people with mental illness.

Websites

National Institute of Mental Health—http://www.nimh.nih.gov

National Alliance on Mental Illness—http://www.nami.org

Mental Health America—http://www.nmha.org/index.cfm

Mental Health Net—http://www.mentalhelp.net

Glossary

Nonmedical roles: A set of activities and behaviors carried out by mental health providers across disciplines in a practice context.

Psychiatric medication: Refers to medications in five general classes (antidepressants, mood stabilizers, antianxiety, antipsychotic, and psychostimulants) used in primary care and psychiatry, and intended to alter mood, thoughts, or behavior.

Psychopharmacotherapy: The practice of implementing and monitoring a regimen of psychiatric medication with an individual client.

References

Andreasen, N. C., & Black, D. W. (2006). *Introductory textbook of psychiatry* (4th ed.). Washington, DC: American Psychiatric Publishing.

Bentley, K. J. (2010). The meaning of psychiatric medication in a residential program for adults with serious mental illness. *Qualitative Social Work, 9*(4), 479–499.

Bentley, K. J., & Kogut, C. P. (2008). Psychopharmacology and contemporary social work. In T. Mizrahi & L. Davis (Eds.), *Encyclopedia of social work* (20th ed., pp. 467–476). New York: Oxford University Press. Retrieved from http://www.socialworkers.org/pubs/encyclopedia.

Bentley, K. J., & Walsh, J. (2006). *The social worker and psychotropic medication: Toward effective collaboration with mental health clients, families and providers.* Belmont, CA: Wadsworth.

Bentley, K. J., Walsh, J., & Farmer, R. (2005a). Referring clients for psychiatric medication: Best practices for social workers. *Best Practices in Mental Health, 1*(1), 59–71.

Bentley, K. J., Walsh, J., & Farmer, R. (2005b). Roles and activities of clinical social workers in psychopharmacotherapy: Results of a national survey. *Social Work, 50*(4), 295–303.

Browne, C., & Mills, C. (2001). Theoretical frameworks: Ecological model, strengths perspective and empowerment theory. In R. Fong & S. Furuto (Eds.), *Culturally competent practice: Skills, interventions and evaluations* (pp. 10–32). Needham Heights, MA: Allyn & Bacon.

MacKain, S. J., Liberman, R. P., & Corrigan, P. W. (1994). Can coping and competence override stress and vulnerability in schizophrenia? In R. P. Liberman & J. Yager (Eds.), *Stress in psychiatric disorders* (pp. 53–82). New York: Springer.

Onken, S. J., Craig, C. M., Ridgway, P., Ralph, R. O., & Cook, J. A. (2007). An analysis of the definitions and elements of recovery: A review of the literature. *Psychiatric Rehabilitation Journal, 31*(1), 9–22.

Saleebey, D. (Ed). (2006). *The strengths perspective in social work practice.* Boston: Pearson/Allyn & Bacon.

Sands, R. G., & Gellis, Z. D. (2012). *Clinical social work practice in behavioral mental health: Toward evidence-based practice* (3rd ed.). Boston: Pearson.

Solomon, P. (2004). Peer support/peer provided services underlying processes, benefits and critical ingredients. *Psychiatric Rehabilitation Journal, 27*(4), 392–401.

Walsh, J., Farmer, R., Taylor, M. F., & Bentley, K. J. (2003). Ethical dilemmas of practicing social workers around psychiatric medication: Results of a national study. *Social Work in Mental Health, 1*(4), 91–105.

3

Illness Management and Recovery

Kim T. Mueser and Susan Gingerich

The Illness Management and Recovery (IMR) program is a standardized intervention designed to help people with severe mental illness set personally meaningful goals based on their own concept of recovery, and then to learn strategies for managing their illness more effectively in the process of pursuing those goals. The IMR program incorporates five empirically supported strategies for teaching people how to manage a severe mental illness, including psychoeducation about the disorder and its treatment, behavioral tailoring to include taking medication as part of the individual's daily routine, developing a relapse prevention plan, teaching coping skills for persistent symptoms, and social skills training to improve social support. The program is organized into ten different topics or modules that can be taught in an individual or group format, and it usually requires nine to ten months of weekly sessions to complete. Research supports the feasibility of implementing the IMR program in routine mental health treatment settings and suggests that it is effective at improving illness self-management and functioning. We begin this chapter with a case review of Mark (see box 3.1) and his experience with participating in five of the IMR modules.

> **Box 3.1. Case Study: Mark**
>
> Mark was twenty-four years old and lived with his parents when he first began receiving services at the community mental health center. When he was twenty-two, he started to hear voices saying that people were "out to get him," he stopped seeing friends, and he had difficulty carrying out his job as a waiter. When his symptoms became severe, he stopped going to work and began staying in his room most of the time, sometimes even refusing to eat meals that his family prepared. Mark's parents

became very concerned, and at the advice of their family doctor, they helped him schedule and attend an evaluation at the mental health center. He received a diagnosis of schizophrenia, and at the recommendation of a psychiatrist, he began to take medication to help him reduce his symptoms. He also was assigned a case manager, Elisha.

Mark improved significantly while taking medication, but he continued to hear voices when under stress and had difficulty socializing and going back to work. He relied on his family's financial support. He told his case manager Elisha that he felt "stressed out" and "stuck" at this point in his life and that he wanted to be doing the same thing as other people his age, including having his own apartment. Elisha suggested joining the Illness Management and Recovery (IMR) group of seven members that was just getting started at the community mental health center, where he could learn more about managing his illness (including strategies for reducing stress and coping with symptoms such as hearing voices) and work on personal goals with the support of others. At the time of this case illustration, Mark had completed five of the ten IMR modules and had been participating in the program for six months.

For the first IMR module, Recovery Strategies, Mark and the other group members spent four sessions talking about what recovery meant to them and developing their own definitions of recovery. In addition, they talked about areas of life they were satisfied with and areas of life they would like to improve. For the areas of life that they would like to improve, each group member used the IMR Goal-Tracking Sheet to define a long-term meaningful goal and break it down into smaller goals. Then they broke down the smaller goals into a series of manageable steps.

Mark identified "getting my own apartment" as his long-term goal, and with the help of the group leader and fellow group members, he identified three short-term goals related to it: getting a part-time job, learning ways to cope with stress, and learning how to cook for myself. Each short-term goal was broken down into three or four smaller steps. For example, getting a job included "make an appointment with the support employment specialist," "make a list of jobs I had in the past and the skills I have," "talk to my parents and relatives about job leads," and "look online for job openings." Mark was interested to learn that other group members had the long-term goal of getting jobs and getting their own apartments. The group leader told the members that in each of the following sessions of the group they would take time to review the steps group members had taken toward their goals and would review with two or three members their overall progress toward their long-term goals. The group leader led a brief discussion about how reviewing goals on a regular basis provides opportunities for group members to encourage one another and celebrate progress, as well as to help one another solve problems or overcome obstacles they encountered.

The group spent four sessions on module 2 (Practical Facts about Mental Illness) discussing the symptoms of their mental illnesses and how to recognize when they were experiencing them. It was surprising to Mark that other group members experienced symptoms (e.g., hearing voices) when they were under stress, and he was interested to hear what they did to cope with stress and to cope with their symptoms. As in all other modules, at the end of session, the group members developed home assignments that included taking steps toward their goals and/or putting into practice something they had learned in the session. For example, as a home assignment during module 2, Mark worked on his goal of getting part-time work by meeting with the supported employment specialist, and he talked to his family (parents and brother) about possible job leads. He also talked to his family about his participation in IMR and told them that he would like them to understand more about his illness. He gave them the handout "Practical Facts about Mental Illness" and drew their attention to the section that focused on schizophrenia. He promised to bring them the handout "Recovery Strategies," from the first module he had completed in the group, as well as handouts from modules he would complete in the future.

In module 3, the Stress-Vulnerability Model, the group spent three sessions talking about what causes psychiatric symptoms and what people can do to address both stress and biological vulnerability, and understanding the treatment options that are available based on the stress-vulnerability model. During this module, Mark continued to complete home assignments related to his goal of finding a part-time job (including the step of looking online for job openings) and started working on the goal of learning ways to cope with stress by making a list of situations that typically cause stress for him and thinking of ways of handling them so they wouldn't be so stressful. For example, he identified that he feels stressed when he is bored, especially on the weekends, and he decided to address this situation by making plans in advance to do something active, such as taking a walk in an interesting neighborhood or getting involved with artwork, which is something he used to enjoy. His home-practice assignment included taking a walk with a family member on Saturday and doing artwork on his own on Sunday.

Module 4, Building Social Support, was of special interest to Mark and several other group members, who described how they often felt lonely and did not know what to say to people. Over the course of seven sessions, the group identified areas they would like to improve in their social life and then learned and practiced skills that they could use to start conversations, to meet new people, and to get closer to people they already know. Mark especially found it helpful to role-play how to get back in touch with friends, including what he could say to start a conversation with them. As a home assignment, he called up an old friend from a painting class and suggested getting together for coffee. During this module, Mark continued to work on his goal of getting a part-time job by meeting with the supported employment specialist, visiting possible job settings, and role-playing how he might respond to questions in a job interview. Mark continued to work on his goal of reducing stress by taking regular walks and doing artwork, and he began to work on his goal of learning to cook by asking his father to teach him how to make his specialty dish, cheese omelets.

Mark found module 5, Using Medication Effectively, helpful in understanding more about the medication he was taking and its dual role in both improving acute symptoms and preventing future relapses. He developed a behavioral tailoring strategy (i.e., fitting the taking of medication into one's regular daily routine) to remember to take his medication daily, which involved placing his medication bottles next to his toothbrush so he could remember to take his pills in the evening as part of his bedtime routine. As one of his home-practice assignments, he put this strategy into place. During this module Mark made progress on his goals of getting a part-time job (going on two job interviews at local restaurants), coping with stress (walking daily and going running once a week with his brother), and learning to cook (cooking dinner for his family once a week). He continued to give his family members the handouts he worked on in IMR and invited them to join the Friends and Family Recovery Support Group at the mental health agency.

After completing the first five IMR modules, Mark reported to his case manager Elisha that he was feeling less "stuck" and "more in charge of what I'm doing in my life." He expressed interest in the remaining five modules (Drug and Alcohol Use, Reducing Relapses, Coping with Stress, Coping with Problems and Persistent Symptoms, and Getting Your Needs Met in the Mental Health System), and he identified ways that these modules could help him learn strategies and skills that would further his progress toward personal goals.

Background

Over the past several decades, the outlook has improved for people with severe mental illnesses (SMIs), such as schizophrenia, bipolar disorder, and major depression. The primary locus of treatment has shifted from long-term, institutionalized custodial care in state hospitals to the community, with services often provided in or close to individuals' living environment. Significant advances have been made in pharmacological treatment and psychiatric rehabilitation, thereby reducing the burden of symptoms and improving psychosocial functioning, including social relationships, independent living, and the ability to work or attend school.

However, despite this progress, people with SMI often know little about their psychiatric disorder or the principles of its treatment, and they often lack basic illness self-management skills for using medication effectively and dealing with challenges such as stress and persistent symptoms. Many clients are not actively involved in establishing their treatment goals or making decision with clinicians and family members about their own care. All too often clients have a passive role in their own treatment, which leads to either nonadherence to recommended treatments or dependency on others and low self-esteem. As a result of this lack of involvement in one's own treatment and poor illness self-management skills, people with SMI are often prone to medication nonadherence, disruptive symptoms, and frequent relapses and rehospitalizations.

Illness self-management refers to a core knowledge base and set of skills that can enable individuals with SMI to minimize their symptoms, reduce distress or interference caused by persistent symptoms, and prevent or limit the severity of relapses and hospitalizations. Information and skills for managing a psychiatric disorder can be taught by mental health professionals, other people with the disorder (i.e., consumers), or a combination thereof. Teaching illness self-management in the context of providing treatment can foster the development of a mutually respectful, collaborative therapeutic relationship. The Illness Management and Recovery program was developed as a standardized but personally tailored intervention for achieving this aim.

Theoretical Perspective

The Illness Management and Recovery Program draws its theoretical orientation from the field of social learning theory (Bandura, 1986), the stress-vulnerability theory of severe mental illness (Liberman et al., 1986; Nuechterlein & Dawson, 1984), the transtheoretical model of change (Prochaska & DiClemente, 1984), and self-determination theory (Ryan & Deci, 2000).

Principles
The IMR Program

The IMR program was developed on the basis of research evaluating different approaches to teaching illness self-management to people with SMI (Gingerich & Mueser, 2010, 2011). In a comprehensive review of controlled research on illness self-management, Mueser et al. (2002) identified five empirically supported methods for improving the course of SMI: psychoeducation, behavioral tailoring, relapse prevention training, coping skills training, social skills training. These methods are also the basis of core principles or values of the IMR program:

- *Principle of psychoeducation*—Providing clients with information about their psychiatric disorder and its treatment through didactic and interactive teaching strategies, such as reviewing educational handouts. People with SMI can learn and retain information about their psychiatric illness and its treatment, and play an active role in shared decision-making regarding their own treatment.

- *Principle of behavioral tailoring*—A strategy for increasing medication adherence and decreasing relapses by teaching clients how to develop natural prompts in their daily routine that remind them to take their medication as prescribed. For example, clients who take medication in the morning and evening can attach their toothbrush to their pill dispenser with a rubber band to prompt them to take their medication when they brush their teeth.

- *Principle of relapse prevention (training)*—Teaches people how to identify situations that have triggered relapses in the past, identify and monitor early warning signs of relapse, and develop a plan for immediately responding to early warning signs and averting a possible relapse (e.g., seeing the psychiatrist for a temporary increase in medication dosage). Supportive people such as family members can play a key role in helping clients develop effective relapse prevention plans.

- *Principle of coping skills training*—Systematically teaches strategies for coping with persistent symptoms such as hallucinations (e.g., shifting attention), depression (e.g., positive self-talk, scheduling pleasant events), and anxiety (e.g., relaxation). The more coping skills someone has, the greater is his or her coping efficacy, and the less distress and interference that person experiences from symptoms.

- *Principle of social skills training*—Teaches more effective interpersonal skills by breaking complex social behaviors into smaller steps and teaching those skills through a combination of modeling, repeated role-play practice followed by positive and corrective feedback, and homework to practice skills on one's own. Improving social relationships can bolster social support, which serves to protect people with SMI from stress-induced relapses.

Steps for Implementing IMR and Recovery Curriculum

The IMR program was developed as a curriculum-based approach to teaching illness self-management that incorporates the five empirically supported strategies described earlier. The IMR program does not assume that all clients with SMI are motivated to learn how to better manage their illnesses. Rather, motivation is instilled by first helping individuals explore the concept of recovery, and then helping them develop personally meaningful goals based on what recovery means to them. Goals are then broken down into steps, which are worked on throughout the course of the program, with motivation to learn illness self-management harnessed by exploring how it could help the person achieve those goals.

The curriculum taught in the IMR program is organized into ten modules, which are summarized in table 3.1. Between three and six sessions are usually spent on

Table 3.1. Overview of Topics for IMR Program Modules

Module	Topic	Goals
1	Recovery strategies	• Engage client in program • Explore different meanings of recovery • Set personal recovery goals • Develop plans for achieving goals
2	Practical facts about SMI	• Identify symptoms associated with schizophrenia, schizo-affective disorder, bipolar disorder, and major depression • Dispel myths about SMI • Address stigma • Help clients become aware of people with SMI who have led productive lives
3	Stress-Vulnerability Model and treatment strategies	• Explain that stress and biological vulnerability cause symptoms of SMI • Discuss strategies for reducing stress and vulnerability • Inform clients about treatment options
4	Building social support	• Discuss how building social support can facilitate recovery • Teach strategies for increasing support, such as finding places to meet people, conversation skills, and getting closer to people
5	Using medications effectively	• Teach client about benefits and side effects of medications • Increase skills for discussing medication issues with prescriber • Help clients weigh pros and cons of taking medications • Teach strategies to facilitate medication adherence
6	Drug and alcohol use	• Provide information on the effects of substance use on mental illness • Explore reasons for using substances • Weigh the pros and cons of continued use versus sobriety • Develop a personal sobriety plan
7	Reducing relapses	• Teach clients that relapses are predictable and preventable • Develop an individual relapse prevention plan
8	Coping with stress	• Inform clients that they can reduce stress and improve their ability to cope with it effectively • Identify and practice strategies to prevent and cope with stress
9	Coping with problems and persistent symptoms	• Teach structured problem-solving method • Help clients identify common problems and symptoms that cause distress • Practice strategies for coping with persistent symptoms
10	Getting your needs met in the mental health system	• Review different mental health services • Identify insurance benefits clients are entitled to • Help clients identify strategies to advocate for themselves in mental health system

each module, with the entire program requiring nine to ten months of weekly sessions (or four to five months of biweekly sessions) to complete.

All topics are taught with a combination of three different teaching strategies:

1. Psychoeducation involves providing information about illness self-management using a variety of formats (e.g., handouts, discussion), interactive presentation

of material to help clients relate information to their own experiences, use of clients' language to facilitate their understanding, and the asking of questions to evaluate comprehension and retention of material.

2. Motivational enhancement involves exploring how learning illness self-management skills can help clients achieve personal recovery goals, weighing the pros and cons of behavior change, exploring concerns or ambivalence about change, and promoting the client's active role in shared decision making about treatment options while avoiding coercive tactics.

3. Cognitive-behavioral therapy strategies are based on learning theory and include methods such as social skills training, systematic teaching of relaxation skills and strategies for coping with symptoms, use of the environment to cue illness self-management behaviors (e.g., medication adherence), and development of a relapse prevention plan.

In the IMR program personal goals are set and broken down into smaller goals and steps, which are tracked over the program and updated and problem solved as needed. At the end of each session, the client and clinician collaborate on developing a home assignment aimed at taking steps toward a goal, following up on illness self-management material taught in the session, or both, which are followed up on in the subsequent session. Clients are encouraged to involve significant others in supporting their work in the IMR program. Support can be provided in a variety of ways, such as helping the client follow-through on home assignments, reviewing information taught in the program, having regular phone calls with the clinician to review the client's progress, participating in occasional IMR sessions, and helping to develop a relapse prevention plan.

Logistics

The IMR program was designed primarily for people with schizophrenia, schizoaffective disorder, major depression, or bipolar disorder. Recognizing that one has a psychiatric illness (or a specific disorder) is not a prerequisite for participating in or completing IMR. Any person with a major mental illness who wants to improve his or her quality of life can benefit from the IMR program, regardless of the severity of symptoms, functional impairment, lack of insight, or cognitive impairment.

The IMR program can be provided in an individual or group format. For group IMR, group size is limited to four to eight clients, depending on symptom severity and attention capacity. This ensures that everyone has the opportunity to explore the relevance of each topic to their goals and experiences, and to practice skills. The IMR groups can be run as either closed (i.e., the same group of clients begin and end the program together) or open (i.e., new clients can join the group at the beginning of any module and remain in the group for a full cycle of all the modules). When IMR is provided in open groups, before a client joins an ongoing group the first module (recovery strategies) is taught to the client on an individual basis to identify personal recovery goals that the individual can begin working on as soon as he or she joins the group.

The IMR program can be provided in a wide range of settings, including at outpatient clinics, day treatment programs, residences, inpatient units, on assertive community treatment teams, and in forensic mental health settings. The frequency of IMR sessions usually depends on the intensity of other treatments provided to clients in the same setting. When moderately intensive services are provided to clients, such as in day treatment or inpatient programs, multiple IMR sessions per week are desirable to maximize learning. In less intensive treatment settings, such as outpatient clinics, weekly sessions may be preferred, as they provide more time to practice skills between sessions.

What's the Evidence?

The IMR program was designed to target factors that influence symptoms, relapses, and hospitalizations associated with SMI. Motivation to learn how to manage one's mental illness more effectively is developed by helping clients articulate and make progress toward their own personal recovery goals. Finally, because poor illness self-management can have drastic effects on functioning, the program may lead to improved psychosocial functioning. All these areas are important outcomes of the IMR program.

The IMR program was designed in 2003 to incorporate empirically supported methods for teaching illness self-management, and it is based on a comprehensive review of forty randomized controlled trials (Mueser et al., 2002). Some research on the overall IMR program has recently been completed, and multiple other studies are currently under way. Recent research findings are briefly summarized here.

The IMR program has been implemented successfully in multiple settings with a broad range of persons with SMI. Surveys of participants in IMR indicate relatively low rates of dropout and high satisfaction with the program. Furthermore, clients

Do you know what that mean

have reported that participation in IMR is empowering and has helped them achieve personal goals, with other gains in areas such as the ability to cope with symptoms (Mueser et al., 2006). These surveys indicate that IMR is feasible and is associated with promising improvements in illness self-management and recovery.

The implementation and sustainability of evidence-based practices in routine mental health treatment settings is of critical importance. One study evaluated the implementation of IMR and four other evidence-based practices for psychosocial treatment of SMI across fifty-three community treatment settings (McHugo et al., 2007). The IMR program was implemented in twelve centers, with assessments of fidelity to the program model conducted before training in the model and at six-month intervals for two years following training. The results indicated that the IMR program can be implemented and sustained with good model fidelity in routine treatment settings.

Three randomized controlled trials of IMR have been completed. The first study was conducted at twelve community mental health centers in Israel and found that participants in group IMR had greater gains in illness self-management than did those who did not receive IMR (Hasson-Ohayon, Roe, & Kravetz, 2007). The second study was conducted at a supported-housing setting in New York City and found that clients who received group IMR had greater gains in illness self-management, reductions in anxiety and depression, and better functioning than did those who received usual services (Levitt et al., 2009). The third study was conducted in Sweden (Färdig, Lewander, Melin, Folke, & Fredriksson, 2011) and found that clients randomized to IMR improved more in illness self-management, symptoms, suicidal thinking, and coping strategies than did clients randomized to receive usual services. These findings provide support for the effectiveness of the IMR program at improving illness self-management and other outcomes.

Assessment and Evaluation

Illness management outcomes can be tracked by measures of symptom severity, relapses, and rehospitalizations. The emphasis in IMR on recovery signifies the importance of not focusing narrowly on illness and pathology, and instead bolstering the individual's personal sense of recovery, including hope, empowerment, and progress toward personally meaningful goals. A variety of measures can be employed to evaluate progress toward recovery, such as the Recovery Assessment Scale (Corrigan, Salzer, Ralph, Sangster, & Keck, 2004). Last, gains in psychosocial functioning can be evaluated by measures designed to tap specific domains, such as independent or community living; social relationships; and role functioning in work, school, or parenting (Bilker et al., 2003; Goodman, Sewell, Cooley, & Leavitt, 1993).

Specific illness self-management factors that can be monitored include knowledge of the psychiatric disorder, medication adherence, having a relapse prevention plan, avoiding or minimizing substance use, social support, stress management skills, coping skills for persistent symptoms, and involvement in meaningful structured roles. The IMR Scale is a fifteen-item scale (with parallel clinician and client versions) that taps these factors and has been shown to be reliable, valid, and sensitive to change in the IMR program (Mueser & Gingerich, 2005). Using the IMR scale throughout the course of the program (e.g., every three months) can provide useful clinical information that can be incorporated into the teaching of information and skills.

Implementation Issues

The IMR program can be used in a wide range of treatment settings to help people learn how to manage their mental illness and move forward in their personal recovery. The IMR program has been implemented with clients from many different cultures within the United States (e.g., Hispanic, African American, Hmong, Somali) and has been adopted by mental health practitioners in a growing number of other countries, including Denmark, Israel, Australia, Sweden, Canada, the Netherlands, Japan, and Great Britain.

The steps for implementing IMR are listed here, followed by a short description:

1. Development of an organizational structure and formation of an IMR team

2. Scheduling training in the basics of IMR

3. Setting expectations for number of clients to whom IMR will be provided;

4. Conducting weekly IMR team supervision and meeting regularly with agency or clinical director

5. Ongoing evaluation and improvement of IMR services, including planning for expansion

6. Scheduling training in advanced skills for providing the IMR program

An IMR team is composed of several clinicians (e.g., between three and eight) who provide IMR, the IMR supervisor, the IMR director, and the agency or clinical director. In some agencies, the IMR supervisor may also be the IMR director, or there may be multiple IMR teams and supervisors but only one IMR director. The clinicians and the supervisor receive formal IMR training from a trainer who has personal experience delivering IMR, starting with the two-day IMR Basics workshop. During the first year of implementation, each clinician is usually expected to engage three or four individuals in IMR or to conduct two to three IMR groups. Supervisors usually work with one or two individuals or colead one to two groups. The formation of an IMR advisory board is recommended to oversee the introduction and ongoing implementation of IMR at the agency.

The clinicians on IMR teams receive weekly supervision on IMR together, provide cross-coverage for each other, and develop and maintain a process for identifying and referring clients to IMR services. The IMR director meets regularly (e.g., monthly) with the agency or clinical director, who supports and encourages provision of IMR by practitioners at the agency, troubleshoots obstacles to providing IMR, reviews overall IMR implementation at least twice a year, and develops a plan either to maintain IMR at the present level or to expand its provision. When practitioners have several months of experience providing IMR and receiving supervision, they benefit from additional training on topics such as motivational enhancement, cognitive-behavioral therapy, working with cognitively impaired or severely symptomatic clients, developing IMR graduation groups to support gains made in IMR, and training other clinicians in IMR.

Research indicates that IMR implementation is facilitated by the following factors: strong and active leadership, an organizational culture that promotes innovative services, training provided by experienced and supportive trainers, and staff members who are strongly committed to recovery and are receptive to learning new clinical strategies and skills (Whitley, Gingerich, Mueser, & Lutz, 2009).

Provider Competencies

The IMR providers come from a variety of disciplines, including social work, case management, psychology, nursing, occupational therapy, psychiatric rehabilitation, and counseling. In some settings, peer specialists receive training and supervision in providing the IMR program alone or in collaboration with clinicians (e.g., coleading groups, helping clients identify and pursue personal goals, assisting with home assignments, helping clients build and practice specific skills, providing outreach).

Competent provision of IMR requires that clinicians are able to do the following:

- Develop rapport with clients and convey confidence that they can make important change in their lives

- Take a strengths-based approach to working with clients rather than focusing on pathology and deficits

- Reach out to family members and other supporters

- Assist clients in identifying personally meaningful goals

- Help clients break down their goals into manageable steps

- Structure sessions in order to maintain focus on the topic

- Use interactive teaching strategies to convey information in the IMR modules

- Take a systematic, cognitive-behavioral approach to teaching relaxation techniques, coping skills for persistent symptoms, social skills, and behavioral tailoring for medication

- Assist clients in developing and practicing a relapse prevention plan

- Help clients develop meaningful home assignments to put into practice what they learn in IMR sessions

Future Directions

The IMR program is still relatively new to the field, and thus there are many possible future directions for clinical adaptations of the model and research. We briefly consider three potential future directions here. First, most implementations of IMR have occurred in outpatient treatment settings, and there is a need to adapt the program to different inpatient settings. Long-term inpatient psychiatric settings present a special challenge because they are often custodial in nature, and the concept of recovery may be either alien or threatening to staff members. Involving all hospital employees in implementing and supporting IMR may be critical to creating a milieu in which clients are encouraged to take more responsibility for managing their illness and in which staff members can be actively involved in helping clients pursue personal goals (Bartholomew & Kensler, 2010). Implementing IMR in correctional settings involves many of these same challenges, as well as addressing the criminal justice context, in which clients are often perceived primarily in terms of the threat they pose to others rather than as individuals with psychiatric illnesses in need of treatment (MacKain & Mueser, 2009).

Second, research is needed to further evaluate the impact of IMR on the broad range of functioning that is often impaired in people with SMI and to better understand how IMR can be coordinated with other evidence-based practices for this population. For example, can the provision of IMR increase interest or involvement in work, and does combining IMR with supported employment improve vocational outcomes? Can IMR increase motivation for clients to work on their substance abuse problems, and how can it be optimally combined with integrated treatment for co-occurring mental health and substance abuse problems? Family psychoeducation and IMR overlap in the curriculum on managing psychiatric illnesses, which leads to the question of how to optimally integrate the two approaches into a seamless intervention.

Third, little is known about how IMR works. Research is needed to evaluate whether IMR succeeds in activating clients to be more involved in their own treatment with doctors and other clinicians. Research is also needed to determine whether and how IMR influences clients' perceptions of themselves, their concepts of recovery, and their self-efficacy for achieving personal goals. In addition, research is needed to examine the processes by which IMR helps clients achieve social reintegration and become active members of their community.

Websites

The Substance Abuse and Mental Health Services Administration (SAMHSA) provides downloadable copies of the revised implementation resource kit for IMR, including a manual for practitioners as well as information sheets to give to clients, family members, and staff members—http://store.samhsa.gov/product/SMA09-4463

The Dartmouth Evidence-Based Practices Center facilitates the implementation of evidence-based practices (EBPs) in public mental health systems and agencies across the country. On the website one can find descriptions of EBPs, including

IMR, and can order DVDs with an introductory video and a practice demonstration video (showing clinicians working with clients using the EBP)—http://www
.dartmouth.edu/~prc/

At the website for *Psychiatric Services*, one can download the review article "Illness Management and Recovery: A Review of the Research" and the article "A Randomized Controlled Trial of the Effectiveness of the Illness Management and Recovery Program," which describes the five empirically supported clinical practices for teaching illness self-management to clients (Mueser et al., 2002)—http://psych
services.psychiatryonline.org/cgi/content/full/53/10/1272 and http://psychservices
.psychiatryonline.org/cgi/content/abstract/58/11/1461

At the website of *Schizophrenia Bulletin*, one can download the article presenting data from the United States and Australia on the effects of individual- and group-based treatment over the nine-month program and over a three-month follow-up (Mueser et al., 2006)—http://schizophreniabulletin.oxfordjournals.org/content/
32/suppl_1/S32.full

Glossary

Illness Management and Recovery (IMR): A step-by-step program that helps people set meaningful goals for themselves, acquire information and skills to develop more mastery over their illness, and make progress toward their own personal recovery.

Illness Management and Recovery (IMR) team: Clinical and consumer staff providers of IMR, supervisor, coordinator, and agency director.

Severe mental illnesses: Schizophrenia, schizoaffective disorder, bipolar disorder, major depression.

References

Bandura, A. (1986). *Social foundations of thought and action: A social cognitive theory*. Englewood Cliffs, NJ: Prentice-Hall.

Bartholomew, T., & Kensler, D. (2010). Illness Management and Recovery in state psychiatric hospitals. *American Journal of Psychiatric Rehabilitation, 13*, 105–125.

Bilker, W. B., Brensinger, C. M., Kurtz, M. M., Kohler, C. G., Gur, R. C., & Siegel, S. J. (2003). Development of an abbreviated schizophrenia Quality of Life Scale using a new method. *Neuropsychopharmacology, 28*, 773–777.

Corrigan, P. W., Salzer, M., Ralph, R., Sangster, Y., & Keck, L. (2004). Examining the factor structure of the Recovery Assessment Scale. *Schizophrenia Bulletin, 30*, 1035–1041.

Färdig, R., Lewander, T., Melin, L., Folke, F., & Fredriksson, A. (2011). Evaluating the Illness Management and Recovery program for schizophrenia: A randomized controlled trial. *Psychiatric Services, 62*, 606–612.

Gingerich, S., & Mueser, K. T. (2010). *Illness Management and Recovery Implementation Resource Kit* (rev. ed.). Rockville, MD: Center for Mental Health Services, Substance Abuse and Mental Health Services Administration.

Gingerich, S., & Mueser, K. T. (2011). *Illness Management and Recovery: Personalized skills and strategies for those with mental illness* (3rd ed.). Center City, MN: Hazelden.

Goodman, S. H., Sewell, D. R., Cooley, E. L., & Leavitt, N. (1993). Assessing levels of adaptive functioning: The Role Functioning Scale. *Community Mental Health Journal, 29*, 119–131.

Hasson-Ohayon, I., Roe, D., & Kravetz, S. (2007). A randomized controlled trial of the effectiveness of the illness management and recovery program. *Psychiatric Services, 58*, 1461–1466.

Levitt, A., Mueser, K. T., DeGenova, J., Lorenzo, J., Bradford-Watt, D., Barbosa, A., et al. (2009). A randomized controlled trial of illness management and recovery in multi-unit supported housing. *Psychiatric Services, 60*, 1629–1636.

Liberman, R. P., Mueser, K. T., Wallace, C. J., Jacobs, H. E., Eckman, T., & Massel, H. K. (1986). Training skills in the psychiatrically disabled: Learning coping and competence. *Schizophrenia Bulletin, 12*, 631–647.

MacKain, S., & Mueser, K. T. (2009). Training in illness self-management for people with mental illness in the criminal justice system. *American Journal of Psychiatric Rehabilitation, 12*, 31–56.

McHugo, G. J., Drake, R. E., Whitley, R., Bond, G. R., Campbell, K., Rapp, C. A., et al. (2007). Fidelity outcomes in the National Implementing Evidence-Based Practices Project. *Psychiatric Services, 58*, 1279–1284.

Mueser, K. T., Corrigan, P. W., Hilton, D., Tanzman, B., Schaub, A., & Gingerich, S. (2002). Illness management and recovery for severe mental illness: A review of the research. *Psychiatric Services, 53*, 1272–1284.

Mueser, K. T., & Gingerich, S. (2005). Illness Management and Recovery (IMR) Scales. In T. Campbell-Orde, J. Chamberlin, J. Carpenter, & H. S. Leff (Eds.), *Measuring the promise: A compendium of recovery measures* (Vol. 2, pp. 124–132). Cambridge, MA: Evaluation Center @ Human Services Research Institute.

Mueser, K. T., Meyer, P. S., Penn, D. L., Clancy, R., Clancy, D. M., & Salyers, M. P. (2006). The Illness Management and Recovery program: Rationale, development, and preliminary findings. *Schizophrenia Bulletin, 32*(Suppl. 1), S32–S43.

Nuechterlein, K. H., & Dawson, M. E. (1984). A heuristic vulnerability/stress model of schizophrenic episodes. *Schizophrenia Bulletin, 10*, 300–312.

Prochaska, J. O., & DiClemente, C. C. (1984). *The transtheoretical approach: Crossing the traditional boundaries of therapy*. Homewood, IL: Dow Jones/Irwin.

Ryan, R. M., & Deci, E. L. (2000). Self-determination theory and the facilitation of intrinsic motivation, social development and well-being. *American Psychologist, 55*, 68–78.

Whitley, R. E., Gingerich, S., Mueser, K. T., & Lutz, W. J. (2009). Facilitators and barriers to the implementation of the Illness Management and Recovery program in routine mental health settings. *Psychiatric Services, 60*, 202–209.

Best Practices for Improving the Health of Persons with Serious Mental Illness and Comorbid Physical Health Conditions

Sara Bressi Nath

Throughout adulthood, persons with severe mental illnesses are more likely to have physical health problems than are those without mental disorders. However, prior studies have suggested that persons with severe mental illness are often unable to access quality health services. Research-based principles for improving the health of this vulnerable population aim to improve access to continuous, coordinated, and comprehensive health services. Using prior literature, this chapter outlines these principles, as well as best practices to achieve this aim, including integrated behavioral and medical services, health promotion, shared decision making, and support for informal or family caregivers. We begin this chapter with a case review of Ms. Jones (see box 4.1) and her experience with both health and mental health conditions.

Box 4.1. Case Study: Ms. Jones

Ms. Jones is a fifty-five-year-old African American woman with schizophrenia and comorbid type II diabetes mellitus. She lives in a group home, and her children and grandchildren live close by. Ms. Jones meets weekly with an outpatient therapist at her local community mental health center and regularly sees a psychiatrist at the same center for management of her psychotropic medications. However, Ms. Jones has difficulty with managing the daily tasks related to her diabetes, such as monitoring her blood sugar, watching her diet, and taking her medications. As a result, she has gained a significant amount of weight over time, and she physically doesn't feel well. In addition, she has a primary-care physician, but she often doesn't feel like spending money on transportation to the appointments, as she doesn't really like her doctor, and the crowded waiting room makes her anxious.

Background
Severe Mental Illness and Comorbid Physical Health Conditions

For many people with severe mental illness, such as schizophrenia and major affective disorders, the burden of having a mental illness is compounded by poor physical health (Dixon, Wohlheiter, & Thompson, 2001). Chronic illnesses such as diabetes, cardiovascular disease, and hypertension are common in this population and contribute to premature mortality, diminished quality of life, admission to a nursing home, and longer hospital stays (Brown, 1997; Dixon, Goldberg, Lehman, & McNary, 2001; Miller & Rosenheck, 2006; Nath, Marcus, & Solomon, 2006; Simpson & Tsuang, 1996). Unfortunately, these health problems also have the potential to inhibit the effectiveness of recovery-oriented services.

Several factors explain the prevalence of comorbid physical disease. First, functional impairments associated with mental illness increase persons' vulnerability to poverty, chronic unemployment, homelessness, and substandard housing, which in turn put them at risk for poor health outcomes. In addition, side effects of psychotropic medications, as well as lifestyle factors, such as poor diet, high rates of tobacco use, substance abuse, and risky sexual behaviors, also contribute to chronic health problems in this population (Alison, Mackell, & McDonnell, 2003; Blank, Mandell, Aiken, & Hadley, 2002; Brown, Birtwistle, Roe, & Thompson, 1999; Daumit et al., 2003; Lyon, 1999; RachBeisel, Scott, & Dixon, 1999; Sussman, 2001).

Access to Quality Health Services and Comorbid Physical Health Conditions

The majority of the comorbid health conditions prevalent among persons with mental illnesses are preventable, manageable, or curable with the appropriate medical intervention. However, prior studies have suggested that persons with severe mental illness have difficulties accessing preventive, primary, and specialty health services. For example, a comparative study reported that persons with any axis I disorder visited the doctor less over the course of one year than did persons without a psychiatric disorder (Cradock-O'Leary, Young, Yano, Wang, & Lee, 2002). Other research has suggested that these individuals may not have a regular source of medical care or be able to readily identify their primary-care provider (Berren, Santiago, Zent, & Carbone, 1999; Levinson-Miller, Druss, Dombrowski, & Rosenheck, 2003). Furthermore, even after accessing care, the quality of care, and in turn the effectiveness of the health care received by persons with severe mental illness, may be compromised (Druss, Bradford, Rosenheck, Radford, & Krumholz, 2001). For example, these persons may be less able to access specialized procedures that are considered best practices for the treatment of cardiovascular disease and diabetes than are those without mental disorders (Desai, Rosenheck, Druss, & Perlin, 2002a; Druss, Bradford, Rosenheck, Radford, & Krumholz, 2000; Jones, Clarke, & Carney, 2004).

A variety of person, provider, and system-level factors may inhibit health services utilization among persons with severe mental illness. Although lack of health insurance is less likely to be a barrier to accessing health services for low-income, aged, or disabled populations because of the availability of coverage by Medicare and Medicaid, the extent to which these programs cover services and the degree to which patients are responsible for paying for treatment varies. Consumers may delay visits to their doctors to avoid copays and other costs (Dickerson et al., 2003; Druss & Rosenheck, 1998; O'Day, Killeen, Sutton, & Iezzoni, 2005). The symptoms of particular psychiatric disorders coupled with physical distress may also deter help seeking. First, symptoms of mental illness such as cognitive disturbances, disruptive auditory hallucinations, social isolation, and paranoia may inhibit persons with mental illness from recognizing illness or presenting for care (Phelan, Stradins, & Morrison, 2001). These symptoms and the stigma associated with mental disorder may also limit the ability to adequately communicate symptoms and medical history to medical providers or may diminish the capacity of providers to accurately assess and diagnose medical illness in this population. Finally, persons with mental illness may have difficulty negotiating the bifurcated and complex health-care and mental health-care systems, making or presenting for appointments, or managing health or treatment regimens.

Theoretical Perspective

Most interventions that address comorbid health and mental health conditions operate from an ecological perspective and seek to integrate systems of care, to bolster social support, and to improve interactions with formal and informal caregivers.

Research-Based Principles

Improving the health of persons with severe mental illnesses and comorbid physical health conditions requires strategies that enhance the ability of these persons to access quality health services. Existing evidence suggests that quality health services should be based on the following core principles: continuous, coordinated, and comprehensive. Figure 4.1 illustrates the three principles, along with related best-practice strategies and implementation approaches.

Figure 4.1. Principles, Strategies, and Approaches for Improving the Health of Persons with Serious Mental Illness and Comorbid Physical Health Conditions

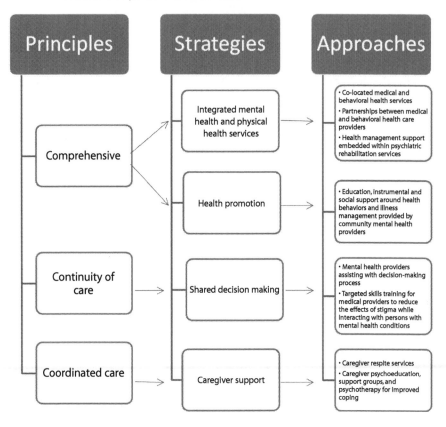

These principles of quality have been applied in prior studies on defining quality primary-care services (Levinson-Miller et al., 2003; Shi, Starfield, & Xu, 2001; Shi, Starfield, Xu, Politzer, & Regan, 2003), but they are also helpful for conceptualizing quality in health services more generally, as they reflect core aims of quality improvement strategies outlined by the Institute of Medicine, other key stakeholders, and research that examines best practices for managing chronic illness (Institute of Medicine, 2001; National Advisory Mental Health Council, 1993; President's New Freedom Commission on Mental Health, 2003; Wagner, Austin, & Von Korff, 1996):

Principle of continuity—Continuous care offers services that are ongoing within the context of relationships with health-care providers (IOM, 2001; Levinson-Miller et al., 2003). A continuous relationship with a health-care provider is important for avoiding repetition of painful life histories, for enhancing the development of trust, and for partnering in making decisions (Lester, Tritter, & Sorohan, 2005). A high degree of longevity with a health professional, or the degree to which a professional serves as the provider of care over time, predicts greater utilization of preventive and curative health services (Druss, 2002; Gallagher, Andersen, Koegel, & Gelberg, 1997; Hayward, Bernard, Freeman, & Corey, 1990). With continuity of care, providers are able to know their patients better and to reflect on their medical history in making treatment decisions. The continuity of the care clients receive is likely to be strained in publicly financed systems that are increasingly operating under the constraints of managed care and thus are more often exposed to large group practices and increasing rates of primary care provider turnover because of dissatisfaction related to reimbursement rates. Individuals with mental illness may also become dissatisfied with a physician if the provider does not demonstrate concern for patients' well-being or include patients as active participants in medical decision making (Lester, Tritter, & Sorohan, 2005). The quality of relationships with providers is hindered by providers' stereotyped beliefs about mental illness, as well as by symptoms of mental illness that may affect communication with providers, such as depressed mood and paranoia (Corrigan et al., 2003; Desai, Stefanovics, & Rosenheck, 2005).

Principle of coordinated care—Coordinated care requires providers to work toward a set of common goals and to access reliable information concerning the health promotion and illness management activities of their patients. The complexity of the health needs among persons with mental illness involves treatment from numerous providers, which makes coordination of care for these persons particularly relevant to positive health outcomes. Coordinated health services for this population are also essential for avoiding medical error, duplication of services, and increased burden on consumers. However, the bifurcated nature of behavioral and medical treatment systems is an important barrier to care that is coordinated among providers and forces individuals with mental illness to navigate two different processes for help seeking (Koyanagi & Alfano, 2004; Lester, Tritter, & England, 2003).

Principle of comprehensive care—Comprehensive care addresses the full range of health needs and provides referral or access to resources in response to those needs.

Comprehensive care may include assessment and treatment of chronic health problems as well as support with health promotion strategies (Dhooper, 1997; Vandiver, 2009). However, prior research has demonstrated that community mental health centers have a limited capacity to assess, treat, and refer clients for medical care (Druss et al., 2008). In addition, although persons with mental illness desire access to health promotion activities, such as support with diet and exercise and smoking cessation, these resources may not be offered or available (Carney, Allen, & Doebbeling, 2002; DiFranco, Bressi, & Salzer, 2006). For example, Desai, Rosenheck, Druss, and Perlin (2002b) reported that those with a mental disorder and comorbid hypertension or diabetes were less likely than a comparison group to receive nutrition and exercise counseling from their health providers. In addition, health professionals holding stigmatized beliefs about persons with mental illness may be reluctant to refer consumers to these services because of a belief that these persons will not succeed or follow through with their recommendations (Lyon, 1999).

Steps for Implementing Best Practices for Health and Mental Conditions

A set of best practices and several approaches to implementing these best practices have emerged in the health and mental health services evidence base. These practices seek to improve access to continuous, coordinated, and comprehensive services for persons with mental illness in an effort to improve the health of this population and to include integrated behavioral and medical services, health promotion, shared decision making, and caregiver support. Figure 4.1 outlines these practices, approaches to implementing these practices, and their relationship to the research-based principles discussed here.

What's the Evidence?
Integrated Behavioral and Medical Services

Integrated mental and physical health care has been proposed as the solution for ensuring that persons with mental illness receive adequate levels of quality coordinated and comprehensive care (Druss, Rohrbaugh, Levinson, & Rosenheck, 2001; Grazier, Hegedus, Carli, Neal, & Reynolds, 2003). We know from research in primary care that comprehensive care involving interventions such as information technology (e.g., e-mailing, text messaging) and educational approaches (e.g., booklets, health trackers, simple leaflets) can be used to successfully treat hypertension, an all-too-common condition among individuals with mental illness (Dawes, Kaczorowski, Swanson, Hickey, & Karwalajtys, 2010; Hanna, May, & Fairhurst, 2012). Integrated behavioral and medical services have the potential to yield positive outcomes, including decreased psychiatric symptoms, increased utilization of health services, and improved overall functioning (Druss et al., 2001; Lin et al., 2003; Williams et al., 2004).

Several strategies have emerged as important implementation approaches for improving the integration of health services for persons with mental illness (Bartels, 2004; Druss & Mauer, 2010; Grazier et al., 2003). First, colocated health services aim to integrate care by offering behavioral and physical health services at a single site. Persons with mental illness are often engaged in specialty mental health services, and thus bringing primary medical care into this arena uses an existing supportive environment to improve access to medical care (Alakeson, Frank, & Katz, 2010). In a randomized trial by Druss et al. (2001), patients with mental illness treated by primary care that was colocated in a mental health clinic visited the doctor more frequently than those who received usual care.

Other approaches to integration include partnerships between behavioral and medical service providers that involve risk sharing and reorganization of existing care systems in an effort to provide integrated care to persons with mental illness (Grazier et al., 2003). Furthermore, medical case management or health management support offered in community mental health settings have been proposed as other strategies that enhance the existing care system to improve integration of care. For example, Bartels et al. (2004) indicated that among older adults with mental illness, a health management intervention offered by a community support program improved access to preventive health care. In this intervention, a nurse case manager offered support to consumers with monitoring and coordinating general and preventive medical care. Utilization of medical case management models in community mental health services has the potential to help consumers formulate a comprehensive plan of care, provide tangible support with implementing this plan, and monitor progress with goals (Bartels, 2003).

Health Promotion

Health promotion "transcends narrow medical concerns and embraces less well defined concepts of wellness, self-growth, and social betterment" (Dhooper, 1997, p. 207). Thus, in an effort to offer services that comprehensively address the full range of health needs among persons with severe and persistent mental illness, health promotion emerges as an important target for interventions to improve health (Vandiver, 2009). Community mental health providers might invest resources into strategies for offering primary prevention techniques, such as interventions that improve diet and exercise among consumers, as well as secondary and tertiary prevention efforts, such as psychoeducational programming aimed to provide the knowledge and skills needed to slow the progression of disease or reduce risky health behaviors.

Hutchinson et al. (2006) suggest that health education is the "cornerstone" of health promotion for persons with psychiatric disabilities (p. 247). In addition, interventions that utilize other core components of psychiatric rehabilitation including instrumental and social support are effective strategies for encouraging health promotion among persons with severe mental illness (Corrigan, 2003). For example, Brown, Goetz, Van Sciver, Sullivan, and Hamera (2006) examined the effects of a twelve-week manualized intervention to encourage weight loss among persons with psychiatric disabilities. This intervention involved meal planning, dietary education, psychosocial support, and exercise support. Results of this study suggest this kind of intervention may be effective at promoting weight loss among this group. Furthermore, Richardson et al. (2005) suggested that mental health providers in community settings can effectively provide training and support for consumers to utilize and self-monitor moderate intensity physical activity.

Shared Decision Making

Shared decision making requires patients and medical providers to collaborate in making medical decisions with the goal of promoting productive and continuous relationships with providers, adherence to treatment regimens, and in turn health outcomes (Hamann et al., 2009). This collaboration is in line with the mandate of psychiatric rehabilitation to empower persons with mental illness to be involved in every aspect of life, and it is desirable among persons with mental illness (Corrigan, 2003; Drake & Deegan, 2009; Lester, Tritter, & England, 2003). For these individuals there may be specific barriers to shared medical decision making because of providers' stigmatized assumptions about mental illness that preclude active involvement in care and psychiatric symptoms such as hostility, depressed affect, and paranoia, which may make communication with providers difficult. For example, Lester, Tritter, and England (2003) reported that persons with mental illness in primary care often felt that they had little agency in the process of making medical decisions. Other research has suggested that psychiatrists are reluctant to use shared decision making in medical and legal decisions with consumers (Hamann et al., 2009).

Shared decision making may be enhanced by psychiatric rehabilitation providers, case managers, and therapists guiding consumers through the process of understanding the pros and cons of medical interventions, as well as their values and attitudes toward this care (Epstein, Alper, & Quill, 2004). This will allow consumers to have more agency in their interactions with health professionals. In addition, targeted skills training may also be effective for reorienting health professionals toward a recovery perspective that raises their expectations about what persons with severe mental illness may achieve, as well as about strengths and abilities among this population.

Caregiver Support

Informal caregivers are a crucial aspect of a support system that promotes and maintains health among adults with mental illness and comorbid physical health conditions, in part by assisting consumers in accessing continuous, coordinated, and comprehensive care. Persons with mental illness without available informal caregivers may be less likely to seek needed medical care and are more likely to be admitted to a nursing home (Meeks & Murrell, 1997; Miller & Rosenheck, 2006). However, the demands of caregiving for persons with severe mental illness often create emotional and physical distress, which in turn lessens the availability of caregivers over time (Cummings & MacNeil, 2008).

A recent policy analysis for the President's New Freedom Commission on Mental Health calls for enhanced support for caregivers of adults with mental illness, in particular those who are elderly (Bartels, 2003). In a study examining caregivers for older adults with mental illness, Cummings and MacNeil (2008) reported that caregivers did not receive the desired level of support and information from mental health providers. Effective interventions for informal caregivers may involve the provision of respite or assistance oriented toward improving well-being and coping skills (Sorenson, Pinquart, Habil, & Duberstein, 2002). These interventions often employ psychoeducation, support groups, psychotherapy, or a multicomponent frame. Caregivers for those with mental illness may benefit from these kinds of interventions directly targeted to the complex needs of this population and the challenges of caring for these persons over time. For example, Cohen et al. (2000) suggested that caregivers of older adults with schizophrenia may benefit from psychoeducational programs that train families how to manage mental health and health concerns simultaneously. Kopelowicz and Liberman (2003) reported that involving families in illness management improved consumer knowledge of the symptoms of schizophrenia and treatment regimen.

Assessment and Evaluation

Existing literature has examined the efficacy of the presented best practices through assessing key outcomes including health-care utilization rates among persons with mental illness, as well as changes in their subjective and objective health status. However, the quantity of services utilized does not always reflect the quality of the services that this vulnerable group receives. Thus, efforts to assess these best practices requires that researchers and service providers develop appropriate quality care measures for use in myriad service contexts, including community mental health settings, and primary care.

Several existing measures are helpful for assessing aspects of these identified interventions. For example, the Adult Primary Care Assessment Tool, which measures the degree to which primary health services are accessible, comprehensive, coordinated, and continuous, has been used to assess the outcomes of integrated health services (Shi et al., 2001). For examining outcomes of caregiver support models, the Pearlin Caregiver Stress Scale is useful for measuring caregiver stress related to primary and secondary stressors among informal caregivers (Pearlin, Mullen, Semple, & Skaff, 1990). Finally, in the literature, health promotion and shared decision making have been measured through an examination of a variety of constructs, including decisional capacity, patient knowledge, values, motivation, perceived roles and preferences, and patient satisfaction (e.g. Adams, Drake, & Wolford, 2007).

Implementation Issues

A variety of system-, provider-, and person-level factors complicate implementation of the outlined strategies for improving the health of persons with mental illness. For example, systemic barriers to integrated care models include complex and bifurcated reimbursement structures, limitations in the existing structures that train behavioral and medical providers, physical plant constraints, and a lack of available community providers (Druss et al., 2008). Furthermore, many of the best practices proposed require consumer engagement with specialty mental health providers or community level services. As a result, there are many contexts amenable to intervention, including residential settings, community mental health centers, and primary care. However, harder-to-reach populations of persons with mental illness, such as those who are chronically homeless, may be less able to access these best practices. Finally, person-level factors also significantly affect help seeking from formal systems of care, and behavioral and medical professionals should consider them in designing interventions that target health-care utilization and quality. For example, because of institutionalized barriers, health-care utilization rates vary by race and ethnicity, and help seeking is greatly influenced by cultural norms around the concepts of health and well-being.

Provider Competencies

Overall, these best practices require that the behavioral health-care workforce be trained in the nature of common medical issues among persons with mental illness, as well as the resources and practices available to assess and treat these problems. Medical providers need to be well versed in the symptoms of major mental disorders, and training that reduces the stigma of providers toward the capabilities of persons with mental illness is imperative. Finally, for integrated care and other strategies to function effectively, behavioral and medical care providers require advanced skills in interdisciplinary collaboration, including knowledge of professional roles, flexibility, and the ability to reflect on process (Bronstein, 2003).

Future Directions

As outlined here, persons with mental illness are prone to comorbid health conditions and often are unable to access quality medical care. Considering the vulnerabilities of persons with severe mental illness, and the rapidly changing context of health care in the United States and abroad, promoting and maintaining health among consumers is critical. Practitioners, in a variety of behavioral and medical treatment settings, may potentially improve the health of these persons by using best practices to diminish barriers to delivery of continuous, coordinated, and comprehensive health services.

Websites

Institute of Medicine, *Crossing the Quality Chasm: A New Health System for the 21st Century*—http://www.iom.edu/~/media/Files/Report%20Files/2001/Crossing-the-Quality-Chasm/Quality%20Chasm%202001%20%20report%20brief.pdf

President's New Freedom Commission Report on Mental Health—http://www.store.samhsa.gov/product/SMA03-3831

Glossary

Medical comorbidity: Medical conditions that are present in conjunction with a major mental illness.

Persons with severe mental illness: Persons with a major mental disorder who have multiple acute illness episodes that result in persistent limits on social and psychological functioning.

Quality health services: Health and mental health services that are coordinated and comprehensive, and that encourage continuity of care with providers and health management or treatment regimens.

References

Adams, J. R., Drake, R. E., & Wolford, G. L. (2007). Shared decision-making preferences of persons with serious mental illness. *Psychiatric Services, 58(9)*, 1219–1221.

Alakeson, V., Frank, R. G., & Katz, R. E. (2010). Specialty care medical homes for people with severe, persistent mental disorders. *Health Affairs, 29*(5), 867–873.

Alison, D., Mackell, J., & McDonnell, D. (2003). The impact of weight gain on quality of life among persons with schizophrenia. *Psychiatric Services, 54*, 565–567.

Bartels, S. J. (2003). Improving the system of care for older adults with mental illness in the United States. *American Journal of Geriatric Psychiatry, 11*(5), 486–497.

Bartels, S. J. (2004). Caring for the whole person: Integrated health care for older adults with severe mental illness and medical comorbidity. *Journal of the American Geriatrics Society, 52*(12), 249–257.

Bartels, S. J., Forester, B., Muerser, K. T., Miles, K. M., Dums, A. R., Pratt, S. I., et al. (2004). Enhanced skills training and health care management for older persons with severe mental illness. *Community Mental Health Journal, 40*(1), 75–90.

Berren, M. R., Santiago, J. M., Zent, M. R., & Carbone, C. P. (1999). Health care utilization by persons with severe and persistent mental illness. *Psychiatric Services, 50*, 559–561.

Blank, M. B., Mandell, D. S., Aiken, L., & Hadley, T. R. (2002). Co-occurrence of HIV and serious mental illness among Medicaid recipients. *Psychiatric Services, 53*(7), 868–873.

Bronstein, L. R. (2003). A model for interdisciplinary collaboration. *Social Work, 48*(3), 297–306.

Brown, C., Goetz, J., Van Sciver, A., Sullivan, D., & Hamera, E. (2006). A psychiatric rehabilitation approach to weight loss. *Psychiatric Rehabilitation Journal, 29*(4), 267–273.

Brown, S. (1997). Excess mortality of schizophrenia. *British Journal of Psychiatry, 171*, 502–508.

Brown, S., Birtwistle, J., Roe, L., & Thompson, C. (1999). The unhealthy lifestyle of people with schizophrenia. *Psychological Medicine, 29*, 697–701.

Carney, C. P., Allen, A., & Doebbeling, B. N. (2002). Receipt of clinical preventive medical services among psychiatric patients. *Psychiatric Services, 53*(8), 1028–1030.

Cohen, C. I., Cohen, G. D., Blank, K., Gaitz, C., Katz, I. R., Leuchter, A., et al. (2000). Schizophrenia and older adults: Directions for research and policy. *American Journal of Geriatric Psychiatry, 8*(1), 19–28.

Corrigan, P. (2003). Towards an integrated structural model of psychiatric rehabilitation. *Psychiatric Rehabilitation Journal, 26*(4), 346–358.

Corrigan, P., Thompson, V., Lambert, D., Sangster, Y., Noel, J. G., & Campbell, J. (2003). Perceptions of discrimination among persons with serious mental illness. *Psychiatric Services, 54*(8), 1105–1110.

Cradock-O'Leary, J., Young, A. S., Yano, E. M., Wang, M., & Lee, M. L. (2002). Use of general medical services by VA patients with psychiatric disorders. *Psychiatric Services, 53*, 874–878.

Cummings, S. M., & MacNeil, G. (2008). Caregivers of older clients with severe mental illness: Perceptions of burdens and rewards. *Families in Society, 89*(1), 51–59.

Daumit, G. L., Clark, J., Steinwachs, D. M., Graham, C., Lehman, A., & Ford, D. E. (2003). Prevalence and correlates of obesity in a community sample of individuals with severe and persistent mental illness. *Journal of Nervous and Mental Disease, 191*(12), 799–805.

Dawes, M. G., Kaczorowski, J., Swanson, G., Hickey, J., & Karwalajtys, T. (2010). The effect of patient education booklet and "BP" trackers on knowledge about hypertension: A randomized controlled trial. *Family Practice, 27*(5), 472–478.

Desai, M. M., Rosenheck, R. A., Druss, B. G., & Perlin, J. B. (2002a). Mental disorders and quality of diabetes care in the Veterans Health Administration. *American Journal of Psychiatry, 159*, 1584–1590.

Desai, M. M., Rosenheck, R. A., Druss, B. G., & Perlin, J. B. (2002b). Receipt of nutrition and exercise counseling among medical outpatients with psychiatric and substance use disorders. *Journal of General Internal Medicine, 17*, 556–560.

Desai, M. M., Stefanovics, E. A., & Rosenheck, R. (2005). The role of psychiatric diagnosis in satisfaction with primary care. *Medical Care, 43*(12), 1208–1216.

Dhooper, S. S. (1997). *Social work in health care in the 21st century*. Thousand Oaks, CA: Sage.

Dickerson, F., McNary, S. W., Brown, C. H., Kreyenbuhl, J., Goldberg, R., & Dixon, L. B. (2003). Somatic healthcare utilization among adults with serious mental illness who are receiving community psychiatric services. *Medical Care, 41*(4), 560–570.

DiFranco, E., Bressi, S. K., & Salzer, M. S. (2006). Understanding consumer preferences for communication channels to create consumer-directed health promotion efforts in psychiatric rehabilitation settings. *Psychiatric Rehabilitation Journal, 29*(4), 251–257.

Dixon, L., Goldberg, R., Lehman, A., & McNary, S. (2001). The impact of health status on work, symptoms, and functional outcomes in severe mental illness. *Journal of Nervous and Mental Disease, 189*(1), 17–23.

Dixon, L., Wohlheiter, K., & Thompson, D. (2001). Medical management of persons with schizophrenia. In J. A. Lieberman & R. M. Murray (Eds.), *Comprehensive care of schizophrenia: A textbook of clinical management* (pp. 281–292). Malden, MA: Dunitz.

Drake, R. E., & Deegan, P. E. (2009). Shared decision making in an ethical imperative. *Psychiatric Services, 60*(8), 1007.

Druss, B. G. (2002). The mental health/primary care interface in the United States: History, structure, and context. *General Hospital Psychiatry, 24,* 197–202.

Druss, B. G., Bradford, D. W., Rosenheck, R. A., Radford, M. J., & Krumholz, H. (2000). Mental disorders and use of cardiovascular procedures after myocardial infection. *JAMA, 283*(4), 506–511.

Druss, B. G., Bradford, D. W., Rosenheck, R. A., Radford, M. J., & Krumholz, H. (2001). Quality of medical care and excess mortality in older patients with mental disorders. *Archives of General Psychiatry, 58*(6), 565–572.

Druss, B. G., Marcus, S. C., Campbell, J., Cuffel, B., Harnett, J., & Ingoglia, C. (2008). Medical services for clients in community mental health centers: Results from a national survey. *Psychiatric Services, 59*(8), 917–920.

Druss, B. G., & Mauer, B. J. (2010). Health care reform and care at the behavioral health-primary care interface. *Psychiatric Services, 61*(11), 1087–1092.

Druss, B. G., Rohrbaugh, R. M., Levinson, C. M., & Rosenheck, R. (2001). Integrated medical care for patients with serious psychiatric illness: A randomized controlled trial. *Archives of General Psychiatry, 58,* 861–868.

Druss, B. G., & Rosenheck, R. (1998). Mental disorders and access to medical care in the United States. *American Journal of Psychiatry, 155*(12), 1775–1777.

Epstein, R. M., Alper, B. S., & Quill, T. E. (2004). Communicating evidence for participatory decision-making. *JAMA, 291*(19), 2359–2366.

Gallagher, T. C., Andersen, R. M., Koegel, P., & Gelberg, L. (1997). Determinants of regular source of care among homeless adults in Los Angeles. *Medical Care, 35*(8), 814–830.

Grazier, K. L., Hegedus, A. M., Carli, T., Neal, D., & Reynolds, K. (2003). Integration of behavioral and physical health care for a Medicaid population through a public-public partnership. *Psychiatric Services, 54*(11), 1508–1512.

Hamann, J., Mendel, R., Cohen, R., Heres, S., Ziegler, M., & Buhner, M. (2009). Psychiatrists' use of shared decision making in the treatment of schizophrenia: Patient characteristics and decision topics. *Psychiatric Services, 60*(8), 1107–1112.

Hanna, L., May, C., & Fairhurst, K. (2012). The place for information and communication technology-mediated consultation in primary care: GPs' perspectives. *Family Practice, 29*(3), 361–366.

Hayward, R. A., Bernard, A. M., Freeman, H. E., & Corey, C. R. (1990). Regular source of ambulatory care and access to health services. *American Journal of Public Health, 81*, 434–438.

Hutchinson, D. S., Gagne, C., Bowers, A., Russinova, Z., Skrinar, G. S., & Anthony, W. (2006). A framework for health promotion services for people with psychiatric disabilities. *Psychiatric Rehabilitation Journal, 29*(4), 241–250.

Institute of Medicine. (2001). *Crossing the quality chasm: A new health system for the 21st century*. Washington, DC: Author.

Jones, L., Clarke, W., & Carney, C. (2004). Receipt of diabetes services by insured adults with and without claims for mental disorders. *Medical Care, 42*(12), 1167–1175.

Kopelowicz, A., & Liberman, R. P. (2003). Integrating treatment with rehabilitation for persons with major mental illnesses. *Psychiatric Services, 54*(11), 1491–1498.

Koyanagi, C., & Alfano, E. (2004). *Get it together: How to integrate physical and mental health care for people with serious mental disorders*. Washington, DC: Bazelon Center for Mental Health Law.

Lester, H. E., Tritter, J. Q., & England, E. (2003). Satisfaction with primary care: The perspectives of people with schizophrenia. *Family Practice, 20*(5), 508–513.

Lester, H. E., Tritter, J. Q., & Sorohan, H. (2005). Patients' and health professionals' views on primary care for people with serious mental illness: Focus group study. *British Medical Journal, 330,* 1122.

Levinson-Miller, C., Druss, B. G., Dombrowski, E. A., & Rosenheck, R. A. (2003). Barriers to primary medical care among patients at a community mental health center. *Psychiatric Services, 54*(8), 1158–1160.

Lin, E., Katon, W., Korff, M. V., Tang, L., Williams, J., Kroenke, K., et al. (2003). Effect of improving depression care on pain and functional outcomes among older adults with arthritis: A randomized controlled trial. *JAMA, 290*(18), 2428–2434.

Lyon, E. R. (1999). A review of the effects of nicotine on schizophrenia and antipsychotic medications. *Psychiatric Services, 50*(10), 1346–1350.

Meeks, S., & Murrell, S. A. (1997). Mental illness in late life: Socioeconomic conditions, psychiatric symptoms, and adjustment of long-term sufferers. *Psychology and Aging, 12*(2), 296–308.

Miller, E. A., & Rosenheck, R. A. (2006). Risk of nursing home admission in association with mental illness nationally in the Department of Veterans Affairs. *Medical Care, 44*(4), 343–351.

Nath, S. B., Marcus, S. C., & Solomon, P. L. (2006). The impact of psychiatric comorbidity of general hospital length of stay. *Psychiatric Quarterly, 77,* 203–209.

National Advisory Mental Health Council. (1993). Health care reform for Americans with severe mental illnesses: Report of the National Advisory Mental Health Council. *American Journal of Psychiatry, 150*(10), 1447–1465.

O'Day, B., Killeen, M. B., Sutton, J., & Iezzoni, L. I. (2005). Primary care experiences of people with psychiatric disabilities: Barriers to care and potential solutions. *Psychiatric Rehabilitation Journal, 28*(4), 339–345.

Pearlin, L. I., Mullen, J. T., Semple, S. J., & Skaff, M. M. (1990). Caregiving and the stress process: An overview of concepts and their measures. *Gerontologist, 30*(5), 583–594.

Phelan, M., Stradins, L., & Morrison, S. (2001). Physical health of people with severe mental illness. *British Medical Journal, 322,* 443–444.

President's New Freedom Commission on Mental Health. (2003). *Achieving the promise: Transforming mental health care in America.* Rockville, MD: Substance Abuse and Mental Health Services Administration. Retrieved from http://mentalhealthcommission.gov.

RachBeisel, J., Scott, J., & Dixon, L. (1999). Co-occurring severe mental illness and substance abuse disorders: A review of recent research. *Psychiatric Services, 50*(11), 1427–1432.

Richardson, C. R., Faulkner, G., McDevitt, J., Skrinar, G. S., Hutchinson, D. S., & Piette, J. D. (2005). Integrating physical activity into mental health services for persons with serious mental illness. *Psychiatric Services, 56*(3), 324–331.

Shi, L., Starfield, B., & Xu, J. (2001). Validating the Adult Primary Care Assessment Tool. *Journal of Family Practice, 50*(2).

Shi, L., Starfield, B., Xu, J., Politzer, R., & Regan, J. (2003). Primary care quality: Community health center and health maintenance organization. *Southern Medical Journal, 96*(8), 787–794.

Simpson, J. C., & Tsuang, M. T. (1996). Mortality among patients with schizophrenia. *Schizophrenia Bulletin, 22*(3), 485–499.

Sorenson, S., Pinquart, M., Habil, D., & Duberstein, P. (2002). How effective are interventions with caregivers? An updated meta-analysis. *Gerontologist, 42*(3), 356–372.

Sussman, N. (2001). Review of atypical antipsychotics and weight gain. *Journal of Clinical Psychiatry, 62,* 5–12.

Vandiver, V. (2009). *Integrating health promotion and mental health: An introduction to policies, principles, and practices.* New York: Oxford University Press.

Wagner, E. H., Austin, B. T., & Von Korff, M. (1996). Organizing care for patients with chronic illness. *Milbank Quarterly, 74*(4), 511–544.

Williams, J., Katon, W., Lin, E., Noel, P. H., Worchel, J., & Cornell, J. (2004). The effectiveness of depression care management on diabetes-related outcomes in older patients. *Annals of Internal Medicine, 140*(12), 1015–1024.

Harm Reduction in Mental Health Practice

*Katie Witkiewitz, Justin Walthers, and
G. Alan Marlatt*

Harm reduction has been characterized as a public health model, a specific or general policy initiative, a therapeutic style and type of psychotherapy, and an approach toward thinking about human behavior. For the purposes of this chapter we define harm reduction as a pragmatic approach toward helping individuals who engage in some problem behavior (e.g., abuse of substances, binge drinking, excessive gambling) to minimize the hazards that are often associated with problematic behaviors (e.g., overdose, infectious disease transmission, drunk driving), without requiring abstinence from those behaviors as an ultimate goal. Harm reduction strategies can be implemented on societal, community, and individual levels, but for the purposes of this chapter we focus explicitly on harm reduction at the individual level. The chapter provides a brief overview of the history of harm reduction, research, practice-based principles that may guide practitioners in using harm reduction, research outcomes in harm reduction programs, steps for implementing a harm reduction approach, evaluation of harm reduction strategies, provider competencies, and a look to the future. We begin this chapter with a case study of Jane (see box 5.1) and her experience working with a provider who implemented a harm reduction approach to address alcohol use.

> **Box 5.1. Case Study: Jane**
>
> Jane, a fifty-one-year-old unemployed, divorced woman, was self-referred to an outpatient psychotherapy clinic because she was concerned that she was drinking too much and that her alcohol use was interfering with her life goals. After an initial assessment of Jane's history of substance use, current level of use and problems associated with her

This chapter is dedicated to the memory of Alan Marlatt, who passed away suddenly on March 14, 2011, during the preparation of this chapter. Alan Marlatt was a true visionary in the field of addictive behaviors, and his commitment to harm reduction serves as our ongoing inspiration for conducting this work.

alcohol use, psychosocial stressors, motivation to change, and the risk and protective factors for her success in treatment, it was determined that Jane had a current diagnosis of alcohol dependence and that she might benefit from a harm-reduction approach.

She was drinking six nights per week and drank at least a bottle of wine (seven to ten drinks) on occasion. Jane would experience terrible sleep disruption when she drank heavily, and she reported that heavy bouts of drinking would also result in her experiencing a more depressed mood the following day. She indicated that at times she would feel suicidal the day after heavy drinking, although she did not have a specific plan or a strong intention to commit suicide. Most recently, she had been drinking more by herself, and this affected her ability to share alcohol with friends. She stated that she was embarrassed that she drank much more than her friends and so decided most nights to stay home and drink by herself.

Jane was very motivated to reduce her drinking, and she wanted to experience fewer alcohol-related consequences, but she was not prepared to give up drinking alcohol for numerous reasons. Her primary concern was that she had a history of depressed mood, and she viewed alcohol use as an important "treatment" for her mood disorder. Indeed, Jane met criteria for a current diagnosis of dysthymia on the basis of her reporting a sad mood on most days for the previous five years, as well as chronic feelings of hopelessness, difficulty sleeping, and low self-esteem. Her secondary concern was that she had been struggling with feelings of loneliness and inadequacy since her divorce with her husband, and she reported that purchasing expensive wine at her favorite wine store (operated by one of her "dear friends") and sharing wine with friends were her two social outlets. Thus, the case formulation was that Jane was using alcohol to regulate her mood and as part of her social life, yet she was experiencing a few consequences that reducing her alcohol use could minimize.

The first short-term treatment goal was to identify the situational and contextual factors that precipitated heavy drinking nights, as well as the factors that predicted evenings when she did not drink. To accomplish this goal, Jane self-monitored her moods, thoughts, feelings, and settings every day for the first two weeks of treatment and reviewed her daily diary during twice weekly fifty-minute individual counseling sessions. The second short-term treatment goal was to identify and practice alternative skills for coping with negative moods. In collaboration with Jane, it was decided that she would begin a daily mindfulness practice of thirty minutes of guided breath meditation per day, as well as mini-meditations at times when she was feeling sad.

At the outset of her treatment planning Jane agreed on a long-term treatment goal of reducing her alcohol use to no more than two glasses of wine per night and reducing her days of alcohol use to four nights per week. By the fifth week of treatment, Jane had reduced her drinking to fewer than four glasses of wine, and she drank only three or four nights per week. Jane stated that journaling her moods and daily mindfulness practice were extremely helpful in regulating her moods. In the sixth week of treatment Jane experienced a lapse, whereby she drank a bottle and a half of wine in one evening. She was devastated. A functional analysis of the lapse revealed numerous factors that could have contributed to it, including hormonal changes associated with menopause, a fight with a family member that led to her feeling extreme anger, and not practicing meditation that day. Using the lapse as an example, we created lapse-warning cards that reminded Jane of these risk factors, and she placed the cards in numerous places around her house. Over the four weeks following the lapse Jane reduced her drinking to one or two glasses of wine, only two or three days per week, and she drank only in the company of friends. We terminated treatment after ten weeks, with the invitation that Jane was welcome back to the clinic at any time if she experienced a lapse or found herself at risk for lapsing again on the basis of the factors we identified. During termination, Jane mentioned that she was afraid at the outset of treatment that we would require her to attend Alcoholics Anonymous meetings and quit drinking all together. She explicitly stated that such an approach would have "driven her over the edge" and that she needed to take the small steps toward change that we encouraged as part of the treatment plan. She also mentioned that she was thinking about not drinking all together and that she would start working on that goal independently.

The case of Jane epitomizes a harm-reduction intervention, in that we took a compassionate, nonjudgmental approach to her drinking and identified alternative strategies for Jane to practice to reduce her drinking, without requiring that she identify abstinence as an ultimate goal. By the end of treatment Jane was drinking at unharmful levels and was not experiencing consequences associated with her alcohol use. She was also willing to consider abstinence in the future, something that was unthinkable to her at the start of treatment.

Background

As noted in the introduction, we define harm reduction as a pragmatic approach toward helping individuals who engage in some problem behavior (e.g., abuse of substances, binge drinking, excessive gambling) to minimize the hazards that are often associated with problematic behaviors (e.g., overdose, infectious disease transmission, drunk driving), without requiring abstinence from those behaviors as an ultimate goal.

The harm reduction movement largely originated in England and Europe during the early to mid-twentieth century, with England initiating a program in 1926 that would provide prescription cocaine and opium derivates to individuals with stimulant and opiate dependence, and in 1976 the Netherlands passed the Dutch Opium Act, which decriminalized the use of marijuana and other "soft" drugs (Collins et al., 2012). In 1984, the Netherlands was the first nation to provide government funding for needle-exchange programs, which were programs to allow injection drug users to receive a clean needle in exchange for a used needle, a program that significantly reduces the transmission of HIV (Mathers et al., 2010).

The implementation of harm reduction in psychotherapy is a recent development that largely originated in the United States as part of a movement focused on developing treatments for alcohol-use disorders that did not require abstinence goals (e.g., Hester & Miller, 1989; Miller & Marlatt, 1984; Sobell & Sobell, 1973). In many ways the harm reduction psychotherapy movement was assisted by new ideas in the addiction research and treatment community that proposed a compassionate, nonconfrontational approach to the treatment of substance use disorders as more effective and more humane (e.g., Miller & Rollnick, 1991).

Harm reduction psychotherapy grew out of these earlier movements in the United States, but it was not formally implemented as a specific treatment approach until the late 1990s (Marlatt, 1998) and early 2000s (Denning, 2000; Tatarsky, 2002). Today, harm reduction psychotherapy is practiced across the United States and internationally. The Harm Reduction Psychotherapy Center (http://www.harm reductiontherapy.org), developed by Patt Denning and Jeannie Little, describes harm reduction psychotherapy as a multidimensional approach that uses a combination of evidence-based treatment and public health principles. Harm Reduction Psychotherapy and Training Associates, directed by Andrew Tatarsky and Mark Sehl, describes harm reduction psychotherapy as a "pragmatic and compassionate approach to reducing alcohol and drug-related harm to the individual user and those in his or her family and community" (http://www.harmreductioncounseling .com, n.p.; see also Tatarsky, 2003).

Theoretical Perspective

Harm reduction can actually be described as a metatheory, rooted in the basic principle of minimizing harm through any means possible and within any theoretical perspective. In general, harm reduction psychotherapists may vary in theoretical perspective and clinical approach, although many harm reductionists are rooted in behavioral change theories. Behavior change theories provide models of individual behavior change, such as social-learning theory (Bandura, 1977), theories of reasoned action and planned behavior (Ajzen, 1985), and stages-of-change theory (Prochaska & DiClemente, 1986). For example, from a social-learning perspective the harm reductionist draws from a vast literature on the role of behavioral learning in a social environment, whereby individuals often learn from the behavior of individuals around them. The harm reduction psychotherapist who draws from social-learning theory may focus on minimizing harm by helping clients change their social environment or by helping clients obtain new social models of healthy, nonharmful behaviors.

Principles

Tatarsky (2002) outlined six core ideas of harm reduction psychotherapy: tailoring treatment to the individual, targeting treatment goals based on the client's individuals needs and willingness, acknowledging and supporting client strengths, accepting small changes as steps in the right direction, never making abstinence (or another preconceived treatment goal) a precondition for therapy, and building a collaborative and empowering relationship with the client. Elaborating on these core ideas, Denning (2000) described ten principles of harm reduction that provide the theoretical basis for the harm reduction psychotherapy techniques that we describe in the current chapter.

Practice Principles of Harm Reduction

- Harm reduction includes any action that reduces the harm associated with addictive behaviors.

- Personal decisions to use a drug or engage in an addictive behavior should not be criminalized or demonized.

- Individuals have various reasons for engaging in addictive behaviors, and engaging in drug use or other behaviors (e.g., gambling) does not necessarily imply abuse.

- Individuals can make rational decisions even if they are under the influence of drugs.

- Individuals are not in "denial"; rather, the expression of denial is a product of shame and sanctions that are associated with drug use.

- Ambivalence to change is normal. The therapist's job is to work with ambivalence or resistance to change.

- Addiction is a biopsychosocial problem, not a disease.

- Many individuals have attachments to substance use, and treatment must work to provide support that will offer those individuals an opportunity to detach from substance use.

- A client's motivation toward change is the responsibility of the therapist and the client.

- Success is any positive change in the direction of less harmful behavior. Recognizing that change is often slow and with setbacks.

As seen in these core ideas and practice principles, the goal is to help individuals minimize the negative consequences of their behavior, without requiring them to abstain from the behavior, and to acknowledge that change is difficult and to support individuals in all efforts toward change. As Marlatt (1998) has noted, "The aims of harm reduction psychotherapy are to find methods that work for the client in terms of his or her goals, and not to blame the client for failure to change" (p. 22). This last aspect, not blaming clients for failure to change, is one of the more important elements of taking a harm reduction approach. Changing behavior, particularly addictive behaviors, is incredibly difficult, and forcing or demanding change is not typically very effective. Furthermore, if a client makes some progress toward change, then it is critical to remember and acknowledge that having a "lapse" (i.e., setback, or initial return to problematic behavior) is the most common outcome following behavior change attempts (Polivy & Herman, 2002). Many providers and treatment models in the substance abuse field are afraid to discuss the probability of a lapse with recently abstinent clients and often consider lapses to be failures. A harm reduction practitioner is more likely to take a pragmatic stance by acknowledging that there is a fairly high probability of lapsing and by viewing a lapse as a learning experience.

To consider all these core ideas, we provide a simple acronym, *PRACTICE*, for introducing and thinking about the principles of harm reduction psychotherapy. Harm reduction psychotherapy is a *pragmatic* approach to *reduce* harm. It is *adaptable* and requires great *compassion*. It acknowledges the importance of the *therapeutic* relationship and the need for an *individualized* and *collaborative* focus with great *empathy* toward the client's endeavors to change. We use the word *practice* because it is well known that learning a new skill often requires practice. Similarly, learning to change your behavior often takes multiple attempts and the practice of several new skills. Harm reduction psychotherapy also requires practice on the side of the practitioner, particularly the practices of acceptance, compassion, and empathy.

Steps for Implementing Harm Reduction Psychotherapy

Although the steps for implementing a harm reduction approach are a challenge to apply in a linear fashion, clinicians can use the following six steps as a guideline for practice. These steps are carry out an assessment; establish a hierarchy of problems; develop a treatment plan; enroll in a standardized treatment protocol or work with the initial assessment to determine when treatment can begin; reevaluate hierarchies of problems, harms, goals, and capabilities; and plan for relapse prevention. The following sections summarize these steps.

Step 1:   Carry Out an Assessment

The first step in implementing harm reduction psychotherapy is to do a thorough assessment of the individual (see later in this chapter for methods of assessment). Typically, we begin by taking a thorough history of the individual's substance use and mental health, focusing specifically on recent problems and any attempts (prior or current) to change their behavior.

Step 2:   Establish a Hierarchy of Problems, Related Harms, Goals, and Capabilities

It is important to consider problems, related harms, goals, and capabilities separately, as a client's number-one problem (e.g., legal prosecution for drug offense) is not always harmful and is often unrelated to his or her goals (e.g., to reduce drug use and visit children). Likewise, a person might have a goal that is incompatible with the real world; thus, it is important to consider what a person wants (as a goal) as separate from what he or she can do realistically in the current moment (i.e., capabilities). It is often useful to begin by brainstorming lists of problems, harms, goals, and capabilities, but without assigning value to the items on the lists. Then the client and therapist can work together to establish a hierarchy by assigning values and rating each problem, harm, goal, and capability from most (problematic, harmful, desirable, capable) to least (problematic, harmful, desirable, capable).

Step 3:   Develop a Treatment Plan

The hierarchy can then be used to develop a treatment plan for each individual client. Consistent with the theme of harm reduction, the goal of the treatment plan is to work toward the most desirable goals that reduce harm and are within a person's capabilities while also acknowledging any ancillary problems that might interfere with those goals. With many clients it is often helpful to revisit their hierarchies throughout treatment.

Step 4:   Enroll Client in a Standardized Treatment Protocol or Work with the Initial Assessment to Determine When Treatment Can Begin

This step of harm reduction psychotherapy is very much dependent on the individual needs of each client. As noted earlier, harm reduction psychotherapy is best described as an amalgam of evidence-based treatments, and specific interventions might be more or less appropriate for individual clients. For some clients the subsequent steps are to enroll them in a standardized treatment protocol; for other clients there are multiple steps between an initial assessment and when treatment can begin.

Step 5: Reevaluate

In the closing stages of treatment, harm reduction psychotherapy should include a final reevaluation of the hierarchies of problems, harms, goals, and capabilities that brought the person in for treatment.

Step 6: Plan for Relapse Prevention

The final step involves planning for the future. Often, relapse prevention planning is an important step as treatment is coming to an end. Also, note that relapse prevention includes relapse to any changed behavior; harm reduction psychotherapy does not require abstinence before the development of a relapse prevention plan.

What's the Evidence?

Unlike many mental health and substance abuse treatments, harm reduction psychotherapy—as an individual treatment for substance users—has not been widely evaluated in large-scale randomized clinical trials. However, the research data in support of harm reduction approaches (including individual-level, community-level, and societal-level harm reduction efforts) have received considerable support for their efficacy and effectiveness in a wide range of populations. For example, Larimer et al. (2009) found that a housing-first program, which provided housing to a group of individuals with continuous alcohol problems, without a stipulation of abstinence and with the acceptance of drinking alcohol at the housing facility, resulted in significant cost savings (53 percent cost reduction for housed participants relative to a control group who did not receive housing) and significant reductions in alcohol use.

A recent Cochrane Review (Mattick, Breen, Kimber, & Davoli, 2009) concluded that individuals with heroin dependence who received methadone maintenance therapy (methadone is considered a less harmful opiate than heroin), had significantly less heroin use and better treatment retention than did individuals who received nonpharmacological approaches to heroin treatment (including detoxification, drug-free rehabilitation, and placebo medication). Wodak and Cooney (2006) provided ample evidence that needle- or syringe-exchange programs reduce HIV infection among injecting drug users, and Van Den Berg, Smit, Van Brussel, Coutinho, and Prins (2007) found that participation in a harm reduction program that consisted of both needle exchange and methadone maintenance was associated with a lower incidence of HIV infection and hepatitis C.

The effectiveness of harm reduction approaches has been demonstrated across numerous behaviors (e.g., alcohol use, drug use, self-harm), in diverse populations (e.g., adolescents, ethnic and racial minority groups), and across multiple settings (e.g., schools, clinics, community centers). We refer the interested reader to a recent edited volume evaluating the effectiveness of harm reduction across these different behaviors, populations, and settings (Marlatt, Larimer, & Witkiewitz, 2012), as well as to recent review articles (e.g., Marlatt & Witkiewitz, 2002; Ritter & Cameron, 2006; Witkiewitz & Marlatt, 2006).

Assessment and Evaluation

There are two levels of assessment and evaluation in harm reduction psychotherapy. First, there is the individual-level assessment and evaluation of treatment progress. To our knowledge, there are only a few individual assessment and evaluation tools that are specific to harm reduction psychotherapy; most harm reduction psychotherapists rely on existing assessment tools that are well established and have been shown to be valid. Generally, it is recommended that harm reduction psychotherapists use a motivational interviewing style in conducting an assessment of the client's history and existing problems (Miller & Rollnick, 1991, 2012; see also chapter 13). Motivational interviewing, as part of the assessment process, refers to an approach to facilitating change that uses four processes: engaging, focusing, evoking, and planning (Miller & Rollnick, 2012). Another tool that is often used is the decisional-balance matrix, shown in figure 5.1 in the form of a worksheet, which includes a list of the pros and cons of their current patterns of substance use, as well as the pros and cons of making any changes to their current substance use.

Some specific assessment tools for harm reduction with injection drug users include the Harm Reduction Self-Efficacy Questionnaire (Phillips & Rosenberg, 2008), which is a self-report questionnaire of an injection drug users' confidence to employ fifteen harm-reducing coping skills (e.g., "Choose a safe place to inject that is private, clean, well lit, and warm"), and the Injecting Risk Questionnaire (Stimson, Jones, Chalmers, & Sullivan, 1998), which measures the extent and nature of needle sharing and related behaviors. A recently developed assessment device for examining perceived moderate drinking capability is the Alcohol Reduction Strategies—Current Confidence Scale (Bonar et al., 2011), which involves an individual

Figure 5.1. Decisional Balance Worksheet

Instructions: In the sections below, write the pros and cons of continuing to use alcohol and drugs or abstinence/recovery.

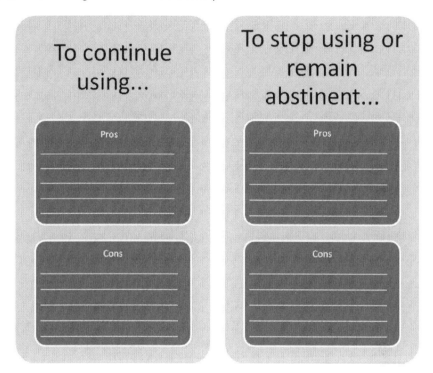

rating his or her confidence in the ability to use cognitive-behavioral strategies to limit quantity or frequency of drinking.

Assessment and evaluation can also occur at the programmatic level. One example is the Harm Reduction Self-Assessment Checklist, developed by the Eurasian Harm Reduction Network and available online (http://www.harm-reduction.org/images/stories/library/ngo_self_assessment_checklist_en.pdf). The Harm Reduction Self-Assessment Checklist is meant to be self-administered by an organization or program and includes questions about general organization, management, harm reduction principles, harm reduction components and services, and advocacy. There is also a section for developing an action plan to make improvements in a particular area. Similarly, the Harm Reduction Coalition provides guidelines for government or community groups to evaluate and monitor the implementation of harm reduction policies that incorporates five standards:

1. *Human dignity*—Provision of inclusive, respectful, equitable services

2. *Common sense*—Programs and services based on realistic and achievable and measurable objectives

3. *Focus on harms*—Acknowledgment that harms occur in a social context that includes determinants of health and provision of basic needs

4. *Balanced*—Services provided from a balanced approach and based on sound evidence and ongoing evaluation

5. *Dealing with priority issues*—Services provided along a continuum of care that addresses the needs and priorities of the client

The full assessment, which provides several assessment questions, is available online (Harm Reduction Network, n.d.).

Implementation Issues

The biggest challenges for implementing harm reduction psychotherapy include existing policies and models of substance use that are focused on a zero-tolerance, abstinent-only approach to alcohol and drug use; the misconceived perception that harm reduction approaches "enable" continued problematic use; and the lack of systematic, manualized intervention manuals to guide the implementation of harm reduction psychotherapy. Numerous recommendations for implementing harm reduction therapy into traditional substance abuse treatment programs and for developing new harm reduction programs can be found in a special section of the *Journal of Psychoactive Drugs* (Gleghorn, Rosenbaum, & Garcia, 2001), which covers a group of presentations from a conference titled "Bridging the Gap in San Francisco: The Process of Integrating Harm Reduction and Traditional Substance Abuse Services." Among the many benefits of implementing harm reduction psychotherapy, Marlatt, Blume, and Parks (2001) concluded that one of the most significant is the opportunity to expand availability and acceptability of substance abuse and mental health treatment services to those individuals who have not benefitted from or are unwilling to attend abstinence-based treatment programs.

An added benefit is that harm reduction psychotherapy is often a compatible approach for working with diverse populations, including Asian Americans (Osilla, Wong, & Zane, 2012), Hispanic and Latino populations (Blume & Resor, 2012), African Americans (Andrasik, Woods, & George, 2012), homeless individuals (Larimer et al., 2009), adolescents (Kelly, 2012), and individuals with dual diagnoses of substance abuse and mental health disorders (Denning, 2012). Traditional addiction treatment services have underserved many of the individuals in these diverse groups, and harm reduction programs specific to these groups have already been shown to be effective (Marlatt et al., 2012).

Provider Competencies

To be an effective provider of harm reduction psychotherapy, it is imperative that the provider embrace and genuinely value each characteristic of the PRACTICE acronym: pragmatism, reducing harm, adaptable, compassionate, therapeutic relationship, individualizing treatment, collaborative focus, and empathy. All these characteristics will help a provider be an effective practitioner of harm reduction psychotherapy. We have also identified acceptance of the client, regardless of the client's problems, goals, and capabilities, as a core competency. The phrase that is commonly used to describe competent harm reduction services are those services that embrace the notion of "come as you are"—in other words, the services and providers accept the individual however he or she might be at the time of approaching the treatment services or provider (Marlatt et al., 2001). It is important to note that a solid foundation in motivational interviewing as a therapeutic style is often sufficient for making the transition to becoming a provider of harm reduction psychotherapy, although other resources are also recommended (Denning, 2000; Tatarsky, 2002).

Future Directions

The landscape of substance abuse treatment is changing in the United States, and in general, harm reduction is becoming much more accepted among policy makers and service providers. For example, the number of individuals enrolled in methadone maintenance programs has more than doubled between 1998 and 2007 (Walthers, Weingardt, Witkiewitz, & Marlatt, 2012), and the Obama administration recently signed into law a repeal of the federal funding bans for needle-exchange programs (Office of National Drug Control Policy, 2010). As the broader community embraces more harm reduction policies, further research on the effectiveness of each policy is imperative. In particular, it is an important limitation that no randomized clinical trials to date have examined individual harm reduction psychotherapy in comparison to an abstinence-based, empirically supported treatment, although studies that have compared treatments with moderation goals to treatments with abstinence goals have generally found that they are equally effective in helping people reduce their use (Graber & Miller, 1988; Sanchez-Craig, Annis, Bornet, & MacDonald, 1984).

A huge challenge for all empirically supported treatments, including harm reduction psychotherapy, is the dissemination of programs to more communities and individuals, particularly individuals in rural areas. Future research on strategies for dissemination and training is essential to help the professional community of harm reduction psychotherapists grow. To have the broadest reach, it would be useful for harm reduction mutual-support organizations (e.g., moderation management) to grow in availability and frequency of meetings.

Websites

The Harm Reduction Coalition provides information about local harm reduction resources in the United States—http://www.harmreduction.org

The Harm Reduction Therapy Center provides training and resources, as well as harm reduction therapy for individuals in the San Francisco Bay area—http://www .harmreductiontherapy.org

Harm Reduction Psychotherapy and Training Associates provides training and resources, as well as harm reduction therapy for individuals in the New York City area—http://www.harmreductioncounseling.com

The International Harm Reduction Association provides information about local harm reduction resources internationally—http://www.ihra.net

Glossary

Compassionate approach: Acknowledging the difficulty of change and providing genuine empathy toward the client's struggles and problems.

Harm reduction: A pragmatic approach toward helping individuals who engage in some problem behavior (e.g., abuse of substances, binge drinking, excessive gambling) to minimize the hazards that are often associated with problematic behaviors.

Success in harm reduction psychotherapy: Any positive change in the direction of less harmful behavior, and the recognition that change is often slow and with setbacks.

References

Ajzen, I. (1985). From intentions to actions: A theory of planned behavior. In J. Kuhl & J. Beckman (Eds.), *Action-control: From cognition to behavior* (pp. 11–39). Heidelberg, Germany: Springer.

Andrasik, M. P., Woods, B., & George, W. H. (2012). The need for culturally competent harm reduction and relapse prevention interventions for African Americans. In G. A. Marlatt, M. E. Larimer, & K. Witkiewitz (Eds.), *Harm reduction: Pragmatic strategies for managing high-risk behaviors* (2nd ed., pp. 247–271). New York: Guilford Press.

Bandura, A. (1977). Self-efficacy: Toward a unifying theory of behavioral change. *Psychological Review, 84*, 191–215.

Blume, A. W., & Resor, M. R. (2012). Harm reduction among Hispanic and Latino populations. In G. A. Marlatt, M. E. Larimer, & K. Witkiewitz (Eds.), *Harm reduction: Pragmatic strategies for managing high-risk behaviors* (2nd ed., pp. 272–290). New York: Guilford Press.

Bonar, E. E., Rosenberg, H., Hoffmann, E., Kraus, S. W., Kryszak, E., & Young, K. M. (2011). Measuring university students' self-efficacy to use drinking self-control strategies. *Psychology of Addictive Behaviors, 25*, 155–161.

Collins, S. E., Clifasefi, S. L., Logan, D. E., Samples, L., Somers, J., & Marlatt, G. A. (2012). Harm reduction: Current status, history and basic principles. In G. A. Marlatt, M. E. Larimer, & K. Witkiewitz (Eds.), *Harm reduction: Pragmatic strategies for managing high-risk behaviors* (2nd ed., pp. 1–33). New York: Guilford Press.

Denning, P. (2000). *Practicing harm reduction psychotherapy: An alternative approach to addictions.* New York: Guilford Press.

Denning, P. (2012). Defining the treatment of dual disorders. In G. A. Marlatt, M. E. Larimer, & K. Witkiewitz (Eds.), *Harm reduction: Pragmatic strategies for managing high-risk behaviors* (2nd ed., pp. 229–243). New York: Guilford Press.

Gleghorn, A., Rosenbaum, M., & Garcia, B. (Eds.) (2001). [Special issue]. *Journal of Psychoactive Drugs, 33*(1), 1–7.

Graber, R., & Miller, W. (1988). Abstinence or controlled drinking goals for problem drinkers: A randomized clinical trial. *Psychology of Addictive Behaviors, 2*(1), 20–33.

Harm Reduction Network. (N.d.). *Guidelines for evaluating harm reduction services.* Retrieved from http://harmreductionnetwork.mb.ca/docs/policy evaluationguidelines.pdf.

Hester, R. K., & Miller, W. R. (1989). *Handbook of alcoholism treatment approaches: Effective alternatives.* Elmsford, NY: Pergamon Press.

Kelly, A. (2012). Adolescent alcohol-related harm reduction: Realities, innovations, and challenges. In G. A. Marlatt, M. E. Larimer, & K. Witkiewitz (Eds.), *Harm reduction: Pragmatic strategies for managing high-risk behaviors* (2nd ed., pp. 318–336). New York: Guilford Press.

Larimer, M. E., Malone, D. K., Garner, M. D., Atkins, D. C., Burlingham, B., & Lonczak, H. S. (2009). Health care and public service use and costs before and after provision of housing for chronically homeless persons with severe alcohol problems. *JAMA, 301*, 1349–1357.

Marlatt, G. A. (1998). *Harm reduction: Pragmatic strategies for managing high-risk behaviors.* New York: Guilford Press.

Marlatt, G. A., Blume, A., & Parks, G. A. (2001). Integrating harm reduction therapy and traditional substance abuse treatment. *Journal of Psychoactive Drugs, 33*, 13–21.

Marlatt, G. A., Larimer, M. E., & Witkiewitz, K. (2012). *Harm reduction: Pragmatic strategies for managing high-risk behaviors* (2nd ed.). New York: Guilford Press.

Marlatt, G. A., & Witkiewitz, K. (2002). Harm reduction approaches to alcohol use: Health promotion, prevention, and treatment. *Addictive Behavior, 27,* 867–886.

Mathers, B., Degenhardt, L., Ali, H., Wiessing, L., Hickman, M., & Mattick, R. P. (2010). HIV prevention, treatment, and care services for people who inject drugs: A systematic review of global, regional, and national coverage. *Lancet, 375,* 1014–1028.

Mattick, R. P., Breen, C., Kimber, J., & Davoli, M. (2009). Methadone maintenance therapy versus no opioid replacement therapy for opioid dependence. *Cochrane Database of Systematic Reviews.* Retrieved from http://summaries .cochrane.org/CD002209/methadone-maintenance-therapy-versus-no-opioid-replacement-therapy.

Miller, W. R., & Marlatt, G. A. (1984). *Manual for the comprehensive drinker profile.* Odessa, FL: Psychological Assessment Resources.

Miller, W. R., & Rollnick, S. (1991). *Motivational interviewing: Preparing people for change.* New York: Guilford Press.

Miller, W. R., & Rollnick, S. (2012). *Motivational interviewing: Helping people change.* New York: Guilford Press.

Office of National Drug Control Policy. (2010). *National drug control strategy for 2010.* Retrieved from http://www.ondcp.gov.

Osilla, K. C., Wong, E. C., & Zane, N. (2012). Harm reduction for Asian American and Pacific Islander populations. In G. A. Marlatt, M. E. Larimer, & K. Witkiewitz (Eds.), *Harm reduction: Pragmatic strategies for managing high-risk behaviors* (2nd ed., pp. 291–317). New York: Guilford Press.

Phillips, K., & Rosenberg, H. (2008). The development and evaluation of the harm reduction self-efficacy questionnaire. *Psychology of Addictive Behaviors, 22,* 36–46.

Polivy, J., & Herman, C. (2002). If at first you don't succeed. False hopes of self-change. *American Psychologist, 57,* 677–689.

Prochaska, J. O., & DiClemente, C. C. (1986). Toward a comprehensive model of change. In W. R. Miller & N. Heather (Eds.), *Treating addictive behaviors: Processes of change* (pp. 3–27). New York: Plenum Press.

Ritter, A., & Cameron, J. (2006). A review of the efficacy and effectiveness of harm reduction strategies for alcohol, tobacco, and illicit drugs. *Drug and Alcohol Review, 25,* 611–624.

Sanchez-Craig, M., Annis, H. M., Bornet, A. R., & MacDonald, K. R. (1984). Random assignment to abstinence and controlled drinking: Evaluation of a cognitive-behavioral program for problem drinkers. *Journal of Consulting and Clinical Psychology, 52*(3), 390–403.

Sobell, M. B., & Sobell, L. C. (1973). Individualized behavior therapy for alcoholics. *Behavior Therapy, 4,* 49–72.

Stimson, G. V., Jones, S., Chalmers, C., & Sullivan, D. (1998). A short questionnaire (IRQ) to assess injecting risk behaviour. *Addiction, 93,* 337–347.

Tatarsky, A. (2002). *Harm reduction psychotherapy.* Northvale, NJ: Aronson.

Tatarsky, A. (2003). Harm reduction psychotherapy: Extending the reach of traditional substance use treatment. *Journal of Substance Abuse Treatment, 25,* 249–256.

Van den Berg, C., Smit, C., Van Brussel, G., Coutinho, R., & Prins, M. (2007). Full participation in harm reduction programmes is associated with decreased risk for human immunodeficiency virus and hepatitis C virus: Evidence from the Amsterdam Cohort Studies among drug users. *Addiction, 102,* 1454–1462.

Walthers, J., Weingardt, K., Witkiewitz, K., & Marlatt, G. A. (2012). Harm reduction and public policy. In G. A. Marlatt, M. E. Larimer, & K. Witkiewitz (Eds.), *Harm reduction: Pragmatic strategies for managing high-risk behaviors* (2nd ed., pp. 339–379). New York: Guilford Press.

Witkiewitz, K., & Marlatt, G. A. (2006). Overview of harm reduction treatments for alcohol problems. *International Journal of Drug Policy, 17,* 285–294.

Wodak, A., & Cooney, A. (2006). Do needle syringe programs reduce HIV infection among injecting drug users: A comprehensive review of the international evidence. *Substance Use and Misuse, 41,* 777–813.

PART II
Community-Oriented Best Practices

Community-oriented best practices are those interventions and strategies delivered primarily in community settings and designed to support individuals', families', coworkers', and community members' abilities to collectively determine their own health and mental health. A universal component of these best practices is that they emphasize the development of life skills and confidence in a manner that is culturally competent and ultimately leads to improved personal and community health. In community-oriented best practices, the primary point of provider and client engagement occurs in community settings or environments rather than in-office clinics.

Part 2 introduces the reader to five core best practices that have a strong community presence. These include a community-based equine program for tribal youth, an assertive community treatment program, supported housing, housing first, and supported employment.

In chapter 6, "Tribal Best Practices: A Native American Horsemanship Program for Indian Youth," Spence and Vandiver describe a culturally specific, tribal best-practice equine program for at-risk Indian youth that has been developed through tribal initiatives and recognized by state government. In chapter 7, "Assertive Community Treatment and Recovery," Salyers, Stull, and Tsemberis provide an overview of a well-researched recovery program that uses a wraparound team of staff to support individuals with mental illness to live safely and productively in community settings. In chapter 8, "Supported Housing," Wong and Lee explore the role of supported housing as a means to address homelessness and housing instability for individuals with mental illness. In chapter 9, "Housing First: Homelessness, Recovery, and Community Integration," Tsemberis and Henwood expand the model of supported housing discussed earlier by reviewing a model for housing that does not require sobriety or participation in psychiatric treatment yet offers intensive treatment and support services for people moving from the street directly to their own apartments. In chapter 10, "Supported Employment," Kukla and Bond review the strategies for helping individuals with mental illness obtain and maintain competitive employment, which includes rapid job search, ongoing support, and supportive mental health services.

Tribal Best Practices: A Native American Horsemanship Program for Indian Youth

John Spence and Vikki L. Vandiver

Emerging epidemiological research illustrates that Indian youth are disproportionately at risk for suicide, incarceration, substance use, family disruption, and tribal dissonance. Tribal and governmental leaders are calling for an increase in the delivery and evaluation of culturally specific, evidence-based interventions to resolve these disparities. In Oregon, one such youth program developed through tribal and state government collaboration is the Horse Program, a Native American equine program centering on Indian youth and the time-honored relationship that Indian people have with horses. Recognized as a tribal best practice, this program is a culturally specific, equine-assisted intervention that merges Indian values (e.g., tradition with the horse) and Western counseling practices. This chapter reviews a history of the challenges facing Indian youth and their families, describes the development of tribal best practices through policy initiatives, overviews guiding principles and values inherent to the Horse Program, and illustrates the steps and goals of the curriculum. Additional discussion involves a review of research, assessment, and evaluation protocols specific to conducting research in Indian country. We close with a review of provider competencies and future directions. We begin this chapter with a case review of Joseph (see box 6.1), who describes his first experience with the Horse Program and a mustang named Chance.

> **Box 6.1. Case Study: Joseph and Chance**
>
> "My name is Joseph and I want to tell you about me and my new horse friend, Chance. Me and my family were at the Grande Ronde Pow Wow last week when some friends told me about a horse program they were going to each week at a place called Mustangs and MOHR down in Dallas, Oregon. They said it was a small ranch that worked with rescued mustangs and Indian kids just like me. They got to brush the horses, clean out

stalls, bridle horses, and even ride them. I don't know about that stall-cleaning business, but I like the idea of riding a mustang. My grandfather use to tell me stories about great warriors who rode on mighty horses and that horses were a part of my heritage (Warm Springs). I've never been around a horse since I live in the city. I always thought they were really big and smelly, but my grandfather thinks I should learn to be around them. My counselor at Polk County Day Treatment also told me about this horse program and asked if I wanted to attend. Since my friends were going I said yeah. So I had my counselor contact Debbie, who runs the program, to see if I could attend. She said yes and to come out this week. My mom took me to the ranch, we met Debbie, some of her horse handlers, and then we met all her mustangs. They were really cool and very calm. I know the one I want to work with—his name is Chance. He has big, soft brown eyes, a beautiful black and tan coat, and he even sniffed my hair when I walked up to him. Debbie says that he used to run away from people . . . just like I used to . . . but now he trusts people and will stay with them[,] . . . and now maybe he'll stay for me. Debbie said I could come any day and that I would have a horse handler with me each time teaching me about horsemanship. The next day my mom brought me, and I met up with some of my friends from Grand Ronde. We all started with a tour of the ranch and met each horse and heard their story. Debbie explained that each session has four steps but that we work at our own pace. We get to do welcoming and introductions, meaning that we meet new horses and old horses and catch up on weekly barn and horse news, then we do safety checks. She teaches us about horse safety and communication. Then we do horse care—like cleaning out our horse's stalls. This sounds yucky, but I really liked being around the horse when I cleaned their stalls—they were quiet and I got quiet. Then we learned how to bridle, lead, and walk our horses. At the end of two hours, I was actually up on a horse—riding Chance! I was so proud of me and my horse. This is the first time I have done something like this, and it makes me feel proud of who I am (Indian, Warm Springs), and I know it makes my mom proud."

Background

The current epidemic rates of youth suicide in Indian country have prompted tribes and state and federal agencies to recognize and support the integration of culturally based, traditional healing practices and Western treatment, also known as practice-based evidence (Centers for Disease Control and Prevention, 2011; Cross, Earle, Echo-Hawk Solie, & Manness, 2000; Oregon Department of Human Services, 2011; Substance Abuse and Mental Health Services Administration, 2010; Walker, 2005). The psychological, social, and cultural needs of Indian youth are substantial: between 1994 and 2004, suicide or alcohol-related deaths among Indian youth ranked as the second leading cause of death for those between the ages of ten and thirty-four. In addition, males between the ages of fifteen and twenty-four had the highest suicide rate (27.99 per 100,000) compared to whites (17.54 per 100,000). These same youth are reported to have more serious mental health problems than non-Indian youth related to suicide, including anxiety, substance abuse, depression, and isolation. Although Native Americans represent 1 percent of the US population, Indian youth are two to three times as likely as whites to be arrested, and they are often placed in adult correctional or juvenile justice facilities for reasons chiefly due to social and mental health issues (e.g., truancy, parent behaviors, drug overdose). Consequently, Indian children are often taken out of their community and offered non-culturally-specific services as individuals (i.e., not in conjunction with their family, tribe, or Indian culture). This removal occurs even when tribal services are available. These placements often dislocate youth from their tribes, traditions, communities, and families (Centers for Disease Control and Prevention, 2011; Cross et al., 2000; Davis et al., 2002; First Nations Behavioral Health Association, 2009; Substance Abuse and Mental Health Services Administration, 2010).

Families themselves are often struggling and in need of services, but they often experience available services as disrespectful, culturally inappropriate, and unfriendly. Collectively, these risk factors undermine tribal unity and remove many safeguards that significantly affect Indian youths' mental and physical health status and cultural identity (Cross et al., 2000).

In contrast, research has suggested the following protective factors as ways to promote Indian youth health and healing: connectedness to family, emotional health, and culturally specific programs that strengthen family ties and spiritual orientation (Centers for Disease Control and Prevention, 2011). It is the goal of tribal communities to help reconnect Indian youth to traditional ways (e.g., horses) that are valued as avenues to developing life skills, commitment to community, and participation in traditional ways (i.e., customs). This important goal helps nurture and shape family relationships, as well as creates resiliency and the capacity to meet

life challenges. One way to achieve this goal is by offering Indian youth an opportunity to participate in equine-assisted activities such as the Horse Program.

Emergence of Tribal Best Practices

Although Oregon's Department of Human Services—Addictions and Mental
Health is recognized as a national leader in identifying, funding, and supporting
mainstream evidence-based practices and programs for use in state agencies that
serve at-risk mental health populations, the agency has lagged in developing
evidence-based services for minority populations, particularly Native American
populations. This gap started to change with the introduction of tribal-initiated
practice-based evidence protocols developed through a coalition of tribal elders,
the nine federally recognized tribes, and the State Department of Mental Health
and Addiction Services (Cruz & Spence, 2005). One protocol recently approved by
the Oregon Health Authority is the Horse Program, an equine-assisted activity
(http://cms.oregon.gov/OHA/amh/ebp/native-american/na-horse-pro.pdf). This
is also the first practice protocol in Oregon to undergo evaluation. The Horse Program fits well with tribal culture in that it helps strengthen the commitment of
youth to community, family, and culture by connecting them directly with horses,
which have a long and time-honored history and tradition among Indian people.

Why Horses?

Of all the practice-based evidence protocols to develop, why horses? Let's look to
history. Horses have a distinguished place in history with Indian people, especially
tribes from the Northwest (e.g., Nez Percé). Working with and around horses has
always been an important part of Indian life. However, this history has been lost to
many youth who do not have access to horses because of urbanization policies and
a host of other barriers: poverty, incarceration, unemployment, a disconnect from
traditional ways, and lack of established evidence-based treatment protocols that
incorporate equine-assisted activities.

Although research in human-animal interaction is gaining recognition through
federal initiatives (Kazdin, 2010), research in equine-assisted therapy programs is
in the early stages, and very little empirical data exist. Of the available research,
many studies are limited by their design and small sample sizes (Smith-Osborne &
Selby, 2010). Even less available is research with culturally specific equine-assisted

programs. What makes the Horse Program unique among equine-assisted programs is that it is designed specifically for Indian youth by Indian people.

Program Description

The Native American Horse Program described here is one of two equine tribal best practices currently endorsed by the Oregon Health Authority for Indian communities. The only other horse program currently available in Oregon for tribal youths is an Equine Assisted Psychotherapy (EAP) program, which is located in Silverton, Oregon, and is used by the Cedar Bough residential treatment program. Both programs serve Indian youth, but their methods, described here, are distinct.

The Horse Program described in this chapter operates out of a community-based, nonprofit community organization, Mustangs and MOHR (Mustangs Offering Hope and Renewal). The Confederated Tribes of Grand Ronde's Tribal Social Services Department contracted the program to provide therapeutic and recreational horsemanship sessions with tribal foster children. The program has at any one time about fifteen rescued mustangs, other horses, and burros, all of which are involved in some capacity with the youth.

The Horse Program affiliated with Mustangs and MOHR represents what the field of animal-assisted research and practitioners refer to as an animal-assisted activity (AAA) (Kruger & Serpell, 2010). This means that an AAA program is typically designed to provide opportunities for motivational, educational, recreational, and/or therapeutic benefits to enhance quality of life and well-being for its participants. The program can be delivered in a variety of environments by specially trained professionals, paraprofessionals, and/or volunteers. Academic credentials, certification, and professional titles are not a necessary requirement for horse handlers or volunteers. In an AAA program there is no emphasis on clinical record keeping; diagnosis; or identification of individual, psychodynamically oriented therapeutic "treatment" goals. The goals instead are oriented toward youth engagement, wellness, education, and recreation, and they are measured through the choices that youth determine for themselves.

These methods are in sharp contrast to traditional equine-assisted psychotherapy (EAP) programs that use an established curriculum, employ licensed mental health professionals cross-trained as horse handlers (or vice versa), and tend to emphasize psychodynamic growth through the use of the horse as a tool of interpretative metaphor (e.g., talk therapy). For example, a youth would be asked how he or she feels when a horse walks away when approached. The Mustangs and MOHR method, which emphasizes gentle and high contact between youth and horse, goes far beyond the traditional EAP approach. The focus is very youth-centric in the sense that the youth themselves determine the pace for participating in the horse curriculum activities (described later in this chapter).

What distinguishes the two methods is that the youth in most EAP programs do not usually learn to clean stalls, feed and water horses, groom, clean hooves, or learn to lead horses, and they are not allowed to bridle, saddle, or ride horses. The AAA model encourages very hands-on interaction between horses and humans, whereas the EAP model is more a mode of participant observer and interpretative. Both have solid benefits (Kruger & Serpell, 2010), but the AAA model, we argue, seems more culturally suited for Indian youth.

Theoretical Perspective

There are two related theories influencing tribal equine-assisted interventions: attachment theory and community empowerment theory. Attachment theory asserts that disruptions in early attachment experiences between child and caregiver(s) create later life problems in interpersonal relationships and sense of self, particularly as youth progress into adulthood (Melson & Fine, 2010). This theory offers insight into historical abuses in which Indian youth, now adults, were separated from families and traditions (e.g., horses) through segregated educational policies, such as boarding schools, and more recently youth incarceration in settings far away from family and tribal lands.

A second, more global theory and one that is more explanatory of the Indian worldview is community empowerment theory. Community empowerment is a concept that is both process and outcome, and it focuses on both individual and community change (Wallerstein & Bernstein, 1994). Community empowerment theory as applied to equine-assisted activities with Indian youth involves several themes: connectedness to others, critical thinking, the building of personal and social capacity, and the transformation of power relations. Both of these theories offer an explanatory lens for working with Indian youth and horses, and they are illustrated in the principles that guide the Horse Program.

Principles

There are three core principles that offer fundamental guidelines for tribal and nontribal leaders who are involved in the development, evaluation, and dissemination of equine-assisted tribal best practices, such as the Horse Program, in Indian country. These are the principles of balance, culture as prevention, and life teachings:

- *Principle of balance*—In keeping with the historical and cultural worldview, tribal best practices have identified a number of values inherent to the Horse Program: respect, patience, personal responsibility, and generosity. These values merge with more global principles such as mentoring, relating with the natural world, commitment to others, leadership skills and being compassionate, and calmness and self-control (see figure 6.1). Each of these principles corresponds to activities associated with the Horse Program curriculum. These values and principles are summarized in the principle of balance, which incorporates all aspects of spirit, mind, body, and environment (family and community or context) (Cross et al., 2011).

- *Principle of culture as prevention*—This principle is based on the notion that culture is a protective factor against many problem issues, including substance abuse, and that culture should be a part of all aspects of tribal based research efforts (Walker, 2005). Walker (2005) maintains that Native American traditional practices such as talking circles and sweat-lodge ceremonies are powerful healing techniques and may even be more powerful than the use of non-Indian therapy approaches. He notes the importance of the inclusion of cultural and/or spiritual beliefs as integral to any prevention and treatment program in tribal communities. In times past, Indian people were more in tune with horses, and that holistic and spiritual partnership is what the Horse Program is helping tribal youths to regain. This amounts to a prevention and treatment program that is culturally based to help address the many health disparities experienced in tribal communities

- *Principle of life teachings*—Life teaching is based on the notion that there are guiding principles or themes related to the four levels of life's teachings: belonging (a time when infants and children learn who they are, where they belong, and a sense of protection), mastery (a time when adolescents and young adults learn to understand their gifts, their vision, where they come from, and how to master their talents), interdependence (a time for adulthood, responsibility to others, and an interconnectedness with all things), and generosity (a time when a person learns to give back to family and community through sharing wisdom, teachings, culture, rituals, stories, and songs) (Gathering of Native Americans, 1999). These guidelines are used in community gatherings as a tool to help frame the meeting. The life teachings also characterize the natural rhythm of life that horses represent to Indian people.

Steps for Implementing the Horse Program

The curriculum used in the Horse Program consists of four main activities: "Welcome and Orientation," "Horse Care: The Art of Quiet Movement," "Holistic Horsemanship: Safety and Trust"; and "Horse Riding: Of One Spirit." These activities are typically sequential but can also vary according to a youth's interest and need (for a review of the curriculum, see figure 6.1).

Figure 6.1. Horse Program Curriculum and Principles

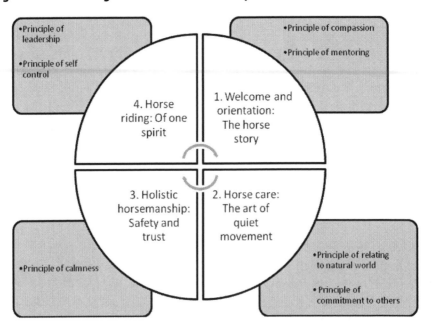

Each session follows the same weekly format and can last from two to four hours, depending on interests and the comfort level of youth. The program director and/or horse trainer, with a host of counselors and horse volunteers, administers the daily program. Generally, each youth is matched with his or her own horse and a volunteer. As older youths progress through the program, they can, in turn, become mentors to younger youths. Steps and goals for each session include the following:

Step 1: Welcome and Orientation—Youth tour the facility, meet the horses, and learn each horse's story; each youth is matched up with a horse. The goals of this session are to begin socialization and building empathy by listening to each horse's story (which for abandoned, abused, or neglected horses often parallel those stories of the youth) and to enhance group cohesion and awareness of others' needs.

Step 2: Horse Care: The Art of Quiet Movement—Referred to as cleaning house and getting down and dirty, youth begin to learn horse care from the ground up, starting with mucking the stall and then moving to in-hand work such as foot care, grooming, and leading. The goals for this session are to learn to care about a living being; attuning to another being; making "safe" mistakes; developing confidence; and as one youth stated, "simply being with the horse."

Step 3: Holistic Horsemanship: Safety and Trust—Youth continue to learn more basics about horse and human safety (trust) and communication. Instructional topics include teaching of safety checks (e.g., use of helmets, closing gates) and respect for animals' body space. Communication strategies include knowledge of equine and human body language, with examples such as how to safely approach and establish trust with horses and overcome one's own fear. The goals for this session are to learn respect for the horse's behavioral choices and boundaries, thus enhancing body and sensory awareness and learning to focus.

Step 4: Horse Riding: Of One Spirit—Youth advance to learning appropriate bridling, saddling, mounting, and horse riding (e.g., walk, trot, canter optional); mastering the physical aspects of riding; and learning to achieve desired outcomes by changing (riding) approaches as the situation requires. The goal of this session is to promote and reflect on aspects of patience, rhythm (e.g., physical, psychological), responsibility, respect, self-confidence and commitment to others, and successfully being a "leader" with the horse.

What's the Evidence?

Now that we have made the argument for connecting Indian youth with horses as a means to promote individual, family, and tribal health and well-being, what do we know empirically about the role of horses and youth? Let's first look to mainstream studies for a review of psychosocial outcomes. Documented knowledge of the helping role of companion animals with children dates back to Florence Nightingale in 1860. In the past forty years, clinicians from various fields of social work, nursing, and psychology have studied the psychosocial benefits of horseback riding among children with disabilities (All, Loving, & Crane, 1999). Smith-Osborne and Selby (2010) completed an extensive review of the theoretical and empirical literature on the psychosocial effects of equine-assisted activities for children and youth. In summary, they found that horses effect "socialization and companionship, self-esteem enhancement, improvement in personal space/boundary issues and other attachment-related problems, reduction in emotional blunting and incongruence and improvement in meta-cognition and reflectivity" (p. 292). They noted, however, that much of the literature also reflects a combination of enthusiastic anecdotal reports and wide variation in study methodology and designs; confounders related to severity, diagnoses, and presenting problem; and vague descriptions of program goals and curriculum. Virtually none of these reports included culturally specific, evidence-based interventions with Indian youth populations.

In Oregon, the Horse Program is the first tribal best practice to undergo evaluation. In particular, two equine tribal best-practices programs, Mustangs and MOHR and the Grand Ronde Saddle Club, have participated in three preliminary program evaluation surveys conducted by tribal elders and leaders (e.g., John Spence, Gros Vente, Sioux, and Thomas Crofoot, Colville) and funded solely through tribal organizations (e.g., Confederated Tribes of Grande Ronde Social Services Department, Native American Center for Excellence). The Grand Ronde Saddle Club is an informal equine youth program that is sponsored by the tribe and that connects young people with horses through adult volunteers. Youth referrals to the two programs were made through a variety of tribal sources: the Confederated Tribes of Grande Ronde Social Services Department, the Cedar Bough/Christie Care Residential Program for Indian Youth, the Confederated Tribes of Siletz Mental Health Department, and the Native American Rehabilitation Association.

Tribal researchers used data from the Relational Worldview Questionnaire (Cross et al., 2011) to evaluate program satisfaction and several other variables among youth attending the Saddle Club and Mustangs and MOHR. Preliminary findings suggest that Indian youth felt positive about their experiences with the program and would return (Crofoot & Spence, 2010). Two separate evaluations of the Horse Program conducted by Spence (2011a, 2011b) used the Relational Worldview Questionnaire (Cross, 1995) and the Companion Animal Bonding Scale (Poresky, Hendrix, Mosier, & Samuelson, 1987). Preliminary findings suggest that tribal youth have reported strong relationships between self-image and a life summarized as balanced and spiritual. Two more mixed-methods study designs to evaluate program outcomes are under way.

Assessment and Evaluation

Assessment and evaluation initiatives in Indian country require researchers to acknowledge value structures and worldviews of tribal communities, which include emphasis on child, extended family, community health, and tribal traditions. Running Wolf et al. (2002) have noted that both tribal and nontribal researchers should be aware of research issues related to tribal sovereignty, tribal government permission to conduct research, data ownership, isolation, cultural barriers, and concerns over methodology and dissemination.

Strategies for Culturally Competent Assessment and Evaluation

Along with understanding value structures and worldviews, researchers must also check their theoretical perspectives. Although much of Western psychological theory holds a disability (e.g., mental illness, addictions) view of research participants, this concept has little meaning in Indian community. In fact, the concept of illness (cognitive, emotional, physical, and spiritual) is often grounded in a worldview that is cyclical in nature and not related to individual disability but instead considered "special" or a stage that one is passing through (Cross, 1986). Consequently, assessment and evaluation strategies must address underlying issues of how illness is defined, other underlying issues (e.g., poverty, racism), expectations for behavior, and change among program participants. Instruments that focus on kinship, extended family, beliefs, cultural wellness, and community health and resiliency are preferred. Evaluation protocols need to be culturally sensitive using local-level evaluation plans that answer questions the tribal communities pose themselves.

With these points in mind, the assessment and evaluation examples here describe two instruments: one is a culturally sanctioned measure as applied to Indian communities, the Relational Worldview (Cross et al., 2011); the other is the Companion Animal Bonding Scale. Both instruments are useful measures for assessing youths' sense of balance and relationship with the horse.

Instruments

The Relational Worldview (Cross et al., 2011) is used to measure cultural health and wellness, and it is intended to be a reflection of the Native American concept of balance as the basis of health. Developed by Terry Cross (Seneca), director of the National Indian Children Welfare Association (NICWA), and used by NICWA staff and researchers, the instrument covers four domains: context (e.g., family, community), body, mind, and spirit. The instrument is designed to tap into beliefs and values considered important to Indian people. The Relational Worldview can be accessed at the NICWA website (http://www.nicwa.org). Spence and Crofoot (Crofoot & Spence, 2010; Spence, 2011a, 2011b) have successfully incorporated this questionnaire, along with qualitative questions, into all three of their Horse Program surveys.

A second instrument that is in the process of being incorporated into equine research projects is the Companion Animal Bonding Scale (Poresky et al., 1987). The eight-item measurement instrument is designed to measure the extent of human-animal bonding. Both instruments are considered acceptable measures of youth connectedness in relation to their exposure to the Horse Program. Tribal advisory members are currently reviewing other measures for consideration in future projects. Last, virtually all surveys have qualitative questions as a means to capture the voice of Indian youth through the oral tradition.

Implementation Issues

There are two core implementation issues that influence the success of equine-assisted activities with Indian youth: lack of culturally specific services and limited guidance for evaluating tribal best practices.

Most states are woefully lacking in culturally specific services that target non-mainstream, diverse populations, such as Indian youth and their families. This gap in culturally appropriate services is particularly harmful for Indian youth who come from their tribes and enter mental health, social service, or substance abuse treatment settings or face incarceration as well as the prevalent threat of suicide. When ethnic or culture specific services are available, such as equine-assisted best practices for tribal youth, getting mainstream providers to refer to these programs can be challenging.

In addition, little guidance is available for tribal and nontribal practitioners in how to create, implement, and evaluate equine-assisted activities. Without evaluating these protocols, introducing them alone does not provide a full understanding of what works, whether suicide rates decrease and tribal traditions increase, or any other outcome factors considered meaningful to the tribes. This issue is further voiced by tribal leaders like Cross (1986), who maintains that most evidence-based interventions ignore the spiritual aspect of community development.

Provider Competencies

In general, basic minimum competencies required for service providers involved in an equine-assisted program are an awareness and experience in working with at-risk tribal youth. Certification requirements of the counselors and therapists at each of the partner tribal organizations are determined by each of the tribal providers who refer and transport youths to the Horse Program. Some of the referral partners are certified as chemical dependency counselors at the bachelor degree level and others are masters' level practitioners. The Horse Trainers/Counselors who work with the tribal youths must not only possess a high degree of experience working with horses, but also the cultural sensitivities necessary to work with the target population of at-risk tribal youths. The optimal combination of competencies for both tribal and non-tribal horse handlers would include: training in the field of child and youth development and mental health, crisis intervention skills, horsemanship and equine management background, and certification in one or more behavioral health fields (e.g., social work, child welfare, psychiatric nursing, substance abuse, counseling, recreation, psychology, and/or family studies).

Future Directions

The future of equine tribal best-practice activities rests on four strategies: the ability to build the evidence; to provide quality education for interdisciplinary investigators and program developers; to disseminate equine programs across different tribal and nontribal communities; and to promote the benefits of equine-assisted activities as a means of helping tribes interested in saving horses and promoting their use in a wide variety of rehabilitation, social services, mental health, forensic, and wellness programs.

First, efforts must be made to empirically support the tenets of equine-assisted programs and particularly those that offer their services to high risk youth populations, such as Indian youth.

We have much to learn about what does and does not work with Indian youth, and about what is the best kind of equine-human partnership for addressing certain issues. Although Indian people have for hundreds of years culturally validated the benefits of horses with tribes, other communities could benefit from additional means of evidence. The Horse Program provides an opportunity to fill a large gap in the cross-cultural, evidence-based-practice literature. By combining two upcoming fields, culture-specific treatment programs and human-animal interaction, the Horse Program will provide empirical support for contemporary practices that have, to date, little evidence.

Second, personnel (e.g., researchers) involved in evaluating equine tribal best practices will need to work closely with the equine staff (e.g., horse handlers) to understand the goals and objectives of the program, and vice versa. The field of animal-assisted therapies and recreation draws a rich variety of personnel from a variety of disciplines, skill levels, training levels, and settings. If equine-assisted activities are to gain credibility in the world of science, then cross-training of personnel will be necessary. Personnel can gain knowledge from researchers about research protocols, researchers can learn about equine behaviors, and both can learn from youth participants about what is meaningful in the human-equine interaction. In this case, Indian youth have much to tell elders, horse personnel, and researchers about what is a meaningful equine experience for them.

Third, the ability to disseminate the program's model across different communities is a core goal of any best-practice initiative. We want to be able to share the good, and even not-so-good, and known aspects of the Horse Program so that it may benefit other communities. In Indian country, the various tribes may not adopt what one tribe does totally, but if we can find universal elements of a successful program, like youth mentoring other youth, these can then be shared across tribes and non-Indian tribes. For example, if the shared goal of tribal communities is to help reconnect Indian youth to traditional ways and customs, then core elements of any tribal equine program could be emphasized while still allowing for tribal distinctions.

Fourth, it is anticipated that equine tribal best practices will soon become the norm, not the exception, when it comes to recognizing and disseminating evidence-based-practice interventions. This means that programs like the Horse Program will represent one of many tribally developed, culturally sanctioned programs that serve the special needs of tribal youth. Equally as important is the recognition that tribes can develop their own cultural best practices and can provide documentation to show that their programs are effective. The Horse Program is currently developing its own evaluation criteria using scientific standards and protocols generated from the community, not imposed by funding agencies, which do not understand Indian worldviews or values.

In closing, the future of equine-based programs in tribal communities depends on actions taken right now. It is imperative that tribes, equine advocates, and researchers promote the benefits of equine-assisted activities as a means of encouraging tribes to become interested in saving horses; rehabilitating them as much as possible; and promoting their use in a wide variety of rehabilitation, social services, mental health, forensic, and wellness programs. Like Indian youth, many noble horses are undervalued for their assets, hidden gifts, and continuing ability to participate and contribute to community. Equine-related tribal best practices, in this regard, are more than just a policy or intervention; they are about saving lives, both human and equine.

Websites

Oregon Department of Mental Health and Addictions, Evidence-based practice list of twenty programs approved by Tribal Review Panel—http://cms.oregon.gov/dhs/mentalhealth/pages/ebp/main.aspx

National Indian Child Welfare Association, "Projects and Initiatives," site for culturally specific, practice-based evidence—http://www.nicwa.org/projects_initiatives

One Sky Center, a national resource center—http://www.oneskycenter.org

Glossary

Animal-assisted (equine) activity: Provides opportunities for motivational, educational, recreational, and other therapeutic benefits to enhance quality of life in association with equines; key features include the absence of specific treatment goals and the fact that volunteers and treatment providers are not required to take detailed notes.

Equine-assisted psychotherapy (EAP): A psychotherapeutic program or session that includes the use of a horse as part of the therapeutic team consisting of licensed, credentialed mental health professionals working with appropriately credentialed equine professionals.

Tribal best practices: Those practices (also known as interventions) that are culturally sanctioned by tribes on the basis of the following criteria: longevity of practice in Indian country, teachings on which practice is based (e.g., stories), values incorporated in practice (e.g., respect, patience), principles incorporated into practice (e.g., mentoring), elder's approval of practice (e.g., informal approval by tribal elders), and community feedback and evaluation of practice (e.g., emerging data, evaluation, youth stories).

References

All, A. C., Loving, G. L., & Crane, L. L. (1999) Animals, horseback riding and implications for rehabilitation therapy. *Journal of Rehabilitation, 65*, 49–57.

Centers for Disease Control and Prevention, National Center for Injury Prevention and Control. (2011). *Injury Prevention and Control: Data and Statistics (WISQARS)*. Retrieved from http://www.cdc.gov/ncipc/wisqars.

Crofoot, T., & Spence, J. (2010). *Program evaluation of Native American therapeutic horsemanship program using Relational Worldview Questionnaire with youth attending Mustangs and MOHR* (Unpublished report). Salem, OR: Author.

Cross, T. L. (1986). *Gathering and sharing: An exploratory study of service delivery to emotionally handicapped children*. Portland, OR: Research and Training Center to Improve Services for Seriously Handicapped Children and Their Families; Regional Research Institute for Human Services, Portland State University; and Northwest Indian Child Welfare Institute.

Cross, T. L. (1995). *Relational Worldview Questionnaire*. Washington, DC: National Indian Child Welfare Association.

Cross, T., Earle, K., Echo-Hawk Solie, H., & Manness, K. (2000). *Cultural strengths and challenges implementing a system of care in American Indian communities*. Washington, DC: Center for Effective Collaboration and Practice, American Institutes for Research.

Cross, T. L., Friesen, B. J., Jivanjee, P., Gowen, K., Bandurraga, A., Matthew, C., et al. (2011). Defining youth success using culturally appropriate community-based participatory research methods. *Best Practices in Mental Health, 7,* 94–114.

Cruz, C., & Spence, J. (2005). *Oregon Tribal evidence based and cultural practices* (Report prepared for Office of Addictions and Mental Health Services, Oregon Department of Human Services). Retrieved from http://cms.oregon.gov/oha/amh/ebp/native-american/presentation.pdf.

Davis, J. D., Erickson, J. S., Johnson, S. R., Marshall, C.A., Running Wolf, P., & Santiago, R. L. (2002). *Workgroup on American Indian research and program methodology: Symposium on research and evaluation methodology—Lifespan issues related to American Indians/Alaska Natives with disabilities.* Tucson: American Indian Rehabilitation Research and Training Center and Northern Arizona University.

First Nations Behavioral Health Association. (2009). *Catalogue of effective behavioral health practices for tribal communities report.* Portland, OR: Portland State University.

Gathering of Native Americans. (1999). *Substance abuse prevention curriculum.* Indian Health Service—Mental Health Programs Branch, Special Initiatives Team. Rockville, MD: Substance Abuse and Mental Health Services Administration.

Kazdin, A. E. (2010). Methodological standards and strategies for establishing the evidence base for animal-assisted therapies. In A. H. Fine (Ed.), *Handbook on animal-assisted therapy: Theoretical foundations and guidelines for practice* (pp. 519–546). Burlington, MA: Academic Press/Elsevier.

Kruger, K., & Serpell, J. (2010). Animal-assisted interventions in mental health; definitions and theoretical foundations. In A. H. Fine (Ed.), *Handbook on animal-assisted therapy: Theoretical foundations and guidelines for practice* (pp. 33–48). Burlington, MA: Academic Press/Elsevier.

Melson, G. F., & Fine, A. H. (2010). Animals in the lives of children. In A.H. Fine (Ed.) *Handbook on animal-assisted therapy: Theoretical foundations and guidelines for practice* (pp. 223–246). Burlington, MA: Academic Press/Elsevier.

Oregon Department of Human Services, Addictions and Mental Health Branch. (2011). *Evidence-based practices.* Retrieved from http://www.oregon.gov/ DHS/mentalhealth/ebp/main.shtml.

Poresky, R. H., Hendrix, C., Mosier, J. E., & Samuelson, M. L. (1987). The Companion Animal Bonding Scale: Internal reliability and construct validity. *Psychological Reports, 60,* 743–746.

Running Wolf, P., Soler, R., Manteuffel, B., Sondheimer, D., Santiago, R., & Erickson, J. S. (2002). In J. Davis, J. Erickson, S. Johnson, C. Marshall, P. Running Wolf, & R. Santiago (Eds.), *Symposium on research and evaluation methodology: Lifespan issues related to American Indians/Alaska Natives with disabilities: Monograph* (pp. 32–49). Washington, DC: American Indian Rehabilitation Research and Training Center.

Smith-Osborne, A., & Selby, A. (2010). Implications of the literature on equine-assisted activities for use as a complementary intervention in social work practice with children and adolescents. *Child and Adolescent Social Work, 27,* 291–307.

Spence, J. (2011a). *Evaluation of Horse Program curriculum for Warm Springs youth attending Summer Youth Culture Camp* (Unpublished report). Salem, OR: Author.

Spence, J. (2011b). *Program evaluation of Native American Therapeutic Horsemanship Program with youth participating in Grande Ronde Saddle Club and Mustangs and MOHR* (Unpublished report). Salem, OR: Author.

Substance Abuse and Mental Health Services Administration. (2010). *Suicide among American Indians/Alaska Natives: Report from the Suicide Prevention Resource Center.* Washington, DC: Author.

Walker, D. (2005). *American Indian Community Suicide Prevention Assessment Tool: The American Indian/Alaska Native National Resource Center for Substance Abuse and Mental Health Services.* Retrieved from http://www.oneskycenter.org.

Wallerstein, N., & Bernstein, E. (1994). Introduction to community empowerment, participatory education, and health. *Health Education Quarterly, 21,* 141–148.

Assertive Community Treatment and Recovery

Michelle P. Salyers, Laura Stull, and Sam Tsemberis

In this chapter, we provide an overview of assertive community treatment (ACT), a widely implemented and rigorously studied mental health practice that can help support recovery in adults with severe mental illnesses. We briefly review the history of ACT, overview key evidence-based principles of the ACT model, and describe core steps and activities associated with delivery of an ACT program. In addition, we provide a review of the effectiveness of ACT, with a focus on adaptations to changing populations and contexts; implementation issues incorporate a recovery orientation into ACT teams. We begin this chapter with a case review of Mary (see box 7.1), who is actively working with an ACT team.

> **Box 7.1. Case Study: Mary**
>
> Mary is a forty-two-year-old woman who was diagnosed with schizophrenia fifteen years ago. After graduating from college, Mary enjoyed several years of stability in employment, family relationships, and living situation. However, Mary's mental health began to deteriorate, and her struggle to cope with schizophrenia ended in an incarceration that lasted for eight years. Mary was released from prison about two years ago and has been served by an assertive community treatment (ACT) team since that time.
>
> Mary set several goals soon after joining the ACT team, and with their assistance she has been able to achieve all of those goals. Mary's goals included addressing some serious physical health problems, "finding a place to live," becoming "more assertive," and doing more things on her own. Mary said, "The ACT team, they didn't help in one area. The ACT team helped all areas." According to one staff member on Mary's ACT team,

"She went from a person, an individual who did not know how to do a lot of things[,] . . . to a person who does just about everything independently." Mary recently stated, "I tell the ACT team all the time, 'You guys are great!' I don't know what they do for others, but what they've done really has made a difference in my life."

The ACT team fully joined Mary along her path of recovery. They helped her to feel hopeful and designed their services to help her meet her goals. The team worked closely with her to address basic needs first: finding her housing, helping her get physical health concerns taken care of, managing medications to help her psychiatric symptoms, and ensuring that she had access to benefits and transportation. They also helped her navigate the legal system and work with the courts after her release from prison. The team provided supportive therapy and a peer recovery specialist who worked with her on the illness management and recovery program. The team was very conscious of avoiding doing things for Mary that she could do on her own, teaching her how to do things when she did not know how to do them, and helping her identify opportunities to be more independent. Gradually, by mutual consent, the team decreased the intensity of services. Currently, the team recognizes that Mary is ready to graduate from their program and begin receiving less intensive services elsewhere. Mary states that she does not feel ready to move on from the team currently, but she also says, "I know that I am stronger; I've achieved a lot with their help. Now I have to go to the next step and let somebody else have their help."

Background

Since the initial demonstration study (Stein & Test, 1980), ACT has proved a remarkably robust and flexible model of treatment for people with severe mental illnesses. Numerous research studies have noted its effectiveness in the treatment and support of consumers with extensive psychiatric hospitalizations (Coldwell & Bender, 2007; Dixon et al., 2010). Assertive community treatment is also remarkable for the unusually clear articulation of its structural and functional features, as well as for having a widely used fidelity scale to measure quality of implementation. In the past decade there has been a surge of interest in ACT, owing in part to the identification of ACT as one of six evidence-based practices endorsed by the Substance Abuse and Mental Health Services Administration (2010) and vigorous advocacy by the National Alliance on Mental Illness. Implementation has also been facilitated in states where Medicaid approves ACT team services for reimbursement. Today, ACT is extremely well known and has been disseminated throughout the world.

Assertive community treatment as a model of community treatment for persons with mental illness first began with the inception of the Training in Community Living (TCL) program in Madison, Wisconsin. A dedicated and insightful group of clinicians working in an inpatient psychiatric unit realized that, to develop an effective approach to help consumers repeatedly admitted and discharged from the hospital remain successfully in the community, they would have to provide treatment and support in the community. They created a team modeled after the staffing pattern of the inpatient unit (a "hospital without walls"). This team comprised multiple disciplines that worked together, met daily, and coordinated care for a specified group of consumers. Then and now, the ACT team assumes full professional responsibility for addressing clinical needs and providing concrete assistance in the skills of daily living (e.g., budgeting, shopping). Assertive community treatment services are intensive (e.g., visits may occur daily for some people) and take place primarily in consumers' homes or in the community. By taking that bold step out of the comfort of their institutional setting and into their consumers' communities, the innovators of ACT took a major step forward in reducing hospitalization, thereby increasing consumers' community tenure and their possibilities for recovery.

Assertive community treatment programs typically serve the most vulnerable and severely disabled consumers. Although specific admission criteria may vary across service systems or programs, ACT services are usually reserved for consumers with an axis I diagnosis of a severe mental illness (e.g., schizophrenia or schizoaffective disorder, bipolar disorder, major depression). Admission criteria for ACT typically include behavioral indicators such as frequent hospital inpatient or emergency-room use, arrests or incarceration, and homelessness. Mental health and court systems also frequently use ACT teams as a means of fulfilling treatment requirements for involuntary outpatient treatment programs.

Theoretical Perspective

Most ACT interventions utilize a pragmatic approach, rather than following a specific theoretical orientation. The idea is to do whatever it takes to help consumers live independently in the community. Though not emphasized in this chapter, readers are referred to the literature on the strengths perspective (Saleebey, 2006), which emphasizes that each client has strengths that are the basis of effective community functioning (Sands & Gellis, 2012).

Principles

As ACT has been studied for more than thirty years, several researchers have attempted to identify the critical ingredients of the ACT model. These components have been highlighted through surveys of experts, clinicians, and consumers and through comparison with similar approaches. Some of the key features or principles guiding the ACT approach are summarized here:

- *Principle of transdisciplinary staff*—Transdisciplinary staffing that includes staff in psychiatry, nursing, social work, vocational services, substance abuse treatment, peer specialists, and related fields; some teams integrate a primary care specialist.

- *Principle of team approach*—Staff share caseloads and participate in daily team meetings.

- *Principle of low client-staff ratios*—The desired client-staff ratio is 10:1.

- *Principle of community*—Locus of contact is in the community, and about 80 percent of contacts are in the community.

- *Principle of intensive contact*—Frequent contacts include from one to four times per week, depending on the consumer.

- *Principle of assertive outreach*—Team members are actively engaged with the consumer in his or her community.

- *Principle of wellness*—Focus is on symptom management and everyday problems in living.

- *Principle of access*—Ready access in times of crisis, which includes twenty-four-hour on-call availability.

- *Principle of time-unlimited services*—Depending on the state, some have limits but when possible, services are provided as long as needed.

Steps for Implementing ACT

Most ACT teams are designed to serve consumers who are not effectively engaged with treatment and are frequent users of acute care systems including psychiatric hospitals, substance abuse treatment centers, jails, shelters, and other facilities. Some consumers are assigned to ACT services as part of a mandatory outpatient commitment order. In efforts to address these challenges, ACT teams utilize various engagement and retention strategies that include repeated attempts to contact consumers despite their refusals, outreach to families and significant others, close monitoring of medication compliance, behavioral contracting, use of outpatient commitment, and representative payeeship. Some critics have suggested that ACT teams are paternalistic or coercive and therefore anti-recovery. Although control methods may contradict recovery-oriented practice values of consumer choice, empowerment, and responsibility, there are certainly times when such mechanisms are needed, as when a consumer is posing a threat to him- or herself or others. The key becomes knowing when and how to use such strategies, and maintaining respect and fairness during those times. There are also preventive planning strategies such as wellness recovery action plans (Copeland, 1997), advanced directives, and other relapse prevention plans that the consumer can help develop so that his or her wishes are taken into account during times when the consumer may not be able to clearly articulate his or her wishes.

What's the Evidence?

Although the ACT model is a comprehensive program consisting of numerous components, researchers have yet to determine the individual contribution of each of the components. One study examined the relationship between core ingredients identified on the basis of expert ratings and client outcomes (McGrew, Bond, Dietzen, & Salyers, 1994) and found that the presence of a nurse on the team, working with shared caseloads, holding daily team meetings, having twenty-four-hour availability, and a high frequency of consumer contacts were significantly related to the reduction in hospital days.

Initially, ACT was designed to reduce the recidivism rates of consumers who were frequent users of inpatient psychiatric services. Not surprising, then, a hallmark outcome for ACT programs across many controlled research studies has been the reduction of hospitalizations and an increase in community tenure. In addition, ACT programs have been very successful in improving independent living, reducing psychiatric symptomatology, and improving quality of life in general (Bond, Drake, Mueser, & Latimer, 2001). Most ACT programs tend to be expensive, relative to simple case management, given the multidisciplinary teams composed of highly trained professionals (e.g., psychiatrists, nurses, social workers) and the fact that there are program features that are time consuming but not billable (e.g., travel time to visit consumers in the community, assertive engagement of consumers who are not yet enrolled in services, daily team meetings). However, costs for ACT teams must be considered in the context of the entire mental health system and their effectiveness in successfully treating consumers with histories of high acute and long-term hospitalizations. In this context, well-implemented ACT programs significantly reduce costs and improve outcomes, particularly when targeting consumers with high hospital use (Burns et al., 2007; Latimer, 1999).

Although ACT is an evidence-based practice, and is seen as effective in general, other recovery-related goals, such as employment (see chapter 10), education (see chapter 16), and improved relationships have not been consistently realized using this model. In the current era of recovery-focused mental health services, ACT programs are expected to address a much broader spectrum of needs. However, moving toward a recovery-oriented approach presents several challenges for ACT teams that have been traditionally clinician driven. Because ACT may be best understood as a way of organizing services (through integration of disciplines, teamwork, and continuity of care), the model is flexible enough to incorporate skills and strategies used in other evidence-based practices. For example, motivational interviewing (see chapter 13) and cognitive-behavioral therapy are core clinical skills in several disciplines and can be used to help engage people, identify recovery-based goals, and teach consumers skills needed to reach those goals. We have seen the synergistic effects of ACT with supported housing (see chapter 8) (Stefancic & Tsemberis, 2007; Tsemberis, Gulcur, & Nakae, 2004), supported employment (see chapter 10), integrated dual-disorders treatment (see chapter 1), family psychoeducation (see chapter 17), and most recently illness management and recovery (see chapter 3) (Salyers et al., 2010).

Although there are valid concerns about the ACT model, most empirical research supports the possibility that ACT can be consistent with a recovery orientation (see chapter 12). For example, there is great variability across programs in how ACT teams exert control in working with consumers, and level of control appears unrelated to fidelity to the model (Moser & Bond, 2009). Practitioners of ACT report using coercive techniques sparingly, focusing more on "friendly persuasion" as their primary means of therapeutic limit setting (Neale & Rosenheck, 2000). Consumers generally report high levels of satisfaction with ACT services, and when asked what they like least about ACT, few consumers indicate that ACT staff are coercive (McGrew, Wilson, & Bond, 2002).

Assessment and Evaluation

The most widely used fidelity scale to assess and evaluate ACT is the Dartmouth Assertive Community Treatment Scale (DACTS; Teague, Bond, & Drake, 1998)—twenty-eight items organized into three subscales: human resources, organizational boundaries, and nature of services. The DACTS has been shown to discriminate between ACT and other approaches to care and to predict better outcomes. However, some of the items on the DACTS as currently worded may be in contention with recovery-oriented practice. For example, the item of time-unlimited services specifies a small number of graduates of the ACT program per year. Although this item ensures that the team will not be quick to discharge consumers until they are ready, consumers can and do successfully graduate from ACT programs (Salyers, Masterton, Fekete, Picone, & Bond, 1998). The possibility of recovery, and consumer choice about service provision, will require this item to include language concerning discharge policies that shift expectations from lifelong service to planning for future graduation and emphasize the role of consumers' choice in this key decision. A team of investigators is updating the DACTS to be more recovery oriented (Monroe-DeVita, Teague, & Moser, 2011).

Implementation Issues

The ACT model has clear criteria for implementation, that is, fidelity standards that specify structures or services for a team to be identified (or certified) as an ACT program (Allness & Knoedler, 2003). Explicit monitoring of program fidelity is increasingly recognized as an important quality assurance technique, and greater fidelity to ACT standards has been related to positive outcomes such as reduced hospitalization. In some states, mental health departments have adopted these fidelity standards as a certification tool to license teams and to help pay for ACT services.

Despite some potential clashes with fidelity, ACT implementation can still be particularly well suited to a recovery orientation. A primary goal of ACT is to assist people to participate fully in their communities. In addition, many fidelity standards support a recovery orientation. For example, the community-based and in-home services provide an optimal approach for assisting consumers to integrate into their communities. The flexibility in the service approach of ACT is consistent with a fluctuating and nonlinear process of recovery for some individuals. It allows for the development of deeply supportive relationships, the ability to learn effective self-management skills, and flexibility in setting a pace for treatment and allowing for relapse. The integration of multiple disciplines on the team can particularly help facilitate recovery in areas of employment, relationships, artistic and cultural activities, management of home and budget, keeping substance use from interfering with life, and management symptoms. When team composition also includes peer specialists, messages of hope and possibility of recovery are woven into the very fabric of the team and serve to remind the staff and consumers that recovery is possible.

Provider Competencies

Providers must be able to work well in teams and to share responsibilities with others on the team. A significant shift is necessary from being an independent practitioner or multidisciplinary team member to a transdisciplinary team member who functions collaboratively in assessing and planning to meet the consumer's needs. Effective communication skills are a must for the transdisciplinary approach to work well. Table 7.1 illustrates these functions and distinctions between both

Table 7.1. Differences between Multidisciplinary and Transdisciplinary Teams

	Multidisciplinary	Transdisciplinary
Team composition	Clinicians from multiple disciplines.	Clinicians from multiple disciplines.
Assessment	Each team member does a separate assessment, often not shared between team members.	Team members conduct comprehensive, integrated assessment. Assessments are conducted within discipline, integrated across the team, and processed collaboratively.
Planning and providing services	Each individual team member plans and implements a specialized part of treatment.	Team members are jointly responsible for planning and implementing integrated services.
Communication	Informal conversations about shared consumers on the team.	Regular meetings with ongoing transfer of information and skills.

approaches. Although it is often difficult for providers to make this shift, an effective team approach can result in decreased individual burden and staff burnout, increased knowledge and problem solving, and built-in peer support.

A newer practitioner competency for ACT is the provision of services that are recovery focused (Salyers & Tsemberis, 2007). Recovery focused practice requires a shift from clinician-as-expert to a practice in which clinicians are in full partnership with consumers and families, and develop individualized treatment plans in which consumers choose who, what, and how treatment will be provided (President's New Freedom Commission on Mental Health, 2003). In addition, in embracing recovery-oriented practices, providers must recognize that individuals can and do recover from severe mental illness and consistently convey the message of hope that plays such an integral part in the individual's recovery.

Assertive community treatment teams are expanding their competencies by adding some new specialist roles to their teams. Some ACT teams that target homeless individuals have an identified housing specialist on the team. Similarly, teams that target consumers with extensive legal involvement often have forensic specialists or even probation officers as part of the team. Specialists take the lead for the services in their area and provide cross-training to other staff on the team. Peer specialists (consumer providers of services) are increasingly being incorporated into ACT team staffing (Wright-Berryman, McGuire, & Salyers, 2011). Peer specialists are uniquely qualified to empathically understand the experience of mental illness, and their presence can be a challenge and a message to the other team members that the distance between consumers and team members is indeed small; "we are all more the same than different." The peer's presence is a visible manifestation for what people diagnosed with severe mental illness can accomplish. Without speaking, the peer is saying, "You too can master your symptoms, have a productive life, belong to another community, and have a different role in this world." This influence can be particularly powerful when peer recovery specialists use their own experiences to help others manage their illnesses more independently, such as by providing Illness Management and Recovery or facilitating wellness recovery action plans.

Future Directions

The ACT model continues to be a viable approach to serving people with psychiatric disabilities. There are several ways in which ACT teams can continue to adapt to the changing context of providing recovery-oriented care. The integration of other evidence-based practices has been one effective approach. Assertive community treatment programs can use tools to monitor their current level of practice and use the feedback to guide improvements in recovery orientation similar to the use of fidelity scales as developmental tools. Along with monitoring and feedback, we also recommend ongoing training and supervision not only in clinical practice skills but also to develop, foster, and reinforce the attitudinal and value shifts required for a recovery-oriented practice. Finally, consumer providers are a natural way to enhance recovery orientation. The work of Solomon and Draine (1995) has established that case management teams comprising consumers can be as effective as teams comprising nonconsumer professionals, and there is evidence that consumer peer specialists on an ACT team can have a positive impact on the outcomes for service recipients and non-consumer providers. Although recovery-oriented practice and ACT have sometimes been viewed as incompatible, the ACT model can provide an ideal platform for incorporating the principles identified by the recovery movement: consumer choice, hope, respect, patience, and compassion.

Websites

ACT Center of Indiana—http://www.psych.iupui.edu/ACTCenter

President's New Freedom Commission on Mental Health—http:/store.samhsa .gov/product/SMA03_3831

Substance Abuse and Mental Health Services Administration—http://www .samhsa.gov

Glossary

Evidence-based practices: Services that have a strong base of research supporting their effectiveness, as well as clear implementation criteria and a specified target population.

Fidelity: The degree to which a program follows a model as intended. Fidelity scales provide a structured way to assess fidelity and give feedback on performance.

Transdisciplinary teams: Teams that involve staff from multiple disciplines who are integrating their work in all phases of assessment, planning, and service provision. Team members also contribute knowledge, support, and cross-training to other team members.

References

Allness, D. J., & Knoedler, W. H. (2003). *The PACT model of community-based treatment for persons with severe and persistent mental illness: A manual for PACT start-up*. Arlington, VA: National Alliance on Mental Illness.

Bond, G. R., Drake, R. E., Mueser, K. T., & Latimer, E. (2001). Assertive community treatment for people with severe mental illness: Critical ingredients and impact on patients. *Disease Management and Health Outcomes, 9*, 141–159.

Burns, T., Catty, J., Dash, M., Roberts, C., Lockwood, A., & Marshall, M. (2007). Use of intensive case management to reduce time in hospital in people with severe mental illness: Systematic review and meta-regression. *British Medical Journal, 335*(7615), 336.

Coldwell, C. M., & Bender, W. S. (2007). The effectiveness of assertive community treatment for homeless populations with severe mental illness: A meta-analysis. *American Journal of Psychiatry, 164*, 393–399.

Copeland, M. E. (1997). *Wellness recovery action plan*. Brattleboro, VT: Peach Press.

Dixon, L. B., Dickerson, F., Bellack, A., Bennett, M., Dickinson, D., Goldberg, R., et al. (2010). The 2009 Schizophrenia PORT psychosocial treatment recommendations and summary statements. *Schizophrenia Bulletin, 36*(1), 48–70.

Latimer, E. (1999). Economic impacts of assertive community treatment: A review of the literature. *Canadian Journal of Psychiatry, 44*, 443–454.

McGrew, J. H., Bond, G. R., Dietzen, L. L., & Salyers, M. P. (1994). Measuring the fidelity of implementation of a mental health program model. *Journal of Consulting and Clinical Psychology, 62*(4), 670–678.

McGrew, J. H., Wilson, R., & Bond, G. R. (2002). An exploratory study of what clients like least about assertive community treatment. *Psychiatric Services, 53*, 761–763.

Monroe-DeVita, M., Teague, G. B., & Moser, L. L. (2011). The TMACT: A new tool for measuring fidelity to assertive community treatment. *Journal of the American Psychiatric Nurses Association, 17*(1), 17–29.

Moser, L. L., & Bond, G. R. (2009). Scope of agency control: Assertive community treatment teams' supervision of consumers. *Psychiatric Services, 60*(7), 922–928.

Neale, M. S., & Rosenheck, R. A. (2000). Therapeutic limit setting in an assertive community treatment program. *Psychiatric Services, 51,* 499–505.

President's New Freedom Commission on Mental Health. (2003). *Achieving the promise: Transforming mental health care in America* (DHHS Pub. No. SMA-03-3832). Rockville, MD: Substance Abuse and Mental Health Services Administration.

Saleebey, D. (2006). The strengths perspective: Possibilities and problems. In D. Saleebey (Ed.), *The strengths perspective in social work practice* (4th ed., pp. 279–303). Boston: Pearson/Allyn and Bacon.

Sands, R., & Gellis, Z. (2012). *Clinical social work practice in behavioral mental health: Toward evidence-based practice.* Boston: Pearson/Allyn and Bacon.

Salyers, M. P., Masterton, T. W., Fekete, D. M., Picone, J. J., & Bond, G. R. (1998). Transferring clients from intensive case management: Impact on client functioning. *American Journal of Orthopsychiatry, 68*(2), 233–245.

Salyers, M. P., McGuire, A. B., Rollins, A. L., Bond, G. R., Mueser, K. T., & Macy, V. R. (2010). Integrating assertive community treatment and illness management and recovery for consumers with severe mental illness. *Community Mental Health Journal, 46*(4), 319–329.

Salyers, M. P., & Tsemberis, S. (2007). ACT and recovery: Integrating evidence-based practice and recovery orientation on assertive community treatment teams. *Community Mental Health Journal, 43*(6), 619–641.

Solomon, P., & Draine, J. (1995). The efficacy of a consumer case management team: Two-year outcomes of a randomized trial. *Journal of Mental Health Administration, 22,* 135–146.

Stefancic, A., & Tsemberis, S. (2007) Housing first for long-term shelter dwellers with psychiatric disabilities in a suburban county: A year study of housing access and retention. *Journal of Primary Prevention, 28*(3–4), 265–279.

Stein, L. I., & Test, M. A. (1980). An alternative to mental health treatment. I: Conceptual model, treatment program, and clinical evaluation. *Archives of General Psychiatry, 37,* 392–397.

Substance Abuse and Mental Health Services Administration. (2010). *Evidence-based practices: Shaping mental health services toward recovery—assertive community treatment.* Rockville, MD: Author. Retrieved from http://mental health.samhsa.gov/cmhs/community-support/toolkits/community.com.

Teague, G. B., Bond, G. R., & Drake, R. E. (1998). Program fidelity in assertive community treatment: Development and use of a measure. *American Journal of Orthopsychiatry, 68*(2), 216–232.

Tsemberis, S., Gulcur, L., & Nakae, M. (2004). Housing first, consumer choice, and harm reduction for homeless individuals with a dual diagnosis. *American Journal of Public Health, 94*(4), 651–656.

Wright-Berryman, J. L., McGuire, A. B., & Salyers, M. P. (2011). A review of consumer-provided services on assertive community treatment and intensive case management teams: Implications for future research and practice. *Journal of the American Psychiatric Nurses Association, 17*(1), 37–44.

8

Supported Housing

Yin-Ling Irene Wong and Sungkyu Lee

Housing is an essential component of mental health services and a critical factor affecting community integration of persons with psychiatric disabilities. In the past two decades, supported housing has evolved from a paradigmatic model to an empirically supported intervention for addressing homelessness and housing instability. Best practices related to supported housing have been identified, accompanied by expanded funding through permanent supported-housing (PSH) initiatives from federal and state government agencies. Future efforts should focus on promoting community integration of supported housing residents and applying the supported-housing principles to the transformation of other housing programs in local behavioral health systems. We begin the chapter with a case study of Mr. Johnson (see box 8.1), whose experience with supported housing shows a new level of personal and community stability.

Box 8.1. Case Study: Mr. Johnson

Mr. Johnson is a forty-seven-year-old man diagnosed with schizophrenia and substance use disorders. He had been chronically homeless since age thirty-one. Before entering a permanent supportive housing program in 2006, Mr. Johnson was hospitalized because of psychiatric problems eight times during the past three years, accumulating 168 inpatient days. He moved twice since obtaining his first apartment through the permanent supportive housing program because of drug-trafficking concerns in the first neighborhood and disputes with his neighbors in the second. Mr. Johnson has been staying in his current apartment for more than two years and has not experienced psychiatric hospitalization or homelessness since entering the program. He sees his case manager once every two weeks, attends a Narcotics Anonymous group twice a week, and is a volunteer for a homeless advocacy group.

Background

Supported housing, which is considered the housing approach most conducive to the goals of consumer empowerment and community integration, refers to long-term and affordable housing coupled with the provision of community-based mental health services (Carling, 1992). This housing approach is based on the premise that individuals with psychiatric disabilities can assume roles and lifestyles as community members in a normal, integrated housing setting when they are given flexible, voluntary, and individualized support services. Three key factors contributed to the emergence of supported housing as a preferred housing and service approach for persons with psychiatric disabilities:

1. *Critique of the residential continuum model*—Proponents of supported housing criticize the residential continuum model (also referred to as continuum of care or continuum housing) for its emphasis on the residential facility as the primary location for mental health treatment and rehabilitation, residential instability and loss of social supports associated with moves along the continuum, and the questionable assumption that consumers do not need mental health services once they "graduate" to independent housing (Ridgway & Zipple, 1990).

2. *Persistence of homelessness and federal efforts in ending chronic homelessness*— Homelessness has prevailed as a major social problem in the United States since the early 1980s. Subsequent to the passage of the McKinney-Vento Homeless Assistance Act in 1987, increased attention has been paid to maintaining long-term community tenure for homeless persons with psychiatric disabilities through subsidized housing and community support services. Recently, federal efforts on significantly reducing or ending chronic and family homelessness have put permanent supportive housing as the central antidote to homelessness.

3. *Assertive Community Treatment (ACT) model*—As an evidence-based intervention, the ACT model has proved effective in enabling persons with serious and persistent mental illness to live in normalized community settings. An ACT team consists of a transdisciplinary staff, including social workers, nurses, a psychiatrist, and other specialists, such as vocational and substance abuse counselors, and housing specialists. The ACT teams offer treatment, support, and other services to consumers seven days a week, twenty-four hours a day. Since the 1990s, the ACT model has been extended as an outreach service strategy for

the homeless mentally ill population, with demonstrated effectiveness in increasing residential stability, reducing homelessness, and reducing hospitalization. The ACT model has been adapted as a service approach in supported housing (see chapter 7).

Theoretical Perspective

The concept of supported housing originally draws from the notions of normalization and nonrestrictive environment in the field of developmental disabilities, and the independent living movement in the field of physical disabilities. The concept predicates that having a regular, stable home in the community is a basic right for persons with psychiatric disabilities and that a normal home environment is requisite to recovery (Ridgway & Zipple, 1990).

Principles

Drawing from the work of Carling (1992) and Ridgway and Zipple (1990), Wong, Filoromo, and Tennille (2007) identified four core principles and five operational domains of the supported-housing approach. Domains are listed in the next section of this chapter under "Steps for Implementing Supported Housing" (see figure 8.1 for an illustration of both concepts). The principles are discussed here:

- *A home in the community as a basic right for persons with severe disabilities*—Premised on the notion of common citizenship, access to decent, safe, and affordable housing is considered a universal right regardless of an individual's disability status and the level of support and services that the individual needs to maintain community tenure.

- *Normal roles of psychiatric consumers as regular tenants and community members*—Persons with psychiatric disabilities in supported housing are regular tenants to be treated in the same manner as market-rate renters. Emphasis is placed on integration of supported-housing residents with their non-disabled neighbors in normalized settings as equal members of the community.

- *Functional separation between housing and mental health support*—Following the principle of right to housing, tenancy is not contingent on engagement in treatment services. Persons with psychiatric disabilities can refuse or discontinue support services and remain in housing so long as they fulfill their obligations as ten-

Figure 8.1. Principles and Operational Domains of Supported Housing

Domains Related to Housing & Tenancy

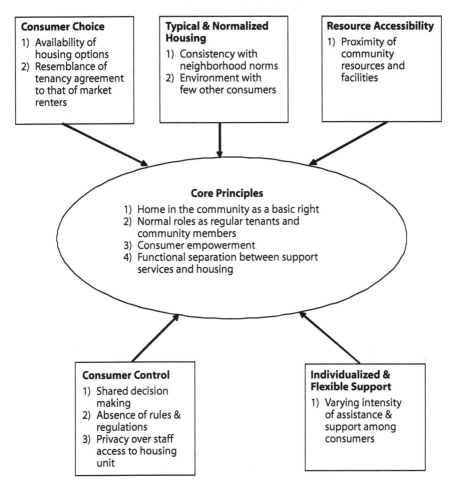

Consumer Choice
1) Availability of housing options
2) Resemblance of tenancy agreement to that of market renters

Typical & Normalized Housing
1) Consistency with neighborhood norms
2) Environment with few other consumers

Resource Accessibility
1) Proximity of community resources and facilities

Core Principles
1) Home in the community as a basic right
2) Normal roles as regular tenants and community members
3) Consumer empowerment
4) Functional separation between support services and housing

Consumer Control
1) Shared decision making
2) Absence of rules & regulations
3) Privacy over staff access to housing unit

Individualized & Flexible Support
1) Varying intensity of assistance & support among consumers

Domains Related to Mental Health Support

Source: Wong, Y. L. I., Filoromo, M., & Tennille, J. (2007). From principles to practice: A study of implementation of supported housing for psychiatric consumers. *Administration and Policy in Mental Health and Mental Health Services Research, 43*(1), pp. 13–28; figure on p. 16.

ants by paying rent on time and taking proper care of the rental unit. Simply put, provisions of appropriate housing and flexible support services are independent of each other.

- *Empowerment as a practice goal in defining the relationship between consumers and their support staff*—Service providers of supported housing are expected to empower residents in exercising consumer choice and control through forging a consumer-provider relationship that is based on mutual trust and respect, as well as by enabling consumers to build and maintain individualized support networks through accessing community-based services and other community resources.

Steps for Implementing Supported Housing

From principles emerge practice approaches. Carling (1992), Ridgway and Zipple (1990), and Wong, Filoromo, and Tennille (2007) identify five operational domains of the supported housing approach that can guide mental health providers in developing supported housing.

Operational Domains of Supported Housing

- *Consumer choice*—Consumer values and preferences are central in determining the location of consumers' residences, as well as with whom and how the consumers will live. In operational terms, consumer choice is indicated by the availability of different housing options and the extent to which the tenancy agreement resembles that of regular market-rate tenants.

- *Typical and normalized housing*—Typical and normalized housing is a housing environment that is considered conducive to the goal of community integration. Typical housing refers to a residence whose physical appearance is consistent with neighborhood norms, and normalized housing refers to the extent to which the resident's housing unit is located in an environment where there are few other individuals with psychiatric disabilities.

- *Resource accessibility*—Resource accessibility refers to proximity to community resources and facilities that may promote contact and interaction with neighbors and participation in community activities. Neighborhoods that have a rich array of community resources, include a range of public meeting places, and have easy access to public transportation are likely to provide more opportunity for neighborhood interaction, facilitate the learning of practical living skills, and help residents to assert independence.

- *Consumer control*—Consumer control refers to the degree of independence supported housing residents have in their relationship with mental health support staff and their living environments. Consumer control is indicated by the extent to which decision making between residents and staff is shared, the absence of rules and regulations as conditions of staying in the housing, and the level of privacy consumers have over staff access to their housing unit.

- *Individualized and flexible support*—Individualized and flexible support refers to the extent to which mental health support and services are provided according to the specific needs of a given psychiatric consumer. Mental health services that are individualized and flexibly offered are indicated by varying intensity of service contacts that staff provide to different supported housing residents.

Examples of Supported Housing

Examples of these domains are illustrated in two nationally recognized supported-housing programs: Pathways to Housing and the Department of Housing and Urban Development's Veterans Affairs Supportive Housing (HUDS-VASH) program.

Supported housing was originally promulgated as a paradigm shift in the field of community mental health (Ridgway & Zipple, 1990). A parallel line of development emerged out of the movement to combat homelessness through increasing the supply of affordable housing. These two "genealogies" of housing traditions shared some similarities but had their own distinct features (Hopper & Barrow, 2003). Published literature that systematically assessed the effectiveness of supported housing programs was limited until the late 1990s. In the past ten years, two best practices have been identified for addressing the housing and service needs of homeless persons with severe and persistent mental illness.

New York City Pathways to Housing Program

The New York City Pathways to Housing (Pathways), founded in 1992, is designed to address the housing and treatment needs of chronically homeless individuals with a dual diagnosis of severe mental illness and substance use problems (Tsemberis, Gulcur, & Nakae, 2004). It is the pioneer of the housing-first model, a housing and service approach characterized by immediate access to housing for consumers without the requirement of participation in psychiatric services or treatment for sobriety. Pathways is premised on the perspective of the right to housing and the notion of consumer choice in the delivery of support and clinical services. The program has its own housing staff to help consumers locate apartments and to liaise with landlords and housing management companies for day-to-day repairs, maintenance, and emergencies. Treatment and support services are provided through an ACT or a modified ACT team. Unlike conventional residential services programs, which make access to housing contingent on abstinence and sobriety, Pathways adopts a harm-reduction approach in its clinical and supportive services. The US Department of Health and Human Services has named the housing-first model an evidence-based practice (see chapter 9).

HUD-VASH Program

The Housing and Urban Development Veterans Affairs Supported Housing program (HUD-VASH), also established in 1992, is a joint initiative of the Department of Housing and Urban Development and the Veterans Affairs (VA) Department to provide housing and case management assistance to homeless veterans with psychiatric or addictive disorders or both. Over the past eighteen years, the capacity of HUD-VASH program has expanded twenty-fold, from about one thousand to twenty thousand housing vouchers. In 2008, 132 VA medical centers were identified to participate in the program, ensuring at least one program site in each of the fifty states and in the District of Columbia and Puerto Rico. Housing vouchers are to be administered by local public housing authorities, which authorize rental payment of no more than 30 percent of the participants' income and approve selected rental units (Rosenheck, Kasprow, Frisman, & Liu-Mares, 2003). The case management approach represents a modification of the ACT model with an interdisciplinary staff and a maximum caseload of twenty-five clients. Similar to the housing-first model, retention of housing is not contingent on involvement in VA treatment, and inability or unwillingness to maintain sobriety does not result in discharge if clients can maintain housing. Fostering community integration and independence is a goal of case management service.

What's the Evidence?

Experimental and quasi-experimental designs have been employed to examine the efficacy of an array of interventions broadly labeled as "supported housing." Two recent meta-analytic studies provided empirical support for the effectiveness of supported housing in reducing residential instability and increasing residential satisfaction.

Nelson, Aubry, and Lafrance (2007) reviewed sixteen outcome evaluations of housing and support interventions for people with serious mental illness who were previously homeless. They found that when compared with providing ACT alone or intensive case management alone, supported housing (housing coupled with support services) is more effective in maintaining residential stability. The authors also noted the absence of fidelity assessment in all the studies they reviewed, which makes it difficult to determine the extent to which components of the housing models were implemented in the interventions.

Based on thirty studies that examined forty-four community housing programs, Leff et al. (2009) conducted a meta-analysis of four categories of housing: residential care and treatment, residential continuum, permanent supported housing, and nonmodel housing. They found that although permanent supported housing is associated with the strongest effects in residential stability and housing satisfaction, residential care and treatment is the only housing model that showed a significant effect in reducing psychiatric symptoms.

Despite being few in number, cost-effectiveness studies have suggested that supported housing results in favorable housing outcomes with modest societal costs. Culhane, Metraux, and Hadley (2002) examined the public investment of supported housing in New York City for homeless persons with psychiatric disabilities using a case-control design and retrospective administrative data. Clients placed in the New York–New York housing initiative were matched with individuals who were homeless but not placed in housing. Both groups were tracked on their utilization of public shelters, public and private hospitals, and correctional facilities. Cost data suggested that the reductions in shelter use, hospitalizations, length of time per hospitalization, and time incarcerated result in substantial savings in service costs, which in turn offset the cost of providing supported housing.

Rosenheck et al. (2003) assessed the cost effectiveness of the HUD-VASH program to a diagnostically heterogeneous group of homeless veterans with psychiatric and/or substance use disorders (including those who are dually diagnosed). The study used a randomized experimental design with four cost perspectives examined: the VA, the total health-care system (VA and non-VA), the government (or taxpayers), and society as a whole. Outcome measures include the incremental cost-effectiveness ratio, which is defined as "the ratio of the difference between groups in costs to the difference in effectiveness," and cost-effectiveness acceptability curves, or the probability that benefits equal costs plotted "across a range of possible shadow prices for a day of independent housing" (Rosenheck et al., 2003, p. 943). The study found HUD-VASH to be more costly than standard care, and depending on the value of a day of independent housing for the target population, the program can be an effective investment. The strengths of the HUD-VASH study pertain to the comparison of costs prospectively between randomly assigned treatment groups, thereby minimizing the selection bias of nonexperimental studies and the availability of rich information through interviews and access to administrative data from the VA and other systems.

Assessment and Evaluation

Three fidelity scales used to evaluate supported housing are discussed here: the Housing Fidelity Rating Scale, the Dartmouth ACT Fidelity Scale, and the Fidelity Scale Protocol.

The study by McHugo et al. (2004) of integrated housing (i.e., a single mental health agency providing both intensive case management services and congregate supervised housing) vis-à-vis parallel housing (supported housing) used two fidelity measures—the Housing Fidelity Rating Scales and the Dartmouth ACT Fidelity Scale—to address implementation issues of the two programs. The study found that the two groups differ consistently on three of seven dimensions of housing fidelity: housing control, integration within housing, and landlord's decisions. The two groups, however, provided similar case management services, given their average scores on the ACT Fidelity Scale. Whereas the parallel housing services teams scored higher on items measuring the interdisciplinary approach, the integrated housing services teams scored higher on individualized substance abuse treatment and dual-disorder treatment groups (McHugo et al., 2004).

In 2010, the Center for Mental Health Services released the Permanent Supportive Housing (PSH) Knowledge Informing Transformation (KIT) guide (http://home less.samhsa.gov/channel/Permanent-Supportive-Housing-KIT-557.aspx). The PSH-KIT provides a guiding framework for developing and evaluating PSH programs. The Fidelity Scale Protocol, included in the kit, specifies seven dimensions as integral to the implementation of supported housing: choice of housing; functional separation of housing and services; decent, safe, and affordable housing; housing integration; rights of tenancy; access to housing; and flexible and voluntary services.

In addition to meta-analytic and cost-effectiveness studies on key residential outcomes such as housing stability, a growing body of research literature has focused on psychosocial outcomes, such as participation in meaningful and productive activities, adaptive role functioning, social network and social support, perceived quality of life, and sense of community. This body of literature may be subsumed under the theme of community integration or community inclusion, which has been considered a major goal of disability policy in the United States. A promising avenue of research in this arena involves incorporating protective factors and barriers, measured at the housing and neighborhood levels, in predicting community integration of residents in supported housing. Newly applied data collection methods, including Geographic Information Systems and participatory mapping, have been used to measure housing and neighborhood characteristics considered pertinent to integration (Townley, Kloos, & Wright, 2009).

Implementation Issues

Systematic efforts to assess the implementation of supported housing programs are relatively uncommon (Nelson, Aubry, & Lafrance, 2007). An early example is found in a multisite evaluation of supported housing funded by the Center for Mental Health Services (CMHS). Using a quasi-experimental design comparing among 172 supported and comparison housing programs in six study sites, the CMHS Housing Initiative was an attempt to establish a comprehensive framework for assessing the fidelity fit of housing programs to supported housing (Rog & Randolph, 2002). The CMHS initiative identifies seven dimensions as core to supported housing.

An implementation study of twenty-seven supported independent living (SIL) programs in Philadelphia, Pennsylvania, using the principles and operational domains outlined in the section "Research-Based Principles," suggests that the programs did not adopt a unitary approach but exhibited substantial variation in housing and tenancy and mental health support characteristics (Wong et al., 2007).

Findings from the Philadelphia study are consistent with those from the CMHS Housing Initiative, which suggests that in real-world settings, a continuum of supported housing may exist rather than one ideal model (Rog & Randolph, 2002). It is also worth noting that supported housing has been implemented with ethnically diverse populations and that race/ethnicity has not emerged as a key factor in determining the effectiveness of the model.

Provider Competencies

Provider competencies for supported housing can be categorized into three key areas: competencies in assertive community treatment (or ACT-modified case management approach), competencies in facilitating community integration, and competencies in working with landlords and neighbors.

Competency 1: Competencies in ACT or ACT-Modified Case Management Approach

Providers of ACT work with mental health consumers in a multidisciplinary team environment. The competencies listed in the following pertain to both working with teammates and with consumers (Substance Abuse and Mental Health Services Administration, 2008):

- Communicate and share their own expertise, professional knowledge, and prior experience, and collaborate with team members to assess clients' needs and come up with treatment strategies

- Provide practical, hands-on, in vivo, and side-by-side support, drawing on resources from consumers' natural support systems and advocating for consumers' rights

- Be innovative and creative, with a problem-solving approach

- Facilitate the exercise of choice, and forge a working relationship based on dignity and respect, while considering cultural competence and focusing on consumers' strengths

Competency 2: Competencies in Facilitating Community Integration

Community integration involves participation in community activities and use of community resources, engagement in social relationships in normalized settings, and development of a sense of community with neighbors and other community members. Consumer empowerment is requisite to providers' competencies in facilitating community integration of supported-housing residents. The competencies required are as follows:

- Develop a working knowledge of resources available to consumers in their neighborhoods, as well as in other communities of interests, including those based on faith, hobbies, and cultural identities.

- Encourage consumers to plan enjoyable things to do and enable them to do so through procuring the needed pecuniary and other resources.

- Facilitate the development of consumers' interpersonal skills and encourage consumers to expand their social circle by making friends and getting along with others.

- Help consumers cope with anxiety, upsets, and distress emanating from their interactions with family, friends, neighbors, and other community members.

Competency 3: Competencies in Working with Landlords and Neighbors

Landlords and neighbors play critical roles in affecting consumers' community tenure, rehabilitation, and social integration. Three areas of competencies are identified for providers in working with landlords and neighbors:

1. Coordination and collaboration with landlords and housing management agencies in addressing day-to-day repairs and maintenance issues, as well as resolving problems pertaining to consumers' tenancy, such as extended absence from the rental unit because of consumers' medical issues (it should be noted that release of medical information is to be compliant with consumers' rights to privacy and confidentiality);

2. Enabling consumers to pay rent and bills on time, to respect the rights of other tenants and community residents, and to keep their rental units in good condition

3. Identification and addressing of problems that may affect consumers' tenancy, and if necessary, serving as mediator with landlords and neighbors on behalf of consumers

Future Directions

Supported housing has evolved from a paradigmatic model based on the principles of universal housing rights, community integration, and consumer choice to an evidence-based intervention to address homelessness and housing instability, with significant funding support from the US Department of Housing and Urban Development, the Substance Abuse and Mental Health Services Administration, the Department of Veterans Affairs, and state and local mental health systems. One of the distinct features in this housing model pertains to the functional separation between housing and services, a principle in sharp contrast to the rehabilitation model of providing a residential continuum with facility-based residential treatment programs varying in intensity of care to match with consumers' treatment needs and psychiatric impairment. Although the effectiveness of supported housing has been ascertained by its favorable housing outcomes relative to alternative housing programs, the extent to which community integration is achieved through the supported-housing approach has not been adequately examined. Social isolation that consumers experience in supported independent-living arrangements has been a concern among service providers and behavioral health administrators. Increasing attention needs to be paid to identifying challenges to community inclusion among supported-housing residents, as well as program and neighborhood characteristics associated with residents' sense of belonging and social integration. Given the salutary residential outcomes of supported housing and considering the compatibility between its core principles and values and those of mental health professionals, policy makers and service providers in local behavioral health systems should consider the adaptation of supported housing principles and operational framework in transforming conventional residential continuum services to a recovery-oriented model.

Websites

Corporation for Supportive Housing—http://www.csh.org

HUD-VASH Vouchers—http://www.hud.gov/offices/pih/programs/hcv/vash/

Substance Abuse and Mental Health Services Administration Homelessness Resources Center—http://homeless.samhsa.gov/channel/Permanent-Supportive-Housing-KIT-557.aspx

Supported Housing Guideline, New York State, Office of Mental Health—http://www.omh.state.ny.us/omhweb/adults/SupportedHousing/supported housingguidelines.html

US Department of Veteran Affairs, Homeless Veterans, and Housing Support Services—http://www.va.gov/HOMELESS/housing.asp

Glossary

Assertive community treatment: A multidisciplinary team approach to service delivery designed for enabling people with severe and persistent mental illness to live in normalized community settings.

Community integration: A multidimensional construct: physical (physical presence of persons with disabilities in ordinary, normalized settings, activities, and contexts); social (involvement in social relationships that are culturally normative); and psychological (perception of community membership and sense of empowerment).

Consumer empowerment: The forging of resident-staff working relationships characterized by mutual trust, mutual respect, and consumer control, to enable residents to build and maintain individualized support networks through accessing community-based mental health services and other community resources.

Residential continuum (continuum of care): A rehabilitation model to housing that provides an array of facilities varying in intensity of care and levels of restrictiveness to match with consumers' treatment needs and psychiatric impairment. Housing is provided on condition that consumers are engaged in behavioral health treatment.

Supported housing: Long-term, decent, safe, and affordable housing coupled with community-based mental health services; housing and services are functionally separate in that access to and retention of housing is not contingent on participation in treatment.

References

Carling, P. J. (1992). Homes or group homes? Future approaches to housing, support, and integration for people with psychiatric disabilities. *Adult Residential Care Journal, 6*(2), 87–96.

Culhane, D. P., Metraux, S., & Hadley, T. (2002). The impact of supportive housing for homeless people with severe mental illness on the utilization of the public health, corrections, and emergency shelter systems: The New York–New York Initiative. *Housing Policy Debate, 13*(1), 107–163.

Hopper, K., & Barrow, S. M. (2003). Two genealogies of supported housing and their implications for outcome assessment. *Psychiatric Services, 54*(1), 50–54.

Leff, H. S., Chow, C. M., Pepin, R., Conley, J., Allen, I. E., & Seaman, C. A. (2009). One size fits all? What we can and can't learn from a meta-analysis of housing models for persons with mental illness. *Psychiatric Services, 60*(4), 473–482.

McHugo, G. J., Bebout, R. R., Harris, M., Cleghorn, S., Herring, G., Xie, H., et al. (2004). A randomized controlled trial of integrated versus parallel housing services for homeless adults with severe mental illness. *Schizophrenia Bulletin, 30*(4), 969–982.

Nelson, G., Aubry, T., & Lafrance, A. (2007). A review of the literature on the effectiveness of housing and support, assertive community treatment, and intensive case management interventions for persons with mental illness who have been homeless. *American Journal of Orthopsychiatry, 77*(3), 350–361.

Ridgway, P., & Zipple, A. M. (1990). The paradigm shift in residential services: From the linear continuum to supported housing approaches. *Psychosocial Rehabilitation Journal, 13*(4), 11–31.

Rog, D. J., & Randolph, F. L. (2002). A multisite evaluation of supported housing: Lessons learned from cross-site collaboration. *New Directions for Evaluation, 94*, 61–72.

Rosenheck, R., Kasprow, W., Frisman, L., & Liu-Mares, W. (2003). Cost-effectiveness of supported housing for homeless persons with mental illness. *Archives of General Psychiatry, 60*, 940–951.

Substance Abuse and Mental Health Services Administration. (2008, October). *Assertive Community Treatment: Evidence-based practices KIT—Training frontline staff* (Publication No. SMA08-4345-04). Retrieved from http://store .samhsa.gov/shin/content//SMA08-4345/SMA08-4345-04-TrainingFrontline Staff-ACT.pdf.

Townley, G., Kloos, B., & Wright, P.A. (2009). Understanding the experience of place: Expanding methods to conceptualize and measure community integration of persons with serious mental illness. *Health and Place, 15,* 520–531.

Tsemberis, S., Gulcur, L., & Nakae, M. (2004). Housing first, consumer choice, and harm reduction for homeless individuals with a dual diagnosis. *American Journal of Public Health, 94,* 651–656.

Wong, Y. L. I., Filoromo, M., & Tennille, J. (2007). From principles to practice: A study of implementation of supported housing for psychiatric consumers. *Administration and Policy in Mental Health and Mental Health Services Research, 34*(1), 13–28.

9

Housing First: Homelessness, Recovery, and Community Integration

Sam Tsemberis and Benjamin Henwood

Housing first is an evidence-based intervention combining housing, intensive community-based treatment, and a consumer-driven philosophy that effectively ends homelessness for individuals with psychiatric disabilities and co-occurring addiction disorders. A key feature of housing first is that it does not require sobriety or participation in psychiatric treatment as a precondition for housing. Consumers move directly into independent apartments of their own and are provided with intensive treatment and support services. These services embody recovery principles by honoring consumer choice and facilitate community integration by offering consumers permanent, affordable housing that is integrated into the community. Housing-first programs are widely implemented across the United States, Canada, and Europe. Research studies in several cities examining the effectiveness of housing first are finding the same 85 percent housing-retention rate that was achieved by the original housing-first program originated by Pathways to Housing. This chapter describes the program's essential components and how the model can most effectively be implemented to best serve consumers in a variety of settings. We begin this chapter with a case study of Mike (see box 9.1) and his experience with the Pathways team as they supported his efforts in obtaining housing, sobriety, and connections with family.

Box 9.1. Case Study: Mike

Mike was homeless for more than ten years. When the Pathways team met him, he was sleeping on the street, somehow managing to survive even while struggling with bipolar disorder—some days feeling very depressed and other days feeling manic. He was tormented because he believed that people were following him or talking to him on the street. He had not received any psychiatric treatment. Mike also drank alcohol on a daily basis. He began drinking when he was fifteen years old; he is now fifty-two. The team helped Mike move directly from the street into his own fully furnished apartment in October 2006. Since that time he has been receiving psychiatric treatment from the team psychiatrist and now reports that he no longer experiences mood swings or delusions. He has a phone in his apartment and plans to reconnect with his fifteen-year-old daughter, with whom he has not had contact since she was two years old. Treatment services have also connected him with a primary medical care provider. He has not had a drink in more than ninety days. Mike would like to work toward becoming a peer counselor to "give back" for what he has received.

Background

More than four hundred cities in the United States and Canada have completed ten-year plans to end chronic homelessness, which was once believed to be an impossible task (US Interagency Council on Homelessness, 2008). About 67 percent of these plans include a housing-first program. In July 2008, the US Department of Housing and Urban Development (HUD) reported that the number of chronically homeless people living in the nation's streets and shelters had dropped by about 30 percent—from 175,914 to 123,833—between 2005 and 2007, and administration officials "attribute much of the decline to the *Housing First* strategy" (Swarns, 2008, p. 30). In June 2010, the US Interagency Council listed housing first as one of its five effective strategies for ending chronic homelessness. How does a housing-first program provide housing and support to people with severe psychiatric disabilities who had previously remained homeless for years? How does it achieve residential stability for people who traditional homeless providers have considered "not housing ready" or "hard to house"? What does a housing-first program do that effectively engages into treatment people whom traditional service providers had labeled "treatment resistant"? How does the program assist with managing mental health and addiction problems and improve the quality of their lives? These are typical questions posed about this model, and they are discussed in this chapter.

Before there was housing first, permanent, independent housing—consumers' most coveted good—was offered only after consumers had successfully "graduated" from a series of programs that typically starting with outreach or drop-in centers and completing a successful stay in transitional housing by demonstrating compliance with treatment and sobriety (for an example of the traditional steps toward residential care, see figure 9.1).

Figure 9.1. Typical Services Approach

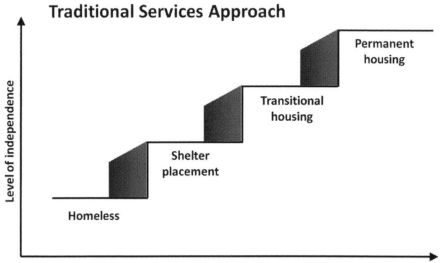

Even for successful consumers, permanent housing is often defined as a studiolike unit in a building inhabited either exclusively or predominantly by other people with psychiatric disabilities. Most supportive-housing programs combine housing and treatment services under a single roof with service providers located on-site. In these programs, consumers with co-occurring diagnoses must first demonstrate that they are "housing ready" by participating in psychiatric treatment and attaining a period of sobriety before they are admitted. Although housing first is gaining popularity and is effective in reducing chronic homelessness, the treatment first approach still dominates the field despite the fact that it is founded on several empirically untested assumptions, including the following: clinicians are the experts and must therefore determine the type of housing best suited to consumers' needs, most consumers require around-the-clock supervision, consumers with a diagnosis of severe mental illness are not able to manage independent housing, consumers with co-occurring addiction disorders must first be clean and sober before they can be housed, and consumers must first receive skills training to learn to live in independent housing.

The treatment-first model persists even in light of a growing body of research evidence indicating that consumers can set and attain their own goals and, with supports, can live independently, effectively managing their housing, mental health, addiction, job, and much more. The research on psychiatric rehabilitation (see chapter 15) shows that the best place to learn the skills necessary for living independently in an apartment is the community. In addition, studies of people who remain homeless for long periods of time have found that programs requiring treatment compliance and sobriety as preconditions for housing preclude many of them from accessing housing. For consumers that do access housing in programs that require treatment compliance and sobriety as a condition for continued tenure a relapse can result in a loss of housing and return to homelessness.

If the treatment-tied-to-housing approach is fraught with erroneous clinical assumptions and creates barriers to access for the very people it seeks to serve, why does it persist? Part of the answer concerns the enormous discrepancy between the supply of affordable supportive housing and the demand. For every open supportive-housing slot there can be literally hundreds of applicants. Thus, providers can easily meet their census target and still select only those applicants who can successfully meet their treatment and sobriety prerequisites. Consumers who cannot or will not meet these requirements continue to remain homeless for years, often cycling in and out shelters, emergency rooms, hospitals, detox centers, and jail (Hopper, Jost, Hay, Welber, & Haugland, 1997).

Continued exposure to homelessness has profoundly adverse effects on a person's physical, psychological, social, economic, legal, and spiritual well-being. Ordinary day-to-day tasks of survival, such as getting a meal or sleep, become a challenging and exhausting ordeal. Being homeless exposes individuals to extremes of weather, dangerous or life-threatening situations, increased opportunities for infection, drug use, and arrests, and it is associated with a high incidence of acute and chronic health problems, victimization, and premature mortality (Barrow, Herman, Cordova, & Struening, 1999).

Ironically, providing affordable housing with support services does not necessarily increase overall costs to society. Chronic homelessness is also associated with increased utilization of acute-care systems, such as emergency rooms and inpatient psychiatric services, detox centers, and incarceration resulting in extremely high service-utilization costs. Consumers who remain chronically homeless comprise only about 10 percent to 20 percent of the total homeless population, but they use as much as 50 percent of the system's resources (Culhane, Metraux, & Hadley, 2002).

Born out of the limitations of the traditional treatment-first approach, the housing-first model, developed by Pathways to Housing in 1992, has changed the landscape of what is considered possible for people with psychiatric disabilities who have remained chronically homeless. The program provides immediate access to permanent affordable housing (one's own apartment) along with support and treatment services. Figure 9.2 illustrates this trajectory from homeless to housing.

Figure 9.2. Housing First Model

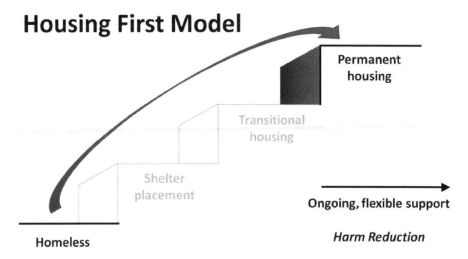

The program effectively ends homelessness by using a consumer-directed service approach and providing consumers what they want most—an apartment of their own—without requiring up-front treatment and sobriety or any other proof of housing "readiness." It supports people with psychiatric disabilities to set their own goals and priorities. Finally, it is based on a belief that housing is a basic human right rather than a reward for treatment compliance.

Theoretical Perspective

The housing-first philosophy derives its theoretical perspective from psychiatric rehabilitation, the consumer movement, harm reduction, and a human rights and social justice perspective that holds that housing is a basic human right and a recovery orientation.

Principles

There are four fundamental principles associated with housing first: consumer choice, separation of housing and services, recovery orientation, and community integration:

- *Principle of consumer choice*—Consumers should have a choice in the housing and services they receive and that services should be geared toward supporting their recovery.

- *Principle of separation of housing and services*—This housing model is consistent with research findings on consumers' housing preferences, as most consumers want to have an apartment of their own.

- *Principle of recovery orientation*—This orientation focuses on hope, consumer choice, and shared decision making in all interventions.

- *Principle of community integration*—Promotes the social inclusion of people with psychiatric disorders, through building community relationships and support networks.

Principle of Consumer Choice

A fundamental principle of the program is that consumers should have a choice in the housing and services they receive and that services should be geared toward supporting their recovery. Making choices about important aspects of one's life and experiencing the consequences of those choices are fundamental to the process of learning and recovery. Most traditional supportive programs are highly structured and offer a narrow range of choices to consumers. Housing-first programs, however, are driven by consumer choice. The starting point of the program is to ask consumers what they want; almost everyone says "a place to live," and the program begins by honoring and fulfilling that request. Consumers actively participate and work with program staff to select the neighborhood they wish to live in, choose their apartment, pick out furniture and household items, and live with someone if they wish.

Once housed, consumers continue to choose the type, sequence, and intensity of services. Clinicians use a harm-reduction approach (see chapter 5) when addressing substance use and mental health issues and incorporate a stages-of-change approach (see chapter 13) when addressing most life domains, including employment, family reconnection, and health. Staff encourages increased participation in mental health treatment and offers suggestions for reducing the risks and harmful behaviors associated with drug abuse. Consumers are not required to accept any formal clinical services such as taking psychiatric medication, seeing a psychiatrist, or working with a substance use specialist.

All consumers are required to meet with the program staff for regularly scheduled home visits, typically two to four times per month. A typical home visit consists of a conversation between the consumer and staff. The home visit provides an opportunity to observe the consumer's environment and to assess his or her general well-being, and most important, to keep open the channels of communication between the consumer and staff. Staff trained in techniques of engagement and motivational interviewing respectfully introduce questions, suggestions, and ideas to help the consumer consider the next step in improving their physical, social, psychological, emotional, educational, economic, or spiritual well-being. Staff visits also serve the purpose of offering assistance with any domain the consumer wishes to address, from apartment repairs to mending broken ties with family members.

Home visits and honoring consumer choice are especially important in times of difficulty or crisis such as when a consumer runs out of money, is under threat of eviction by their landlord, or when they have relapsed into addiction. Unless there is a danger to the consumer or to others, staff resist urges to take control of or fix a chaotic situation and make every effort to remain in communication with the consumer, exploring options but allowing the consumer to make the difficult choices. For example, if a consumer is facing eviction by the landlord because he or she has invited too many homeless friends to stay in the apartment, staff should work with the consumer to determine the best course of action: "What shall we do here? The landlord is pushing for eviction. Do you want to try to negotiate with the landlord? Ask your friends to leave? Leave this apartment and start over in another apartment?" And after the crisis is settled: "Let's figure out how you lost control of this apartment and see what you can do to prevent that from happening again." By continuing to support consumers in making their own decisions under difficult circumstances, consumers can benefit from their experience and learn to make good decisions on their own. The process in which consumers are supported in making their own decisions and experiencing the consequences of those decisions is one of the cornerstones of developing mastery, self-determination, and recovery.

Principle of Separation of Housing and Services

Pathways' housing-first program uses a scattered-site apartment model, renting affordable, decent apartments from landlords in the community. This housing model is consistent with research findings on consumers' housing preferences: the top choice for most consumers is to have an apartment of their own. This housing type maximizes individual approaches to treatment and support services because it provides consumers and staff maximum choice. The program makes every effort to ensure the integration of people with psychiatric disabilities into the community; the program does not rent more than 20 percent of the units in any one building. Consumers have the same rights and responsibilities as all other tenants holding a standard lease, and they are required to pay 30 percent of their income toward rent (which typically consists of Supplemental Security Income). The program uses a variety of government subsidies to pay the remainder (and bulk) of the rent. If consumers are having difficulty paying their rent or budgeting, the program may become a consumer's representative payee or offer other budgeting services to help ensure that bills (especially the rent) are paid. In housing-first programs, loss of housing occurs only for lease violations, not for treatment noncompliance or hospitalization. Some consumers lose their apartment after they relapse, stop paying bills, and are evicted by the landlord. The program works with the consumer to address these issues and help the consumer secure another apartment. The team is already off-site and separate from the housing so that the team can flexibly provide continuity of support when a consumer has to move to a different apartment.

Housing-first consumers have access to several other evidence-based practices that have proved effective for this population, including integrated dual-diagnosis treatment and comprehensive support services. This is usually provided through a multidisciplinary team approach, such as assertive community treatment (ACT; see chapter 7). The ACT team is located off-site but is available on-call twenty-four hours a day, seven days a week, and provides most services in a client's natural environment (e.g., apartment, workplace, neighborhood). The service is time-unlimited in that it is offered as long as a consumer needs that level of support. Assertive community treatment is an evidence-based practice that has been incorporated into the housing-first model. It is also an efficient platform from which to provide other evidence-based practices, including supported employment (see chapter 10), integrated dual-disorder treatment (see chapter 1), and illness management and recovery (see chapter 3). Consumers participate in treatment to address their clinical issues, and treatment considerations are separate from their housing issues. For example, if a consumer needs to be hospitalized, he or she goes to the hospital; after the hospitalization, the consumer returns home to his or her apartment.

By separating the criteria for getting and keeping housing from a consumer's treatment status (yet maintaining a close, ongoing relationship between the two components), housing-first programs help prevent the recurrence of homelessness when consumers relapse into substance abuse or a psychiatric crisis. When necessary, team members can provide intensive treatment by facilitating admission to a detox center or hospital to address the clinical crisis—after the treatment is completed, the person is helped to return home. There is continuity of treatment and no need for eviction.

Principle of Recovery Orientation

Housing-first embodies a recovery orientation (see chapter 12) that is now the cornerstone of mental health service reform (New Freedom Commission on Mental Health, 2003). The ACT team services are characterized by a recovery-oriented practice philosophy that places the conveyance of hope, consumer choice, and shared decision making at the forefront of all interventions. Service plans are not based on clinician assessments of consumers' needs but are derived from consumers' setting of their own goals. This flexible, respectful, consumer-driven approach to clinical practice helps ensure that consumers remain engaged with the team, particularly during crisis. The harm-reduction approach creates an open atmosphere in which consumers can begin to trust staff and can have an open and honest exchange about drug or alcohol use because they understand that using is not linked to eviction from housing.

Principle of Community Integration

Housing first promotes community integration by using the scattered-site apartment model, as mentioned earlier, which promotes the social inclusion of people with psychiatric disorders. Program staff encourage and foster normative relationships with landlords, neighbors, family, and other natural support networks that increase contact with people outside the mental health system and promote community living. This scattered-site housing design renders consumers' residential status virtually indistinguishable from any other neighborhood residents with similar socioeconomic and ethnic-racial characteristics. Consumers are not living in programs; they are living in the community. The model is also consistent with antidiscriminatory legislation such as the Americans with Disabilities Act and the *Olmstead* Supreme Court decision, which mandates that people with disabilities live in the least restrictive settings, both of which aim to promote social inclusion and community integration (Vernon, 2005).

Steps for Implementing Housing First

Currently, housing-first programs have been successfully implemented across the United States in cities such as New York City, New York; Washington, DC; Chicago, Illinois; Columbus, Ohio; Denver, Colorado; Oakland, California; Philadelphia, Pennsylvania; Hartford, Connecticut; Fort Lauderdale, Florida; Salt Lake City, Utah; Burlington, Vermont; and New Orleans, Louisiana—as well as in many cities across Canada and Europe. There are three steps housing-first developers take that explain the widespread dissemination of the program: short start-up, established effectiveness, and cost-effectiveness.

First, the program has a very short start-up time. Once funded, an agency simply needs to hire staff, identify eligible consumers (they are usually already well known to the service provider community), and begin renting apartments from private landlords. There is no new construction in this model. There are no lengthy treatment prerequisites. From the time a program is funded to the time of the first consumer being housed as few as three months can pass, and the range is usually from three to five months. Once started, an average program serving seventy-five consumers can begin housing people at the rate of one or two per week. In about one year after start-up the entire program can be filled to capacity.

Second, the program is highly effective. Staff and other stakeholders do not have to wait long for results. People previously believed to be impossible to house begin to get housed and to stay housed. Many cities that began a pilot housing-first program quickly saw its effectiveness, realized 85 percent housing-retention rates at twelve months, and began a second full-scale program on the heels of the first.

Third, the program is cost effective. Policy makers and program planners know that there are considerable savings in acute-care service utilization cost and acute-care staff burden in providing consumers an apartment and providing support services rather than having consumers cycle in and out of emergency rooms, shelters, detox centers, and jails. Given the wide dissemination, there is more work needed to ensure that the program is implemented correctly and is faithful to the philosophy and practice of the model. A housing-first manual and tool kit including a DVD and interactive web-based training is available to assist in the model's implementation (Tsemberis, 2010).

What's the Evidence?

Housing first is recognized as an evidence-based practice by the National Registry of Evidence Based Programs, hosted by the Substance Abuse and Mental Health Services Administration (2007). Research studies have demonstrated overwhelming evidence that housing first is effective for achieving residential stability for people who have remained homeless for years. Initial evaluations of housing first in urban areas with primarily street-dwelling samples have yielded convincing results. Using archival data over a five-year period, 88 percent of housing-first consumers remained housed, compared to 47 percent of consumers in traditional residential treatment (Tsemberis & Eisenberg, 2000). In a randomized clinical trial of housing alternatives, individuals assigned to housing-first programs spent approximately 80 percent of their time stably housed, compared to only 30 percent of participants assigned to traditional services after two years (Tsemberis, Gulcur, & Nakae, 2004).

In 2004, the US Interagency Council on the Homeless launched its national Initiative to Help End Chronic Homelessness, funded by HUD, the Department of Health and Human Services, the Substance Abuse and Mental Health Services Administration, and the Department of Veterans Affairs. Seven of the eleven cities funded used the housing-first model and achieved 85 percent housing retention rates after twelve months (Mares & Rosenheck, 2007). Two years later, HUD published the outcomes of its three-city, twelve-month study of programs (one of which was Pathways to Housing) and reported an 84 percent housing retention rate for twelve months (Pearson, McDonald, Locke, Montgomery, & Burton, 2007). Similar outcomes also held true for consumers who were long-term shelter dwellers in a suburban county, in which approximately 78 percent of housing-first participants remained stably housed over a four-year period (Stefancic & Tsemberis, 2007). This suggests the model's utility for street-dwelling and shelter-using segments of the homeless population and its effectiveness using housing stock in urban and suburban environments.

Although the hallmark of housing first's effectiveness has been assessed through success achieved in residential stability for people other agencies would not house, both quantitative and qualitative research has documented advantages to housing first that go beyond residential stability. For instance, both choice and scattered-site housing, as part of housing first, are significant predictors of consumers' psychological well-being and social integration, respectively (Greenwood, Schaefer-McDaniel, Winkel, & Tsemberis, 2005; Gulcur, Tsemberis, Stefancic, & Greenwood, 2007). Consumers rate housing satisfaction significantly higher when living in more independent supported-housing settings than in congregate or community residences (Siegel et al., 2006). For instance, housing-first consumers describe the importance of having a home in terms of privacy, normalized daily activities, and a secure base for self-discovery, all of which foster a greater sense of belonging in the world (Padgett, 2007). It is important to note that, although some people report feeling lonely in their apartments, they still prefer independent to congregate housing (Yanos, Barrow, & Tsemberis, 2004). In addition, although consumers in traditional programs report higher rates of substance use treatment, housing-first consumers who have lower rates of treatment utilization have no greater rates of alcohol or substance use (Padgett, Gulcur, & Tsemberis, 2006).

In addition to its clinical effectiveness, housing first is also cost effective when compared to most traditional housing and shelter programs and significantly cheaper than having a person remain homeless. A HUD-funded review dating back to 1998 found that the average cost for shelter beds nationally is $13,000 per year, and the price goes up from there depending on the services available. In New York City a service-enriched shelter bed can range from $23,000 to $33,000, and keeping people in institutional settings such as hospitals or jails can quickly reach more than $100,000 per year. Choosing to leave people on the streets also has its price—the combined average annual cost associated with services such as shelters, emergency services, and incarcerations for individuals who are chronically homeless with severe mental illness comes to $40,500. When this same group is provided housing-first services, the annual average cost does not exceed $22,500 (Culhane, Gross, Parker, Poppe, & Sykes, 2007).

In total, the weight of the evidence clearly shows that housing first is an effective program for helping consumers with multiple problems and with little or no likelihood of access to traditional housing programs obtain and maintain independent housing. As housing first becomes more widely disseminated, assessment of residential stability, cost-benefit analysis, and levels of psychiatric symptoms and substance use will continue to be important outcome measures. However, new housing-first programs should expand their repertoire of services to strive to achieve improved outcomes in a number of other domains, including wellness self-management, employment, and social integration, as well as helping consumers identify and realize capabilities that are important to them.

Assessment and Evaluation

Ensuring that programs are implemented and operate according to housing-first principles will ensure the obtaining of successful outcomes. A housing-first fidelity scale was developed to help ensure that programs operate with a high degree of fidelity to the model and thus can expect to achieve the same successful outcomes. The Housing-First Program Fidelity Checklist was developed by interviewing experts from a number of cities operating highly effective housing-first programs. The experts were asked to list the essential ingredients contributing to the program's success. This is the same methodology used to develop the ACT fidelity scale. In addition, the experts were asked to rate the importance of a list of items describing the program. From a pool of sixty items, a total of thirty-eight items were extracted and selected for the fidelity measure because experts across the sites most often repeated them. These items cluster into the essential dimensions discussed in this chapter: consumer choice, separation of housing and treatment, service philosophy (e.g., recovery, harm reduction), service array, and program structure (for a complete list, see Tsemberis, 2010, pp. 215–218).

Measures that are essential in evaluating housing-first program outcomes include evaluating the domains that the program seeks to improve: a measure of residential stability, housing and service choice, mental health symptoms, health status, addiction severity, recovery, and community integration.

Implementation Issues

Housing first began by serving a street-homeless population, but later expanded its methods of referral and intake to include persons with psychiatric disabilities who were living in and out of shelters, living in acute-care and long-term hospital settings, and were either discharged from prison or needed an alternative to incarceration. The model has been effective for a diverse group of mental health consumers (e.g., homeless, people with substance use issues) and has been widely implemented (Pearson et al., 2007).

The major challenges in implementation are that agencies must successfully secure funding for housing (e.g., rent stipends, vouchers) and service support (e.g., grants, Medicaid). This often requires multiple applications, which must be coordinated so that funding start and end dates coincide. Another major challenge is one that is ubiquitous in the mental health and substance abuse system—the paradigm shift needed to change practitioners' philosophy from clinician driven to consumer driven and to practice a harm-reduction approach to housing and services.

Provider Competencies

Providers working in housing-first programs should have a recovery orientation that includes a desire for social justice, a radical acceptance of the consumer's point of view, comfort with consumers' full participation in treatment decisions, and an ability to work in a harm-reduction framework. Clinicians best suited to the program are those whose training includes psychiatric rehabilitation, self-psychology, and other humanistic approaches.

If agencies operating supportive-housing programs that require treatment and sobriety before housing want to transform their practice, they should consider how their program could be transformed and what the new role of the existing employees would be. It would probably be useful to include every stakeholder of the agency, including the board of directors, before deciding to implement a housing-first program.

Allowing clients to make their own decisions and lead the treatment process is a new experience for many clinicians, especially for those in public mental health settings. Pathways' clinicians intervene without consumer consent only in rare instances when the client presents danger to self or others. Consistent with client-driven treatment, the team members apply principles of harm reduction, helping minimize adverse consequences of substance use if consumers choose to continue using substances or to minimize the adverse consequences resulting from psychiatric symptoms if consumers choose not to take medication. When traditionally trained psychiatrists and clinicians, unaccustomed to this stance, join the Pathways team, they receive training in harm-reduction practice and in techniques such as motivational interviewing.

A team approach is extremely useful when applying a harm-reduction approach in which consumers take risks. Team members can support one another when confronted with difficult situations and can continue to allow clients to direct their treatment even when there is a risk of failure. When these difficult situations are confronted in this manner, successful outcomes build clients' confidence in managing their crisis and reinforce the continued use of client-directed interventions by the team. The team provides opportunities for peer learning and peer supervision.

Future Directions

Dissemination of housing first continues across the United States and internationally. A housing-first manual and tool kit including a DVD and interactive web-based training is available to assist the model's replication (Tsemberis, 2010). Further research is needed to better understand the ways housing first promotes community integration and recovery, as well as how consumers who do not do well in housing-first programs (e.g., about 10–15 percent) can find other useful approaches. A national randomized control trial of housing first in Canada is currently under way. The Mental Health Commission of Canada (2011) funded the five-city study, which is examining the housing and clinical outcomes of 2,015 consumers across Canada. In addition, researchers, practitioners, and consumers are exploring ways to understand the most effective supports, including natural supports and peer specialists to effectively assist consumers to graduate from housing-first programs, because unlike with traditional services, graduation from housing first entails that the consumer remains in place (in his or her home) when the support staff walk away.

Websites

HUD Resources for Housing—http://www.huduser.org/Publications/pdf/hsgfirst.pdf

Pathways to Housing—http://pathwaystohousing.org

Program Replications: 5 City Randomized Control Trial by the Mental Health Commission of Canada (Project Name: At Home/Chez Soi)—http://www.mentalhealth commission.ca

Glossary

Consumer-driven (client-driven) services: A fundamental philosophical program approach that invites consumers to be their own decision makers. Consumers largely determine how housing, clinical support, and services will be delivered to them. Consumers are asked for their preference in type of housing (almost all choose an apartment of their own), location, furnishings, and other personal amenities. Consumers also determine the type, sequence, and intensity of services and treatment options rather than the clinician or provider.

Harm reduction: A practical, client-directed approach that uses multiple strategies, including abstinence, to help consumers manage their addictions and psychiatric symptoms. Harm reduction focuses on reducing the negative consequences of harmful behaviors related to drug and alcohol abuse or untreated psychiatric symptoms. Harm reduction is about starting the process of treatment where consumers are at the time and helping them gradually gain control over harmful behaviors.

Recovery orientation: Housing-first services have a recovery orientation. Staff continually convey a message of the belief that recovery is possible and even inevitable. Staff carry positive messages about recovery, convey hope, avoid hierarchical power relationships, and convey true caring and concern. There is no better way to model and promote the concept of recovery than by including peer specialists as staff on housing-first teams. In addition, the program works to expand the variety and scope of services and to include employment support and health and wellness—a comprehensive program that includes nutrition, wellness self-management, diet, cooking, exercise, meaningful leisure, community activities, and spirituality. Most of all, the staff begins every relationship, in the words of one client, "assum[ing] that every person who walks through the door has the potential for recovery. Staff should just automatically assume that recovery is possible."

Scattered-site housing: Apartments rented at fair-market value that meet government housing-quality standards. This housing model—known as scattered-site independent housing—honors consumers' preferences, such as choosing apartments in neighborhoods with which they are familiar. The housing-first program does not own any housing and does not rent more than 20 percent of the units in any one building. Instead, housing-first participants either directly lease or sublease affordable apartments from community landlords and the agency provides a rent subsidy. Consumers pay 30 percent of income toward their rent. Another dimension that comes with scattered-site housing is social inclusion; this is "normal" housing, and the other tenants in the building are regular neighbors who set a community standard for neighborly behavior that helps clients participate in community living in ways that, for some, had never before been available.

References

Americans with Disabilities Act. Pub. L. No. 101-336. 104 Stat. 327 (1990).

Barrow, S. M., Herman, D. B., Cordova, P., & Struening, E. L. (1999). Mortality among homeless shelter residents in New York City. *American Journal of Public Health, 89*(4), 529–534.

Culhane, D. P., Gross, K. S., Parker, W. D., Poppe, B., & Sykes, E. (2007, March 1). *Accountability, cost-effectiveness, and program performance: Progress since 1998.* Paper presented at the National Symposium on Homelessness Research, Washington, DC. Retrieved from http://aspe.hhs.gov/hsp/ homelessness/symposium07/culhane/index.htm.

Culhane, D., Metraux, S., & Hadley, T. (2002). Public service reductions associated with placement of homeless persons with severe mental illness in supportive housing. *Housing Policy Debate, 13*(1), 107–163.

Greenwood, R. M., Schaefer-McDaniel, N. J., Winkel, G., & Tsemberis, S. J. (2005). Decreasing psychiatric symptoms by increasing choice in services for adults with histories of homelessness. *American Journal of Community Psychology, 36*(3–4), 223–238.

Gulcur, L., Tsemberis, S., Stefancic, A., & Greenwood, R. M. (2007). Community integration of adults with psychiatric disabilities and histories of homelessness. *Community Mental Health Journal, 43*(3), 211–229.

Hopper, K., Jost, J., Hay, T., Welber, S., & Haugland, G. (1997). Homelessness, severe mental illness, and the institutional circuit. *Psychiatric Services, 48*(5), 659–665.

Mares, A.S., & Rosenheck, R.A. (2007). *HUD/HHS/VA Collaborative Initiative to Help End Chronic Homelessness: National performance outcomes assessment: Preliminary client outcomes report.* Northeast Program Evaluation Center. Retrieved from http://aspe.hhs.gov/hsp/homelessness/CICH07/outcomes07/ index.htm.

Mental Health Commission of Canada. (2011). *MHCC Newsletter*. Retrieved from http://www.mentalhealthcommission.ca/english/pages/default.aspx.

New Freedom Commission on Mental Health. (2003). *Achieving the promise: Transforming mental health care in America. Final Report* (DHHS Pub. No. SMA-03-3832). Rockville, MD: US Department of Health and Human Services.

Olmstead v. L.C., 527 U.S. 581 (1999).

Padgett, D. K. (2007). There's no place like (a) home: Ontological security among persons with serious mental illness in the United States. *Social Science and Medicine, 64*(9), 1925–1936.

Padgett, D. K., Gulcur, L., & Tsemberis, S. (2006). Housing first services for people who are homeless with co-occurring serious mental illness and substance abuse. *Research on Social Work Practice, 16*(1), 74–83.

Pearson, C., McDonald, W., Locke, G., Montgomery, A., & Burton, L. (2007). *The applicability of housing first models to homeless persons with mental illness.* Office of Policy Development and Research, US Department of Housing and Urban Development. Retrieved from http://www.huduser.org/portal/publications/hsgfirst.pdf.

Siegel, C., Samuels, J., Tang, D., Berg, I., Jones, K., & Hopper, K. (2006). Tenant outcomes in supported housing and community residences in New York City. *Psychiatric Services, 57*, 982–991.

Stefancic, A., & Tsemberis, S. (2007). Housing first for long-term shelter dwellers with psychiatric disabilities in a suburban county: A four-year outcome study of housing access and retention. *Journal of Primary Prevention, 28*, 265–279.

Substance Abuse and Mental Health Services Administration. (2007). *Pathways' Housing First, National Registry of Evidence Based Programs.* Retrieved from http://www.nrepp.samhsa.gov/ViewIntervention.aspx?id=155

Swarns, R. (2008, July 30). US reports drop in homeless population. *New York Times*, p. 30. Retrieved from http://www.nytimes.com/2008/07/30/us/30homeless.html.

Tsemberis, S. (2010). *Housing first: The Pathways model to end homelessness for people with mental illness and addiction.* St. Paul, MN: Hazelden Press.

Tsemberis, S., & Eisenberg, R. F. (2000). Pathways to housing: Supported housing for street-dwelling homeless individuals with psychiatric disabilities. *Psychiatric Services, 51*(4), 487–493.

Tsemberis, S., Gulcur, L., & Nakae, M. (2004). Housing first, consumer choice, and harm reduction for homeless individuals with a dual diagnosis. *American Journal of Public Health, 94,* 651–656.

US Interagency Council on Homelessness. (2008). *Innovations in 10-year plans to end chronic homelessness in your community.* Retrieved from http://www.usich.gov.

Vernon, S. (2005). *Social work and the law* (3rd ed.). New York: Oxford University Press.

Yanos, P., Barrow, S., & Tsemberis, S. (2004). Community integration in the early phase of housing among homeless individuals diagnosed with severe mental illness: Success and challenges. *Community Mental Health Journal, 40*(2), 133–150.

Supported Employment

Marina Kukla and Gary R. Bond

Supported employment is an individualized psychiatric rehabilitation approach designed to help people with severe mental illness obtain and maintain competitive employment. Based on the place-train model in the development disabilities field, supported employment was adapted to psychiatric rehabilitation in the early 1980s. It is an evidence-based practice with research-supported principles. It uses a rapid job-search approach, a service provider offers ongoing support throughout a client's tenure at a job, and it integrates mental health services with employment services. Randomized controlled trials have consistently found that supported employment is more effective than other vocational approaches in helping people with severe mental illness achieve competitive employment. Clients enrolled in supported employment find jobs faster and earn more from employment than do clients receiving other types of vocational services. Future research should focus on financing and organization of supported employment services, job-development strategies, and ways to increase job tenure of clients. We begin this chapter with a case review of Tim (see box 10.1) and the steps he used to achieve successful employment using supported-employment strategies.

Box 10.1. Case Study: Tim

Tim is a forty-five-year-old African American man with a diagnosis of schizoaffective disorder. He often had a disheveled appearance, and he did not shower regularly. He had a history of legal problems, and in the past, he had served three years in prison on a drug-related felony conviction. Recently, he had become stable on his medications, although he occasionally experienced symptoms of auditory hallucinations and periods of mania. Tim had not worked in the past seventeen years, although he desired to get a job. Recently, he spoke of his motivation to work with his case manager at the community mental health center where he received services. She referred him to their supported employment program, and a supported employment specialist spoke with Tim about his job goals, preferences, and strengths. Together the employment specialist and Tim developed a résumé for him, and several job opportunities became available. Tim's employment specialist found several businesses that fit Tim's vocational goals and were understanding of his legal history. After two interviews, Tim got a part-time job working at a paint store a few miles from his home. Tim's employment specialist assisted him in locating the bus schedule and in planning out the route to and from work. In addition, the employment specialist worked with the store manager and arranged a suitable schedule and work environment for him. Tim quickly learned his job tasks and did not require the assistance of the employment specialist thereafter. She continued to visit Tim at work on a monthly basis to check in and provide support when needed. After six months working at the store, Tim was offered a full-time position, at which he remained employed for more than five years.

Several factors led to Tim's success in employment, in addition to his hard work on the job. First, the teamwork between Tim and his employment specialist in identifying Tim's preferences and needs in regard to competitive employment was the initial step in securing a successful placement. Second, the employment specialist's job development, or job search, matching Tim's preferences and other relevant factors (e.g., finding businesses willing to hire persons with former legal issues) was also very important. Third, the employment specialist's work when Tim first obtained the job was crucial to creating a suitable work environment for Tim. Finally, the employment specialist's visits to Tim at the job site ("follow-along support") were critical to effectively addressing issues and significant changes (e.g., a new job supervisor) as they arose and to helping Tim maintain his employment for the long term.

Background

Supported employment refers to rehabilitation services that assist clients with severe mental illness obtain and maintain competitive employment in the community through an individualized approach that emphasizes rapid job search and that de-emphasizes a stepwise approach of intermediate employment prior to placement in a competitive job. It helps to compensate for the challenges presented by mental illness, such as psychotic symptoms, cognitive dysfunction, and a lack of social skills that make obtaining and maintaining employment more difficult. Supported employment services are especially crucial given the finding that the majority of people with severe mental illness want to work, yet most are unemployed (Becker & Drake, 2003). Supported employment programs are present in a variety of settings (e.g., Veterans Affairs medical centers, university-run outpatient clinics), but they are most often found in community mental health centers, which provide mental health counseling, medication management, case management, housing assistance, and other services.

History

Community-based psychiatric rehabilitation services began in the mid-1950s. This era included the deinstitutionalization movement, in which large numbers of people with severe mental illness moved out of inpatient hospitals into the community. One of the earliest forms of community-based psychiatric rehabilitation was the "clubhouse," where people with severe mental illness could go during the day and socialize. Clubhouses fostered the idea that individuals could work and should have an opportunity to work, if they so desired, even if they had spent many years in the hospital and suffered from debilitating psychiatric symptoms. The desire to participate in meaningful, productive activity ultimately led to the provision of specific employment services for this population (Becker & Drake, 2003).

The earliest formulation of supported employment was the place-train approach, first used in the developmental disabilities field (Wehman & Moon, 1988). The place-train approach assumed that rapid placement into a competitive job in the community with appropriate training and support thereafter would lead to better outcomes for people with even severe disabilities than the traditional train-place approach, which required clients to receive pre-employment training prior to placement. Pre-employment training was ineffective because of the lack of generalizability of job skills training and the unrealistic nature of the pre-employment training situation (clients know that it is not the "real world").

Given the shortcomings of the train-place approach, the mental health field began to adopt the principles of Wehman and Moon's (1988) more successful place-train approach in the late 1980s. The most widely studied, used, and standardized supported employment approach for people with severe mental illness is the individualized placement and support (IPS) model (Becker & Drake, 2003).

Theoretical Perspective

Supported employment is an evidence-based practice based on the recovery model. Recovery from mental illness has several definitions, but a commonly used definition is "a deeply personal, unique process of changing one's attitudes, values, feelings, goals, skills and/or roles. It is a way of living a satisfying, hopeful, and contributing life even with limitations caused by the illness. Recovery involves the development of new meaning and purpose in one's life as one grows beyond the catastrophic effects of mental illness" (Anthony, 1993, p. 17). It is widely accepted that work is a crucial part of recovery, as individuals with severe mental illnesses engage in meaningful, personally satisfying roles, such as employment, in the community.

Principles

The IPS model is an evidence-based vocational model. It uses the following research-based principles (Bond, 1998, 2004; Drake, Bond, & Becker, 2012):

- *Principle of zero exclusion*—Individualized placement and support programs serve anyone with severe mental illness who professes an interest in working, regardless of symptoms, work history, lack of skills, strange appearance, or any of the myriad reasons often given for excluding people from vocational services.

- *Principle of goal of competitive employment only*—Employment specialists do not place clients in noncompetitive jobs such as work crews or sheltered workshop positions in which jobs are reserved for those with severe mental illness.

- *Principle of focus on client choice and preferences*—Client job preferences, needs, and abilities receive paramount importance in identifying jobs during the job search and in determining what kinds of help will be provided. For example, if the client prefers not to disclose his or her psychiatric disability to the employer, the supported employment team accommodates this preference.

- *Principle of ongoing, informal assessment*—On the basis of direct observation and conversations with clients and employers, the employment specialist continuously assesses the fit between the client's preferences and capabilities and the environmental demands. Skills needed to perform job duties are only one aspect of this assessment; relationships with supervisors and coworkers are usually crucial. Other life circumstances, including housing and family situations, are also considered.

- *Principle of systematic job development*—Employment specialists build an employer network based on clients' interests, developing relationships with local employers by making systematic contacts. Job development involves cultivating a relationship. Usually the IPS specialist plans the first employer contact to introduce herself/himself to the employer and request another meeting. The second contact is to learn about the employer's business. Future contacts are to discuss potential employees when there might be a good job match.

- *Principle of rapid job search*—The job search begins as soon as the client enters an IPS program. There is no prevocational training or lengthy vocational assessment. Standardized assessment tools are mostly of little value in identifying who is able to work or what jobs to pursue.

- *Principle of time-unlimited, individualized follow-along support*—Ongoing follow-along support provided by the employment specialist may include a variety of interventions, including assisting the client in mastering job duties, consulting with the client's coworkers and supervisors to enhance interactions with the client, and suggesting modifications in the work environment to accommodate the client's needs. Once a client is successfully employed for a period of time (e.g., one year), employment specialists typically taper off support to once a month or less and transition the bulk of support to the clinical treatment team.

- *Principle of benefits counseling*—Individualized placement and support programs provide clients with personalized information regarding the consequences of employment earnings on their Social Security and Medicaid payments.

- *Principle of integrated employment services and mental health treatment*—Staff from IPS programs work closely with mental treatment teams and attend treatment team meetings. Integration of supported employment services and mental health treatment is characterized by employment specialists providing mental health information to mental health clinicians and mental health clinicians providing vocational information to employment specialists. For example, in the case example of Tim, Tim's employment specialist provides information to mental health clinicians about new symptoms Tim experiences on the job or medication side effects that affect his ability to work. Mental health clinicians (i.e., case managers) provide information to Tim's employment specialist about other aspects of his life, such as changes in his residential status or transportation that could affect his vocational status.

Another important component of the IPS model is that employment specialists carry small caseloads (i.e., usually no more than twenty clients). In addition, employment specialists provide employment services only and do not have responsibilities for nonvocational services, such as crisis intervention, housing, or other case management tasks.

Steps for Implementing Supported Employment

The following is a step-by-step description of the IPS employment process. Although the steps may vary somewhat in temporal sequence and nature depending on the individual circumstances of each client, these steps show the rudimentary process for a typical client:

1. The client expresses a desire to work competitively to their mental health team, or the client comes into the community mental health center seeking out help with employment.

2. An employment specialist begins to work with the client, identifying important factors, including the client's preferences, needs, and individual circumstances (e.g., transportation) regarding employment. If the client is receiving disability benefits, the client receives specific information on the financial implications of earnings from employment, both before the job search and after a specific job offer is made. The employment specialist and client discuss options regarding disclosure of mental illness to employers.

3. Although not a requirement for enrollment in supported employment, supported-employment programs often receive funding from the state and/or federal vocational rehabilitation system. Consequently, employment specialists typically work closely with this agency on behalf of their clients, initiating contact before the client obtains a job.

4. Usually within a month's time, the employment specialist and the client together begin the job-development process and search for a suitable job.

5. When the client obtains a job, the employment specialist often works with the supervisor and coworkers to work out a suitable work environment for the client. This role depends on the client's preferences, including whether the client discloses his or her psychiatric disability.

6. The employment specialist makes routine visits to the client at the job site or in the community and intervenes when issues and problems arise throughout the client's tenure at the job. In some instances, the employment specialist is in regular contact with the client's supervisor. Employment specialists also meet often with clients outside the workplace. The job support plan is individualized.

7. If employment ends or the client desires a new job, the employment specialist works with the client to find another job matching his or her job preferences and needs.

What's the Evidence?
Vocational Outcomes

Research has found that supported employment is superior to other employment approaches in improving competitive employment outcomes (Bond, Drake, & Becker, 2012). Fifteen randomized controlled trials have compared the IPS model of supported employment with various other approaches, finding a significant advantage in competitive employment rates for IPS, as shown in figure 10.1.

These studies have also found that clients receiving supported-employment services obtain their first competitive jobs 50 percent faster and have significantly longer job tenure than those clients receiving services in alternative approaches. Studies of day-rehabilitation programs that have converted to supported-employment programs have found that they have been able to do so successfully, with improved competitive employment outcomes for clients (Becker et al., 2001). Moreover, long-term studies indicate that the vocational benefits of supported employment are long lasting (Becker, Whitley, Bailey, & Drake, 2007).

Nonvocational Outcomes

Participation in a supported-employment program does not itself lead to improved nonvocational outcomes. However, research has indicated that clients who obtain employment realize other benefits, including improved self-esteem (Bond et al., 2001; Mueser et al., 1997), fewer symptoms (e.g., Bond et al., 2001; Burns et al., 2009; Kukla, 2010; Mueser et al., 1997), better general functioning (e.g., Burns et al., 2009; Mueser et al., 1997), improved social networks (Kukla, 2010), and higher quality of life (e.g., Twamley, Narvaez, Becker, Bartels, & Jeste, 2008).

Figure 10.1.   Competitive Employment Rates in Fifteen Randomized Controlled Trials of Individual Placement and Support

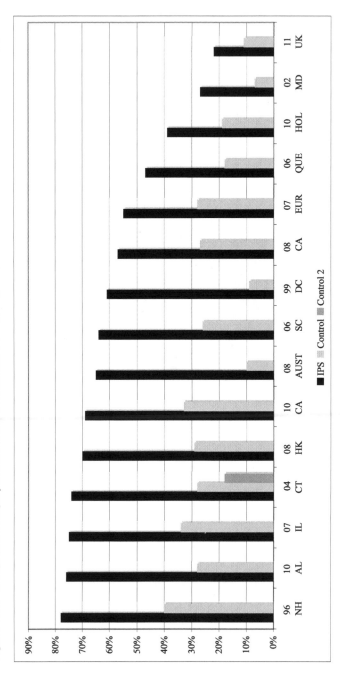

Source: Adapted from Bond, Drake, & Becker, 2012. Reprinted with permission.

Note: On the x-axis, U.S. postal abbreviations are used for states and the District of Columbia. HK = Hong Kong, AUST = Australia, EUR = Europe, QUE = Quebec, HOL = Netherlands, and UK = United Kingdom.

Assessment and Evaluation

Supported-employment studies have typically used objective indicators of competitive employment, such as rates of obtaining employment, time to first job, job tenure, and hours worked per week. Supported employment researchers have often used rigorous research designs, with careful training of clinicians and monitoring of implementation (efficacy methods), conducting these in real-world settings with clients from heterogeneous backgrounds (effectiveness methods) (Bond, Drake et al., 2008). Studies have been conducted in a multitude of settings, including urban and rural areas, and in countries outside the United States with different labor conditions (e.g., Australia, Canada, Hong Kong, several European countries).

It is standard practice in IPS studies to assess fidelity, that is, adherence to the IPS program model using a well-validated fidelity scale (Bond, Becker, Drake, & Vogler, 1997). The IPS fidelity scale comprises fifteen items rated on a five-point, behaviorally anchored scale, with higher scores indicating better fidelity. Fidelity is assessed at the level of the IPS program, and fidelity items cover the primary tenets of the IPS model, such as rapid job search for competitive jobs, agency focus on competitive employment, and zero exclusion criteria (Becker, Swanson, Bond, & Merrens, 2011). Assessing IPS fidelity and making adjustments to practice is also important, given findings that better fidelity to the IPS model leads to better employment outcomes for clients (Bond, Becker, & Drake, 2011).

Implementation Issues

As noted already, systematically assessing and monitoring supported employment fidelity is a crucial implementation strategy. Several other components of effective implementation that relate closely to fidelity include the following (Bond, McHugo et al., 2008):

- Discontinuing non-evidence-based vocational services (e.g., sheltered workshops, train-place vocational approaches)

- Improving the integration of employment services with clinical and mental health services via supervisor leadership

- Changing relevant organizational and structural tasks to be compatible with the supported-employment model, including things such as changing billing processes and procedures, training staff, endorsing the supported employment philosophy organization wide, and changing documentation in client records

- Implementing supported-employment programs at exemplary sites that can be models and opportunities for training for later sites

- Obtaining support and consensus from all stakeholders (e.g., clients, family members, state authorities, practitioners, administrators)

In addition, studies have found that supported employment may be implemented successfully and is widely generalizable and applicable across community settings (rural and urban) and across various ethnic and minority groups (including African Americans, Hispanic Americans, and Asian Americans), among both young and older adults, and with clients with co-occurring substance use (Bond, Drake, & Becker, 2010).

Provider Competencies

Although several provider competencies of employment specialists exist that are necessary for the provision of successful supported-employment services, little research has been conducted in this area. However, some of the most important provider competencies that should be emphasized in practice include the following:

- Hopeful attitudes and the belief that clients with severe mental illness can work (Gowdy, Carlson, & Rapp, 2003)

- The ability to form a good working alliance or relationship with the client (Kukla & Bond, 2009)

- Job-development skills, or the ability to locate and secure numerous and diverse jobs matching client preferences and needs

- Skills encompassed in each specific phase of employment services (e.g., appropriate ongoing job support to the client) (Bond & Kukla, 2011)

- Employment specialist motivation and interest in the field of supported employment

- Employment specialists' focus on working in the community in all phases of employment services rather than in the agency office

Importantly, these are skills and behaviors that can be taught. The research suggests that appropriate supervision, feedback, and leadership provided to the employment specialist by team leaders and other supervisory-level staff make a difference.

Future Directions

Several areas of future research are needed in the supported employment arena, given the paucity of research conducted thus far and/or the need for improvement of supported-employment services in various areas to result in improved client outcomes. Such areas include the following (Drake & Bond, 2008):

- Provider competencies

- Ways to increase job tenure of clients

- Understanding of the overall costs of supported employment and better ways to finance and organize supported employment services

- Better job-development strategies

- Ways to enhance career trajectories of supported-employment clients

- Effective ways to address lack of motivation to work

In addition, in recent years, studies have begun to examine adjuncts to supported employment that are designed to compensate for deficits associated with mental illness. For instance, studies have investigated cognitive remediation and social skills training delivered along with IPS supported employment. To address the educational needs of people with severe mental illness, research has suggested that supported-education services delivered along with supported employment results in promising outcomes, especially for young adults (Nuechterlein et al., 2008). These are fairly new domains of research, however, and future studies should focus on these important areas.

Websites

Dartmouth Psychiatric Research Center, Individualized Placement and Support—http://www.dartmouth.edu/~ips/index.html

Substance Abuse and Mental Health Services Administration (reference to IPS)—http://www.stopstigma.samhsa.gov/topic/employment/brochures.aspx

University of Illinois at Chicago, Department of Psychiatry, Center on Mental Health Services Research and Policy, Employment Intervention Demonstration Program—http://www.psych.uic.edu/eidp

Virginia Commonwealth University's Rehabilitation Research and Training Center, Work Support—http://www.worksupport.com

Glossary

Employment specialist: A vocational or rehabilitation worker who provides employment services to the client; employment specialists work with clients to find jobs (i.e., job development) and provide ongoing follow-along support once the client has gotten a job.

Fidelity: Adherence to the program model. Adherence to the IPS program model is associated with improved outcomes for clients.

Individualized placement and support model: An approach to supported employment that has been shown to be an evidence-based practice in providing services to people with severe mental illness. Individualized placement and support features an individualized approach with an emphasis on competitive employment only, rapid search for a competitive community job, and integrated mental health and employment services.

Job development: The process in which an employment specialist surveys job opportunities in the community and helps clients find jobs matching their preferences. Job development is a key part of supported employment services and has been linked with outcomes in some studies.

Supported employment: Psychiatric rehabilitation services designed to help people with severe mental illness obtain and maintain competitive employment in the community using an individualized service approach. Supported employment services usually occur in an outpatient setting, such as a community mental health center.

References

Anthony, W. A. (1993). Recovery from mental illness: The guiding vision of the mental health service system in the 1990s. *Psychosocial Rehabilitation Journal, 16*(4), 11–23.

Becker, D. R., Bond, G. R., McCarthy, D., Thompson, D., Xie, H., McHugo, G. J., et al. (2001). Converting day treatment centers to supported employment programs in Rhode Island. *Psychiatric Services, 52*, 351–357.

Becker, D. R., & Drake, R. E. (2003). *A working life for people with severe mental illness.* New York: Oxford University Press.

Becker, D. R., Swanson, S., Bond, G. R., & Merrens, M. R. (2011). *Evidence-based supported employment fidelity review manual* (2nd ed.). Lebanon, NH: Dartmouth Psychiatric Research Center.

Becker, D. R., Whitley, R., Bailey, E. L., & Drake, R. E. (2007). Long-term employment outcomes of supported employment for people with severe mental illness. *Psychiatric Services, 58,* 922–928.

Bond, G. R. (1998). Principles of the individual placement and support model: Empirical support. *Psychiatric Rehabilitation Journal, 22,* 11–23.

Bond, G. R. (2004). Supported employment: Evidence for an evidence-based practice. *Psychiatric Rehabilitation Journal, 27,* 345–359.

Bond, G. R., Becker, D. R., & Drake, R. E. (2011). Measurement of fidelity of implementation of evidence-based practices: Case example of the IPS Fidelity Scale. *Clinical Psychology: Science and Practice, 18,* 125–140.

Bond, G. R., Becker, D. R., Drake, R. E., & Vogler, K. M. (1997). A fidelity scale for the individual placement and support model of supported employment. *Rehabilitation Counseling Bulletin, 40,* 265–284.

Bond, G. R., Drake, R. E., & Becker, D. R. (2008). An update on randomized controlled trials of evidence-based supported employment. *Psychiatric Rehabilitation Journal, 31,* 280–290.

Bond, G. R., Drake, R. E., & Becker, D. R. (2010). Beyond evidence-based practice: Nine ideal features of a mental health intervention. *Research on Social Work Practice, 20,* 493–501.

Bond, G. R., Drake, R. E., & Becker, D. R. (2012). Generalizability of the individual placement and support (IPS) model of supported employment outside the US. *World Psychiatry, 11,* 32–39.

Bond, G. R., & Kukla, M. (2011). Impact of follow-along support on job tenure in the individual placement and support model. *Journal of Nervous and Mental Disease, 199,* 150–155.

Bond, G. R., McHugo, G. J., Becker, D. R., Rapp, C. A., & Whitley, R. (2008). Fidelity of supported employment: Lessons learned from the National EBP Project. *Psychiatric Rehabilitation Journal, 31,* 300–305.

Bond, G. R., Resnick, S. G., Drake, R. E., Xie, H. Y., McHugo, G. J., & Bebout, R. R. (2001). Does competitive employment improve nonvocational outcomes for people with severe mental illness? *Journal of Consulting and Clinical Psychology, 69*(3), 489–501.

Burns, T., Catty, J., White, S., Becker, T., Koletsi, M., & Fioritti, A. (2009). The impact of supported employment and working on clinical and social functioning: Results of an international study of individual placement and support. *Schizophrenia Bulletin, 35,* 949–958.

Drake, R. E., & Bond, G. R. (2008). The future of supported employment for people with severe mental illness. *Psychiatric Rehabilitation Journal, 31,* 367–376.

Drake, R. E., Bond, G. R., & Becker, D. R. (2012). *IPS supported employment: An evidence-based approach to supported employment.* New York: Oxford University Press.

Gowdy, E. A., Carlson, L. S., & Rapp, C. A. (2003). Practices differentiating high-performing from low-performing supported employment programs. *Psychiatric Rehabilitation Journal, 26,* 232–239.

Kukla, M. (2010). *The relationship between employment status and nonvocational outcomes for persons with severe mental illness enrolled in vocational programs: A longitudinal study* (Unpublished doctoral dissertation). Purdue University of Indianapolis, IN.

Kukla, M., & Bond, G.R. (2009). The working alliance and employment outcomes for people with severe mental illness receiving vocational services. *Rehabilitation Psychology, 54,* 157–163.

Mueser, K. T., Becker, D. R., Torrey, W. C., Xie, H. Y., Bond, G. R., & Drake, R. E. (1997). Work and non-vocational domains of functioning in persons with severe mental illness: A longitudinal analysis. *Journal of Nervous and Mental Disease, 185*(7), 419–426.

Nuechterlein, K. H., Subotnik, K. L., Turner, L. R., Ventura, J., Becker, D. R., & Drake, R. E. (2008). Individual placement and support for individuals with recent-onset schizophrenia: Integrating supported education and supported employment. *Psychiatric Rehabilitation Journal, 31,* 340–349.

Twamley, E. W., Narvaez, J. M., Becker, D. R., Bartels, S. J., & Jeste, D. V. (2008). Supported employment for middle-aged and older people with schizophrenia. *American Journal of Psychiatric Rehabilitation, 11,* 76–89.

Wehman, P., & Moon, M. S. (Eds.). (1988). *Vocational rehabilitation and supported employment.* Baltimore: Brookes.

PART III
Empowerment-Oriented Best Practices

Empowerment-oriented best practices are those interventions and strategies that support activities associated with promoting personal empowerment, choice, and a sense of hopefulness. These activities include honoring the dignity of the individual, with a focus on the education of self, family members, and caregivers regarding self-advocacy, self-efficacy, resilience, and critical thinking. A key element in the best practices described in this section is skill building for clients and family members while honoring diversity of experience and self-determination.

Part 3 introduces the reader to four core best practices that focus on spirituality, recovery, motivational interviewing, and the valued role of family members and caregivers in the lives of individuals with mental illness.

In chapter 11, "Spirituality and Mental Health," Derezotes discusses the need for mental health practitioners to develop comprehensive assessment, practice and evaluation strategies that incorporate an eco-bio-psycho-social-spiritual approach. In chapter 12, "Recovery-Oriented Services," Stanhope and Solomon overview the recovery model as a person-centered approach in which individuals determine their own path toward health and wellness. In chapter 13, "Motivational Interviewing," McGuire and Gearhart describe the elements of motivational interviewing as a client-centered, directive technique for changing health-related behaviors. In chapter 14, "Best Practices for Family Caregivers of People with Severe Mental Illness," Mason describes practical strategies for reducing stress for family caregivers of people with mental illness.

11

Spirituality and Mental Health
David S. Derezotes

Spiritually oriented mental health practice does not replace traditional theories and methods but adds the spiritual component to all assessments, interventions, and evaluations. The spiritually oriented practitioner uses an eco-bio-psycho-social-spiritual approach to mental health. Informed by both scientific and artistic ways of knowing, this approach views the mental health of individuals as interrelated with their physical, emotional, social, and spiritual health, as well as with the well-being of their family, community, ecosystem, and planet. We begin this chapter with a case study of Joyce (see box 11.1 and table 11.1) and her experience working with a practitioner who uses an eco-bio-psycho-social-spiritual approach.

Box 11.1. Case Study: Joyce

Martha, a licensed clinical social worker, is seeing a thirty-eight-year-old single mother of two at the community mental health clinic. The woman, Joyce, has complained of symptoms of chronic but moderate depression and anxiety. Because Martha is a spiritually oriented practitioner, she includes the spiritual dimension in all her assessments, interventions, and evaluations.

In the history taking, Joyce stated that her husband left her two years ago, when their child was four years old. Joyce's other child, Susan, is from another marriage and is now thirteen years old. Both children live with their mother in their apartment. At the time of the divorce, Joyce was working outside the home but earning only minimum wage at a fast-food restaurant. She had to take on a full-time job to support herself and her family, and she has had ongoing financial, child-care, and housing problems. She has not reconnected with the friends she had before she entered her second marriage, and she stated that her best friend is probably her aging mother, who "is often very critical and demanding of me."

When asked, Joyce said that she feels like she "has become like a robot who feeds, clothes, and chauffeurs the children in between working for money."

Part of the history is also about Joyce's spiritual and religious stories. Martha discovered that, as a child, Joyce grew up attending church with her family. She stopped going to church when she became a young adult but began attending again after she was divorced. The church has provided some resources for Joyce when times were hard, including clothing, food, and money. She commented that her most spiritual moments were when her children were born, but she said that she "has not had many spiritual moments since then."

Using the eco-bio-psycho-social-spiritual assessment (as described in table 11.2), Martha looked at Joyce's physical, emotional, cognitive, social, and spiritual development. Joyce was diagnosed as prediabetic, engages in little physical exercise, and is currently about thirty-five pounds overweight. She denied the abuse of drugs or alcohol. Joyce reported that she cries when she feels angry inside. The assessment also revealed that Joyce has dysthymia with generalized anxiety. Although she is depressed, she denies suicidal ideation. Joyce has above-average intelligence and has no close friends or current lover. Martha believes that Joyce operates primarily at the personal level of development (see table 11.1) and that she struggles to access her prepersonal (e.g., play and spontaneity) and transpersonal (e.g., disidentification) states of consciousness.

Martha uses interventions that integrate spirituality with methods drawn from all four forces of psychology (see Derezotes, 2006). One psychodynamic approach that she uses is a spiritually oriented interpretation, which builds on Joyce's strength of high intelligence. After hearing stories about Joyce's past, Martha suggested to Joyce that she, like many other people today, had lived with a "spiritual hunger" since her childhood. Joyce related to this idea and decided that she wanted to discover what spirituality is, for herself and for the sake of her children.

Martha uses a cognitive-behavioral approach, which also relies on Joyce's intellectual strength. Martha challenged Joyce's belief that there is something seriously "wrong" with her. Instead, she encouraged Joyce to also view her dysthymia as a sign of health, a pain signal from her soul or psyche that she needs to "make friends with" and pay attention to.

Joyce decided that her depression may be partly genetic in nature but that it is also at least in part about how she is much more alone in the world than she wants to be and the fact that she is disconnected from other people and from herself. As they talked about these ideas, Martha helped Joyce realize how much she identifies with her many fears about social rejection and that she is "more" than just her worried thoughts.

Using experiential theory, Martha worked with Joyce's anger. Joyce realized how angry she was at her parents, her former husband, and even God. Martha helped Joyce engage in an empty-chair exercise in which she had a dialogue with God. In the dialogue, Joyce initially told God how sad and angry she was about her life, but eventually she also asked for help in forgiving others and herself. In the following months, Joyce stated that her emotional work seems to gradually help her stay more present with her children and other people, rather than being constantly distracted by feelings and thoughts about the past and future.

Martha also used transpersonal interventions to help Joyce. Martha taught Joyce about the idea of identification and about how she might identify with her mind, her social roles, and her suffering. She taught her a mindfulness exercise that Joyce began to use each day. Joyce started to develop her "observing self" during these exercises, and from that ego state (see table 11.1), she can start to view her identifications directly for herself. Although she still has depressed and anxious states, Joyce has reported that she "is at least aware of them" and that she "even has moments when I briefly feel calm inside." Martha supports Joyce's progress and has suggested that she can have more of those calm moments as she does her spiritual work, which eventually proves true.

Martha also suggested that Joyce consider a biopsychosocial intervention that would integrate her bodywork with her spiritual work. Joyce looked at a number of choices available to her in her community and finally picked a yoga class for women. This class emphasizes stretching and breathing exercises that she enjoys, and Joyce made some new female friends at the meetings. There is also some aerobic workout at the beginning of each class, which helps alleviate Joyce's symptoms of depression and anxiety. Martha also discussed the options of psychopharmacology with Joyce, empowering her to make her own decisions about medication.

Using casework techniques, Martha helped Joyce continue to find resources that could help her with her ongoing needs for financial, child-care, and housing assistance. Martha also has supported Joyce's desire to connect more with the people in her church. They together planned out how Joyce might join the church singles group, and Martha encouraged Joyce as she began to take the risk of going to the group meetings.

Martha evaluates Joyce's progress each session by asking her questions about elements of her multidimensional development (see table 11.2). Martha begins with general questions and then becomes more specific. For example, in one meeting, Martha asked Joyce, "How have our sessions been for you?" Then she followed up by asking Joyce about her physical development, including her yoga program. The next week, they discuss Joyce's progress in her social development and her participation in meetings for singles at her church. Joyce gradually reduced the frequency of her meetings with Martha as she developed a deeper sense of well-being, more confidence in herself, and more social supports.

Table 11.1. Assessing Levels of Consciousness and Functioning

Level of consciousness	Example of healthy functioning	Example of imbalanced (or "stuck") functioning
Prepersonal (child-state dominant)	Client can experience pleasure and have spontaneous and creative experiences.	Client deals with shame by blaming the other and by putting his or her own needs first (may be associated with axis II traits).
Personal (parent-state dominant)	Client is able and willing to control his or her own impulses and be empathic toward the other.	Client deals with shame by blaming him- or herself and putting the other's needs first (may be associated with neurosis).
Transpersonal (observing-self-state dominant)	Client is able and willing to be in the here and now and gradually disidentify from his or her beliefs and roles.	Client may begin to self-identify with his or her own spiritual development or may lose ability to be intimate with other people, living things, and ecosystems.

Background

All mental health practice was originally spiritually oriented. Our earliest ancestors, in practically all localities on the earth, went to shamanic healers for what we would today call mental health issues. These shamans would journey into ecstatic states of consciousness to assist their clients, often using drumming and sometimes sacred medicines to assist in their healing rituals (Harner, 1990).

Although both modern psychology and social work have spiritual and religious roots, most theorists abandoned spirituality and religion, as the helping professions increasingly followed the lead of Western medical science in the nineteenth and twentieth centuries. In social work, concerns about professionalism discouraged some leaders from drawing from the potential benefits of spiritual and religious experiences.

Interest in religion has waxed and waned over time. During the past three or four decades, there has been a new and significant global religious resurgence. More than two-thirds of the human world now self-identifies as religious, more than ever before in history. The top religious affiliations worldwide are with Christianity, Islam, Hinduism, and Buddhism. In this increasingly religious world, the United States is one of the most religious nations (Armstrong, 2006). As a result, the majority of the people whom mental health practitioners see today identify as religious, though not necessarily as spiritual.

Perhaps at least in part in reaction to this religious resurgence, there has also been a renewed interest in spirituality in both psychology and social work. Called the fourth force of psychology (Maslow, 1973), transpersonal psychology has become a leading theoretical influence in spiritually oriented practice. Ken Wilber's (e.g., 2006) work, for example, has provided practitioners with a transpersonal framework that bridges the major religious and psychological wisdom traditions of the world. Hillman's (1975) work helped frame what we call mental health and illness inside a broader framework that is more inclusive and thus transcends the prevailing Western medical model that still informs mental health practice.

Currently, many theoretical differences about spirituality continue to divide practitioners and academics. These divides can be considered a continuation of the centuries-old conflicts that have been fought in the Western world among advocates of science, religion, and spirituality. These conflicts are exemplified today, for example, in the current debates between advocates of evolution and creationism, artistic factors in practice and evidence-based practice, and New Age psychology and fundamentalist religion.

Defining spirituality is somewhat like using words to describe the color green or the taste of a particular vegetable. This is because for most people spirituality is usually not just a mental experience but a whole-body experience that includes all the interrelated dimensions of human development: physical, emotional, cognitive, and social (Piedmont 1999). Attempts to define spirituality include descriptions such as a "personal quest for meaning and understanding of life's ultimate questions" (Koenig, 2005, p. 44) and "a framework that guides individuals in finding meaning in their lives and events" (Cunningham, 2000, p. 65).

A related way to think about spirituality is that it is a dimension of lifelong human development, and in this way, it is similar to the physical, emotional, cognitive, and social dimensions of development. From this perspective, everyone has a spiritual component, but each person has a different set of spiritual experiences and interests. As is the case with any dimension of development, some people may highly value their spirituality while others may devalue or deny their spirituality.

Perhaps the most practical synonym for spirituality is *reverent connectedness*; from this perspective, spirituality can be thought of as the natural desire for a reverent connectedness with the inner world (e.g., the physical, emotional, cognitive) and the outer world (e.g., the other person, another living thing, the ecosystem, the planet) of human existence. Humans can create more reverent connections both individually and collectively through a variety of intentional, meaning-making rituals. Spiritual experiences can also be associated with powerful and unplanned life events, such as marriage, divorce, birth, and death.

Theoretical Perspective

The theoretical perspective of this chapter is that the spiritual perspective is an inclusive perspective, one that connects individual human well-being with intrapsychic, interpsychic, ecological, and global well-being. Because it is inclusive, the spiritual perspective is also a radical perspective that identifies and addresses the multiple root causes of what we today call mental illness.

In contrast with the individual nature of spirituality, religion is a collective experience in which people share rituals, beliefs, and doctrines. Like any other experience, religion may help, inhibit, or both help and inhibit the spiritual development of an individual. Not all religious people consider themselves spiritual, and not all spiritual people identify themselves as religious.

Principles

All mental health assessments, interventions, and evaluations should include a spiritual component that is guided by best-practice principles. Four suggested practice principles are listed here:

- *Principle of wholeness*—Increasing evidence suggests that spiritual issues are related to most biopsychosocial problems and that spiritually oriented intervention can help foster positive outcomes (e.g., Ano & Vasconcelles, 2005; Derezotes, 2006; Pargament, 2007). The spiritually oriented mental health practitioner understands that there is a spiritual component to every human challenge. The spiritually oriented practitioner views mental health as eco-bio-psycho-social-spiritual well-being and views every human challenge as being associated with factors at the individual, family, community, ecological, and global levels.

- *Principle of personal responsibility*—Spiritually oriented practitioners recognize that the client is most responsible for positive outcomes, that relational factors predict outcomes more than method, and that practice-based evidence must be included with traditional evidence-based practice when assessing and evaluating interventions (Duncan, Miller, Wampold, & Hubble, 2010). The practice-based approach essentially values data derived from feedback from and monitoring of clients themselves. Thus, the spiritually oriented professional listens to a client and responds to his or her feedback.

- *Principle of relationship*—The practice-based approach also emphasizes the development of the helping relationship, which is especially built on such factors as genuineness, empathy, and warmth.

- *Principle of feedback*—Finally, the helper continues to seek feedback and uses various monitoring approaches to make sure that he or she understands and values the client's own goals and progress.

Steps for Implementing Spirituality-Based Best Practices

The effective spiritually oriented practitioner is flexible in responding to the unique and constantly changing needs of the client and client system (e.g., couple, family, culture, environment). There are, however, some general approaches that can be followed in spiritually oriented practice.

First, the helper strives to develop a helping relationship with the client. Because, as discussed in this chapter, the genuineness of the helper is especially important in the relationship-building process, the professional brings integrity, honesty, and self-disclosure (as appropriate) to the relationship. We also know that empathy and warmth and presence help predict relational effectiveness. It may be that the most important gifts that the worker brings to the client are caring, listening, and presence.

Second, the practitioner begins an ongoing assessment of the client and client system. The client must always be understood in context, which means in part that the worker views clients as people who are doing the best they can in a situation as they understand it. This context includes the eco-bio-psycho-social-spiritual system that clients have lived in. Both recent and long-term intergenerational issues are included in the assessment, which also considers all elements of human diversity, including religious, cultural, and gender contexts.

Third, the practitioner always strives to value and understand the goals of the client. The professional continues to seek feedback from the client and monitor progress toward goals. The professional may be in situations in which the client has to deal with externally imposed goals, such as those that may result from court-ordered counseling, incarceration, or parental involvement. Even in such "nonvoluntary" situations, the professional still always seeks to treat the client as a human being and spiritual being, and tries to build on the client's strengths and recognize and honor the client's goals.

Fourth, the professional uses both artistic and scientific approaches in the assessments and interventions. Spiritually oriented work also includes all models and theories of counseling. The professional helper draws on all ways of knowing, including intuition and published research, in the assessment. As goals are developed, the professional offers possible approaches and directions to the client. The client and helper scientifically "test" out the approaches and theories together, through trial and error. For example, if the theory is that a client is depressed at least in part because he or she is disempowered, the client may choose to test this out by working on self-empowerment strategies.

Fifth, the worker uses rituals (interventions) that are drawn from myths (theories) that makes sense and feel comfortable to both worker and client. We know that such interventions and theories work best when both client and worker embrace them (Duncan et al., 2010).

Finally, ongoing assessment of progress is measured by such practice-based evidence as client feedback and client monitoring.

What's the Evidence?

Multidisciplinary scholarship in spirituality and mental health practice continues to expand rapidly. Exciting model building, measurement development, and research efforts are under way in many areas of interest to the mental health practitioner. Only a few examples of the relevant research are briefly summarized here.

In the majority of studies, measures of spirituality and religiosity are associated with increases in a number of positive indicators of well-being, including happiness, life satisfaction, life purpose, self-esteem, and optimism. In addition, spirituality and religiosity are correlated with decreases in indicators such as anxiety, depression, substance abuse, criminal activity, loneliness, and marital dissatisfaction (Koenig, McCullough, & Larsen, 2001; Miller et al., 2012; Robinson, Krentzman, Webb, & Brower, 2011).

Scientists have looked at various aspects of spirituality and their relationship to religious traditions. For example, measures of spiritual and religious coping are associated with positive psychological adjustment in more than four dozen studies (Ano & Vasconcelles, 2005). Mindfulness has been shown to improve psychological functioning and to reduce mental health symptoms (Lazar, 2005).

Some scholarship has focused on the biology of spirituality. A school of researchers has found evidence that suggests that the human brain may indeed have a "module" that evolved as our biological spiritual or religious center (Alper, 2001; Hamer, 2004). Other researchers remain skeptical, and others doubt that spirituality will be fully explained by the function of any living tissue or other structures in the material world (Beauregard & O'Leary, 2007).

Assessment and Evaluation

The spiritually oriented mental health practitioner includes the spiritual dimension in formal and informal evaluations. Valid and reliable formal measures of spirituality and religiosity are available to the practitioner, although there are controversies about the meanings of and the relationships between these complex constructs (e.g., King & Crowther, 2004). For example, the Ironson-Wood Spirituality/Religiousness Index (IWSRI; Ironson et al., 2002) is a formal measure of spirituality and religiosity that is frequently cited in the literature. The Intrinsic Spirituality Scale (Hodge, 2003) is a six-item instrument that views spirituality as an internal function that serves as an individual's master motivator. Several experts have suggested that spirituality be included in the five-factor model of personality assessment (MacDonald, 2000). The five factors include openness, conscientiousness, extroversion, agreeableness, and neuroticism. A practice-based evidence approach (discussed earlier) to measuring work with youth might use, for example, the Mental Health Outcomes and Assessment Tools. These standardized instruments can be computerized; are designed for mental health settings; and are administered at intake, discharge, and at regular thirteen-week intervals during treatment (Kelly, Bickman, & Norwood, 2010).

The practitioner can also regularly ask clients to make assessments of the work. As in most mental settings, termination will be discussed and planned during the beginning and middle phases of therapy, and the practitioner may make referrals or do follow-ups as appropriate.

The spiritually oriented mental health practitioner takes an eco-bio-psycho-social-spiritual approach to assessment. As table 11.2 illustrates, this assessment considers elements of multidimensional development (e.g., physical, emotional, cognitive, social, spiritual) and the client's environmental development (e.g., family, local and global community well-being, ecosystem well-being).

The spiritually oriented mental health assessment can be informed by transpersonal theory (Wilber, 2006), which suggests that there are three levels of consciousness available to people. As table 11.3 illustrates, each level of consciousness is associated with different aspects of functioning.

Table 11.2. Elements and Examples of Eco-Bio-Psycho-Social-Spiritual Assessment

Elements	Examples of each element
Physical development	Acceptance of body, physical self-care
Emotional development	Awareness and acceptance of emotions
Cognitive development	Ability to reflect on my own experience and the experience of others
Social development	Ability to be intimate with others
Spiritual development	Ability to disidentify from personality
Family development	The extent to which the family values and supports human diversity (including spiritual and religious diversity)
Local and global community well-being	The extent to which the community values and supports human diversity (including spiritual and religious diversity)
Ecosystem well-being	The extent to which people value and support other living things and the ecosystems that support all life

Table 11.3. Examples of Integration of Spirituality with Traditional Intervention Approaches

Traditional theories and related spiritual interventions	Teaching transformation of externalizing disorders	Teaching transformation of internalizing disorders
Psychodynamic (spiritual momentum)	Respect and responsibility for continuity of life	Healing historical trauma from current and past lifetimes
Cognitive behavioral (mindful daily living)	Mindfulness and right actions toward the other	Mindfulness and disidentification practice
Experiential (spirit with heart)	Gratitude, compassion, and forgiveness for the other	Gratitude, compassion, and forgiveness for self
Transpersonal (religious self)	Rituals from wisdom traditions that promote social and ecological responsibility	Rituals from wisdom traditions that promote spiritual development
Biopsychosocial (body consciousness)	Bodywork that promotes self-awareness and responsibility	Bodywork that helps express and develop spirituality
Community organization (community consciousness)	Cocreation of communities of diversity	Responsibility for stewardship of community
Deep ecology (eco-consciousness)	Valuing and responsibility for other living things and ecosystems	Individual responsibility for stewardship of ecosystem

The practitioner identifies the dominant level of consciousness at which the client and client system is functioning. When a client is "stuck" at one level of functioning, the practitioner helps the client value and access his or her other two more-dormant levels of consciousness. The mentally healthy person is viewed from this perspective as a person who can move wisely and fluidly from one level of consciousness to another as necessary.

Implementation Issues

From the theoretical perspective of this chapter, the spiritually oriented mental health practitioner integrates spirituality with existing intervention approaches. As the examples in table 11.3 illustrate, these integrated interventions can be used in work with both externalizing and internalizing disorders.

Categories in table 11.3 can be further explained and expanded on. Internalizing disorders are those symptoms that are especially experienced and suffered from "inside" the person's psyche, such as shyness, depression, and anxiety (although there may be behavioral correlates, such as social withdrawal and sleeplessness). In contrast, externalizing disorders are those symptoms that are especially experienced by (and associated with suffering inflicted on) other people, such as disruptive, antisocial, or criminal behavior (although there may be internal correlates, such as shame or low self-esteem). In community organization, people come together to empower themselves to learn about their shared issues and take collective actions to remedy these problems. Deep ecology is a form of environmentalism that views people as interconnected with their ecosystems and empowered to take collective actions to enhance and protect that connection.

As noted already, the spiritually oriented mental health practitioner is aware that spirituality is an individual dimension of development that is profoundly related to the person's history, culture, and environment. Practitioners continue to work on themselves, increasing their awareness and acceptance of their own biases about diverse human groups and of their countertransference reactions to individual clients. Such self-awareness and self-acceptance in the practitioner models self-awareness and self-acceptance for the client, and helps build the helping relationship.

The mental health practitioner knows that spiritually oriented practice can be helpful to clients from all walks of life. Studies show that people belonging to oppressed and minority populations can receive significant benefits from spiritual coping (Smith, McCullough, & Poll, 2003). One responsibility of the practitioner is to use language that fits with the spiritual and religious diversity of each client and client system. Thus, for example, if the client is a Christian, Muslim, or Jew who believes in a sacred text, God, and prayer, the practitioner can be flexible enough to use these concepts in the therapy, regardless of his or her own personal beliefs. The practitioner thus always needs to assess and remain sensitive to the unique spiritual and religious beliefs of each individual client.

Provider Competencies

Spiritually oriented mental health practitioners do not need to be "perfect" or "enlightened" to help other people. More important is that practitioners are aware and accepting of who they are in the here and now, including their own strengths and weaknesses. They are able to be "transparent" with the client about who they are, but only when such transparency supports the client's progress. Practitioners have their own spiritual practice(s) that they engage in across their own life span.

Practitioners realize that their relationship with clients is a stronger predictor of successful case outcome than the method they use. Thus, they emphasize the ability to be fully present and conscious with the client in the here-and-now moment. Practitioners respect the diversity of client religiosity and spirituality, and are aware and accepting of their own countertransference reactions, including spiritual and religious countertransference. These reactions can be used as part of the assessment to help practitioners determine who the client is and what he or she is feeling (see Derezotes, 2006).

Practitioners, however, also continue to improve their assessment, intervention, and evaluation skills. Especially important in spiritually oriented practice are the use of imagination, intention, and awareness. Practitioners use existing methods but are open to new approaches and alternative explanation. They also are willing to incorporate the spiritual interventions used by people of different cultures, including those that existed in the past. They are especially skilled at and flexible in using the client's own spiritual and religious language and concepts.

Future Directions

The spiritually oriented mental health practitioner knows that every individual mental health issue is also a global issue. Such awareness will eventually become a foundation of all mental health practice, and mental health will expand into an evolving theory that includes all the dimensions of the eco-bio-psycho-social-spiritual framework.

Spiritually oriented mental health practitioners will continue to have a growing impact on the helping professions. They will, for example, continue to advocate for a more inclusive approach to assessment using the American Psychiatric Association's (2000) *Diagnostic and Statistical Manual of Mental Disorders* (4th ed., text rev.) that truly addresses the eco-bio-psycho-social-spiritual roots and correlates of what we still call mental illness. They will advocate for a more inclusive eco-bio-psycho-social-spiritual approach to intervention as well, which emphasizes the interrelated well-being of person, family, community, ecosystem, and planet.

Websites

Institute of Medicine's site with a report on complementary medicine that includes content on spirituality—http://iom.edu/Reports/2005/Complementary-and-Alternative-Medicine-in-the-United-States.aspx

Study of UCLA students and their spiritual development—http://pewforum.org/events/?EventID=168

Substance Abuse and Mental Health Services Administration's website on sources for spirituality and mental health—http://stopstigma.samhsa.gov/topic/faith/books.aspx

World Health Organization report on spiritual issues in health—http://www.who.int/hia/examples/overview/whohia203/en

Glossary

Mental health: The spiritual perspective views mental health as individual and collective eco-bio-psycho-social-spiritual well-being.

Religiosity: An individual's participation in the sharing of sacred rituals and beliefs.

Spirituality: An individual's development of personally meaningful and reverent connection with self and the world.

References

Alper, M. (2001). *The "God" part of the brain: A scientific interpretation of human spirituality and God*. New York: Rogue.

American Psychiatric Association. (2000). *Diagnostic and statistical manual of mental disorders* (4th ed., text rev.). Arlington, VA: Author.

Ano, G. A., & Vasconcelles, E. B. (2005). Religious coping and psychological adjustment to stress: A meta-analysis. *Journal of Clinical Psychology, 61*, 1–20.

Armstrong, K. (2006). *The great transformation: The beginning of our religious traditions*. New York: Knopf.

Beauregard, M., & O'Leary, D. (2007). *The spiritual brain: A neuroscientist's case for the existence of the soul*. New York: Harper Collins.

Cunningham, M. (2000). Spirituality, cultural diversity and crisis intervention. *Crisis Intervention, 6*(1) 65–77.

Derezotes, D. S. (2005). *Re-valuing social work: Implications for emerging science and technology*. Denver: Love.

Derezotes, D. S. (2006). *Spiritually oriented social work practice*. Boston: Allyn and Bacon.

Duncan, B. L., Miller, S. D., Wampold, B. E., & Hubble, M. A. (2010). *The heart and soul of change: What works in therapy.* Washington, DC: American Psychological Association.

Hamer, D. (2004). *The God gene: How faith is hardwired into our genes.* New York: Doubleday.

Harner, M. (1990). *The way of the shaman.* New York: HarperOne.

Hillman, J. (1975). *Re-visioning psychology.* New York: Harper and Row.

Hodge, D. R. (2003). The intrinsic spirituality scale: A new six-item instrument for assessing salience of spirituality as a motivational construct. *Journal of Social Service Research, 30,* 41–61.

Ironson, G., Solomon, G. F., Balbin, E. G., O'Cleirigh, C., George, A., Kumar, M., et al. (2002). The Ironson-Woods Spirituality/Religiousness Index is associated with long survival, health behaviors, less distress and low cortisol in people with HIV/AIDS. *Annals of Behavioral Medicine, 24,* 34–38.

Kelly, S. D., Bickman, L., & Norwood, E. (2010). Evidence-based treatments and common factors in youth psychotherapy. In B. L. Duncan, S. D. Miller, B. E. Wampold, & M. A. Hubble (Eds.), *The heart and soul of change: Delivering what works in therapy* (2nd ed., pp. 325–355). Washington, DC: American Psychological Association

King, J. E., & Crowther M. R. (2004). The measurement of religiosity and spirituality: Examples and issues from psychology. *Journal of Organizational Change Management, 17*(1), 83–101.

Koenig, H. G. (2005). *Faith and mental health: Religious resources for healing.* West Conshohocken, PA: Templeton Foundation Press.

Koenig, H. G., McCullough, M. E., & Larsen, D. B. (2001). *Handbook of religion and health.* Oxford: Oxford University Press.

Lazar, S. W. (2005). Mindfulness research. In C. K. Germer, R. D. Siegel, & P. R. Fulton (Eds.), *Mindfulness and psychotherapy: Mindfulness research* (pp. 220–238). New York: Guilford Press.

MacDonald, D. A. (2000). Spirituality: Description, measurement, and relation to the five factor model of personality. *Journal of Personality, 68,* 149–197.

Maslow, A. (1973). *The farther reaches of human nature.* New York: Viking.

Miller, L., Wickramaratne, P., Gameroff, M., Sage, M., Tenke, C., & Weissman, M. (2012). Religiosity and major depression in adults at high risk: A ten-year prospective study. *American Journal of Psychiatry, 169*(1), 89–94.

Pargament, K. I. (2007). *Spiritually integrated psychotherapy: Understanding and addressing the sacred.* New York: Guilford Press.

Piedmont, R. L. (1999). Does spirituality represent the sixth factor of personality? Spiritual transcendence and the five-factor model. *Journal of Personality, 67,* 985–1013.

Robinson, E., Krentzman, A., Webb, J. R., & Brower, K. J. (2011). Six-month changes in spirituality and religiousness in alcoholics predict drinking outcomes in nine months. *Journal of Studies of Alcohol and Drugs, 72*(4), 660–668.

Smith, T. B., McCullough, M. E., & Poll, J. (2003). Religiousness and depression: Evidence for a main effect and the moderating influence of stressful life events. *Psychological Bulletin, 129,* 614–636.

Wilber, K. (2006). *Integral spirituality: A startling new role for religion in the modern and postmodern world.* Boston: Shambhala.

12

Recovery-Oriented Services

Victoria Stanhope and Phyllis Solomon

The mental health recovery movement is changing the way the mental health system approaches care for people with severe mental illnesses. By challenging the notion that severe mental illnesses are chronic and that services should focus primarily on symptoms, recovery represents a major shift from the traditional medical model approach to mental health care that has been predominant throughout the twentieth century. Based on the experiences of service users and research that demonstrates that recovery is possible for everyone, recovery-oriented services have been implemented throughout the United States. For practitioners, recovery means delivering person-centered care that acknowledges and embraces the unique path that each person takes toward his or her own recovery. We begin this chapter with a case review of Townsend (see box 12.1), a service user and social worker, who describes what it's like to work with a case manager who uses a recovery orientation (Townsend & Glasser, 2003).

Box 12.1. Case Study: Townsend and Glasser

In this case example, Townsend, a social worker and a service user, and his colleague Glasser (Townsend & Glasser, 2003) demonstrate what it means to use a recovery orientation in practice. Townsend's goal was to be an astronaut. He was assigned two case managers, who both interpreted his desire as symptomatic of his illness and failed to take his aspirations seriously. Instead, they documented in progress notes that the service user was uncooperative and delusional when he refused to modify his goals. As a result, he did not progress in his recovery. However, the service user was then assigned a case manager, Glasser, who listened to him and suggested that he research what was involved in becoming an astronaut. On finding that it required a good deal of work to become an astronaut, the service user decided that being an astronaut was not for him, but he still had a passion for space travel. The case manager worked with him to obtain a job in a company that contracted with NASA, which resulted in him becoming competitively employed in an environment that inspired him. He was thus able to modify his goal and progress in his own recovery. This case example illustrates the "heart and soul" of recovery-oriented treatment. At the same time, readers will recognize the use of supported employment as a means of assisting the client in pursuing his dreams. In this case, the practitioner enters into the dreams of their service users and does not reframe their aspirations as symptoms of their disorders but accompanies them on their unique journey. Furthermore, this exemplar demonstrates how taking a recovery orientation can result in far more successful outcomes than a traditional clinical or psychodynamic approach.

Background

In 2002 President George W. Bush appointed the New Freedom Commission on Mental Health to reform the mental health care system in the United States. The commission stated that the ultimate goal for mental health reform was to promote recovery, which was the first time that the federal government had endorsed the belief that recovery was possible for everyone suffering from severe mental illnesses (Department of Health and Human Services, 2003). As a result, the recovery vision represents a major shift from the traditional medical model approach to mental health care, which has focused mainly on symptom reduction. There is no consensus as to the precise definition of mental health recovery. The concept often has variant meanings for different people, and the continuing ambiguity has provided a challenge to implementing recovery-based services. The Substance Abuse and Mental Health Services Administration defines mental health recovery as "a process of change through which individuals improve their health and wellness, live a self-directed life, and strive to reach their full potential" (Vecchio, 2012, n.p.)

Recovery, as a mental health concept, emerged from two different historical roots. One is the psychosocial rehabilitation movement, currently referred to as psychiatric rehabilitation, and the other is the mental health advocacy movement, which comprises service users and psychiatric survivors. The psychiatric rehabilitation movement (see chapter 15) started with a group of ex–hospital patients who formed the self-help group We Are Not Alone in the mid-1940s, which later evolved into Fountain House, the first clubhouse program. Psychiatric rehabilitation brought attention to the fact that mental illness affects all aspects of a person's life; therefore, assessment of service users' needs and treatment based solely on intensity of symptoms is inadequate. The psychiatric rehabilitation centers were ideologically opposed to the medical model approach to treatment, employing a strengths-based approach rather than a deficit one. They spoke of community role outcomes, consumer choice, and person-centered planning (Anthony, 2007). Psychiatric rehabilitation broadened from the centers' orientation to incorporate theories from physical rehabilitation, to develop the idea of functionality with a psychiatric disability. Recovery was viewed in terms of a service user's ability to function in the major domains of life: work, housing, relationships, and recreation. Psychiatric rehabilitation programs emphasized the value of community inclusion for persons with severe mental illnesses. Understanding severe mental illnesses as a psychiatric disability changed the way service users and practitioners viewed treatment goals: their focus was on moving toward attaining one's own goals while adapting to the illness and the consequent limitations of the disability.

The ex-patient and/or survivor and consumer movement was the other major influence that shaped the concept of recovery. In the 1970s, more service users, who had previously been viewed as passive recipients of treatment, started to speak out about their experiences of mental illness. Inspired by the civil rights movement of the 1960s, service users challenged the medical establishment's portrayal of mental illness as chronic and hopeless. Service users' narratives powerfully depicted the inadequacies and abuses of the mental health system and claimed their role as experts in their own mental health recovery. These narratives have become an essential part of the current recovery movement. Deegan (1996), who has written eloquently of her own experiences in the mental health system, declared that "the concept of recovery is rooted in the simple yet profound realization that people who have been diagnosed with mental illness are human beings" (p. 92).

To understand the concept as it relates to mental health services, it is important to distinguish the meaning of recovery from its use in other contexts. Davidson O'Connell, Tondora, Lawless, and Evans (2005) illustrate how recovery can also be applied to physical illness, chronic illness and/or disability, trauma, and substance abuse. In relation to physical illness, recovery is usually associated with a return to the physical condition one had before illness. With chronic illness or disability, living with the illness or disability and its consequences is an ongoing process. In relation to trauma, recovery means that one has integrated traumatic events so as to mitigate their negative impact and allow for a fulfilling life, but unlike recovery from physical illness, this is often an ongoing process throughout one's life. People most often associate the term *recovery* with substance abuse, where it means maintaining abstinence from drugs and alcohol. Like recovery from trauma and chronic illness, recovery in substance abuse is characterized as an ongoing process; although one may not be actively using, one has to continue to work to maintain sobriety because of an ongoing vulnerability to addiction. Recovery for people with severe mental illnesses is distinct in that recovery does not depend on control of, remission, or a cure for one's symptoms but rather a reshaping of one's life to accommodate mental illness. In this respect, recovery conceptualizes mental illness as a disability and draws on notions from the disability rights movement, which claims that recovery is possible because it is not contingent on physical or mental ability. But, as in three of these four domains, there is recognition of the ongoing nature of the process involved in living and functioning with the illness, disability, or event.

Theoretical Perspective

Most recovery-oriented services are informed by theories that emphasize the role of self-determination, natural supports, and community integration in people's quest for a meaningful life. These include capabilities theory, social supports, and ecological or systems theory (Hopper, 2007; Sands & Gellis, 2012). Each of these theoretical perspectives reflects a positive orientation that involves viewing recovery as a journey of healing and transformation that enables a person to live a meaningful life in their community while striving to achieve their full potential.

Principles

The concept of recovery lends itself to two core practice principles: capability and dimensionality.

- *Principle of capability*—Recovery has often been framed with regard to the individual, thus placing the onus on each person to identify and pursue his or her own path to recovery. Underlying this approach is the assumption that people have the capability to make choices and move ahead with their recovery. More recently, advocates and researchers have drawn attention to factors both at the individual and the societal level that can prevent people from working on their recovery. Stigma, marginalization, and poverty are frequently major barriers to recovery. Also, persons with severe mental illnesses have a significantly lower life expectancy than average, and poor health often precludes them from pursuing desired activities. Therefore, a prerequisite to having meaningful choices in life is having basic human needs met, such as a safe place to live, education, an adequate income, and access to quality health and mental health services. Only when these needs are met can an individual contemplate choices about education, career, and family. Capabilities theory is now being applied to the concept of recovery to illustrate how "substantial" freedoms to pursue individual choices are predicated on having the necessary psychological, social, and material resources (Hopper, 2007).

• *Principle of dimensionality*—In an effort to capture the many aspects of recovery, Whitley and Drake (2010) have posited a dimensional approach to recovery. The dimensions are clinical, existential, functional, physical, and social, and together they create a framework that helps guide practice and research.

Steps for Implementing Recovery-Oriented Services

A panel of experts, including service users, family members, researchers, and practitioners, identified ten fundamental components of recovery: self-direction, individualistic and person centered, empowerment, holistic, nonlinear, strengths based, peer support, respect, responsibility, and hope (see figure 12.1).

The components of recovery are defined in terms of what it means to lead a meaningful life for a person who has experienced severe mental illness. This phenomenological approach to mental illness stresses that recovery is unique to the individual; for some, recovery is about alleviating symptoms through the use of medications, but for others, it may be pursuing their spirituality or overcoming the effects of societal stigma. The conceptual ambiguity of recovery lies in the fact that it is as much a process as an outcome; its course is often nonlinear; and most important, recovery is specific to every service user. People often describe themselves as being "in" recovery, which encompasses the individual path with symptoms and functioning varying over time depending on myriad personal, social, and material factors, but it essentially means that one has autonomy and is working

Figure 12.1. Ten Components of Recovery

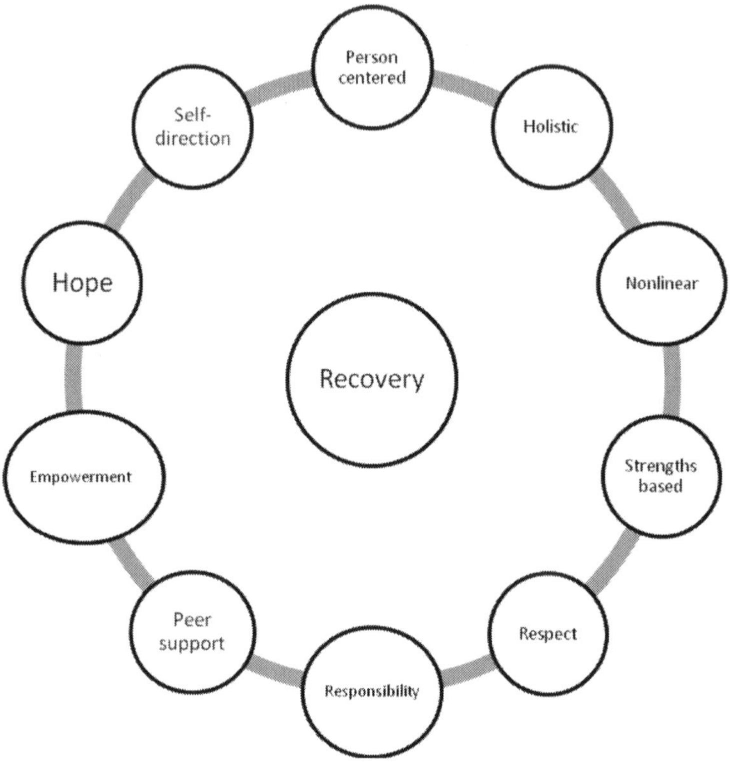

Source: Department of Health and Human Services (2004). *National consensus statement on mental health recovery* (Rockville, MD: Substance Abuse and Mental Health Services Administration).

toward reclaiming one's own life. The fact that people can experience sudden improvements as often as sudden setbacks should help both people in recovery and practitioners have a sense of hope and optimism about the future.

What's the Evidence?

The knowledge base for recovery has been both experiential and empirical. Service user narratives have played a central role in informing the movement, illustrating the nonlinear and essentially unique nature of the recovery path. Service users describe how being labeled with a mental illness can bring about despair and a sense of helplessness. In turn, they describe how reclaiming their own sense of identity, being heard by mental health professionals, and becoming active in one's own recovery is the key not only to healing but also to thriving. Researchers have employed qualitative methods to capture the subjective and dynamic nature of recovery. This research has demonstrated how recovery comes out of taking an active role, understanding one's capabilities with respect to change, and using a sense of self as a resource. Onken, Craig, Ridgway, Ralph, and Cook (2007) describe the process as reauthoring, which allows service users to uncover inherent strengths and resources both for themselves and for a broader audience. In this way, the narrative process itself is transformative, as it integrates the trauma of mental illness and creates new meanings within one's life. However, one criticism has been that the personal stories informing the recovery movement have been primarily from those well into their recovery, and as a result, they set up unrealistic expectations for many service users. What has been missing from the research is the voices of the more marginalized who are still trying to gain stability while coping with multiple adversities, including poverty, homelessness, and oppression (Padgett, 2007).

The empirical basis for recovery has also emerged from studies that support the notion that severe mental illnesses are not as chronic and persistent as the traditional Kraepelin view of mental illness has claimed (Sadock & Sadock, 2002). A longitudinal study in Vermont followed up on 262 patients, diagnosed with schizophrenia, who had been hospitalized for an average of six continuous years before being released into the community upon their completion of a hospital-based rehabilitation program. The researchers found that after thirty-six years in the community, 34 percent of former patients made a full recovery with regard to the presence of symptoms and social functioning (Harding, Brooks, Ashikaga, Strauss, & Breier, 1987). Overall, research conducted both in the United States and abroad between the late 1960s and early 2000s has demonstrated that between one-half to two-thirds of people diagnosed with severe mental illnesses experience full recovery or have only mild impairment. The conclusion drawn from these studies is that schizophrenia and other severe mental illnesses are far more heterogeneous both in their manifestation and in their outcome than was originally believed (Sands & Gellis, 2012).

Recovery also challenges the way research is conducted and the criteria for determining the effectiveness of mental health services. Researchers are examining the extent to which services promote recovery-oriented outcomes rather than focusing on pathology. Previously, outcome measures in mental health services research reflected the goals of symptom management, such as relapse, recidivism, length of hospitalization, and presence of symptoms. Recovery-oriented research evaluates care on its capacity to promote service users' choice and collaborative decision making, as well as outcomes that represent the pursuit of a meaningful life, such as empowerment, sense of hope, quality of life, community integration, and citizenship.

The evidence base for recovery-oriented services is still being gathered. However, initial findings are promising for programs such as wellness recovery action planning, which is a peer led self-management intervention that helps people develop individualized plans of care that may or may not include formal mental health services. Peers must not only be involved in the delivery of services but also must participate as partners in conducting research. The inclusion of service users in the development and implementation of research ensures that the scientific task is accountable to recovery principles and that the choice of study methods and outcomes reflects service users' perspectives (Solomon & Stanhope, 2004).

Assessment and Evaluation

The Evaluation Center at the Human Services Research Institute has developed a collection of recovery measures titled *Measuring the Promise: A Compendium of Recovery Measures* (Campbell-Orde, Chamberlin, Carpenter, & Leff, 2005). The purpose of these measures is to provide stakeholders and practitioners with tools for research on and evaluation of adult mental health services. The measures specifically focus on the recovery orientation of services and identifying evidence-based practices. The instruments assess recovery both at the individual and at the organizational level. Also *Review of Recovery Measures* (Burgess, Pirkis, Coombs, & Rosen 2010) provides an assessment of recovery measures with an appendix of the measures.

Implementation Issues

Recovery cannot be implemented without change at the systems level. The Freedom Commission on Mental Health (Department of Health and Human Services, 2003) generated a federal action agenda based on its recommendations, and since that time many states have launched initiatives to overhaul their mental health systems according to recovery planning. Transformation has entailed comprehensive reform involving the following:

• Development of new values and principles

• Training of practitioners

• Changing programs and structures

• Alignment of funding streams to support recovery programs

• Integration of recovery services into existing ones

• Evaluation of process and outcomes of services using a recovery perspective

• Advocacy for people in recovery

One of the key issues has been to address the problem of fragmentation, moving from a system that divides itself according to the varying needs of persons with severe mental illnesses, such as categorizing services into mental health, substance abuse, financial assistance, housing, and physical health, to one that treats service users holistically. Service delivery systems, as well as practitioners, must move beyond diagnostic and categorical services to treat individual service users and their multiple needs. Another essential part of the reform process has been the participation of services users in all aspects of planning and implementation, which ensures that the transformation process itself is person centered.

At the program level, transformation means either developing or adapting interventions to reflect the values and goals of recovery. Concurrent with recovery initiatives are efforts to promote evidence-based practices to ensure that people are receiving high-quality mental health services. Wellness management and recovery, supported employment (see chapter 10), and integrated dual-diagnosis treatment (see chapter 3) are three examples of evidence-based programs that clearly embrace a recovery orientation. Wellness management and recovery, which originally educated service users on medication adherence and symptom management, has been expanded to focus on the more holistic goal of wellness, which includes having a sense of self-efficacy and self-esteem that allows service users autonomy and choice. Integrated dual-diagnosis treatment (see chapter 1) fits the recovery model by taking a holistic approach that reflects how service users experience severe mental illnesses and addiction. Supported employment, another evidence-based practice, has proved successful in helping service users enter into the competitive job market with flexible supports. Other programs can be adapted, such as assertive community treatment (ACT; see chapter 7), a transdisciplinary team case management model, which has the structure and flexibility to integrate a recovery orientation (Salyers & Tsemberis, 2007). Through training and monitoring, implementing other recovery-oriented evidence-based practices, and hiring service users as team members, the ACT model can incorporate recovery-oriented practice principles.

Service users as mental health practitioners are a vital component of any recovery-based system. Hiring service user practitioners into existing mental health programs offers service users receiving services the added value of peer support and role models for their own recovery. Service user practitioners also play a valuable role in educating other practitioners about the recovery experience and can bring about reform from within the system. A recovery-based system also provides service users with broader treatment options than conventional clinical and rehabilitative programs. Services run by service users themselves are one such example; such as independent agencies providing drop-in centers, residential services, outreach, and vocational programs. As with mutual support groups, these services give service users the opportunity to be active in their treatment and to benefit from instrumental and emotional support available from their peers.

Provider Competencies

Advocates have emphasized that recovery is possible without formal mental health services. Therefore, a system that is truly recovery oriented must integrate the use of informal supports into its approach and honor service users' choices even when that means choosing informal over formal supports. However, when service users choose professional supports, their relationship with their practitioner is often central to their recovery process. Practitioners, therefore, need to reorient themselves from the mind-set of traditional mental health services, which have perceived service users largely in terms of their symptoms. Seeing beyond the symptoms to the uniqueness of each service user puts a premium on the relationship, thus requiring practitioners to invest time and energy into clients so they can accompany their clients on their own recovery journey. Building such relationships means the following:

- Valuing people as human beings

- Accepting, understanding, and believing in a person's abilities and potential

- Attending to people's priorities and interests

- Allowing people to take risks and accepting their setbacks

- Finding ways of sustaining hope and guarding against despair

- Believing that practitioners learn and benefit from the experience of the service user

The traditional hierarchical relationships between the expert professional and the passive service user cannot sustain a recovery orientation. The recognition that service users are experts in their own mental health care has led agencies to adopt a person-centered planning approach to treatment. Person-centered planning as a practice is when "a highly individual comprehensive approach to assessment and services is used to understand each individual's and family's history, strengths, needs, and vision of their own recovery including attention to issues of culture, spirituality, trauma and other factors" (Adams & Grieder, 2005, p. 21). As a result, practitioners collaborate with service users to develop customized plans that identify life goals and potential barriers rather than focusing on symptom relief. Person-centered plans also ensure that services are oriented to a person's life goals rather than generic outcomes. Another technique that focuses on collaboration between the practitioner and the service user is shared decision making. Using this modality, practitioners play the role of a consultant: they provide information, help clients weigh different treatment options according to their values and preferences, and support their final decisions (Adams & Drake, 2006). To assist in this process, decision aids can help service users be fully informed about the risks and benefits of treatment choices. Decision aids can come in a variety of mediums, including brochures, computer-based programs, videos, audio materials, and workbooks.

Future Directions

As recovery becomes a reality in many agencies, practitioners are having to reorient themselves to a person-centered model of care. In many cases this necessitates a reconciliation of professional values and medical-model approaches that are well ingrained in practitioners and the system with those of a recovery orientation.

Although many practitioners have embraced this shift in relationship with their clients, they often feel that they do not have the tools and skills to implement this new paradigm of care. Workforce training, therefore, must not only increase knowledge and skills but also help practitioners negotiate the challenging transition from a medical model to a recovery model. Sustainable change is rooted in the new generation of practitioners, and social work and psychiatry training programs are starting to integrate recovery materials into their educational curricula. However, in an era of severe budget cuts for health and human services, mental health reform focusing on recovery efforts may be imperiled. Advocates, therefore, have to demonstrate not only the moral imperative of person-centered care but also how recovery improves the efficiency and quality of mental health care.

Websites

Center to Study Recovery in Social Contexts, a participatory research program dedicated to exploring the meaning and determinants of social recovery for persons diagnosed with severe mental illness—http://recovery.rfmh.org

Center for Adherence and Self-Determination, a research center that aims to promote choice and full engagement in services that help people with serious mental illnesses achieve their recovery goals—http://www.adherenceandselfdetermination.org

Pillars of Peer Support, an initiative designed to develop and foster the use of Medicaid funding to support peer-support services in state mental health systems of care—http://www.pillarsofpeersupport.org

Substance Abuse and Mental Health Services Administration's Partners for Recovery, a federal initiative to support and provide technical resources to those who deliver behavioral health services—http://pfr.samhsa.gov

Substance Abuse and Mental Health Services Administration's Recovery to Practice Resource Center, a resource targeted to mental health professionals to help them understand recovery and its implications for behavioral health practices—http://dsgdev2.dsgonline.com/rtp/

Glossary

Person-centered planning: An individualized approach to assessment and services that orients care to an individual's personal life goals.

Recovery: A journey of healing and transformation enabling a person with a mental health problem to live a meaningful life in a community of his or her choice while striving to achieve his or her full potential.

Shared decision making: An interactive collaborative process between the healthcare practitioner and the service user that is used to make mental health decisions, in which the practitioner becomes a consultant to the service user, helping him or her by providing information and discussing options.

References

Adams, J. R., & Drake, R. E. (2006). Shared decision-making and evidence-based practice. *Community Mental Health Journal, 42*, 87–105.

Adams, N., & Grieder, D. (2005). *Treatment planning for person-centered care: The road to mental health and addiction recovery: Mapping the journey for individuals, families and providers*: San Diego, CA: Academic Press.

Anthony, W. (2007). Giving psychiatric rehabilitation its due. *Psychiatric Rehabilitation Journal, 31*, 95.

Burgess, P., Pirkis, J., Coombs, T., & Rosen, A. (2010). *Review of recovery measures* (Version 1.01). National Mental Health Strategy. (Available free at http://amhocn.org/static/files/assets/80e8befc/Review_of_Recovery_Measures.pdf).

Campbell-Orde, T., Chamberlin, J., Carpenter, J., & Leff, H. (2005). *Measuring the promise: A compendium of recovery measures* (Vol. 2). Cambridge, MA: The Evaluation Center@ HSRI. (Available free at http://www.thecathrsi.org).

Davidson, L., O'Connell, M. J., Tondora, J., Lawless, M., & Evans, A. C. (2005). Recovery in serious mental illness: A new wine or just a new bottle. *Professional Psychology: Research and Practice, 36*, 480–487.

Deegan, P. (1996). Coping with: Recovery as a journey of the heart. *Psychiatric Rehabilitation Journal, 19*(3), 91–97.

Department of Health and Human Services. (2003). *New Freedom Commission on Mental Health—Achieving the promise: Transforming mental health care in America, final report* (DHHS Pub. No. SMA-03–3832). Rockville, MD: Author.

Department of Health and Human Services. (2004). *National consensus statement on mental health recovery.* Rockville, MD: Substance Abuse and Mental Health Services Administration.

Harding, C. M., Brooks, G. W., Ashikaga, T. S., Strauss, J. S., & Breier, A. (1987). The Vermont Longitudinal Study of Persons with Severe Mental Illness. *American Journal of Psychiatry, 144,* 718–726.

Hopper, K. (2007). Rethinking social recovery in schizophrenia: What capabilities approach might offer. *Social Science and Medicine, 65,* 868–879.

Onken, S. J., Craig, C. M., Ridgway, P., Ralph, R. O., & Cook, J. A. (2007). An analysis of the definitions and elements of recovery: A review of the literature. *Psychiatric Rehabilitation Journal, 31*(1), 9–22.

Padgett, D. K. (2007). There's no place like (a) home: Ontological security among persons with serious mental illness in the United States. *Social Science and Medicine, 64*(9), 1925–1936.

Sadock, B. J., & Sadock, V. A. (2002). *Kaplan and Sadock's synopsis of psychiatry: Behavioral Sciences/Clinical Psychiatry* (9th ed.). Philadelphia: Lippincott Williams and Wilkins.

Salyers, M. P., & Tsemberis, S. (2007). ACT and recovery: Integrating evidence-based practice and recovery orientation on assertive community treatment teams. *Community Mental Health Journal, 43*(6), 619–641.

Sands, R. G., & Gellis, Z. D. (2012). *Clinical social work practice in behavioral mental health: Toward evidence-based practice* (3rd ed.). Boston: Allyn and Bacon/Pearson.

Solomon, P., & Stanhope, V. (2004). Recovery: Expanding the vision of evidence based practice. *Crisis Intervention and Brief Treatment, 4,* 311–321.

Townsend, W., & Glasser, N. (2003). Recovery: The heart and soul of treatment. *Psychiatric Rehabilitation Journal, 27,* 83–86.

Vecchio, P. (2012, March 23). SAMHSA's working definition of recovery updated. *SAMHSA blog.* Retrieved from http://blog.samhsa.gov/2012/03/23/defintion-of-recovery-updated/.

Whitley, R., & Drake, R. E. (2010). Recovery: A dimensional approach. *Psychiatric Services, 61*(12), 1248–1250.

13

Motivational Interviewing

Alan B. McGuire and Timothy D. Gearhart

Motivational interviewing (MI) is a client-centered, directive technique for changing health-related behavior that builds on the client's internal motivation for change. More than seventy-two randomized clinical trials have demonstrated the efficacy of MI in changing a range of behaviors. This chapter delineates the essential spirit of MI and techniques that allow clinicians to join with their clients in the journey toward change. In addition, the chapter discusses issues in implementation and future directions of research. Because mastering MI requires continuous practice and refinement, this chapter serves as an introduction and primer for interested clinicians. We begin this chapter with a case review of Dave (see box 13.1) and his experience with a provider who offered an MI approach to his ambivalence regarding medication usage.

Box 13.1. Case Study: Dave

Dave is a sixty-five-year-old man who lives independently in his own apartment. He was diagnosed with schizophrenia in his midtwenties. He considers himself retired and greatly values his relationships with his card-playing partners at the senior center. Dave has been hospitalized four times in the last year because of psychiatric relapses. All four of these occurrences were subsequent to discontinuation of his psychiatric medications. He reported that he no longer wanted to take medications because of the uncomfortable side effects.

Upon discharge from the hospital the first three times, Dave was required to attend meetings at which clinicians lectured him on the reasons taking his medications were important. The more the clinicians presented the reasons for adhering to medicine, the more he saw reasons against taking them. Staff who worked in this program viewed Dave as resistant and "noncompliant." Dave just did not like being told what to do! He knew that the staff cared about him, but he did not feel respected by them.

After the fourth discharge from the hospital, Dave was referred to a clinician who used motivational interviewing. This clinician did not try to tell Dave all the reasons he should take his medications. He asked Dave why he might want to take medications while expressing understanding for Dave's ambivalence. Over the course of a few sessions, Dave discovered how medications were related to the things that he valued, like independence, autonomy, and relationships. He realized that abruptly stopping his medication regimen did, in fact, lead to his hospitalizations. Once he resolved his ambivalence, he was ready to reconsider his commitment to taking his medications.

Dave was finally allowed the space to make his own decision about taking medications while feeling respected and autonomous. After sorting through the pros and cons of taking medications, it was clear to Dave how medications could assist him in the pursuit of his personal goals. The clinician understood what intrinsically motivated Dave, and collaboratively they examined how medications were related to those motivations.

Background

Motivational interviewing is "a client-centered directive method for enhancing intrinsic motivation to change by exploring and resolving ambivalence" (Miller & Rollnick, 2002, p. 25). Although Miller and Rollnick first developed MI to enhance motivation to quit substance use, the method has expanded to be used to enhance myriad health (Rollnick, Miller, & Butler, 2008) and mental health (Arkowitz, Westra, Miller, & Rollnick, 2008) behaviors.

Theoretical Perspective

The theoretical origins of MI derive from the person-centered therapy style of Carl Rogers (1951). Unlike Rogers, though, MI works toward a predetermined client change. The more contemporary theory of motivational interviewing is built on the transtheoretical model of change set forth by Prochaska and DiClemente (1983). This model is based on a synthesis of psychological and sociological studies of how people change their behavior or the behavior of others.

Principles

The following factors, as Miller and Rollnick (2002) delineated, are considered central principles to the practice of MI. In fact, some literature supports the importance of adhering to the spirit of MI over and above faithful application of specific MI techniques and skills (Moyers, Miller, & Hendrickson, 2005):

- *Principle of autonomy versus authority*—In general, people do not like being told what to do. In MI, it is important to understand and embrace that the responsibility for change rests solely on the individual receiving services. Embracing this concept not only is powerful for the individual but can be powerful for the clinician as well. Many times clinicians feel responsible for the progress, or lack thereof, of the individuals with whom they are working. This concept helps clinicians understand that they are not responsible for change, which frees them from that burden that sometimes leads to burnout.

- *Principle of collaboration versus confrontation*—The relationship between the clinician and client is critical in MI and should be characterized as a collaborative partnership. Therefore, it is essential that the clinician not take on the role of expert, with an authoritarian position. The clinician's spirit ought to be one of exploration and wondering.

- *Principle of evocation versus education*—Motivational interviewing assumes that each individual is intrinsically motivated. It is the MI clinician's job to elicit the case for change from the individual instead of expertly developing the case on his or her behalf.

Steps for Implementing Motivational Interviewing

This section reviews three different step-by-step approaches to offering MI to clients. First, we review philosophical steps, which is followed by a review of person-centered skills and directive approaches. Beginning with the underpinning philosophy, there are four specific steps or strategies used in supporting the principles of autonomy, collaboration, and evocation.

1. *Develop discrepancy*—Developing discrepancy means allowing a person to explore how a particular behavior may be interfering with progress toward a personally relevant goal or value. This heightens natural ambivalence around change and provides momentum toward change.

2. *Express empathy*—It is essential for the social worker to be empathetic and understanding of individuals' frame of reference and displaying a nonjudgmental attitude toward their views. Acceptance is a key ingredient to displaying empathy. Empathy is focused on the individual's conflicting thoughts and feelings about the targeted behavior.

3. *Roll with resistance*—Resistance is a normal response to being pressured to change. When resistance occurs, the clinician needs to be careful to not fall into the trap of arguing for change while the client defends the status quo. The MI clinician skillfully allows the client to find flaws with the status quo as opposed to pointing those flaws out for the client. It might be helpful to think of resistance as momentum of a river flowing. If you wish to change the direction of the river, you must first embrace the current direction and then provide opportunities for the water to begin moving in a different direction—a river does not just reverse course when a dam is built.

4. *Support self-efficacy*—The more people believe in their ability to successfully make a change, the more likely they are to bother trying (Bandura, 2001). It is essential for the therapist or interviewer to believe in the client's ability to make a change; this is partly because of the impact of self-fulfilling prophecies. It is in this step that hope has tangible relevance to the impact of the intervention.

Person-Centered Skills Used in MI

Person-centered skills are another set of steps or strategies helpful in the application of MI. The person-centered counseling skills used in MI can be summarized using the acronym OARS (open-ended questions, affirmation, reflection, summary). These are consistent with the skills taught in Rogers's (1951) client-centered therapy. Competence in OARS is essential to practicing MI in accordance with fidelity (Moyers, Martin, Manuel, Hendrickson, & Miller, 2005).

Open-Ended Questions

Open-ended questions encourage more than a one-word answer such as yes or no. They allow the respondent to answer without the constraints of a predetermined set of possible choices. Some examples of open-ended questions are "What do you make of that?" or "How does that relate to your goals?" By not limiting the number of possible ways that any given question can be answered, the direction of the conversation can be led in a person-centered direction instead of allowing for the interviewer to impose possible biases.

Affirmation

Affirmations are used as ways to encourage individuals and the content they are sharing. They can be considered opportunities to reinforce and thus shape conversations. Some examples of affirmations are "That makes a lot of sense" and "That is pretty impressive."

Reflection

"The essence of a reflective listening response is that it makes a guess as to what the speaker means" (Miller & Rollnick, 2002, p. 69). Skillful use of reflective statements is vital to the practice of MI. Reflections alone seem very nondirective, but they are used to subtly direct the focus and course of the interaction. The clinician should focus on reflecting change talk.

Summary

Essentially, a summary is a collection of reflective responses. After gathering information from the client, summaries can serve to put the information together into a coherent picture for the client. It might be helpful to think of a summary as a collection of reflections. As with reflections, summaries should provide a collection of the individual's change talk.

Directive Aspects of MI

In MI, clients make their own case for change. So, when clinicians hear words that represent change (i.e., change talk), they can assume that those statements are part of the individual's case for change. Change talk leads to commitment language, which has been directly linked to behavior change (Amrhein, Miller, Yahne, Palmer, & Fulcher, 2003). The key job for the clinician, then, is to elicit and support change-talk statements. Types of change-talk statements are categorized with the acronym DARN-C (Miller & Rollnick, 2002), as follows (these categories are not exclusive in nature, and some statements can fall in more than one category):

- *Desire*—Statements that refer to things people want (e.g., "I want . . . ," "I'd like . . .")

- *Ability*—Statements that reflect a person's perceived ability (confidence) in making a change regarding the target behavior (e.g., "I could do this if . . . ," "I can do . . .")

- *Reason*—Statements that include reasons for making a change (e.g., "I'd like things to be different because . . .")

- Need—Statements that imply necessity (e.g., "I must . . . ," "I need . . . ," "I have to . . .")

- *Commitment*—(e.g., "I will . . . ," "I might . . . ," "Perhaps I'll . . .")

If you were to break up change talk into only two categories, those would be "importance" and "confidence." Desire, reason, and need all represent the importance for change. Ability represents the confidence in one's ability to make a change. A practical way to elicit and illustrate change talk statements is through the readiness rulers, as demonstrated here.

"On a scale of 0 (least important) to 10 (most important), where would you rate how important this change is to you?" Allow for a response and provide an affirmation. "Why are you not a 0?" The response here is typically change talk. This is a statement that you may want to reflect on after hearing: "What would make you rate this change as a 10?" Again, what follows is typically change talk. At this point, it may be helpful to provide a nice summary so that the client has the opportunity to hear again why making this change is important to him or her.

The decisional balance (see figure 13.1) is a visual illustration of weighing the pros and cons of change: "What are the positive reasons to continue this behavior?" (pros) versus "What are the costs of continuing this behavior?" (cons). One may

Figure 13.1. Decisional Balance

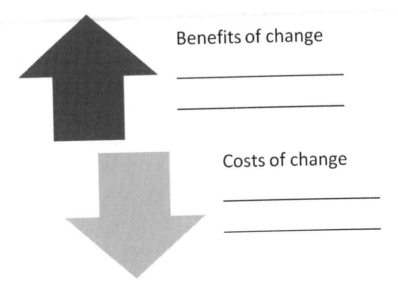

Benefits of change

Costs of change

choose to use the decisional balance when there is a large amount of resistance to change. It is typically not recommended to have an individual discuss reasons for not changing, except in the case of trying to develop an empathetic relationship and decreasing resistance.

What's the Evidence?

The efficacy of MI has been supported by more than seventy-two randomized controlled trials (see Hettema, Steele, & Miller, 2005; Rubak, Sandbaek, Lauritzen, & Christensen, 2005). In brief, MI is efficacious across several delivery methods and presenting problems. However, Smedslund et al. (2011) have noted significant variance between trials, which has led to preliminary research on factors that affect the impact of MI.

Research has supported the efficacy of MI in changing broad health-related behaviors (e.g., diet, exercise), substance use, and other mental health behavior (e.g., medication adherence, purging, engagement in PTSD treatment). Positive results have been found not only in self-reported indications of behavior but also in more objective indicators, such as blood glucose levels or length of hospital stay. As with other interventions, the effects of MI are strongest in the period immediately after follow-up. Importantly, though, when MI is combined with another intervention (e.g., relapse prevention training, a twelve-step program, cognitive therapy), the effect is maintained longer (Hettema et al., 2005).

Although studies have supported the overall efficacy of MI, significant variation still exists between studies (Hettema et al., 2005). As noted earlier, the addition of a complementary intervention explains some of the inconsistency. Another important factor is the number of client encounters, with increased numbers of encounters associated with increased size of effect (Rubak et al., 2005). Encouragingly, research based in minority populations also has shown positive results, and in some studies an even greater effect than with Caucasians. Unexpectedly, studies using treatment manuals have met less success; this may be a result of manuals that do not allow sufficient flexibility for clinicians to adhere to the spirit of MI.

Assessment and Evaluation

Assessment of the outcomes of MI depends on the behavior that the intervention is targeting. Motivational interviewing was originally developed in a substance abuse context; therefore, many studies have used substance abuse questionnaires as the outcome of interest. In addition to the readiness ruler described earlier as a means of fidelity measurements, The Stages of Change Questionnaire (McConnaughy, Prochaska, & Velicer, 1983) can be adapted to assess change in readiness toward a change of interest. When using MI as an intervention to engage clients in subsequent services, objective indicators such as "show rates" (i.e., keeping of appointments) are appropriate indicators. Clinicians may also want to assess and evaluate their own skills for applying MI techniques.

A formal instrument such as the MI Treatment Integrity scale (MITI; Moyers, Miller, & Hendrickson, 2005) can provide structured feedback to clinicians. The benefits of clinical supervision are discussed in the following sections.

Implementation Issues

Many clinicians get excited about promising new practices, only to become frustrated when attempting to implement the practice in the "real world." There are several issues that clinicians and organizations planning on adding MI to their clinical repertoire must address. The first is how clinicians are to become proficient in the practice of MI. Consistent evidence has shown didactic trainings alone to be ineffective in changing practitioners' behaviors (Davis et al., 1999), and the same is true for MI (Miller, Yahne, Moyers, Martinez, & Pirritano, 2004). Rather, effective implementation of MI requires two components: introduction to the materials and ongoing feedback. Most implementations adequately address the first component but woefully neglect the latter.

Several options are available for aspiring MI clinicians to gain feedback on their practice. First, and perhaps ideally, clinicians should seek out a clinician experienced in MI who is willing to review his or her practice. This should take the form of reviewing audio- or videotapes of sessions. As mentioned earlier, using a formal instrument such as the MI Treatment Integrity Scale (MITI; Moyers et al., 2005) can provide structured feedback to clinicians. Supervision allows for constant refinement of a clinician's skills and prevents treatment drift in more seasoned clinicians. When an appropriate supervisor is not readily available, supervision can be sought on a consulting basis through the MI Network of Trainers (see the section "Websites").

Beyond the issues facing the individual clinician, health-care organizations also face systematic decisions regarding MI. As noted already, organizations must establish infrastructure that supports clinicians such as regular supervision and quality assurance mechanisms. Furthermore, organizations must decide on the format in which they will offer MI. Motivational interviewing is maximally effective when paired with another appropriate treatment (e.g., cognitive-behavioral therapy, relapse prevention training). In some cases, this may involve referring clients to another service. Potential gaps in service or non-MI-oriented clinicians in the referent service can easily cause clients' motivation to revert.

Many organizations and clinicians have increasingly moved toward group formats for treatment. Group formats, as well as being cost effective (an important factor in today's managed care environment), provide an opportunity for clients to interact with peers. Peers can provide additional motivation for change. However, peers can also provide additional reasons for maintaining the status quo. Although some preliminary guidelines are available for providing MI in groups (Arkowitz, Westra, Miller, & Rollnick, 2008), and research is emerging, the bulk of the MI literature focuses on its provision in an individual format.

Provider Competencies

To effectively practice MI, providers must begin and end with basic therapeutic skills—warmth, empathy, and genuineness. Beyond that, the practitioner must evoke and recognize change talk, develop discrepancy between current actions and desired goals, maintain the direction of the session (i.e., on the desired change), and roll with resistance. Meanwhile, the practitioner must maintain a spirit of collaboration and emphasize the client's autonomy.

Future Directions

Extant research has shown the superiority of MI when used as a precursor to another standardized treatment (Hettema et al., 2005). This research provides a promising model of MI working synergistically with other best practices. However, not enough is known about the universality of the effectiveness of MI as an antecedent to other treatments. This dearth necessitates further research that determines for which interventions MI can be used to enhance treatment effects. More specifically, motivational interventions such as illness management and recovery (Mueser et al., 2002) and integrated dual-disorder treatment (Drake et al., 2001) are included as components to several of the Substance Abuse and Mental Health Services Administration's evidence-based tool kits. Despite the inclusion of MI in these manuals, no research has specifically addressed the role or additive effectiveness of MI in these evidence-based practices.

In addition, although excellent research has begun to dissect both the change process and the effects of MI on that process (e.g., Arkowitz et al., 2008; Moyers et al., 2005), more work is yet to be done. For instance, Moyers et al. (2005) found that varying from MI-specific techniques can lead to better results when the spirit of MI is maintained. Nonetheless, this leaves clinicians with vexingly unclear guidelines. Early findings argued against the use of practice manuals (Hettema et al., 2005), but would refined practice manuals that adhere to the spirit of MI by providing flexibility in application attenuate this gap in effectiveness while providing necessary consistency? Finally, all best practices labor under a common yoke of poor dissemination and implementation; future research in MI must further solidify methods for training practitioners in MI and maintaining fidelity in practice.

Websites

ACT Center of Indiana—http://www.psych.iupui.edu/ACT/

Addiction Technology Transfer Center Network—http://www.attcnetwork.org

Center on Alcoholism, Substance Abuse, and Addictions—http://.casaa.unm.edu/intro.asp

Motivational Interviewing site—http://www.motivationalinterviewing.org

Glossary

Ambivalence: A natural part of the change process in which a client experiences both sides of the decisional balance. Change occurs through the resolution of ambivalence.

Change talk: A client's vocalization of reasons not to maintain the status quo or to make a desired change.

Decisional balance: The relative importance of the costs and benefits of changing a given behavior.

Resistance: A client's communication of motivation to maintain the status quo; this reaction should cue the clinician to do something different.

References

Amrhein, P. C., Miller, W. R., Yahne, C. E., Palmer, M., & Fulcher, L. (2003). Client commitment language during motivational interviewing predicts drug use outcomes. *Journal of Consulting and Clinical Psychology, 71,* 862–878.

Arkowitz, H., Westra, H. A., Miller, W. R., & Rollnick, S. (2008). *Motivational interviewing in the treatment of psychological problems.* New York: Guilford Press.

Bandura, A. (2001). Social cognitive theory: An agentive perspective. *Annual Review of Psychology, 52,* 1–26.

Davis, D., O'Brien, M. A., Freemantle, N., Wolf, F. M., Mazmanian, P., & Taylor-Vaisey, A. (1999). Impact of formal continuing medical education: Do conferences, workshops, rounds, and other traditional continuing education activities change physician behavior or health care outcomes? *JAMA, 282,* 867–874.

Drake, R. E., Essock, S. M., Shaner, A., Carey, K. B., Minkoff, K., Kola, L., et al. (2001). Implementing dual diagnosis services for clients with severe mental illness. *Psychiatric Services, 52,* 469–476.

Hettema, J., Steele, J., & Miller, W. R. (2005). Motivational interviewing. *Annual Review of Clinical Psychology, 1,* 91–111.

McConnaughy, E. A., Prochaska, J. O., & Velicer, W. (1983) Stages of change in psychotherapy: Measurement and sample profiles. *Psychotherapy: Theory, Research, and Practice, 20,* 368–375.

Miller, W. R., & Rollnick, S. (2002). *Motivational interviewing: Preparing people for change* (2nd ed.). New York: Guilford Press.

Miller, W. R., Yahne, C. E., Moyers, T. B., Martinez, J., & Pirritano, M. A. (2004). A randomized trial of methods to help clinicians learn motivational interviewing. *Journal of Clinical and Consulting Psychology, 72,* 1050–1062.

Moyers, T. B., Martin, T., Manuel, J. K., Hendrickson, S. M., & Miller, W. R. (2005). Assessing competence in the use of motivational interviewing. *Journal of Substance Abuse Treatment, 28,* 19–26.

Moyers, T. B., Miller, W. R., & Hendrickson, S. M. (2005). How does motivational interviewing work? Therapist interpersonal skill predicts client involvement within motivational interviewing sessions. *Journal of Consulting and Clinical Psychology, 73*, 590–598.

Mueser, K., Corrigan, P., Hilton, D., Tansam, B., Schaub, A., Gingerich, S., et al. (2002). Illness management and recovery for severe mental illness: A review of the research. *Psychiatric Services, 53*, 1272–1284.

Prochaska, J. O., & DiClemente, C. C. (1983). Transtheoretical therapy: Toward a more integrative model of change. *Psychotherapy: Theory, Research and Practice, 19*, 276–288.

Rogers, C. R. (1951). *Client-centered therapy*. Boston: Houghton-Mifflin.

Rollnick, S., Miller, W. R., & Butler, C. C. (2008). *Motivational interviewing in health care: Helping patients change behavior.* New York: Guilford Press.

Rubak, S., Sandbaek, A., Lauritzen, T., & Christensen, B. (2005). Motivational interviewing: A systematic review and meta-analysis. *British Journal of General Practice, 55*, 305–312.

Smedslund, G., Berg, R. C., Hammerstrom, K. T., Steiro, A., Leikner, K. A., Dahl, H. M., et al. (2011). *Motivational interviewing is a short psychological treatment that can help people cut down on drugs and alcohol.* Retrieved from http://summaries.cochrane.org/CD008063/motivational-interviewing-is-a-short-psychological-treatment-that-can-help-people-cut-down-on-drugs-and-alcohol.

14

Best Practices for Family Caregivers of People with Severe Mental Illness

Susan E. Mason

Family caregivers of people with mental illness face challenges that clinicians can be called on to ameliorate. Interventions that work can reduce stress for the entire family so that they can better care for their ill family member. Services shown to be successful are suggested in this chapter in the context of a typical case, the Rodríguez family. Not all of the suggested interventions are available in every community, and every family has unique needs, but using this case as a model, the clinician, together with caregivers, can devise a workable plan. We begin this chapter with a brief overview of the Rodríguez family and their teenage son, Luis (see box 14.1), who has just been diagnosed with schizophrenia, leaving the family wondering what next steps to take in caring for him, his sibling, and themselves.

Box 14.1. Case Study: The Rodríguez Family

María and Tomás Rodríguez were shocked to hear from their local clinic's psychiatrist that their eighteen-year-old son, Luis, was diagnosed as having schizophrenia. They were uncertain about how Luis came to have schizophrenia and were not at all sure what this meant for his and their future. The clinician recommended that Luis attend a day program, take his medication, and look into vocational options.

María and Tomás are concerned about their ability to care for Luis; the family's financial future; and the effects that Luis's illness will have on his sister, who does not have any sign of the illness. They are also worried about how their friends, extended family members, and neighbors will react to Luis's diagnosis. María and Tomás are in good health now, but María has had bouts of depression in the past and is concerned that caregiving responsibilities may bring them back. Tomás wants to be sure that María is not overly burdened, as she will be the primary caregiver.

Background

The Stresses of Caring for a Family Member with a Severe Mental Illness

Family caregivers of people with severe mental illness often require a variety of clinical services to alleviate the stress of caring for their family member in their home. Caregivers may also be coping with stigma attached to severe mental illnesses, and they may need help in accessing resources for alleviating stress and feelings of being not accepted in their community. Clinicians who are aware of the challenges faced by caregivers of people with severe mental illnesses can intervene in ways that have been shown to overcome the difficulties associated with the caregiver role.

In this case, María and Tomás Rodríguez are beginning their caregiver roles and are expressing realistic concerns related to having a person with severe mental illness living in their family home. It is likely that Luis has been displaying symptoms of schizophrenia for many months before he received the diagnosis. Often, it takes about two years between the initial onset of the illness and the assessment by a qualified mental health provider. Nevertheless, hearing the diagnosis can be perceived as a shock, one that reverberates throughout the entire family. In this case the designated caregiver is María, the mother, but in many situations it can be grandparents, spouses, siblings, and children who have accepted the caregiver responsibility. Stressors that caregivers experience may include confusion about the source and treatment of mental illness; fear about what the future holds for themselves, other family members, and the person they are caring for; and concern about their own mental status. Caregivers may also experience feelings of stigma and burden, and they need to be able to identify and access suitable resources.

Defining the Severe Mental Illnesses

Mental illnesses that are considered severe are those that cause symptoms and behaviors that are often difficult to live with and are not always easily controlled even when medications are taken and counseling appointments are kept. When there is nonadherence to treatment, the situation can become considerably worse. It is important for families to remember that the behaviors are caused by symptoms that patients may have little control over or that the behaviors themselves are the symptoms. In both situations, it is likely that the person with a severe mental illness is not acting out but, instead, is not in control of his or her actions. A partial list of the severe mental illnesses includes, schizophrenia, schizoaffective disorder, bipolar I (major depression plus mania), major depression, anorexia, dissociative identity disorder (formerly known as multiple personality disorder), and intractable forms of posttraumatic stress disorder. There are others, and the *Diagnostic and Statistical Manual of Mental Disorders* (4th ed., text rev.; *DSM-IV-TR*) can be consulted as a reference (American Psychiatric Association, 2000).

Family and Sibling Caregiver Stress Associated with Severe Mental Illnesses

There is evidence to show that family caregivers of people with severe mental illness, siblings, and even extended family members endure high levels of stress sometimes accompanied with feelings of resentment for being burdened (Shankar & Muthuswamy, 2007). Let's look at the unique issues these three family units face.

Family caregivers. Feelings of stress and resentment seem to increase when the mentally ill family member does not appear to improve in symptoms and functioning, and caregivers respond with criticisms and negativity toward the person (McFarlane & Cook, 2007). Family caregivers sometimes experience feelings of guilt and shame, such as when they may speak harsh words to the family member who is ill. They may also feel isolated or lonely, and they can report feelings of loss and grief. Not every caregiver experiences all or even some of these feelings, but for those who do, when the feelings are not easy to express, their own health may be in jeopardy (Curtin & Lilley, 2001).

Siblings. The designated caregiver may not be the only family member who feels stress. In families in which the caregivers are the parents, there may be other children who feel neglected or resentful of having to help out with the tasks related to care giving. Sometimes siblings feel guilty, "why him or her and not me," and at other times they may be ashamed of the ill family member or reluctant to bring friends home (Miller & Mason, 2005). Siblings, especially teenagers, can display hostile or erratic behavior without being fully aware of how their behavior is connected to feelings toward the ill family member.

Extended family members. Well adult siblings may expect to take on the role of caregivers as their parents age. They may not be currently living in the same household as their parent caregivers and the unwell sibling, but they may plan to take their brother or sister to their home in the future (Jewell & Stein, 2002). For this reason, clinicians may want to explore the caregiving options of the extended family (e.g., in-laws). Interventions to alleviate stress can be offered to all family members who have direct contact with the person who is ill, not just current primary caregivers. The clinician's role is to provide caregivers with knowledge about mental illness and how to best care for their diagnosed family member. Proven interventions for alleviating burden and stress are the groundwork of clinical practice with caregivers of people with severe mental illness.

Theoretical Perspective

Ideally, family support interventions use an empowerment theory perspective; they seek to increase family members' sense of control and hopefulness. Empowerment theory emphasizes the taking of control of one's situation in the face of obstacles, gathering up one's resources, and moving forward to achieve goals (Lee, 1996). Empowerment theory focuses on the client, but the clinician can help get the process started and then hand off the work. The clinician serves as a resource for support and consultation as families face the challenges inherent in caring for their designated family member.

Principles

Three core principles guide family-support interventions: partnership, strengths, and education.

- *Principle of partnership*—Clinicians and families work together as equal partners in the care and treatment of the family member with mental illness.

- *Principle of strengths*—Families have strengths and limitations, and interventions should be designed to support the caregiver and the person with the mental illness according to each member's abilities.

- *Principle of education*—Clinicians offer guidance and concrete educational and informational resources to help support the caregiver and ill family member.

Steps for Implementing Family Support Interventions
Evidence-Based Interventions to Reduce Caregiver Stress

Reducing caregiver stress is an important priority that can be addressed with several interventions that are evidence based. Here is a list of the most commonly accepted approaches for maintaining a person with a severe mental illness in the home or other supportive and stable housing, thereby relieving family stress caused by an ill family member:

- (Family) psychoeducation

- Assertive community treatment (ACT) teams

- In-home crisis care, sometimes referred to as mobile crisis units

- Spirituality, connections with places of worship and spiritual activities

Family Psychoeducation

One of the most researched interventions for alleviating stress related to the severe mental illnesses is family psychoeducation. Psychoeducation (see chapter 17) has been shown to benefit people who have a severe mental illness such as schizophrenia or bipolar I, and it can be designed to benefit families (McFarlane, Dixon, Lukens & Lucksted, 2003). Psychoeducation groups with families, such as the Psychoeducational Multifamily Group (PMFG; McFarlane, 2002), vary in format. Some include the family member who is ill, and others include multiple families meeting together without the unwell persons, and other groups rotate between the two formats at specified times. The main goals of these groups are to support the family caregivers and to achieve the best possible outcome for the identified patient, whether living full-time or part-time in the family. These groups also provide a safe space for family members to learn about mental illnesses and to work on collaborating with mental health professionals. Psychoeducation groups can also help reduce the guilt that many parents feel as a result of the incorrect but often-held belief that they did something to their child that caused the mental illness. When guilt is reduced, caregivers can work with treatment teams to encourage medication adherence and to monitor their ill family member for signs of wellness and for symptoms.

Assertive Community Treatment Teams

Assertive community treatment (ACT; see chapter 7) teams provide medications, counseling, and rehabilitative services to people with mental illness. Team members may make home visits periodically to check on patients, especially when they miss appointments or when caregivers voice a concern. Family caregivers are often the most stressed when their ill family member's symptoms bring about behavior that is disruptive to the rest of the family. These behaviors can vary and may include bothersome activities such as playing loud music, unexplained outbursts, and being generally disorganized. Aggressive actions are also possible. Most behaviors can be managed successfully in the home with the support the ACT team provides. When the ill family member requires hospitalization, the team takes charge, thereby reducing caregiver stress. There is evidence that the community-centered support that these and similarly structured teams provide reduces rehospitalizations (Malone, Marriott, Newton-Howes, Simmonds, & Tyrer 2007). Fewer hospitalizations can mean a reduction in financial costs of hospital care and fewer disruptions in family routines that are emotionally distressing. With each hospitalization, family caregivers may feel that they cannot provide adequate care, and their hope for full or even partial recovery may seem increasingly remote. The ACT teams that provide periodic assessments, counseling, and medications can take a huge responsibility off individual caregivers, thus making the caregiver role a viable option for people wishing to assume this responsibility for a loved one.

In-Home Crisis Care

In-home crisis care, also known as mobile crisis units, is available in some communities. These mobile units bring medical staff and social workers to the home when needed to calm an agitated person and assess whether hospitalization is required. Often it is not, and families can ride out the difficult times while knowing that if there is a recurrence, the in-home crisis team is available. In-home crisis care units have been shown to reduce hospital admissions (Irving, Adams, & Rice, 2006). Social workers and families can contact their local hospital to check on the availability of this service.

Spirituality

Spirituality (see chapter 11) has been connected to stress reduction among caregivers of people with a severe mental illness. Caregivers with high levels of spirituality and religiosity are reported to experience increased levels of self-esteem and self-care and low rates of depression (Murray-Swank, Lucksted, Medoff, Yang, Wohlheiter, & Dixon, 2006). When appropriate, clinicians may want to encourage families to become involved in spiritual activities. By staying in the bounds of caregivers' wishes and sensitivity to cultural diversity, clinicians can help families reduce stress through outreach and collaboration with religious and spiritual leaders in communities.

Creating a To-Do List for the Rodríguez Family

By way of example, figure 14.1 illustrates how each of these approaches can be incorporated into a helpful, step-by-step resource guide for the family. The clinician offers a list of guided tasks, the to-do list, which the family can accomplish over time. Returning once again to the Rodríguez family, let's look at how these approaches could be presented as a to-do list in a concrete way to the family:

Step 1: Contact mental health provider for emergency phone number.

Step 2: Learn the names of Luis's current medication(s), doses, adherence schedule, and refill information.

Step 3: Research local treatment resources available to Luis, such as day programs, ACT teams, in-home crisis care, help with transportation, and emergency rooms friendly to psychiatric patients.

Figure 14.1. A "To Do" List for the Rodríguez Family

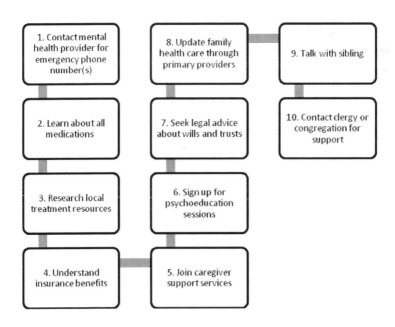

Clinician-guided tasks that can help the Rodríguez family

1. Contact mental health provider for emergency phone number(s)

2. Learn about all medications

3. Research local treatment resources

4. Understand insurance benefits

5. Join caregiver support services

6. Sign up for psychoeducation sessions

7. Seek legal advice about wills and trusts

8. Update family health care through primary providers

9. Talk with sibling

10. Contact clergy or congregation for support

Step 4: Understand the insurance benefits that apply now and in the future for Luis's care.

Step 5: Discover and participate in caregiver support services available in the local community.

Step 6: Sign up for psychoeducation sessions, if available.

Step 7: Get legal advice regarding wills (family and living will), trusts, and Luis's rights.

Step 8: Contact local health providers for updated health exams for all family members, including stress assessments, and schedule counseling services if needed.

Step 9: Have a talk with Luis's sister about her feelings about Luis's illness, and pay special attention to her schoolwork and activities. Provide her with outside support, if needed.

Step 10: Contact clergy person, if this applies, for ideas on how to best get support from the local congregation.

The Rodríguez family was shocked to learn of Luis's diagnosis with schizophrenia. It is likely that they need to learn more about this illness, its cause, its expected progression, and how they can best help Luis. A family psychoeducation program can help. Information about psychoeducation programs can be accessed through their local hospital or the state office of mental health. In addition, they would benefit from the services of an ACT team, and if this is not available, registration with a mobile crisis unit is advised. If they require Spanish-language mental health workers, this can often be provided. The family can be encouraged to attend their local church and bring Luis with them. Potential feelings of stigma are likely to be reduced when friends and neighbors meet and become acquainted with Luis. Then the community will begin to feel comfortable around him. The entire family needs to be evaluated for depression and self-care on a regular basis. An attorney can help Tomás and María by drawing up the necessary papers for future care of Luis. Finally, the family can find out whether Luis is eligible for Medicaid, Medicare, and Social Security benefits. The clinician can inform the family about the possibility of alternative housing for Luis if and when there is a need for respite. In working with Latino families, the social worker needs to be sensitive to their unique needs (Magana, Ramirez Garcia, Hernandez, & Cortez, 2007).

What's the Evidence?

These interventions, though not perfect solutions to caregivers' challenges, have been shown to relieve stress and the accompanying feelings of burden resulting from caring for a family member with a severe mental illness. Meta-analyses are reviews of multiple empirical studies related to a specific intervention and conclude with a report on the overall findings. Readers interested in searching the field of available meta-analyses can access the Cochrane Library (http://www.cochranecollaboration.org). The following interventions, reported in meta-analyses by the Cochrane Reviews, indicate the efficacy of the interventions discussed in this chapter:

* *Psychoeducation*—Decreases relapse rates and readmissions to hospitals for people who are diagnosed with schizophrenia (Pekkala & Merinder, 2002)

* *Community mental health teams (similar to ACT teams)*—Encourage adherence to treatment and likely to reduce hospitalizations and suicides (Malone et al., 2007)

* *In-home crisis care*—Helpful in reducing hospital readmissions when connected with other treatments (Irving et al., 2006)

* *Spirituality*—There are currently no meta-analyses on the benefits of spirituality, though one study cited found it to be helpful (Murray-Swank et al., 2006).

Caregiver support groups such as those offered by the National Alliance on Mental Illness may also be a helpful intervention. The reports of satisfaction surveys on the helpfulness of these groups are positive.

Assessment and Evaluation

The US-government-funded agency National Clearinghouse on Families and Youth (NCFY; http://ncfy.acf.hhs.gov) is devoted to the well-being of families and young people. As part of its mission it maintains an informative website for family members, youth, and clinicians that provides up-to-date research, links to articles and research data, and networking opportunities for agencies and individuals within their localities.

In addition to these services, the NCFY makes available an extensive list of assessment and evaluation tools for adolescents and family life, some in the public domain and some for a fee. There are thirty-nine assessment and screening tools listed at the website http://ncfy.acf.hhs.gov/publications/assessment-screening/ table1. The listing includes a brief description of the assessment or screening tool, the approximate time needed for administration, and whether there is a fee for use. By scanning the table, clinicians can choose the tool that is right for their client or agency use.

Implementation Issues

Most clinicians would agree that stigma is the biggest obstacle when it comes to accessing and implementing services with and on behalf of families who are caregivers of people with severe mental illness. Stigma encourages people to discriminate against those who hold a certain attribute, in this case severe mental illness. Stigma can result in people keeping a distance from individuals and their families, and it can cause a great deal of hurt and unfair treatment. Although there is no clear-cut way to eliminate stigma, when people come in contact with the person who has a mental illness, their negative attitudes and discriminatory behavior can be reduced.

The stigma of mental illness is unfortunately pervasive and often strongly felt by certain ethnic and religious groups. Because stigma is part of a belief system it is difficult to challenge, and families may attempt to hide their negative feelings related to mental illness and their fears of being discriminated against by others in their community. For these reasons, it is essential that mental health providers be professionally and culturally competent.

Provider Competencies

To support caregivers, there are three core competencies that clinicians must possess: understanding and awareness of impact of stigma on accessing interventions, knowledge of symptoms of mental illness (e.g., negative symptoms) to be able to link families with educational resources, and the ability to access and network housing resources. Let's look at these in detail.

Interventions That Challenge the Effects of Stigma for Caregivers

Clinicians and other health professionals have long faced the challenges of stigma in mental illness, which many consider the most difficult obstacle to families. Understanding what caregivers and families are experiencing is the first step in overcoming the harmful effects of stigma. Depending on a family's cultural background, mental illness in a family can result in a great deal of real and perceived discrimination, not only against the identified patient but also against the entire family. Parent caregivers may see the way neighbors avoid their ill child or how their other child's friends have quickly become former friends. The shunning of their family member can be an emotionally difficult process to witness, and caregivers can feel the pain of rejection along with the person they are caring for. One unfortunate reaction is for caregivers to remove the ill family member from treatment to avoid the label "mentally ill." This happens all too often; the shame of having a person in the family with a mental illness may be so strong for people from some cultures that caregivers fail to access needed services (Kokanovic, Petersen, & Klimidis, 2006; Magana et al., 2007).

Although there are no confirmed methods for overcoming stigma, here are several interventions that are widely thought to help:

• Reducing depression in caregivers can result in lower levels of perceived stigma. Counseling and referrals for medication assessment can help.

• Increasing contact with people who have mental illness reduces stigma. There is some evidence that increased contact reduces fear of the person with the illness. Clinicians can encourage caregivers to include the ill family member in social gatherings.

• Meeting with other caregivers in groups or organizations such as the National Alliance on Mental Illness can reduce feelings of being stigmatized.

• Accessing needed services can reduce stress and burden, which is likely to lower perceived stigma. The feeling that someone cares makes a positive difference in stigma reduction (Mason & Miller, 2006).

• Providing access to documents, such as the Surgeon General's report on stigma and mental illness, is an excellent resource for family caregivers and is listed in the resource section of this chapter.

Understanding Mental Illness and Linking Caregiver to Resources

To help caregivers through the confusing array of symptoms and social deficits associated with severe mental illness, clinicians must first possess their own level of competency about such illnesses. Clinicians must steep themselves in the latest knowledge about the medical and social trajectory of recovery, and how to access educational resources to be able to assist caregivers in learning about the illness and its associated features. For example, caregivers are often perplexed by an ill family member who has achieved control over positive symptoms such as hallucinations, delusions, and the like but whose behavior is lethargic, who shows a flat affect, and who displays few emotions (i.e., negative symptoms). Caregivers can lose patience with the family member, who they may view as lazy, uncaring, and even ungrateful. They may not understand that this can be a part of the person's unresolved negative symptoms. Negative symptoms can be more irritating than the acute illness symptoms because they often do not immediately respond to treatments. The same is true of untoward social skills. Caregivers may have to tolerate their family members' poor choice of discussion topics, lack of boundaries, and other behaviors that may at first seem rude. Clinicians can help caregivers access psychoeducation groups, which provide information about negative symptoms and coping mechanisms. In addition, social skills groups can help the identified patient relate more acceptably to others.

Accessing Housing Resources

Clinicians can help families learn about the housing options available to them in their local communities. An option for caregivers is to have the family member with a severe mental illness live in transitional, supportive, or supported housing (see chapter 8). Caregivers can visit at regular intervals and have the family member return home for visits. This allows the caregiving family respite while contact with the ill family member continues. Transitional housing is for people with severe mental illnesses who need a high level of structure or who may be starting to live away from their families for the first time. These group homes usually have time limits for residents with the goal of moving on to supportive or supported housing. Supportive housing offers more privacy and independence, with on-site services that residents are required to attend. Supported housing is the least structured program: residents receive in-home services but otherwise function independently. In all three models twenty-four-hour emergency care is available. Families are encouraged to maintain the relationship with their ill family member by maintaining regular contact and by providing guidance, nurturance, and sometimes financial support.

Future Directions

The challenges that families face when confronted with caring for a family member diagnosed with a severe and persistent mental illness are beyond description. Even with the support of the best behavioral health and social services, there remains a need for individualized counseling and planning. With the diagnosis comes a shift in the family relationship balance. Although it can be said that this occurs with any newly discovered illness, the progression of most severe mental illnesses is especially difficult for families to manage. A son or daughter might appear to be doing fine until the late teenage years, when he or she begins to exhibit odd behavior that worsens over time. At first there is denial—"It is a stage; it will pass"—and only later, after hearing the formal diagnosis does the shock settle in. Culturally based stigmas complicate the already-difficult to comprehend changes in the family member. When the illness affects a young person, as in the example in this chapter, the despair that parents and siblings feel can be overwhelming. This is not to negate family stresses that result in chronic or late-onset mental illnesses, but there is a special heartbreak when one learns that a young person will face a lifetime of living with a treatable but incurable disorder that changes life plans and negatively affects his or her feelings of self-worth and identity.

The bottom line is that these families need help, help that goes beyond what we in the helping professions typically offer today. Ongoing counseling to families as a group and for individuals as needed should be standard care. Financial planning should be included in counseling so that families can best provide realistically for all its members. Caregivers need to be aware of their legal rights and consumer choices, and they need to be kept up-to-date with the latest research on the mental illness that affects their family member. This requires funding to pay designated family clinicians with the skills and knowledge to work effectively with family caretakers. A competent clinical workforce trained to provide families with both clinical and concrete services is called for. The development of programs that support family caregivers may be cost effective if they reduce hospitalization costs and increase the ability of family caregivers to work outside the home.

Websites

Beacon of Hope (for spouse caregivers of people with mental illness)—http://www.lightship.org

National Alliance on Mental Illness—http://www.nami.org

National Family Caregivers Association (family resource for local government agencies)—https://www.thefamilycaregiver.org/about_nfca/

National Mental Health Association—http://www.nmha.org

The Reports of the Surgeon General—http://www.surgeongeneral.gov/library/mentalhealth/chapter1/sec1.html

Schizophrenia.com (for families and caregivers)—http://www.schizophrenia.com/index.php

Glossary

Assertive community treatment (ACT) teams: Teams of behavioral clinicians that provide services to people with severe and persistent mental illnesses in the communities where they live. Team members visit homes, monitor medications, and offer psychological and rehabilitation services with the goal of reducing rehospitalizations and increasing client functioning.

Meta-analyses: A method clinical researchers use to statistically analyze numerous studies on the same topic with the goal of coming to a reasonable conclusion on the value of an intervention. The Cochrane Reports are examples of how meta-analyses can be useful in determining the effectiveness of a variety of interventions for people with severe and persistent mental illnesses. Meta-analyses are statistical reports; individual clinical effectiveness may vary depending on the unique characteristics of patients.

Positive and negative symptoms: Positive symptoms are associated with sensory perceptions, thoughts, and behaviors that are not typically found in most people, for example, a belief that one's ideas are being taken out of one's head and broadcast on television. This would be considered a bizarre delusion and would qualify as a positive symptom. Other examples include hearing voices that others do not hear or exhibiting extreme, disorganized behavior. Negative symptoms are associated with a lack of abilities or emotions that most people are able to demonstrate. Negative symptoms often present in clusters of symptoms, including lack of energy, motivation, emotional expression, and general loss of interest in things that a person once found pleasurable. An example would be a formerly active person not leaving the house all weekend because of lack of interest or motivation. Negative symptoms are especially difficult to treat and often cause a great deal of frustration for caregivers.

Psychoeducation: The process of educating people about the various aspects of mental illness, including symptoms, functioning, use of medications, early warning signs of relapses, and treatment goals and options. Psychoeducation can take place in individual sessions, in groups, and with families. The family member with the illness and caregivers may participate in any one of these formats, depending on choice and availability.

References

American Psychiatric Association. (2000). *Diagnostic and statistical manual of mental disorders* (4th ed., text rev.). Washington, DC: Author.

Curtin, T., & Lilley, H. (2001). *Caring across community, 2000, 2001: Carer education project for carers from culturally and linguistically diverse backgrounds.* Canberra: Carers Association of Australia.

Irving, C. B., Adams, C. E., & Rice, K. (2006). Crisis intervention for people with severe mental illnesses. *Cochrane Database of Systematic Reviews, 4*(Art. No. CD001087). doi: 10.1002/14651858.CD001087.pub3.

Jewell, T. C., & Stein, C. H. (2002). Parental influence on sibling caregiving for people with severe mental illness. *Community Mental Health Journal, 38*(1), 17–33.

Kokanovic, R., Petersen, A., & Klimidis, S. (2006). "Nobody can help me . . . I am living through it alone": Experiences of caring for people diagnosed with mental illness in ethno-cultural and linguistic minority communities. *Journal of Immigrant and Minority Health, 8*(2), 125–135.

Lee, J. A. B. (1996). The empowerment approach to social work practice. In F. J. Turner (Ed.), *Social work treatment* (4th ed., pp. 218–249). New York: Free Press.

Magana, S. M., Ramirez Garcia, J. I., Hernandez, M. G., & Cortez, R. (2007). Psychological distress among Latino family caregivers of adults with schizophrenia: The roles of burden and stigma. *Psychiatric Services, 58*(3), 378–384.

Malone, D., Marriott, S., Newton-Howes, G., Simmonds, S., & Tyrer, P. (2007). Community mental health teams (CMHTs) for people with severe mental illnesses and disordered personality. *Cochrane Database of Systematic Reviews, 3*(Art. No. CD000270). doi: 10.1002/14651858.CD000270.pub2.

Mason, S. E., & Miller, R. (2006). Stigma and schizophrenia: Directions in student training. *Journal of Teaching in Social Work, 26*(1–2), 73–91.

McFarlane, W. R. (2002). *Multifamily groups in the treatment of severe psychiatric disorders.* New York: Guilford Press.

McFarlane, W. R., & Cook, W. L. (2007) Family expressed emotion prior to onset of psychosis. *Family Process, 46*(2), 185–197.

McFarlane, W. R., Dixon, L., Lukens, E., & Lucksted, A. (2003). Family psychoeducation and schizophrenia: A review of the literature. *Journal of Marital and Family Therapy, 29*(3), 223–245.

Miller, R., & Mason, S. E. (2005). Shame and guilt in first episode schizophrenia. *Journal of Contemporary Psychotherapy, 35*(2), 211–221.

Murray-Swank, A. B., Lucksted, A., Medoff, D. R., Yang, Y., Wohlheiter, K., & Dixon, L. B. (2006). Religiosity, psychosocial adjustment, and subjective burden of persons who care for those with mental illness. *Psychiatric Services, 57*(3), 361–365.

Pekkala, E. T., & Merinder, L. B. (2002). Psychoeducation for schizophrenia. *Cochrane Database of Systematic Reviews, 2*(Art. No. CD002831). doi: 10.1002/14651858.CD002831.

Shankar, J., & Muthuswamy, S. S. (2007). Support needs of family caregivers of people who experience mental illness and the role of mental health services. *Families in Society, 88*(2), 302–310.

PART IV
Education-Oriented Best Practices

Education-oriented best practices are those interventions and strategies that focus not only on enhancing individuals' academic education but also on educational opportunities tied to personal growth, interpersonal skill development, and job acquisition. The goal of educationally oriented best practices is to provide skill sets that increase functioning through a variety of meaningful activities so that individuals with mental health conditions are ultimately successful and satisfied in their environments.

Part 4 introduces the reader to three prominent best practices that emphasize education as the core element of service. These include psychiatric rehabilitation, supported education, and psychoeducation.

In chapter 15, "Psychiatric Rehabilitation," Anthony, Forbess, and Furlong-Norman discuss the history of the field of psychiatric rehabilitation and its pivotal role in setting the stage for promoting the recovery philosophy; full community integration; and aiming for quality of life through opportunities for learning, living, and working. In chapter 16, "Supported Education," Unger continues the dialogue on the value of education by describing supported education as a means to helping people develop careers through the use of personal support and coaching. In chapter 17, "Psychoeducation," Walsh describes the various ways that psychoeducation programs enhance participants' education, support, and development of coping skills.

15

Psychiatric Rehabilitation

*William Anthony, Rick Forbess, and
Kathleen Furlong-Norman*

Psychiatric rehabilitation began to emerge as a field of practice and study during the 1970s as a response to the failure of the deinstitutionalization movement, which discharged large numbers of state hospital patients to an unsupportive community. This chapter defines psychiatric rehabilitation, identifies several of the research-based principles on which the psychiatric rehabilitation field is grounded, and describes the empirically based processes and programs that constitute the field and the provider competencies needed to practice most effectively. The chapter also advances challenges to the future growth of the field. We begin this chapter with a case review of Jim (see box 15.1) and his experience with a psychiatric rehabilitation program that supported his interest in attending college.

Box 15.1. Case Study: Jim

Jim is a thirty-five-year-old man who lives with his parents. He has been hospitalized for psychiatric care on six occasions over the past ten years and is currently participating in a community-based psychiatric rehabilitation program four days a week. Except for six months in a college dormitory before his first psychiatric hospitalization, he has lived his entire life with his parents. His work experience has been sporadic and limited to low-paying, nonskilled jobs.

Supported by encouragement from his clinician and other staff, Jim became hopeful about returning to college, and he decided to make that dream the focus of his rehabilitation plan. Initially, he and the staff focused services on gathering information about two aspects of college about which Jim was most concerned. Jim wanted to know about the types of supports that were provided on campus for students with a psychiatric disability and about average classroom sizes. He and his clinician

---

used the Internet and telephone interviews to learn about these two characteristics of several colleges. Heartened by what he learned, Jim decided that he was interested in selecting the college he'd like to attend. With his clinician's assistance, Jim applied a step-by-step decision-making process that included gathering detailed information about three colleges he was particularly interested in and comparing each against his personal criteria for an ideal college setting. After several weeks, he had set his overall rehabilitation goal to begin attending the local community college on a part-time basis in a year.

Jim and his clinician then turned their attention to assessing Jim's ability to use skills and the availability of supports he'd need to function as a part-time student at the community college. On the basis of an analysis of the behavioral expectations for functioning as a student at the college and of Jim's college experience before his first psychiatric hospitalization, they identified and evaluated nine critical skills and six critical supports. For the following several months the clinician and Jim were involved in skill teaching or support development activities. For instance, Jim learned the skill of recognizing stressful situations and practiced applying that skill in situations similar to those he might encounter as a student at the community college. Also, an agreement was brokered with Jim's older brother to be available on a weekly basis to provide encouragement if this support was requested. After Jim began attending classes, the skill and support assessment and development continued on a less frequent basis in response to new or ongoing challenges that Jim and his clinician found to be critical to his ongoing success as a student.

Background

The mission of the field of psychiatric rehabilitation is to help persons with long-term psychiatric disabilities increase their functioning so that they are successful and satisfied in the environments of their choice, with the least amount of ongoing professional intervention (Farkas & Anthony, 1989). The major methods by which this mission is accomplished involve developing the specific skills and/or supports (resources) that people with psychiatric disabilities need to reach their chosen goals. As psychiatric rehabilitation services and concepts have become more common, the necessity of developing a standard definition of psychiatric rehabilitation became apparent. On September 29, 2007, the board of directors of the US Psychiatric Rehabilitation Association (2007, n.p.), the major professional association of the field of psychiatric rehabilitation, approved the following definition:

> Psychiatric rehabilitation promotes recovery, full community integration and improved quality of life for persons who have been diagnosed with any mental health condition that seriously impairs their ability to lead meaningful lives. Psychiatric rehabilitation services are collaborative, person directed and individualized. These services are an essential element of the health care and human services spectrum, and should be evidence-based. They focus on helping individuals develop skills and access resources needed to increase their capacity to be successful and satisfied in the living, working, learning, and social environments of their choice.

Adults diagnosed with severe mental illnesses, such as schizophrenia, bipolar disorder, and major depression, are the primary recipients of psychiatric rehabilitation services. Psychiatric rehabilitation focuses on persons who have experienced severe psychiatric disabilities rather than on individuals who are simply dissatisfied, unhappy, or socially "disadvantaged." Persons with psychiatric disability have diagnosed mental illnesses that limit their capacity to perform certain tasks and functions (e.g., interacting with family and friends, interviewing for a job) and their ability to perform in certain roles (e.g., worker, student, resident).

The psychiatric rehabilitation field developed as a response to the tragedies of the deinstitutionalization movement that started during the 1950s. In essence, deinstitutionalization accomplished a single outcome: the transfer of patients who were severely mentally ill to the community, a relatively easy task in comparison to the goals of rehabilitation. In essence, deinstitutionalization opened the doors of the institutions and literally gave people a prescription for their medicine when they left. Rehabilitation attempts to open the doors of the community and help people figuratively develop a prescription for their lives (Anthony, Cohen, Farkas, & Gagne, 2002).

Theoretical Perspective

Recovery is the theoretical framework that shapes the core foundation of psychiatric rehabilitation. This is a perspective and concept that has been supported by ten longitudinal studies of persons with mental illness both in the United States and abroad (Corrigan, Mueser, Bond, Drake, & Solomon, 2008). By definition, recovery is the process of pursuing a fulfilling and contributing life regardless of the difficulties one faces; restoring and continuing enhancement of a positive identity;

making personally meaningful relationships; and finding supportive environments that provide hope, empowerment, choices, and opportunities that promote people's reaching their full potential (Recovery Advisory Committee, 2007–2008).

Using this definition, recovery is a framework in which psychiatric rehabilitation supports the development of skills and supports that can be implemented in a variety of program models, in many different places or settings, and by most mental health disciplines. That is to say, the psychiatric rehabilitation process can be implemented in any program model, any location or setting, or by any person, as long as the primary outcome is to help people become more successful and satisfied in living, working, learning, and social environments of their choice.

Principles

The research underlying the principles of psychiatric rehabilitation has been reviewed regularly (e.g., Anthony et al., 2002; Corrigan et al., 2008). The following principles are basic to the practice of psychiatric rehabilitation and operate independently of both the settings in which they are practiced and the professional disciplines of practitioners:

• *Principle of promoting client skills and environmental supports*—Interventions that attempt to improve either the person or the person's environment are the time-tested double focus of rehabilitation—be it physical or psychiatric rehabilitation. The focus on changing the person typically involves learning and/or applying the specific skills needed to interact more effectively in an environment. The focus on environmental supports typically involves accessing and/or modifying the environment so it accommodates or supports the person's present level of functioning. The psychiatric rehabilitation approach is based on research that indicates that a person's skills, not symptoms, relate most strongly to rehabilitation outcome. In addition, rehabilitation research has shown that persons with psychiatric disabilities can learn a variety of physical, emotional, and intellectual skills regardless of their symptomatology. Furthermore, these skills, when properly integrated with support for the use of the skills in the community, can have a significant impact on rehabilitation outcome. Psychiatric rehabilitation programs vary in how systematically they approach skill building and environmental support. Skill building and environmental support may be informal and experiential or planned and systematic.

- *Principle of comprehensive outcomes*—Psychiatric rehabilitation aims to improve residential, educational, social, and vocational outcomes for persons with psychiatric disabilities. Rehabilitation helps people gain or regain valued roles in society, such as tenant, homemaker, parent, community member, student, and worker. Rehabilitation research studies have confirmed that the kind of practical outcomes that most people with psychiatric disabilities want reflect these roles and settings (e.g., decent homes, meaningful jobs, a viable social life, educational opportunities).

- *Principle of full participation*—Psychiatric rehabilitation is a person-driven process that includes an active partnership between the service recipient and the practitioner throughout all the phases of rehabilitation. This active partnership and involvement requires rehabilitation procedures that can be explained to and understood by the client. The rehabilitation intervention cannot be mysterious. The practitioner must constantly try to demystify rehabilitation. People do not get rehabilitated; they must be "active and courageous participants in their own rehabilitation" (Deegan, 1988, p. 12). Furthermore, persons in a psychiatric rehabilitation program are viewed as having the right to choose; they are not forced into a specific environment. Aside from the inherent decency of valuing self-determination, it is practical to have people with psychiatric disabilities choose where they live, learn, socialize, and/or work. Research has consistently shown that persons with psychiatric disabilities, like all people, are more apt to strive to succeed when they have been actively involved and supported in making their own choices.

- *Principle of complementary treatments*—Long-term drug treatment is an often necessary but rarely sufficient complement to a rehabilitation intervention. Psychiatric rehabilitation practitioners need to be aware of this principle because, in the past several decades, drug treatment has been provided to support almost everyone with a psychiatric disability. The research literature is clear on this principle: drug treatment without an accompanying rehabilitation intervention cannot bring about rehabilitation outcome, and that holds for the newer antipsychotics as well (Swartz, Perkins, Stroup, & Davis, 2007). The lack of a demonstrated relationship between drug treatment alone and rehabilitation outcome should come as no surprise. Drug treatment does not develop a person's skills, energy, and environmental supports necessary for living, learning, socializing, and working in the community. Although the effect of drug therapy on symptomatic behavior may be viewed as preparing the person for rehabilitation, and particularly so with newer medications, the relationship between drug therapy and rehabilitation also may be viewed in a slightly different way. A rehabilitation intervention can be conceived of as supportive to the withdrawal or reduction of drug therapy. That is, once drug therapy has helped prepare the person for rehabilitation, a successful rehabilitation intervention might prepare the person for the reduction of drug therapy (see chapter 2).

Steps for Implementing Psychiatric Rehabilitation

The field of psychiatric rehabilitation has accumulated an evidence base around the psychiatric rehabilitation process, the competencies of psychiatric rehabilitation practitioners to implement the rehabilitation process, and the various psychiatric rehabilitation programs that are structured to achieve rehabilitation outcomes. Figure 15.1 provides an overview of the diagnostic, planning, and intervention process of psychiatric rehabilitation.

Figure 15.1. Overview of the DPI Planning Process of Psychiatric Rehabilitation

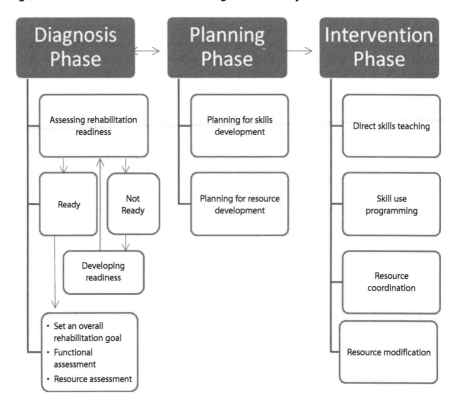

The psychiatric rehabilitation process is based on research literature that shows that it is the person's self determined goals and the presence of the skills and supports necessary to reach those goals, rather than the person's diagnosis and symptomatology that relates most strongly to rehabilitation outcomes. Anthony et al. (2002) have summarized the research literature relevant to the psychiatric rehabilitation process and are generally credited by other psychiatric rehabilitation researchers (Corrigan et al., 2008) with conceptualizing the psychiatric rehabilitation process. The psychiatric rehabilitation process can be best understood by breaking down the process into three phases: diagnostic, planning, and intervention.

The diagnostic phase involves the practitioner (or other form of helper) helping the person to self-determine his or her readiness for rehabilitation, to set goal(s), and to evaluate his or her skill and support strengths and deficits in relation to the goal(s). In contrast to the traditional psychiatric diagnosis that describes symptomatology, the rehabilitation diagnosis yields a behavioral description of the person's current skills and an operational definition of the current level of support needed to be successful in the chosen residential, educational, social, and/or vocational environments. The diagnostic information enables the person to develop a rehabilitation plan in the planning phase. A rehabilitation plan differs from most treatment planning in that the goal of a treatment plan focuses mostly on reducing symptoms. A rehabilitation plan specifies how to develop the person's skills and/or supports to achieve the person's rehabilitation goals. The plan is similar to what sometimes is called an individualized service plan, the major difference being its identification of high-priority skill and resource development objectives and specific interventions for each objective, rather than simply identifying potential service providers or program activities. In the intervention phase, the rehabilitation plan is implemented to achieve the rehabilitation goal(s), by changing the person's skills and/or environmental supports.

What's the Evidence?

The psychiatric rehabilitation field has begun to establish an empirical basis, not only for the aforementioned process and principles but also for specific outcomes and program models that attempt to achieve rehabilitation outcomes. In terms of outcomes, a systematic review of the research literature by Michon, van Weeghel, Kroon, and Schene (2005) found positive results for employment, work performance, and social functioning when psychiatric vocational rehabilitation was offered to individuals with mental health conditions. Two of the evidence-based program models that are most relevant to psychiatric rehabilitation outcomes are supported employment (see chapter 10; Bond et al., 2001) and assertive community treatment (see chapter 7; Mueser, Bond, Drake, & Resnick, 1998). As Corrigan et al. (2008) have detailed, these evidence-based program models are replicable and possess fidelity scales, which measure the degree to which a program meets the empirical and operationalized standards of the program model. In addition, implementation resource kits have been created to facilitate dissemination and replication.

Assessment and Evaluation

The targets of psychiatric rehabilitation outcome assessment are measures of people's vocational, residential, educational, and/or social outcomes. Psychiatric rehabilitation outcomes are defined as the level of success and satisfaction of individuals in the environment of their choice. Success is measured in terms of the person's ability to respond to the demands of the environment, and satisfaction is measured in terms of the person's experience in the environment. The types of outcome measurement currently used indicate increasing sophistication of outcome measures. For example, simple yes-no measures of whether the person is employed have been complemented by measures of the types of employment (prevocational, transitional, supported, and independent), satisfaction with income, productivity, worker self-esteem, and job tenure. With respect to residential functioning, simple measures of institutional recidivism have been all but replaced by counts of number of days in the community, types of community housing, satisfaction with community life, degree of independent living, instrumental role functioning, and so forth. Overall measures that cut across the individual environments reflect the values of psychiatric rehabilitation and include measures of quality of life, empowerment, and recovery.

Implementation Issues

Distilling the experience of three decades of psychiatric rehabilitation dissemination across all continents except Africa, the Center for Psychiatric Rehabilitation has identified three main categories of focus important to a comprehensive implementation plan for introducing psychiatric rehabilitation interventions: culture, commitment, and capacity (Farkas, Ashcroft, & Anthony, 2008). Farkas and Anthony (2010) emphasize the importance of organizing an implementation plan that assesses and then enhances culture while simultaneously ensuring that the organizational structures and ways of "doing business" are consistent with the overall spirit and intent of psychiatric rehabilitation. For example, including service recipients in the design, delivery, and evaluation of services is a critical component of a recovery-oriented service culture like psychiatric rehabilitation (Farkas, Gagne, Anthony, & Chamberlin, 2005). Culture also includes elements related to the introduction of change (e.g., the extent to which an organization is characterized by openness to learning, willingness to entertain challenges, and effective problem solving; Farkas, 1990).

Commitment involves ensuring that all major actors are willing and able to support implementation efforts and activities. Difficulties in stakeholder support (e.g., families, individuals with lived experience, legislators, funding bodies) often reflect inadequate attention being paid to these groups when introducing and implementing innovations. Effectively implementing psychiatric rehabilitation requires the alignment of commitment among the leadership of the critical stakeholder groups so that financial, political, and community support work in concert to ensure implementation of the best practice (Drake, Bond, & Essock, 2009).

Capacity reflects aspects of implementation related to staff knowledge, attitudes, and skills in delivering psychiatric rehabilitation best practice. The Center for Psychiatric Rehabilitation has developed competency-based psychiatric rehabilitation training programs for providers that cover specific skills to enhance the capacity of providers to deliver psychiatric rehabilitation. Practitioner skills that can be taught and implemented in the delivery of psychiatric rehabilitation include how to assess and develop readiness for change, how to help people determine the valued roles they want, how to assess skills and supports relative to a person's valued role aspirations, and how to promote skill generalization.

Provider Competencies

As stated, the practitioner's ability to involve people in the rehabilitation process is facilitated by the practitioner's level of knowledge and skills (i.e., the technology of psychiatric rehabilitation practice). As summarized by Corrigan et al. (2008), there have been numerous attempts to identify provider competencies for psychiatric rehabilitation. However, the mental health research literature has not developed any empirical evidence about what particular knowledge, attitudes, and skills make for an effective psychiatric rehabilitation practitioner.

Anthony (2004) has taken a different approach to the empirical question of what competencies are necessary for effective psychiatric rehabilitation practice. With respect to the field of severe mental illnesses, Anthony (2004) argues that findings in the behavioral science literature on how people in general are helped to change and grow meets the definition of clinically relevant research for the field of psychiatric rehabilitation. Empirically based principles of how people without severe mental illnesses change should also guide the work in the area of helping people with severe mental illnesses to change and grow. Behavioral science has found that people are more apt to change positively in the context of a positive relationship, when they set their own goals, when they are taught skills, when they receive support, when they have positive expectations or hope for the future, and when they believe in their self-efficacy.

This behavioral science research on the facilitators of positive change not only supports many of the components of the psychiatric rehabilitation process as previously described but also suggests the helper competencies that underlie these facilitators of change (e.g., interpersonal skills, goal-setting skills, teaching skills, skills of providing personal support, inspiring skills, and functional assessment skills) (Anthony et al., 2002)

Future Challenges

The past two decades have witnessed an explosion of interest in psychiatric rehabilitation, and as a result, there is now considerable agreement on the fundamental philosophy and process of psychiatric rehabilitation, a significant body of research forms the knowledge base of a credible psychiatric rehabilitation field, model service programs have been demonstrated and disseminated, funding for psychiatric rehabilitation services is provided by Medicaid and departments of mental health, preservice and in-service training programs are in place, and a practitioner technology exists. Yet many current challenges to the further development of the psychiatric rehabilitation field remain. Three of the most fundamental challenges are workforce development, funding, and research.

Unfortunately, workforce development programs have not kept pace with the emerging knowledge base of psychiatric rehabilitation. Preservice programs exist, but not enough to meet the demand, which results in most practitioners developing their knowledge base through experience or agency in-service training programs. As a result, the ability of practitioners to implement the psychiatric rehabilitation process and the leadership capacity to implement best-practice and evidence-based programs is not sufficient (Anthony & Huckshorn, 2008). On a positive note, the US Psychiatric Rehabilitation Association has developed a certification exam for psychiatric rehabilitation practitioners. More than two thousand practitioners have become certified psychiatric rehabilitation practitioners, and this credential (CPRP) has been recognized in regulations in more than a dozen states.

At one time, state and local mental health authorities provided the little money available for psychiatric rehabilitation services. As Medicaid has become a major source of funding for psychiatric rehabilitation services, practitioners need to ensure that the services they provide are reimbursable under Medicaid. Medicaid audits are placing the field on notice that it may have to do a better job of justifying psychiatric rehabilitation services within the Medicaid regulations. Of course, such expert justification necessitates a workforce knowledgeable of psychiatric rehabilitation processes and programs.

Citing the need for more meaningful and rigorous research may be stating the obvious. However, this challenge may be the one that is most easily addressed. In the past several decades, the research focus on psychiatric rehabilitation has increased tremendously. Furthermore, the knowledge base developed in other fields is being translated into psychiatric rehabilitation practice, particularly the implications of behavioral science findings for the psychiatric rehabilitation process and related practitioner competencies.

As the knowledge base continues to expand, the other two challenges must also be met to developing reasonable funding and a more skilled workforce. Each of these challenges complements the others. Progress in all these areas is needed for the psychiatric rehabilitation field to reach its potential in helping people with psychiatric disabilities reach their potential.

Websites

Center for Mental Health Services—http://www.samhsa.gov/about/cmhs.aspx

Center for Psychiatric Rehabilitation—http://www.bu.edu/cpr

US Psychiatric Rehabilitation Association—http://www.uspra.org

Glossary

Psychiatric rehabilitation: Psychiatric rehabilitation promotes recovery, full community integration, and improved quality of life for persons who have been diagnosed with any mental health condition that seriously impairs their ability to lead meaningful lives.

Psychiatric rehabilitation process: The psychiatric rehabilitation process includes the diagnostic, planning, and intervention phases, which focus on helping individuals develop skills and access resources needed to increase their capacity to be successful and satisfied in the living, working, learning, and social environments of their choice.

Psychiatric rehabilitation services: Psychiatric rehabilitation services are collaborative, person directed, and individualized. These services are an essential element of the health-care and human services spectrum, and they should be evidence based.

References

Anthony, W. A. (2004). Expanding the evidence base in an era of recovery. *Psychiatric Rehabilitation Journal, 27*, 1–2.

Anthony, W. A., Cohen, M. R., Farkas, M., & Gagne, C. (2002). *Psychiatric rehabilitation* (2nd ed.). Boston: Center for Psychiatric Rehabilitation.

Anthony, W. A., & Huckshorn, K. (2008) *Principled leadership*. Boston: Center for Psychiatric Rehabilitation

Bond, G. R., Becker, D. R., Drake, R. E., Rapp, C. A., Meisler, N., Lehman, A. F., et al. (2001). Implementing supported employment as an evidence-based practice. *Psychiatric Services, 52*, 313–322.

Corrigan, P. W., Mueser, K. T., Bond, G. R., Drake, R. E., & Solomon, P. (2008). *Principles and practice of psychiatric rehabilitation: An empirical approach.* New York: Guilford Press.

Deegan, P. E. (1988). Recovery: The lived experience of rehabilitation. *Psychosocial Rehabilitation Journal, 11*, 11–19.

Drake, R. E., Bond, G., & Essock, S. M. (2009). Implementing evidence based practices for people with schizophrenia. *Schizophrenia Bulletin, 35*, 704–713.

Farkas, M. (1990, April 3). *Strategic planning and system change: Serving the severely psychiatrically disabled.* Seminar presented at the Netherlands Institute of Mental Health, Utrecht, Netherlands.

Farkas, M., & Anthony, W. A. (1989) *Psychiatric rehabilitation programs: Putting theory into practice.* Baltimore: Johns Hopkins University Press.

Farkas, M., & Anthony, W. A. (2010) Psychiatric rehabilitation interventions: A review. *International Review of Psychiatry, 22,* 114–129.

Farkas, M., Ashcroft, L., & Anthony, W. A. (2008). The 3 C's for recovery services. *Behavioral Healthcare, 28,* 26–27.

Farkas, M., Gagne, C., Anthony, W. A., & Chamberlin, J. (2005). Implementing recovery oriented evidence based programs: Identifying the critical dimensions. *Community Mental Health Journal, 41,* 141–158.

Michon, H. W., van Weeghel, J., Kroon, H., & Schene, A. H. (2005). Person-related predictors of employment outcome after participation in psychiatric vocational rehabilitation programs: A systematic review. *Social Psychiatry and Psychiatric Epidemiology, 40*(5), 408–416.

Mueser, K. T., Bond, G. R., Drake, R. E., & Resnick, S. G. (1998). Models of community care for severe mental illness: A review of research on case management. *Schizophrenia Bulletin, 24,* 37–74.

Recovery Advisory Committee, Philadelphia Department of Behavioral Health (2007–2008). *County mental health plan.* Philadelphia: Author.

Swartz, M. S., Perkins, D. O., Stroup, T. S., & Davis, S. M. (2007) . Effects of antipsychotic medication on psychosocial functioning in patients with chronic schizophrenia: Findings from the NIMH CATIE study. *American Journal of Psychiatry, 164,* 428–436.

US Psychiatric Rehabilitation Association. (2007). *About the US Psychiatric Association, Boston, MA.* Retrieved from http://www.uspra.org.

16

Supported Education

Karen V. Unger

Most people with a serious mental illness are typically unemployed or underemployed, and many live on the margins of society. Although supported employment is available for many clients, it seldom provides jobs that develop into careers. Supported education helps people return to school and develop skills so that they can find work that leads to upward economic mobility. Components of supported education include personal support and coaching, as well as the use of a variety of mental health and community resources. Research has demonstrated that supported education is a very effective intervention to improve recovery and employment outcomes. We begin this chapter with a case review of John (see box 16.1) and his first experience working with a supported-education (SEd) specialist who assisted him in returning to college.

Box 16.1. Case Study: John

John is a twenty-nine-year-old man with a diagnosis of paranoid schizophrenia and multiple-substance dependence that is in remission. He is unmarried, living in supported housing, and receiving Supplemental Security Income. His work history includes janitorial work, clerking in a minimart, and other low-level jobs. He is a high school graduate and became ill his first year in college. His family is very supportive and would like to see him return to school. He has tried taking classes at the local community college but has never completed a course. John would like to get a BA degree, but he says that school makes him too anxious, and he has trouble concentrating and finishing his assignments. His new caseworker at the mental health center referred him to the supported education (SE) program.

John completed an SE program application and discussed his goal of returning to school. He and the SE specialist examined his strengths and needs and developed a plan to move forward. The local community college seemed a good place to begin. The SE specialist helped John complete the financial aid application and the application for admission. He took the placement tests and registered for classes. The SE specialist and John visited the office of disabled student services and requested accommodations. After documenting his disability, John asked for books on tape and extended time for tests.

John and the SE specialist met weekly and checked in by phone or computer every day. Sometimes the SE specialist helped him with a paper or to study for a test. John attended a student support group and made several friends. He and the SE specialist celebrated the completion of his first two courses, in which he earned an A and a B. He has registered for two classes again next term. He attributes much of his success to the help he received from the SE specialist.

Background

Supported education helps people with a mental illness participate in an education program so that they can receive the education and training they need to achieve their learning and recovery goals and/or become gainfully employed in the job or career of their choice. It includes adult basic education, General Education Development (GED), training programs, and colleges and universities.

Supported education began in the early 1980s, when it became clear that young adults did not want the same day-treatment options available to older adults. It was also clear from research that illness had interrupted the education of many. To address these needs, the first supported-education program was begun at Boston University. The pilot program implementation was successful and the outcomes promising. Over time, new programs were developed at other institutions, and three implementation models of supported education emerged: the closed classroom, on-site support, and mobile support (Unger, 1999). Figure 16.1 shows the similarities and differences across the models.

Figure 16.1. **Similarities and Differences of Supported Education Implementation Models**

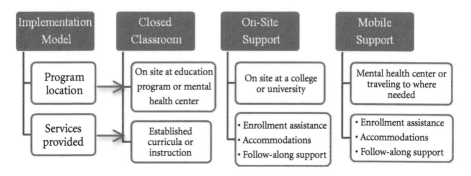

Theoretical Perspective

Supported education derives its theoretical framework from the field of psychiatric rehabilitation (see chapter 15), which supports the belief that people learn new skills with personal support and appropriate resources.

Principles

Supported education is based on a set of principles from which the practice flows. The principles are as follows:

- *Principle of access*—Access to and participation in an education program is the goal.
- *Principle of choice*—Eligibility is based on consumer choice.
- *Principle of timeliness*—Supported-education services begin soon after the person expresses interest.
- *Principle of integration*—Supported education is integrated with ongoing treatment.
- *Principle of continuous support*—Follow-along supports are continuous.
- *Principle of preference*—Consumer preferences guide services.
- *Principle of strengths based.* Supported education is strengths based and promotes growth and hope.

- *Principle of recovery*—The recovery philosophy (see chapter 12) is a guiding component of supported education and is an ongoing process facilitated by meaningful roles.

Steps for Implementing Supported Education

How and where will supported education services be provided? It depends on the setting and the kind of services delivered, and whether it is a closed classroom, an on-site model, or a mobile support model. Each implementation model provides services in a slightly different way. In some cases, services may be combined, as when an introductory or reentry class is provided at the college, but the support services come from a mental health center. Either college staff or a mental health practitioner may provide the instruction. This section reviews nine steps associated with providing supported education services. They are described in the following sections.

Step 1: Referral

A typical supported-education intervention begins when a prospective student is referred to an SEd specialist. An initial interview, often with the referring case manager, is scheduled to determine the student's commitment and readiness to begin an education program. Although the supported-education program is open to all students, a return to college or a postsecondary training program, particularly where financial aid is involved, requires client readiness to take on the responsibility. A program application can be used to assist in this determination if the application reflects the student's education experiences and motivation.

Step 2: Developing an Education Goal

Once the prospective student has been accepted into the supported-education program, he or she decides on an education goal through a process of exploring interests and abilities. Many colleges have career centers that can assist the student in exploring career options. Other career exploration activities are available on the Internet. A client may already have a goal in mind and be ready to enroll in school as soon he or she begins the supported-education program. In either case, the goal may change as the student gains experience.

Step 3: Applying for Admission

Once the student has determined an education goal, the appropriate institution or program needs to be identified. In many cases, a community college is the most appropriate place to begin. The admission process is fairly simple and can often be done online. College application often goes hand in hand with placement tests. Placement tests determine the level of various classes, such as math and English, for which the student is eligible.

Step 4: Applying for Financial Aid

Applying for financial aid may be done before or concurrent with the application process. Sooner is better, as more money may be available earlier. Completing the Free Application for Federal Student Aid (FAFSA) can be a daunting task, and most students need assistance in doing so. The FAFSA determines eligibility for a Pell Grant or other federal financial awards.

Step 5: Registering for Classes and Disability Services

After applying for financial aid and being accepted to the school, the student needs to register. Initial course selection may be determined by placement tests or with the help of an academic adviser at the school. This is also the best time to discuss accommodations. To receive accommodation, a student often must register with the Disability Services Office and provide verification of his or her disability.

Step 6: Learning about the Campus

Students new to campus may benefit from a campus orientation and tour by the SEd specialist. It is helpful to familiarize them with the location of their classrooms, the library, the career and resource center, the student union, and other resources available on campus. This is also a good time to review add and drop policies, withdrawal policies, management of financial aid, and campus rules.

Step 7: Integrating Services

An individual service or treatment plan is often incorporated into the client's case record if the client is receiving services from a mental health agency. It may be part of an overall treatment plan with education goals integrated with other treatment goals.

Step 8: Developing an Education Service Plan

Students who choose to return to school will bring with them academic skills and strengths from their previous experiences. Examples of strengths include the ability to complete assignments, getting along with teachers, asking clarifying questions, and a love of learning. Taking tests, ability to concentrate, or writing papers may be academic issues that require special attention and accommodations.

Issues related to coping with the challenges of returning to school will also need attention. Managing general anxiety, symptom management, lifestyle behaviors, and making friends are examples. Discussing where the problems occur and how to address them is also recorded on the education service plan.

Resources are another area for assessment. Resources include people, places, or things that make it possible for the student to stay in school. Does the student have the support of friends and family? Can he or she buy books, use public transportation, obtain child care, enroll in Supplemental Security Income and Social Security Disability Income, and find appropriate housing? The SEd specialist will manage resource issues on campus. The specialist does not provide therapy but may work closely on school-related issues with a case manager and therapist from the mental health center.

An education service plan includes activities to address the academic and coping issues that the student presents related to school, and it names interventions to address the issues. The plan lists the resources needed and how they will be obtained. It also may list tasks that the SEd specialist will perform, such as wake-up calls. The student's special tasks are also part of the plan. As the semester or quarter of the school year passes, the plan is reassessed and updated. The reassessment becomes an evaluation process to determine what is working and what needs to be revisited.

Step 9: Providing Support

Students who have received supported-education services most often cite personal support as the single most important factor that helps them stay in school. Personal support means that the student has a personal relationship with an SEd specialist whom he or she trusts and can count on for help. Activities like assisting the student to apply for financial aid, registering for classes, advocating for the student with the Disability Services Office to receive accommodations, wake-up calls, accompaniment to classes, and monitoring of homework are examples of supportive activities. Underlying these activities is the fundamental belief of the SEd specialist that the student is a capable and valued person who can succeed.

The relationship between the SEd specialist and the student is often more informal than that with a therapist or a case manager. The SEd specialist is a teacher, advocate, problem solver, mentor, and support person. The SEd specialist is personally invested in the success of the student and will do what is reasonable, helpful, and clinically responsible to help the student succeed. The boundaries between the two are dictated by caring, friendly engagement while maintaining professional standards.

The student is the person most responsible for his or her success. Completing assignments, managing finances, maintaining a healthy lifestyle, being personally responsible, and showing up at class are some of the student's tasks. Although providing assistance and support are important for the SEd specialists, if they are doing more work than the student, it is time for them to reassess their role and the student's commitment.

Roles of Institutions, Services, Funders, and Policies

In supported education, educational institutions and mental health agencies have unique roles. Although few institutions provide the wide range of services that individuals receiving supported education need, there are three that schools are required to provide: academic counseling, financial aid, and reasonable accommodations. In this section, we further examine the unique roles that key institutions (postsecondary education), services (mental health), funders (financial aid), and policies (Americans with Disabilities Act, 1990) play in the ability of a community to offer supported education.

Role of the Postsecondary Institution

Academic counselors on campus help with class selection so the student can meet his or her program requirements. Some colleges, universities, and training programs have a career center to help students with choosing a career and course of study.

The Role of Mental Health Services

The field of mental health is undergoing a major change, from providing traditional services to providing evidence-based practices. Although supported employment (see chapter 10) has become common practice, research indicates that between 41 percent and 77 percent of participants typically terminate employment within six months (Bond, Drake, Mueser, & Becker, 1997). The reasons clients cite indicate that they are being placed in unskilled or entry-level positions. Offering supported-education programs in tandem with supported employment will increase the opportunities for upgrading work opportunities.

To increase the availability of supported-education programs, mental health leaders must change their philosophy of providing services. To respond to both the needs and the interest of the consumers, supported-education programs should be widely available. This requires a change in attitudes and beliefs—people with mental illness can be successful in school and can develop meaningful careers.

To make this paradigm shift, the mission statement of an agency should reflect the importance of education as a rehabilitation intervention. Mental health practices, guided by revised policies and procedures, will modify the services available. Changes in funding streams and billing codes will reflect the need to revise the allocation of resources within the agency.

Some agencies may want to fold supported education into either case management or supported-employment services. Although many skills may be similar, SEd specialists require specific knowledge about the education system and its resources, just as supported-employment specialists require specific information about the world of work and job placement. Case managers have, in some cases, attempted to help their clients return to school. However, because of caseload sizes and the array of services a case manager provides, it has been difficult. An SEd specialist, with a caseload similar to a supported-employment specialist, is the best solution.

Financial Support and Supported Education

Financial aid is available from most education programs and educational institutions. A FAFSA form must be completed if aid is to be requested. This qualifies many applicants for a Pell Grant, the most common form of financial aid for low-income students. Pell Grants vary in amount depending on the postsecondary institution and student's course load. They do not have to be repaid, but certain stipulations apply. The FAFSA also qualifies the student for other grants such as Federal Supplemental Educational Opportunity Grants, work-study, and scholarships. Until a student has a good academic record, it may be unwise to apply for a student loan. Many clients have attempted college previously and may have defaulted on their loans, although loan forgiveness is possible (see the resources at the end of the chapter).

Not all students will choose to attend a college or university or training program. Some may want to complete a GED or adult basic education classes. Financial aid may not be available for these programs, but students are still entitled to receive accommodations.

Role of Americans with Disabilities Act

Accommodations for people with disabilities who are otherwise qualified are guaranteed by section 504 of the 1973 Rehabilitation Act and the Americans with Disabilities Act of 1990. The most common accommodations requested by students with a history of mental illness are use of tape recorders in the classroom, seating modifications, extended time for tests, special parking permits, use of note takers, alternative ways to complete assignments, books on tape, use of cubicles, headphones or alternative test formats, individual rooms during tests, and beverages in class.

To receive accommodations, the student must disclose and verify his or her disability. The requirements for documentation must be reasonable and limited to the need for the modification or the aid requested. Documentation should provide a decision maker with a basic understanding of the individual's disability and enough information to anticipate how the disability is expected to interact with the institution's structure of courses, testing methods, program requirements, and so on. The student's information is confidential and must be kept in a locked file cabinet, available only to the Disability Services Office. Instructors who may be required to provide the accommodations do not have access to this information, with the exception of a description of the accommodation requested. Some students may choose not to disclose their disability because of the stigma surrounding mental illness.

What's the Evidence?

Supported education began as an intervention in the early 1980s, and the first research article to examine outcomes (Unger, Anthony, Sciarappa, & Rogers, 1991) demonstrated the efficacy of the approach. The authors reported that the students had significant increases in pre- and post-class enrollment and competitive employment. Decreased rates of hospitalization and increased self-esteem were also reported. A later follow-up study indicated that these gains were maintained over time (Ellison, Danley, Bomberg, & Palmer-Erbs, 1999).

More recent research shows that students in supported education most often enroll in about six credits, complete 90 percent of their classes, and maintain a grade point average of 3.14 (on a 4-point scale). Their retention rate is comparable to that of other part-time students, and their employment rate before and after being in school is about 42 percent (Unger, Pardee, & Shafer, 2000). Predictors of success were not related to a particular diagnosis such as schizophrenia or bipolar disorder, nor were prior college experience, prior grade point average, or type of institution. Having one's own transportation, degree of severity of the illness, and the leave and reentry policy of the university were the strongest predictors of educational achievement (Smith-Osborne, 2005; Unger et al., 2000).

Students participating in a supported-education program report higher levels of satisfaction with their quality of life and significantly higher levels of self-esteem than those who are working or not enrolled in school or work. They also report higher levels of satisfaction with their living situation, finances, daily activities, social relations, and family contacts than those who are not going to school (Unger et al., 2000).

The most recent research analyzing barriers to employment indicated that low educational achievement was a barrier to paid work (Cook, 2006). A 2006 multisite research study found that those with a more recent work history, younger age, and higher education were more likely to achieve competitive employment and more work hours (Burke-Miller et al., 2006).

Assessment and Evaluation

An initial assessment taken in the first few weeks as the student enters the program can provide basic demographic information. It can also gather previous education history, academic strengths and needs, and resource needs. Students' progress each academic term can be evaluated by the number of courses attempted and completed, as well as grades earned. Program evaluations can be tied to numbers of students referred to the program compared to numbers enrolled, levels of services provided, and whether the program adheres to the stated program principles and practices.

A standardized program evaluation for supported education is available in the Substance Abuse and Mental Health Services Administration's (n.d.) Evidence-Based Practice Kit series.

Implementation Issues

Eligibility for supported-education services may be an issue. Given the principles of practice, anyone who expresses an interest should be considered. However, readiness can be an issue, and preparatory steps to actual enrollment may be helpful. Another implementation issue is where the program should be located and how it will be funded and staffed. Ideally, the employment and education programs would share space and funding, and a uniquely qualified person would staff each. Supported-education programs, provided in tandem with supported-employment services, give consumers choices in their rehabilitation program.

Provider Competencies

Supported-education specialists will be familiar with the postsecondary environment, requirements for financial aid, setting education goals, and linking the student to resources on campus and in the community. They will know the availability and requirements of training programs, GED programs, and adult education opportunities. They can develop collaborative relationships with education staff and can advocate for their clients. These skills and knowledge are overlaid with their primary task of coach and mentor to the student.

Future Directions

Supported education has been shown to be a very effective rehabilitation intervention. It begins by giving clients a new role that is highly valued in our society, that of student. It makes upward economic mobility possible through learning new skills and increasing a sense of efficacy and hope. The Substance Abuse and Mental Health Services Administration (n.d.) has designated supported education as a promising practice, and it is encouraging the development of new programs and research. Clients have often expressed a desire for additional education, seeing it as a way to a new life. With help from a supported-education program, many have realized their dreams.

Websites

Federal Student Aid (information on loan deferment, cancellation, and consolidation)—http://www.studentaid.ed.gov

Free Application for Federal Student Aid (financial aid information)—http://www.fafsa.ed.gov

Health Resource Center at the National Youth Transitions Center, George Washington University (information on disability-related scholarships)—http://www.health.gwu.edu

Supported Education with Dr. Karen Unger—http://www.supportededucation.com

Glossary

Federal Supplemental Educational Opportunity Grant: Similar to the Pell Grant, the Federal Supplemental Educational Opportunity Grant does not have to be repaid. Pell Grant recipients with the lowest expected family contribution are the first students to receive this aid. Amounts vary depending on when students apply, their financial need, and the funding level of the school.

Otherwise handicapped person with a disability for postsecondary education: An individual who meets the academic and technical standards requisite to admission or participating in the recipient's education program or activity.

Reasonable accommodations: Adjustments in a classroom environment, task, or requirement that allow a person with a disability to participate equally with others.

Section 504 and the Americans with Disabilities Act: No otherwise handicapped individual shall solely because of his or her handicap, be excluded from participation in, be denied benefits of, or be subjected to discrimination in any program receiving federal aid. The Americans with Disabilities Act expanded the mandate of section 504 to include other public and private entities (U.S. Department of Justice, 2009).

References

Americans with Disabilities Act. 42 USC §§ 12101 et seq. (1990).

Bond, G. R., Drake, R. E., Mueser, K. T., & Becker, D. R. (1997). An update on supported employment for people with severe mental illness. *Psychiatric Rehabilitation Journal, 48*, 335–346.

Burke-Miller, J. K., Cook, J. A., Grey, D. D., Razzano, L. A., Blyler, C. R., Leff, H. S., et al. (2006). Demographic characteristics and employment among people with severe mental illness in a multi-site study. *Community Mental Health Journal, 42*(2), 143–159.

Cook, J. A. (2006). Employment barriers for persons with psychiatric disabilities: Update of a report for the President's Commission. *Psychiatric Services, 57*, 1391–1405.

Ellison, M. L., Danley, K. S., Bromberg, L., & Palmer-Erbs, V. (1999). Longitudinal outcomes of young adults who participated in a psychiatric vocational rehabilitation program. *Psychiatric Rehabilitation Journal, 22*, 337–341.

Smith-Osborne, A. (2005). Antecedents to postsecondary educational attainment for individuals with psychiatric disorders: A meta-analysis. *Best Practices in Mental Health, 1*(1), 15–30.

Unger, K. (1999). *Handbook on supported education: Providing services to students with psychiatric disabilities.* Towson, MD: Brookes.

Unger, K., Anthony, W. A., Sciarappa, K., & Rogers, E. S. (1991). Development and evaluation of a supported education program for young adults with long-term mental illness. *Hospital and Community Psychiatry, 42,* 838–842.

Unger, K. V., Pardee, R., & Shafer, M. S. (2000). Outcomes of postsecondary supported education programs for people with psychiatric disabilities. *Journal of Vocational Rehabilitation, 14,* 195–199.

U.S. Department of Justice. (2009). *A guide to disability rights laws.* Washington, DC: Civil Rights Division, Disability Rights Section. Retrieved from http://www.ada.gov/cguide.htm#anchor62335.

Vocational Rehabilitation Act. 29 USC §§701 et seq. (1973).

Additional Resources

Mowbray, C. T. (Ed.). (2004). Overview of the special issue on supported education. *American Journal of Psychiatric Rehabilitation, 7*(3), 223–226.

Mowbray, C. T., Brown, K. S., Furling-Norman, K., & Sullivan-Soydan, A. (Eds.). (2002). *Supported education and psychiatric rehabilitation: Models and methods.* Linthicum, MD: International Association of Psychosocial Rehabilitation Services.

Substance Abuse and Mental Health Services Administration. (N.d.). *Supported education: A promising practice.* Rockville, MD: Author. (This publication may be downloaded online or ordered by calling 1-877-726-4727.)

17

Psychoeducation
Joseph Walsh

Psychoeducation describes a range of mental health interventions focused on enhancing participants' education, support, and coping skills development. The modality has become extremely popular in human services practice over the past thirty years. Such programs are delivered in many service settings and with many consumer populations. This chapter includes an overview of the history and definition of the concept, its range of applications, research evidence for its utility, methods for evaluation, implementation challenges, provider competencies, and future directions. We begin our chapter with a case study of Terry (see box 17.1), who was invited to attend a psychoeducation program.

Box 17.1. Case Study: Terry

Terry is a thirty-seven-year-old divorced African American male with no children who has struggled with depression for most of his adult life. He had always been prone to low moods, poor self-esteem, and a pessimistic attitude about his future. Terry's depression has been a factor in his lack of motivation to perform effectively at school and on jobs. Today he manages several Laundromats in a large Midwestern city, a position he fulfills adequately but without much satisfaction. Terry believes that his failed marriage was largely due to his wife's (a high school sweetheart) frustration with his lack of ambition and desire to start a family. Although he had never received professional intervention for his problems, believing that they were merely a part of his personality, Terry accepted the invitation of an uncle to join him in the Coping with Depression program that was opening at a local health clinic. After participating in the twelve-session program, Terry was able to see how self-change skills (e.g., sessions 1 and 2) prompted him to reconsider how he viewed his circumstances and what he could do differently. By sessions 7 and 8, he was able to replace his irrational thought processes (e.g., personal failure due to lack of ambition) with new thought processes accompanied by new skills (e.g., sessions 9 and 10), such as strategies for increasing positive socializing and for making new friends. He credits his uncle with giving him the boost he needed to "do something different," and he credits the group with helping him reconsider his life. Although Terry may continue to experience low moods, the Coping with Depression program provided him with a rich set of skills and behaviors that may serve to buffer future feelings of depression.

Background

Psychoeducation is a term that describes a range of individual, family, and group interventions that are focused on educating participants about a significant challenge in living, on helping participants develop adequate social and resource supports in managing the challenge, and on developing coping skills to deal with the challenge (Walsh, 2010). Additional goals may include reducing participants' sense of stigma, changing participants' cognitions with regard to the issue, identifying and exploring feelings about the issue, and developing relevant problem-solving skills. The targets of change may include the participants themselves or their significant others.

The concept of psychoeducation has evolved over the past forty years. It initially referred either to a process of educating practitioners about the nature of mental, emotional, and behavioral problems or to preparing clients to undergo analytic psychotherapy. Contemporary uses of psychoeducation can be traced back to the 1970s, when knowledge about mental disorders began to focus on biological rather than family processes. Many practitioners became interested in sharing this information with, rather than "treating," consumers and their families. This form of psychoeducation was first implemented for persons with schizophrenia and their families by such pioneers as Hatfield (1979) and Anderson, Hogarty, and Reiss (1980). Other psychoeducation programs were developed for people with bipolar disorders (McFarlane, 2002).

It is difficult to estimate the numbers and types of psychoeducational interventions that are provided in the United States and around the world. A sample of such programs derived from a PsycINFO literature review included the following applications: parenting skills development, persons experiencing mental illness or substance abuse or their family members, families of children with emotional and behavioral problems, families of persons facing chronic and life-threatening physical conditions, permanency planning for the adult offspring of aging parents, trauma recovery for youth in residential treatment, incarcerated male and female inmates, university women who have experienced sexual assault, social workers who experience vicarious traumatization, adolescent girls who experience negative social pressures, persons experiencing bulimia, children of divorce, and youth experiencing bullying behavior (McFarlane, 2002; McFarlane, Dixon, Lukens, & Lucksted, 2003).

Theoretical Perspective

Most psychoeducational interventions utilize a cognitive-behavioral theoretical perspective (Walsh, 2010), as they seek to increase participants' knowledge of a condition and to change their behaviors on the basis of that new understanding. Specifically, new information addresses participants' cognitive deficits and (possibly) distortions (based on previous misunderstandings about an issue), and through problem-solving skill development they may improve their abilities to address challenges related to the condition.

Principle

Because the goals and formats of psychoeducation are so varied, there is no set of distinct research-based principles available to guide all intervention studies. However, one of the core principles of any psychoeducation program is the notion of empowerment:

• *Principle of empowerment*—Rests on the notion that psychoeducational approaches are intended to increase consumers' knowledge of, and insight into, their illness and its treatment. It is assumed that knowledge and insight will enable persons to cope more effectively with their illness. As discussed later in this chapter, research by Landsverk and Kane (1998) concluded that psychoeducation can empower participants to collaborate more fully with health-care providers.

Steps for Implementing Psychoeducational Best Practices

One example of a psychoeducation program is Coping with Depression (CWD). This is a structured psychoeducational course that teaches participants techniques for coping with problems related to their depression. It addresses four areas: discomfort and anxiety in social situations, the importance of pleasant activities, managing irrational thoughts, and developing social skills (Swan, Sorrell, MacVicar, Durham, & Matthews, 2004). The course also promotes improved self-monitoring of mood and personal goal attainment. The CWD program consists of twelve two-hour sessions conducted over eight weeks, and it is provided in group settings that allow participants to practice new interpersonal and other skills. Sessions are held twice weekly for the first four weeks and then weekly afterward (for a summary of each session, see table 17.1).

Table 17.1. The Coping with Depression Program

Sessions 1–2	Presentation of course rules, rationale, and the social-learning view of depression (modeling the behavior of significant others can reinforce different emotional responses); several self-change skills are taught, along with the principles of monitoring behaviors by developing a baseline, goals, plan, and contract for change
Sessions 3–4	Relaxation skills, featuring progressive muscle relaxation
Sessions 5–6	Increasing pleasant activities through a review of a list of potentially pleasant activities provided by the leader
Sessions 7–8	Identifying and changing irrational thoughts
Sessions 9–10	Social skills development, featuring assertion, planning more social activities, and strategies for making new friends
Sessions 11–12	An integration of skills learned and strategies for maintaining gains; each participant develops a personal "emergency plan" to counteract feelings of depression in the future

The CWD groups typically consist of six to ten adults and a single group leader. One- and six-month follow-up sessions are held to help support treatment gains. An instructor's manual is used in the course, as is a textbook from which reading assignments are given.

What's the Evidence?

Psychoeducation is said to be among the most effective of the evidence-based practices in clinical and practice settings (Lukens & McFarlane, 2006). Most studies show that psychoeducation is equal to or superior to alternative interventions. One early review concluded that education is an effective component in a comprehensive treatment approach to mental illness and other problems in living (Landsverk

& Kane, 1998). This review also concluded that psychoeducation is not only an empowering approach with health-care providers; just as important are the skills and attitudes of leaders in the process.

I now turn to several comprehensive reviews that have been undertaken with regard to psychoeducation for persons with schizophrenia or bipolar disorder and their families, which are among the most popular applications of the modality.

Schizophrenia

Psychoeducational approaches to schizophrenia are intended to increase consumers' knowledge of, and insight into, their illness and its treatment. As mentioned earlier, it is assumed that knowledge and insight will enable persons to cope more effectively with their illness. The purpose of one systematic review was to assess the effects of psychoeducational interventions as compared to other types of knowledge provision (Pekkala & Merinder, 2002). The authors located ten relevant randomized controlled trials focusing on psychoeducation for schizophrenia and related serious mental illnesses involving individuals or groups, all of which included family members. In one study of a brief intervention, consumer compliance with medication significantly improved at the one-year follow-up, but other studies produced equivocal results on the same variable. Any kind of psychoeducation, however, significantly decreased relapse and readmission rates at nine to eighteen months follow-up against standard care. Several secondary outcomes (e.g., knowledge gained, mental status, global level of functioning, expressed emotion in family members) were more difficult to summarize. In general, findings were consistent with psychoeducation having a positive effect on a person's well-being. No impact was found on insight, medication-related attitudes, or overall satisfaction with services. It was not possible to analyze which formats of psychoeducation were most effective.

One meta-analysis evaluated the short- and long-term efficacy of psychoeducation, with and without the inclusion of families, with regard to relapse rates, symptom reduction, knowledge, medication adherence, and social functioning (Lincoln, Wilhelm, & Nestoriuc, 2007). Eighteen randomized controlled trials comparing psychoeducation to standard care or nonspecific interventions were included. Independent of treatment modality, psychoeducation produced a medium positive effect at posttreatment for relapse and a small effect for knowledge. It had no effect, however, on symptoms, functioning, and medication adherence. Positive effects remained significant for twelve months after treatment but not for longer follow-up periods. Interventions that included families were more effective in reducing symptoms and in preventing relapse.

Another review summarized the outcome literature on psychoeducation in schizophrenia published during the previous year (Rummel-Kluge & Kissling, 2008). The authors found that studies done in clinical settings showed results comparable to those in experimental settings. They further concluded that brief interventions may have long-term effects on relapse and rehospitalization rates, and the combination of diagnostic groups may be effective in small settings with too few potential members to comprise single-diagnosis groups.

Bipolar

The role of the family is considered essential (see chapter 14) in the care and support of persons with bipolar disorder. One systematic review investigated the effectiveness of any psychosocial family intervention for people with bipolar disorder and their families (Justo, Soares, & Calil, 2007). Of the seven randomized controlled trials included, five compared family interventions against no treatment, and two compared psychoeducation against another family intervention. The authors concluded that the studies provide insufficient evidence to draw conclusions that could be generalized. The purpose of another systematic review and meta-analysis of randomized and quasi-randomized controlled trials was to determine the effectiveness of psychosocial interventions for the prevention of relapse in bipolar disorder (Beynon, Soares-Weiser, Woolacott, Duffy, & Geddes, 2008). The authors concluded that either cognitive-behavioral therapy or group psychoeducation can be effective for relapse prevention in currently stable individuals.

Assessment and Evaluation

Assessment and evaluation of best-practice interventions are crucial to establishing evidence of effectiveness. As discussed previously, there are three clinical categories in which psychoeducational programs, such as the Coping with Depression course, have shown positive outcomes: individuals diagnosed with schizophrenia and/or bipolar disorder and reducing tension among family members who have a relative with mental illness. This section describes three instruments used in the assessment and evaluation of psychoeducational outcomes such as depression, family tension, and life stability. These instruments are the Beck Depression Inventory, the Camberwell Family Interview, and Quality of Life Questionnaire. In particular, discussion is centered on the evaluation of the Coping with Depression program, considered a best practice and the focus of this chapter.

Depression and the Beck Depression Inventory

The Coping with Depression (CWD) course described earlier is the best-studied psychoeducational intervention for the treatment and prevention of depression (Cuijpers, Muñoz, Clarke, & Lewinsohn, 2009). The efficacy of the CWD has been examined in twenty-five randomized controlled trials. The Beck Depression Inventory (BDI) is often used as a pre- and posttest measure with this program. The BDI is a twenty-one-item, four-point Likert scale (Beck & Steer, 1987) that assesses the symptoms of mood, pessimism, sense of failure, self-dissatisfaction, guilt, punishment, self-dislike, self-accusations, suicidality, crying, irritability, social withdrawal, indecisiveness, body image, work difficulty, insomnia, fatigability, loss of appetite, weight loss, somatic preoccupation, and loss of libido. A meta-analysis of six CWD studies aimed at the prevention of new cases of major depression indicated a 38 percent reduced risk among participants developing the disorder. The eighteen studies examining CWD as treatment for depression demonstrated a modest, positive effect; comparisons with other psychotherapies indicated that CWD was equally or more effective.

Family Tension and the Camberwell Family Interview

Some psychoeducation programs for families of persons with schizophrenia include expressed emotion (EE), a measure of family tension, as an outcome variable. The best-known measure of EE is the Camberwell Family Interview (CFI), a semistructured interview that is conducted with the impaired person's relatives (Vaughn & Leff, 1985). The interview includes questions about levels of tension and irritability in the household, the client's participation in routine household tasks, and the daily routines of the client and family members. The CFI makes ratings on five scales, including criticism, hostility, emotional overinvolvement, warmth, and positive remarks. Family members are classified as high or low on EE on the basis of the first three scales.

Life Stability and the Quality of Life Questionnaire

The Quality of Life Enjoyment and Satisfaction Questionnaire is one measure of the impact of psychoeducation on the life stability of persons with bipolar disorder.

This measure contains ninety-three items covering eight scales that assess a person's quality of life functioning across a range of domains, including school, work, and physical health (Endicott, Nee, Harrison, & Blumenthal, 1993).

Implementation Issues

There is great variety in how psychoeducation programs are organized and delivered, which is a major reason the general modality is difficult to evaluate. Programs may be provided in one hour, in one day, or in up to fifteen sessions or more, with open or closed-ended structures. Most psychoeducation services are led by human service professionals, but some are led by consumers or family members of consumers, and others are co-led by professionals and consumers. Psychoeducation can be a stand-alone intervention, but it is often used as one method among several for helping consumers and families with a particular life challenge.

Psychoeducation is easily adapted to the specific needs of participants. As examples, groups have been used successfully with minority populations, including low-income Latino women with HIV/AIDS, Korean American families of persons with mental illness, African American women who are adjusting to college, African American women working to increase their psychosocial competence, schoolchildren facing racial-identity challenges, American Indians seeking stronger identity development, and minority families of mentally ill clients.

Provider Competencies

To be effective psychoeducators, human service professionals must be effective teachers. The psychoeducation literature appears to assume that having knowledge qualifies one to dispense it, but this is not necessarily true. Formal training in psychoeducation seems to be somewhat limited. Interestingly, peer-run programs often include the most extensive leadership training (Rummel, Hansen, & Helbig, 2005). Some major provider competencies include the following (DeLucia-Waack, 2006; Grasha, 1996):

- Knowledge about the subject

- Organization skills (starting and stopping on time, preventing interruptions, maintaining momentum, managing topic transitions)

- Presentation (communication) skills

- Positive attitudes about learners

- The ability to assess learners' motivational level, pace of learning, and moods

- Awareness of different learning styles and the ability to incorporate these into the process

- The ability to think critically about the content area

- The ability to provide opportunities for learners to share concerns

- Evaluation skills (regarding the learning that has taken place, the adequacy of the content, future program needs, and one's own performance)

Providers also need to understand that there are different types of learners. For example, Kolb (1984) categorizes learners into the following types:

> The activist learns best through experimentation of the type found in simulations, case studies, and homework assignments. This person learns by doing rather than by listening.

> The reflector learns best through reflective observations and discussions about a topic. This learner needs time to think about new material and to see how it fits with his or her view of the world.

> The theorist learns best by abstract conceptualization, such as through lectures and supplemental readings that link the material to other ideas.

> The pragmatist learns best with concrete experiences of the type found in laboratories, fieldwork, and personal observations. Activities should be provided that help this learner apply new knowledge and skills.

Future Directions

Psychoeducation is continuing to expand as an intervention modality and will continue to encompass a variety of formats and range of participant goals. It has begun to emerge as both an online modality and an in-person one, and although it once featured exclusively professional leaders, it increasingly includes peer leaders as well. Future research on psychoeducation must focus on the differential effects of consumer versus professional programs, the potential of online programs, and the effects of provider competencies on consumer outcomes.

Psychoeducation represents a practical intervention approach for helping a wide variety of vulnerable populations become better able to address their life challenges. Its popularity and range of uses have proliferated over the past thirty years. A challenge to evidence-based practice is to implement a variety of research methodologies that can capture the range of types of intervention and its goals. Service providers themselves can easily implement single-subject and single group pre- and posttest designs, but experimental designs are impractical at the agency level. Although much more research is required to make generalizations about evidence-based practice, service providers can certainly learn much from the research that has been done to guide their planning and choices of outcome measures.

Websites

Center for Mental Health Services, National Mental Health Information Center, *Evidence-Based Practices: Shaping Mental Health Services Toward Recovery: Family Psychoeducation*—http://store.samhsa.gov/shin/content//SMA09-4423/The Evidence-FP.pdf

National Alliance on Mental Illness—http://www.nami.org

Glossary

Learning styles: The activist (who learns best through simulations, case studies, and homework assignments), the reflector (who learns best through reflective observations and discussion), the theorist (who learns best by abstract conceptualization), and the pragmatist (who learns best with concrete experiences).

Provider competencies: Knowledge about a subject, organizational skills, communication skills, positive attitudes about learners, the ability to assess learners' motivation and pace of learning, awareness of different learning styles, the ability to think critically about the topic, the capacity to provide opportunities for learners to share concerns, and evaluation skills.

Psychoeducation: A range of individual, family, and group interventions that are focused on educating participants about a significant challenge in living, on helping participants develop adequate social and resource supports in managing the challenge, and on developing coping skills to deal with the challenge.

References

Anderson, C. M., Hogarty, G. E., & Reiss D. J. (1980). Family treatment of adult schizophrenic patients: A psycho-educational approach. *Schizophrenia Bulletin, 6*(3), 490–505.

Beck, A. T., & Steer, R. A. (1987). Internal consistencies of the original and revised Beck Depression Inventory. *Journal of Clinical Psychology, 40*(6), 1365–1367.

Beynon, S., Soares-Weiser, K., Woolacott, N., Duffy, S., & Geddes, J. R. (2008). Psychosocial interventions for the prevention of relapse in bipolar disorder: Systematic review of controlled trials. *British Journal of Psychiatry, 192*(1), 5–11.

Cuijpers, P., Muñoz, R. F., Clarke, G. N., & Lewinsohn, P. M. (2009). Psychoeducational treatment and prevention of depression: The "Coping with Depression" course thirty years later. *Clinical Psychology Review, 29*(5), 449–458.

DeLucia-Waack, J. L. (2006). *Leading psychoeducational groups for children and adolescents.* Thousand Oaks, CA: Sage.

Endicott, J., Nee, J., Harrison, W., & Blumenthal, R. (1993). Quality of life enjoyment and satisfaction questionnaire: A new measure. *Psychopharmacology Bulletin, 29,* 321–326.

Grasha, A. F. (1996). *Teaching with style.* Pittsburgh, PA: Alliance.

Hatfield, A. (1979). Help-seeking behaviors in families of schizophrenics. *American Journal of Psychiatry, 7,* 563–569.

Justo, L., Soares, B., & Calil, H. (2007). Family interventions for bipolar disorder. *Cochrane Database of Systematic Reviews* (Vol. 4, Art. No. CD005167).

Kolb, D. A. (1984). *Experiential learning: Experience as the source of learning and development.* Upper Saddle River, NJ: Prentice-Hall.

Landsverk, S. S., & Kane, C. E. (1998). Antonovsky's sense of coherence: Theoretical basis of psychoeducation in schizophrenia. *Issues in Mental Health Nursing, 19*(5), 419–431.

Lincoln, T. M., Wilhelm, K., & Nestoriuc, Y. (2007). Effectiveness of psychoeducation for relapse, symptoms, knowledge, adherence and functioning in psychotic disorders: A meta-analysis. *Schizophrenia Research, 96*(1–3), 232–245.

Lukens, E. P., & McFarlane, W. R. (2006). Psychoeducation as evidence-based practice: Considerations for practice, research, and policy. In A. R. Roberts & K. R. Yeager (Eds.), *Foundations of evidence-based social work practice* (pp. 291–313). New York: Oxford University Press.

McFarlane, W. (2002). *Multiple-family groups and psychoeducation in the treatment of severe psychiatric disorders.* New York: Guilford Press.

McFarlane, W. R., Dixon, L., Lukens, E., & Lucksted, A. (2003). Family psychoeducation and schizophrenia: A review of the literature. *Journal of Marital and Family Therapy, 29*(2), 223–245.

Pekkala, E. T., & Merinder, L. B. (2002). Psychoeducation for schizophrenia. *Cochrane Database of Systematic Reviews* (Vol. 2, Art. No. CD002831).

Rummel, C. B., Hansen, W. P., & Helbig, A. (2005). Peer-to-peer psychoeducation in schizophrenia: A new approach. *Journal of Clinical Psychiatry, 66,* 1580–1585.

Rummel-Kluge, C., & Kissling, W. (2008). Psychoeducation in schizophrenia: New developments and approaches in the field. *Current Opinion in Psychiatry, 21*(2), 168–172.

Swan, J., Sorrell, E., MacVicar, B., Durham, R., & Matthews, K. (2004). "Coping with Depression": An open study of the efficacy of a group psychoeducational intervention in chronic, treatment-refractory depression. *Journal of Affective Disorders, 82*(1), 125–129.

Vaughn, C., & Leff, J. P. (1985). *Expressed emotion in families: Its significance for mental illness.* New York: Guilford Press.

Walsh, J. (2010). *Psychoeducation in mental health.* Chicago: Lyceum Books.

PART V
Children- and Youth-Oriented Best Practices

Children- and youth-oriented best practices are those interventions and strategies that address risk and protective factors, occur in multiple settings (with a focus on schools), and provide comprehensive support systems that focus on peer and parent-child relations and academic performance. These best practices also recognize the importance of information and services provided in an appropriate, equitable, and holistic manner.

Part 5 introduces the reader to two chapters detailing best practices for children and youth. These include a description of an early intervention program for youth at risk for emerging mental illness, followed by a comprehensive review of practices aimed to promote children's mental health.

In chapter 18, "Early Intervention for Youth Psychosis: The Australian Model," McGorry (the program's founder) and Goldstone describe an innovative early intervention center (Early Psychosis Prevention and Intervention Center), which evolved to become Australia's largest specialized youth mental health organization, Orygen Youth Health. The authors provide a detailed review of the program, its multiple components, and its focus on early intervention and prevention across a range of mental and substance use disorders that youth experience. Although first established in Australia, the model is now recognized worldwide. In chapter 19, "Best Practices in Children's Mental Health," Nguyen provides a comprehensive review of epidemiological, clinical, and treatment models associated with best practices for children.

18

Early Intervention for Youth Psychosis: The Australian Model

Patrick McGorry and Sherilyn Goldstone

Mental health difficulties are easily the key health issue that adolescents and young adults face in the developed world today. Epidemiological studies have shown that the incidence and prevalence of mental disorders, as well as their contribution to the overall burden of disease, is highest among those between the ages of fifteen and twenty-four, and yet young people in this age range are the least likely to access services for mental health problems. This is particularly problematic because untreated, or poorly treated, mental disorders are associated with ongoing disability, including impaired social functioning, poor educational achievement, unemployment, substance abuse, and violence, which all too often leads to a cycle of dysfunction and disadvantage that is difficult to break. Young people tend to be reluctant to discuss emotional concerns with a general practitioner, if indeed they have a regular doctor, and the traditional mental health services, which are designed to cater to the needs of children or older adults, are typically alienating to young people. A new approach to mental health services for young people is clearly needed: one that considers young people's unique developmental issues, their help-seeking needs and behaviors, and the complex and evolving patterns of symptoms and morbidity common in this age group. This chapter describes Australian innovation in the provision of youth mental health services, informed by an evidence-based approach and dedicated advocacy, which seeks to contribute to this much-needed reform process. We begin this chapter with a case review of James (see box 18.1), a university student who developed symptoms of mental illness while in school but was able to continue academic studies with the support of an outreach approach offered to him and his family through the Youth Access Team.

Box 18.1. Case Study: James

James is a twenty-year-old student, in his third year of a science degree at university. He lives with his parents and sixteen-year-old brother in Melbourne, Australia. James's family had become increasingly concerned about his unusual behavior over the past two or three months, and when he refused to come out of his room because he believed that Australian intelligence service agents were following him and would try to kill him because he had deciphered the coded messages they had been exchanging about a plan to assassinate the prime minister, they immediately contacted their family general practitioner, who referred them directly to EPPIC, the early psychosis clinic at Orygen Youth Health, a specialized youth mental health clinic. The Youth Access Team from Orygen Youth Health visited James and his family at home, where they were able to assess James's mental state in familiar surroundings that were comfortable to him. After talking with him, they determined that he was experiencing a first psychotic episode. After consultation with James's family it was decided that, although he was reluctant to accept treatment, he did not need hospitalization at this stage, and that the Youth Access Team would visit him daily to monitor his mental state and initiate treatment. James reluctantly accepted this decision, and he agreed to take medication if he could stay at home. The team psychiatrist prescribed James a low dose of an atypical antipsychotic medication and benzodiazepines to help with his agitation. After two weeks of home treatment James's psychotic symptoms had begun to abate, and he was well enough to visit the EPPIC clinic and begin outpatient treatment with the Continuing Care Team. He was assigned a case manager, Lisa, a psychologist, who began by explaining psychosis to James and his family and assuring them that James had a good chance of recovery and returning to his studies. Over the following eighteen months Lisa worked through a program of cognitive therapy with James, to help him understand and manage his symptoms, to deal with stress, and to recognize and manage the early warning signs of a possible relapse. James continued to take his medication, and as his symptoms settled, Lisa encouraged him to join several of the group programs available at Orygen Youth Health. He found that he particularly enjoyed the music group, and the study skills group helped him with returning to university and resuming his studies after deferring his course for the first six months of his illness. He is now in his final year at university, and for the next six months he will continue to see Lisa and his treating psychiatrist at EPPIC. Although his treating team expects him to make an excellent recovery, the team members, James, and his family are aware that he remains at increased risk for another psychotic episode in the future and that he needs to remain vigilant for any signs of relapse. James's treatment team at EPPIC will arrange to meet with him and his family doctor to discuss his ongoing treatment needs before his discharge from the service, and they will remain available to discuss any concerns with his family doctor once James is finally discharged.

Background

Historically, the psychotic illnesses, especially schizophrenia, have been viewed as having an inevitably poor prognosis, in terms of both symptoms and social and economic functioning. As a consequence of this belief and until relatively recently, little real effort has been put into the early recognition and treatment of these illnesses, and thus through poor or even nonexistent treatment, the prevailing belief has largely become a self-fulfilling prophecy.

Careful epidemiological studies have shown that the majority of cases of psychotic illness begin during the developmentally vulnerable adolescent and early adult years. It is well established that the interruption of this crucial period of psychosocial development by untreated, or poorly treated, psychotic illness is largely responsible for the significant social and economic disability associated with psychotic disorders such as schizophrenia. Early case identification and intensive treatment of a first episode of illness were first proposed in the 1990s as a core preventive strategy for the psychotic illnesses, and the first specialized early psychosis clinical services were established, initially in Melbourne, Australia, and soon afterward in many key locations in the United Kingdom, Europe, North America, and Asia. There are now hundreds of early intervention programs worldwide that focus on the special needs of young people facing the onset of a serious mental illness (Edwards & McGorry, 2002).

The Early Psychosis Prevention and Intervention Center (EPPIC) was established in Melbourne, Australia, in 1992, providing the first model of a comprehensive early intervention program for young people with emerging psychosis (McGorry,

Edwards, Mihalopoulos, Harrigan, & Jackson, 1996). Over the past decade, EPPIC has evolved to become Australia's largest specialized youth mental health organization, Orygen Youth Health (OYH), which provides community-based clinical services to young people between the ages of fifteen and twenty-five in a catchment area of approximately one million people in northwestern Melbourne. Orygen Youth Health focuses on early intervention across a range of mental and substance use disorders in young people, working in partnership with existing local agencies where indicated, notably drug and alcohol services. There are two broad clinical streams within OYH: EPPIC, which accepts young people who are either at ultra-high risk of developing a psychotic illness or experiencing a first treated episode of psychosis, and YouthScope, which provides treatment at several specialist clinics for young people experiencing a range of nonpsychotic disorders, predominantly the severe mood and anxiety disorders and emerging borderline personality disorder.

Theoretical Perspective

Most of the early psychosis and intervention services are informed by theories emphasizing prevention, family education, and support and empowerment. These include prevention theory, cognitive-behavioral theory, and empowerment theory.

Principles

Broadly speaking, EPPIC aims to identify and facilitate the treatment of psychosis in a young person as early as possible, to minimize disruption to the young person's functioning and psychosocial development during the critical early years following the onset of a serious mental illness. Given the complex and multifaceted needs of these young people (and those of their families), EPPIC's client services have been designed to promote and support recovery within the practice principles of a comprehensive, integrated, flexible, and responsive approach that considers the phase and severity of illness. There are three key principles underlying the EPPIC program: early detection, evidence based, and recovery:

- *Principle of early detection*—Early detection is an important goal of any EPPIC program and the driving value of service outreach.

- *Principle of evidence-based practice*—Early intervention programs are guided by an understanding of the emerging evidence on brain development and developmental trajectories for youth.

- *Principle of recovery*—Early intervention efforts are cognizant of the importance of the concept of recovery and how this framework respects the young person and engages him or her as an active partner working toward his or her own recovery.

Steps for Implementing the EPPIC Program

The Early Psychosis Prevention and Intervention Center is a long-term, comprehensive intervention program formed around several core components. Services are delivered through a wide array of interdisciplinary teams in both outpatient and inpatient settings (see figure 18.1).

Figure 18.1. Structure of the EPPIC Program

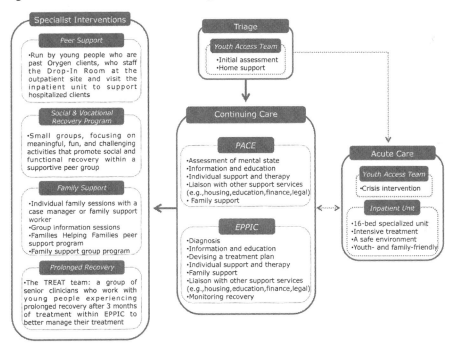

Time Line and Core Components of EPPIC

Treatment at EPPIC is provided for up to two years and is based on the following core components:

- Twenty-four hour access via the dedicated Youth Access Team

- Team-based case management, with a key worker and a team of other clinicians to draw on for specific interventions

- A minimum of a two-year tenure of service

- A dedicated inpatient unit

- A wide range of evidence-based psychosocial interventions

- Involvement of young people (current and former consumers or participants) and family members

- An alumni program for clients

Team Approach

The Early Psychosis Prevention and Intervention Center uses four teams comprised of interdisciplinary staff: the Youth Access Team, the Treatment Resistance Early Assessment Team, the Intensive Case Management Team, and the Platform Team.

The Youth Access Team is available twenty-four hours a day, seven days a week, and is staffed by nurses, occupational therapists, social workers, psychologists, and psychiatrists. The Youth Access Team serves as the first contact point for young people referred to EPPIC, and it serves three main functions: triage, initial assessment, and acute care (whether for ongoing home support or crisis intervention). Referrals can be made by anyone in the community with concerns about a young person, or directly by the young person him- or herself. Triage staff discuss the young person's difficulties with the referrer and make an initial assessment about whether the person requires a specialist mental health assessment, the level of risk, and the urgency of the situation. After assessment, the young person may be referred to one of OYH's clinical programs or to another appropriate community agency.

The Treatment Resistance Early Assessment Team (TREAT) is a panel of consultant psychiatrists, senior multidisciplinary clinicians, and a coordinator who aims to identify and review the clinical management of young people experiencing prolonged recovery at three months after entry into EPPIC. The TREAT coordinator arranges for all EPPIC clients to be screened by their clinical treating team at three months to establish whether the young person is experiencing ongoing psychotic symptoms. If so, the TREAT panel reviews the client's care and makes recommendations to optimize the chances of ameliorating the enduring symptoms. These changes may include changes to medication, referral for cognitive-behavioral therapy designed to reduce ongoing psychotic symptoms, or other psychosocial or family interventions.

The Intensive Case Management Team supports young people who have difficulty engaging with mental health services or those who have more complex needs and require intensive interventions. The Intensive Case Management Team accepts referrals from case managers of young people who attend EPPIC and operates on an outreach model, with a focus on community assessment, treatment, and support for young people and their families and/or caregivers.

The Platform Team is open to all clients and is a group that meets regularly to discuss possible improvements to service. Involvement of young people and their families is welcomed in EPPIC. Peer-support workers, who are all past clients, visit the inpatient unit and staff the platform room to provide support to current clients. All EPPIC peer-support workers are fully trained and supported by mentors in the service, and they are paid for their time. Platform Team members and peer-support workers can also choose to contribute to educating the wider community about mental health issues by speaking at schools or talking to youth workers and the media. Finally, Platform Team members and peer-support workers participate in staff selection by contributing to interview selection panels.

Services

The Early Psychosis Prevention and Intervention Center provides a wide range of services for youth and families, including evidence-based psychosocial interventions, social and vocational recovery programs, family and friend programs, and case management.

Evidence-based psychosocial interventions are available in the EPPIC program, including individual psychotherapy and cognitive-behavioral therapy programs designed to enable the young person to cope better with the symptoms of psychosis and with the stress, depression, anxiety, and substance abuse disorders that commonly accompany a psychotic illness.

Social and vocational recovery programs offered at EPPIC include a unique vocational program for clients wishing to return to work, which is based on the individual placement and support model, and a broader group program that provides a wide range of meaningful, challenging, and fun activities that give young people the opportunity to work on personal issues such as lack of confidence, low self-esteem, anger, and anxiety in a supportive peer-group environment (Killackey, Jackson, Fowler, & Neuchterlein, 2009). These groups are usually small, with four to eight people involved, and include groups focusing on school, study, and work;

groups that focus on better health such as physical fitness, reducing drug use, and stress management; social and leisure groups that focus on self-exploration and expression, such as outdoor adventure, music, and art; and groups that help with management of anxiety about recovery from illness.

The Early Psychosis Prevention and Intervention Center also offers a family program designed for parents, partners, children, siblings, extended family, close friends, and other people who care for an EPPIC client. Peer-family-support workers, who have themselves had experience of EPPIC services, provide phone and face-to-face support to new family caregivers whose relative enters EPPIC. Other services include family-support groups and a family resource room with access to a wide range of information.

Case management is central to EPPIC's outpatient-based continuing care program, and EPPIC currently offers a two-year tenure of service. Each client is assigned an individual case manager, who may be a clinical psychologist, a social worker, an occupational therapist, or a psychiatric nurse, as well as a psychiatrist or psychiatric registrar under the supervision of a consultant psychiatrist. The continuing care team works collaboratively with the young person and his or her family or other caregivers to provide a highly individualized treatment approach, which usually involves a combination of medication and psychosocial interventions that are most appropriate for the young person, depending on the stage of illness. The continuing care team also provides information and education to the young person and his or her family, and its members act as a liaison between the young person and other useful support services (e.g., housing, educational, vocational, financial, legal). The average number of new EPPIC registrations is approximately 260 per year, with an average standing caseload for full-time continuing-care case managers of 30 (Edwards & McGorry, 2002; McGorry et al., 1996).

Clinic and Inpatient Care

The Early Psychosis Prevention and Intervention Center offers two core entry points for youth and family to access services: the Personal Assessment and Crisis Evaluation Clinic and inpatient hospital care.

The Personal Assessment and Crisis Evaluation Clinic (PACE) is an integral part of EPPIC and treats young people considered at ultra-high risk of developing a psychotic illness (Yung et al., 2007). Currently, referrals to PACE typically come from the Youth Access Team. Clients of PACE have access to case management, psychological therapy, and medication when necessary, as well as the full range of psychosocial and family programs offered at OYH. Should a young person being treated by PACE develop a full-threshold psychotic illness, he or she is immediately transferred to EPPIC, which ensures continuity of care.

Inpatient care, when necessary, is provided in a sixteen-bed inpatient service that focuses on acute care, with an emphasis on brief admission to prepare the young person for community support provided by the Youth Access Team or the case manager. The inpatient unit is a youth-friendly environment that is part of a twenty-eight-bed complex for people age twelve to twenty-five; the somewhat different needs of the younger end of this age cohort are managed by the appropriate grouping of patients. Peer-support workers assist nursing staff by bridge building with patients and serving as role models for recovery and progress. Medication is used cautiously in these often drug-naive patients, and despite relatively high levels of initial involuntary status, the unit is unlocked apart from the intensive-care section, which is used as a last resort only. Illicit drug use and the social consequences of homelessness or the risk of homelessness complicate many young people's presentations. They are usually unfamiliar with the mental health system and initially disturbed by the experience of hospitalization. This clientele presents different clinical challenges from those involved in managing older and more "experienced" patients with established mental illnesses, and they need a different context, skill set, and modus operandi.

What's the Evidence?

Evidence has been mounting to show that early intervention not only produces significantly better clinical and functional outcomes for clients but also is much more acceptable to patients and families and considerably more cost effective than standard care (McCrone, Craig, Power, & Garety, 2010; Mihalopoulos, Harris, Henry, Harrigan, & McGorry, 2009). Early intervention aims to prevent, or at the very least delay, the onset of a fully fledged psychotic disorder. If psychosis does occur, early intervention aims to enable the best-possible level of recovery before symptoms and poor functioning become entrenched, thereby preempting and minimizing the disability and adverse health and social impacts associated with a serious mental illness.

Preventive interventions require a detailed knowledge of the risk factors for an illness that can be modified by specifically targeted interventions. As yet, very few modifiable risk factors have been identified for the psychotic illnesses. Although we are currently unable to accurately identify which individuals will develop a psychotic illness, research has shown that it is possible to identify those young people who have a greatly increased risk of psychosis on the basis of defined clinical and functional criteria, called the ultra-high-risk mental state (Yung et al., 2003). These young people can be offered stepwise interventions according to the stage of their illness, with the aim of preventing or delaying the onset of full-threshold psychosis. There remain the normal considerations of risk versus benefit, which apply to all early diagnostic approaches in health care, and the related need to avoid overtreatment, but the advantage of intervention in this ultra-high-risk period is that the length of the stage provides an opportunity for engagement and sequential treatment options, and it allows for natural resolution.

For those young people who have progressed to a fully fledged first episode of psychosis, the most important of the modifiable factors known to influence the outcome of their illness is the duration of their untreated psychosis. It is well established that the longer people go without effective treatment, the poorer their outcome will be (Marshall et al., 2005). Hence, early detection of the onset of psychosis and immediate initiation of broad-spectrum biopsychosocial treatment is central to the success of any treatment regime. The groundbreaking Early Treatment and Intervention in Psychosis Study (TIPS) project in Scandinavia (Melle et al., 2009) has shown the enduring benefits of reducing duration of untreated psychosis, particularly on the level of the notoriously treatment-resistant negative symptoms. There is also good evidence to show that young people need intensive and continuous treatment to achieve an optimal outcome, rather than dipping in and out of care. Where care is provided continuously for two to three years, people have better outcomes than when they access care episodically during this critical period. Furthermore, the first five years after the onset of illness are the most critical in terms of development of disability, and the latest studies have suggested that to consolidate these early gains, many people may require sustained care in a specialized early-psychosis setting for up to five years to ensure that early gains are not lost.

Assessment and Evaluation

As early intervention in mental health expands, services will seek to assess and intervene when people are at risk of developing psychosis, in a possible prodromal phase. One measure used in this phase is the Comprehensive Assessment of At-

Risk Mental States (CAARMS; Yung et al., 2006). The CAARMS was developed with two main purposes: to assess psychopathology thought to indicate imminent development of a first episode of psychotic disorder and to determine whether an individual meets criteria for being at ultra-high risk for the onset of a first psychotic disorder. The instrument has seven categories (i.e., positive symptoms, cognitive change attention and/or concentration, emotional disturbance, negative symptoms, behavioral change, motor and/or physical changes, and general psychopathology) and multiple subscales. The CAARMS displays good to excellent concurrent, discriminant, and predictive validity and excellent interrater reliability (it is available by e-mailing pace@orygen.org.au). Other measures used in the early intervention program are the Brief Psychiatric Rating Scale (Ventura, Green, Shaner, & Liberman, 1993), which uses a twenty-four-item version of the original scale and includes categories such as somatic concern, anxiety, depression, suicidality, guilt, hostility, elevated mood, and grandiosity, to name a few. Delusions and auditory hallucinations are measured by the Psychotic Symptom Rating Scales (Haddock, McCarron, Tarrier, & Faragher, 1999). This instrument is divided into two domains: auditory hallucinations (fifty-nine items) and delusions (thirty items).

Implementation Issues

This model acknowledges the difficulties of service provision in an age group in which comorbidity is the norm; therefore, linkages with other mental health and general support agencies are essential in ensuring quality service provision. Although it might be expected that the care provided in the EPPIC model is more expensive than that provided in the existing system, this is not the case. Secure tenure of care in a specialized, separately streamed treatment system is significantly cheaper than late and periodic bursts of intervention within standard care settings oriented toward older patients with later-stage, enduring illness. The success of the EPPIC model has encouraged the wider application of early diagnosis and specialized treatment for the full range of emerging disorders in young people, including mood and anxiety disorders, substance use disorders, eating disorders, and personality disorders (McGorry, Nelson, Goldstone, & Yung, 2010).

Provider Competencies

The EPPIC team comprises staff from a range of educational, clinical, and allied health backgrounds: teachers, family- and peer-support workers, social workers, occupational therapists, mental health nurses, psychologists, and psychiatrists. The common theme uniting members of the EPPIC team is their interest in young people and their mental health, as well as their commitment to the delivery of evidence-based, effective, and timely interventions in a youth-friendly, stigma-free environment. All EPPIC staff receive specialized training targeted to their role in the EPPIC team, in formal training sessions run by the EPPIC Training and Communications Team or by senior EPPIC clinicians or in the form of individual clinical supervision and mentoring. Additional resources available to EPPIC staff include the EPPIC Clinical Guidelines; the *EPPIC Case Management Manual*; and a range of specific intervention manuals, psychoeducational materials, and audiovisual resources.

Future Directions

The sheer scale of the incidence and prevalence of mental ill health among young people calls for a layered approach to service provision that has both the capacity to deal with the high volumes involved and the depth necessary to manage the diversity of need. A broader range of service levels that cover the entire spectrum of need among young people is needed: from services that benefit the entire community to enhanced primary-care services for those with mild to moderate mental ill health and specialized services, such as EPPIC, for those with complex presentations or more severe illness.

Over the past decade the Australian government has increasingly recognized the need for reform in the provision of mental health services, particularly for young people, and a series of policy frameworks and new programs have been put into place to address this major public health issue. Headspace, the National Youth Mental Health Initiative, was established in 2006 with the mission to promote and support early intervention for young people with mild to moderate mental and substance use disorders (McGorry et al., 2007). A major part of the Headspace mandate is to establish youth-friendly, highly accessible centers offering multidisciplinary models of care that target young people's core health needs by providing an enhanced primary-care structure with close links to locally available specialist services and community organizations. Headspace has opened more than forty clinical centers across Australia over the past five years. Each Headspace center provides four core service streams: mental health, drug and alcohol services, primary care, and vocational and educational assistance, and each is led by a key agency on behalf of a local partnership or consortium of organizations that take on responsibility for the coordination and delivery of the four core streams. This approach is designed to facilitate, as far as possible, the coming together of existing local services that already work well in the region, rather than creating a new service from scratch. As well as providing services in the four core streams, each Headspace center also runs community-awareness campaigns to enhance young people's help-seeking behavior and the capacity of families and local service providers to identify emerging mental health concerns early. Education and training programs are also provided to strengthen local mental health, and primary-care workers' and other workers' understanding and use of evidence-based approaches in mental health care for young people.

In 2011 OYH opened an additional hub, colocated with one of the two Headspace centers in its catchment area. This hub is being established as an exemplar model that will be evaluated to inform the development of a seamless system of mental health care for young people, to be expanded nationwide in the future. This type of colocated model offers the complementary activities of enhanced primary care (Headspace) side by side with a specialized youth mental health clinic (OYH)— together these have the capacity to provide a comprehensive range of services to young people with mental health issues that vary from mild to severe. The primary goals of this model are to provide care in a way that is efficient for the service user, with services best matched to the needs of the individual young person and his or her caregivers while also overcoming the barriers to service that young people with mental health difficulties typically experience. The model will also allow for access to the OYH clinical program for Headspace clients in circumstances in which their mental health deteriorates significantly or risk issues increase. This environment will also provide the opportunity for the conduct of clinical research to improve the evidence base for the utilization of treatments specific to the stage and severity of emerging mental disorders, as well as the trials of methods that foster the efficient take-up of evidence-based treatments and models of care into clinical practice. We expect this model of care to be scaled up across the whole country in the coming years, following the announcement of more than $400 million in the 2011 federal budget to support this reform process.

In conclusion, the construction of a third component of the specialist mental health system, namely a youth mental health stream, sitting between child and older adult psychiatry, is an urgent and achievable goal if we are to deliver appropriate, acceptable, and effective care in the twenty-first century. New initiatives, such as Headspace and OYH in Australia, provide one way of addressing the long-overdue need for reform in service provision for this age group. These initiatives are stimulating or mirrored by similar reforms in other countries, notably Ireland, the United Kingdom, and Canada, and the coming decade should see steady progress in this major domain of health care.

Websites

EPPIC—http://www.eppic.org.au

Headspace—http://www.headspace.org.au

Orygen Youth Health—http://oyh.org.au

Glossary

Early intervention: Intervention that aims to prevent, or at least delay, the onset of a serious mental illness, so as to avoid or minimize the distress and disability that are all too often associated with these illnesses. The cornerstones of this approach are the earliest possible identification of those who are at risk of developing a serious mental illness and the strategic targeting of appropriate evidence-based interventions, depending on the stage of illness and presenting symptoms.

Psychosis: A state of mind in which an individual experiences a loss of contact with reality, characterized by the presence of hallucinations, delusions, and/or disordered thought processes. In addition to these positive symptoms, a person suffering from a psychotic illness may also experience negative symptoms such as affective blunting and loss of motivation, as well as a range of more nonspecific symptoms, including sleep disturbance, depression, anxiety, social withdrawal, and poor functioning.

References

Edwards, J., & McGorry, P. (2002). *Implementing early intervention in psychosis: A guide to establishing early psychosis services*. London: Dunitz.

Haddock, G., McCarron, J., Tarrier, N., & Faragher, E. B. (1999). Scales to measure dimensions of hallucinations and delusions: The Psychotic Symptom Rating Scales (PSYRATS). *Psychological Medicine, 19*, 879–889.

Killackey, E., Jackson, H., Fowler, D., & Neuchterlein, K. (2009). Enhancing work function in early psychosis. In H. Jackson & P. D. McGorry (Eds.), *The recognition and management of early psychosis: A preventative approach* (pp. 331–348). Cambridge: Cambridge University Press.

Marshall, M., Lewis, S., Lockwood, A., Drake, R., Jones, P., & Croudace, T. (2005). Association between duration of untreated psychosis and outcome in cohorts of first-episode patients: A systematic review. *Archives of General Psychiatry*, *62*(9), 975–983.

McCrone, P., Craig, T. K., Power, P., & Garety, P. A. (2010). Cost-effectiveness of an early intervention service for people with psychosis. *British Journal of Psychiatry*, *196*(5), 377–382.

McGorry, P. D., Edwards, J., Mihalopoulos, C., Harrigan, S. M., & Jackson, H. J. (1996). EPPIC: An evolving system of early detection and optimal management. *Schizophrenia Bulletin*, *22*(2), 305–326.

McGorry, P. D., Nelson, B., Goldstone, S., & Yung, A. R. (2010). Clinical staging: A heuristic and practical strategy for new research and better health and social outcomes for psychotic and related mood disorders. *Canadian Journal of Psychiatry*, *55*(8), 486–497.

McGorry, P. D., Tanti, C., Stokes, R., Hickie, I. B., Carnell, K., Littlefield, L. K., et al. (2007). Headspace: Australia's National Youth Mental Health Foundation— Where young minds come first. *Medical Journal of Australia*, *187*(7 Suppl.), S68–S70.

Melle, I., Larsen, T. K., Friis, S., Vaglum, P., Johannesen, J. O., Simonsen, E., et al. (2009). Early detection of first psychosis: TIPS sample five year outcomes. *Schizophrenia Bulletin*, *35*(Suppl. 1), S330.

Mihalopoulos, C., Harris, M., Henry, L., Harrigan, S., & McGorry, P. (2009). Is early intervention in psychosis cost-effective over the long term? *Schizophrenia Bulletin*, *35*(5), 909–918.

Ventura, J., Green, M. F., Shaner, A., & Liberman, R. P. (1993). Training and quality assurance with the Brief Psychiatric Rating Scale: The "drift busters." *International Journal of Methods in Psychiatric Research*, *3*, 221–244.

Yung, A. R., McGorry, P. D., Francey, S. M., Nelson, B., Baker, K., Phillips, L. J., et al. (2007). PACE: A specialised service for young people at risk of psychotic disorders. *Medical Journal of Australia, 187*(7 Suppl.), S43–S46.

Yung, A. R., Phillips, L., Simmons, M. B., Ward, J., Thompson, P., French, P., et al. (2006). *The Comprehensive Assessment of At-Risk Mental States*. Melbourne, Australia: Pace Clinic, Department of Psychiatry, University of Melbourne.

Yung, A. R., Phillips, L. J., Yuen, H. P., Francey, S. M., McFarlane, C. A., Hallgren, M., et al. (2003). Psychosis prediction: 12-month follow up of a high-risk ("prodromal") group. *Schizophrenia Research, 60*(1), 21–32.

19

Best Practices in
Children's Mental Health

Peter V. Nguyen

The untreated or unsuccessful treatment of children with mental disorder(s) is a critical concern in that it influences the potential for successful adult functioning. This chapter assesses the current state of children and mental health in the United States by focusing on evidence about prevalence rates, assessment and evaluation, and evidence-based treatment approaches. Overall, a high number of children suffer from at least one mental illness. Research on this population is limited, and data on effectiveness of treatment are still emerging. Future directions should focus on assessing intervention appropriateness for a diverse population of children, conducting research that addresses methodological challenges, and developing and evaluating strategies for effective intervention. The chapter begins with a case discussion of Max (see box 19.1), a young child diagnosed with a mental health condition and who received a variety of best-practice interventions.

Box 19.1. Case Study: Max

Early in the school year, eight-year-old Max was referred to a clinical social worker for an evaluation by his school counselor. The school counselor stated that Max was a very talented student, but she also informed the social worker that his teachers had observed the following behaviors: outbursts at school against teachers and peers, not being able to maintain attention long enough to complete assigned tasks, inability to follow directions on assignments, talking excessively in class and often interrupting others, and continuous fidgeting and an inability to sit still. Max also had several absences and often reports late to his first class. Further, he appears malnourished and often wears clothes that cover his entire body even though the weather is warm. Max also informed the school counselor that he can't sleep well and doesn't feel safe in his neighborhood since he hears gunshots at night. He also reported witnessing his parents engage in physical and verbal fights. He stated that he is the only child and doesn't have many friends since "they all like to tease and hit" him.

Some of the behavioral symptoms reported by the school counselor are criteria for attention deficit/hyperactivity disorder (ADHD). However, there are other issues involving Max's family and environment that need investigation for an evaluation. For example, his malnourished appearance and wearing clothes that cover his entire body even in warm weather should caution the clinician of possible neglect (malnourished appearance) and even child abuse (body marks). Other issues to explore are possible drug use, exposure to domestic violence, living in an unsafe neighborhood, dealing with bullying, anger, and self-esteem issues.

Although it is important for the clinical social worker to consider some of the problems presented, it is equally important to explore Max's strengths, such as past behaviors and grades, the onset of ADHD symptoms and past coping skills (since he did well in the past), the onset and nature of his parents' fighting, special interests and talents, other support systems such as relatives from whom he seeks guidance, and resources in his community.

After the assessment and evaluation of Max, a treatment plan was created on three levels: individual, familial, and environmental. The treatment plan considered all the factors that play a role in Max's life and was formed under the premise that all factors are interrelated. For the treatment of Max to be successful and sustainable, all factors must be addressed.

On an individual level, it was determined that Max has behaviors that qualify him for the diagnosis of ADHD. The counselor addressed this issue by referring Max to a psychiatrist, who prescribed Ritalin. In addition, Max is receiving individual therapy to explore the source of his anger and low self-esteem. The clinician is also teaching him ways of dealing with the fears of living in an unsafe neighborhood, by promoting positive interaction with peers and handling bullies. The individual therapy sessions also focus on Max's strengths, such as his talents for the arts and music and sports.

On a familial level, working with Max's parents can directly and indirectly help solve some of Max's individual issues. Using this family systems approach, the clinician also enrolled Max's parents in marriage counseling to learn ways to communicate with each other and to avoid physical and verbal altercations, especially in front of Max. Max's parents also need to be educated on his developmental stages and ADHD disorder in order to integrate such knowledge into their parenting. Equally important is family therapy for Max and his parents. This serves as a venue for Max to express his feelings and promotes bonding and communication between parents and child.

Using community resources, the clinician also sought out organizations such as Big Brothers to provide a mentor who serves as a role model for Max since he is an only child. Max also is enrolled in art and sports activities at the local YMCA, which serve as outlets for his creative skills and physical energy. Further, these activities can be venues in which Max applies to a social group setting the interpersonal skills, such as dealing with peers, that he has learned in individual therapy sessions.

Background

According to the Methodology for Epidemiology of Mental Disorders in Children and Adolescents study (InCrisis, 2007), almost 8.4 million children in the United States between the ages of nine and seventeen have a diagnosable mental or addictive disorder associated with at least minimum impairment. The untreated or unsuccessful treatment of children with mental disorder(s) can adversely affect an individual on personal, familial, and societal levels, starting from childhood and moving into adulthood. Thus, the need to address mental health disorders in children is a public health issue that deserves ongoing attention.

Critically important is an accurate assessment that leads to proper diagnosis and ultimately intervention for each child. Therefore, how the prevalence of mental illness in children is determined holds incredible significance for their positive growth and development. Prevalence in mental health is defined as the number of people with a disorder who are present in the general population (InCrisis, 2007). In assessing prevalence, there are three key factors that need to be considered: diagnostic guidelines, recognition of comorbidity, and access to services.

Using Standardized Diagnostic Guidelines to Assess Children's Mental Health

Mental disorders are generally identified by using the guidelines of the *Diagnostic and Statistical Manual*, fourth edition, text revision (*DSM-IV*; American Psychiatric Association, 2000). There are three categories that identify children who have diagnosable mental or addictive disorder(s): those with at least minimum impairment, those with significant functional impairment, and those with extreme functional impairment. Of the 8.4 million children identified in the Methodology for Epidemiology of Mental Disorders in Children and Adolescents study, 21 percent (or one out of five) fall into the first category of minimum impairment. The percentage drops to 11 percent (4.3 million children) in the second category, with the presence of significant functional impairment. Finally, about 5 percent, or 2 million children, fall into the third category of extreme severe functional impairments (InCrisis, 2007). Using the *DSM-IV*, the average prevalence of functionally impairing psychiatric disorders among children in the United States is 12 percent. This median is also comparable to other countries in the world: Brazil, 12.7 percent; Denmark, 10.1 percent; Puerto Rico, 16.4 percent; Taiwan, 20.3 percent; and United Arab Emirates, 10.4 percent (Ezpeleta et al., 2007).

The National Institute of Mental Health (2011) reported that the prevalence rate of mental illness is 46.3 percent for adolescents between the ages of thirteen and eighteen. Moreover, 21.4 percent in the same age range suffer from a serious and debilitating mental disorder. The study reported no difference between males and females suffering from mental illnesses (46.0 percent and 46.7 percent, respectively).

Recognition of the Potential for Comorbidity in Children

Regarding the types of disorder, the Centers for Disease Control and Prevention's National Health and Nutrition Examination Survey, as cited on the National Institute of Mental Health's (2011) website, reports prevalence data for children between the ages of eight and fifteen and found that approximately 13.1 percent of children had a diagnosable mental disorder within the previous year. Attention deficit/hyperactivity disorder ranks the highest by far (13.1 percent) over other disorders (e.g., mood disorders, 3.7 percent; major depression, 2.7 percent; conduct disorder, 2.1 percent; dysthymia, 1 percent; anxiety disorders, 0.7 percent; panic disorders, 0.4 percent). However, it is not uncommon for a child to have more than one disorder. For example, children with conduct disorder are often depressed.

Along the line of multiple disorders, there is growing evidence suggesting that children who have a substance abuse disorder also have an increased risk of having mental disorder(s) or comorbidities (Substance Abuse and Mental Health Services Administration [SAMHSA], 2002). Because large-scale epidemiological studies do not report prevalence rates for children (Hawkins, 2009), several separate smaller studies have found the prevalence of children who use mental health services and also have a substance abuse disorder to be in a range of 43 percent (US Department of Health and Human Services, 1999) to 76 percent (Hawkins, 2009). The most recent data reported by SAMHSA (2011) collected in 2008 reported that commonly abused substances are alcohol, marijuana, and cocaine. In addition, the majority of children with substance abuse disorders have a current anxiety, mood, or disruptive disorder (Wise, Cuffe, & Fischer, 2001).

Raising Awareness about Immigrant Children's Access to Mental Health Services

A population that is worth mentioning and that needs special attention is US-born children of immigrants. It has been predicted that there will be no population majority by the year 2050. Further, first- and second-generation immigrant children are the fastest-growing segment of the US population (Pumariega, 2007). The National Institute of Mental Health (2007) has reported that, overall, immigrants appear to have lower rates of mental disorders than second- or later-generation individuals. However, racial and ethnic minorities are less likely to have access to mental health services and often receive poorer quality of care than the population in general (US Department of Health and Human Services, 2003).

Theoretical Perspective

A core theory associated with working with children is life-span (development) theory, a component of developmental theory (Herschell, McNeil, & McNeil, 2004). When working with children who may have mental health issues, it is extremely important that practitioners are well versed in the developmental stages of these individuals in order to make the correct diagnosis. In other words, it is important not to mistake an appropriate behavior at a certain age of development for a misdiagnosis of mental problem.

Practice Principles

Successful treatment of children who have mental health or comorbidity issues requires an integrative approach that involves more than just the interaction between a professional mental health worker and the child. Thus, there are basic principles that are formed around the importance of multiple levels of intervention. As illustrated earlier in the case of Max, efforts should be taken to ensure that treatment or intervention takes place on individual, family, and community levels. Three principles supporting these levels of intervention focus on life-span development, community resources, and cultural diversity:

- *Principle of life-span development*—On an individual level, in addition to therapeutic techniques and treatment models, professionals should incorporate life-span developmental theory to clearly discern the appropriateness of specific behaviors and multiple changes that apply to a child (Herschell et al., 2004).

- *Principle of community resources*—On a community and societal level, research has shown that comprehensive and integrated programs that involve entities from the legal, health, recreational, educational, group, family, and community areas have yielded success. Awareness of these factors can promote effective intervention with reaching out to resources that are located in the child's natural setting and can help formulate interventions that fit into these contexts (Kazak et al., 2010).

- *Principle of cultural diversity*—Given the increase in the immigrant population, culturally sensitive practice must be incorporated on all levels (individual, familial, community) starting from the assessment phase and ending with the termination phase, to enhance the chance of success. However, for all the factors listed here to be implemented and effective, there should be an emphasis on training the professionals who deliver and work with the children and their families.

Steps for Implementing Best Practices with Children

There are many treatment models for adolescents with mental health issues. However, some work better than others, and there has been an interest in evaluating the effectiveness of treatment or in seeking evidence of practice. This approach is evidence-based practice, and it "can be defined simply as using clinical interventions that have the best scientific support for their effectiveness" (Shipman & Taussig, 2009, p. 418). Table 19.1 describes ten different treatment models and their corresponding components. However, more research needs to be done on these models, as discussed later in this chapter.

Table 19.1. Children's Best-Practice Interventions and Treatment Components for Child Trauma, Maltreatment, and Co-occurring Disorders

Intervention	Core components	Outcomes	Population
Treatments for child-trauma and maltreated children			
Trauma-focused cognitive behavioral therapy (TF-CBT)	Psychoeducation; strategies for managing distressing feelings, thoughts, and behavior; exposure to and processing of trauma-related memories through narrative; enhancing parenting skills and child safety.	Short-term and proven effectiveness maintained at one- and two-year follow-up.	Used with diverse populations and children in foster care.
Parent-child interaction therapy (PCIT)	Teaching parents relationship-building skills (e.g., praise, reflection, imitation, description, enthusiasm) through training and coaching, training and coaching of parent-child interaction to teach skills focusing on positive behavior management (e.g., effective use of commands, strategies for increasing compliance) with the goal of enhancing quality of parent-child relationship and teaching positive approaches to child behavioral management.	Short-term and proven effectiveness can be maintained over time.	Adapted for diverse populations.
Abuse-focused cognitive behavioral therapy (AF-CBT)	Child-directed skills, parent-directed skills, parent-child or family system; intervention is applied in three phases: psychoeducational and engagement, individual and family skills training, and family applications.	Short term.	Used clinically with urban African American families.
Child-parent psychotherapy (CPP)	Emphasis on the importance of treating mental health problems in the context of the parent-child relationship by working with the parent-child dyad; target treatments include safety, affect regulation, quality of parent-child relationship, and processing of trauma experiences.	At 50 sessions, gains maintained at 6-month follow-up.	Clinical trials conducted with diverse populations.
Treatment for co-occurring disorder			
Motivational enhancement treatment/cognitive behavioral therapy 5 (MET/CBT5)	Learning and practicing coping skills to handle high-risk substance use situations and community reinforcement approach and multidimensional family therapy with the focus on moving the adolescent through the stages of change and developing motivation for change.	Findings suggest MET/CBT5 results in reduction in substance use, greater number of youth in recovery, and low cost of intervention per day of abstinence achieved; results achieved with a 12-session MET/CBT and 7-session CBT program.	Adolescents.

Table 19.1. Children's Best-Practice Interventions and Treatment Components for Child Trauma, Maltreatment, and Co-occurring Disorders—(*Continued*)

Intervention	Core components	Outcomes	Population
Seeking safety	Intervention guided by five practice principles: safety as a priority, integrated treatment of both disorders, a focus on ideals to counteract the loss of ideals in both PTSD and substance abuse, four content areas (cognitive, behavioral, interpersonal, and case management), and attention to therapist processes.	Results for PTSD indicate positive outcomes in terms of reductions in substance abuse, trauma-related symptoms, suicide risk, and depression, along with improvements in social adjustment, family functioning, and problem-solving skills.	Highly flexible in individual or group sessions, single or mixed gender, and session length.
Dialectical behavior therapy (DBT)	Blends cognitive-behavioral therapy with mindfulness and meditation practices and focuses on emotional validation and acceptance coupled with skills training via individual and family therapy; primary challenge is to accept people as they are while at the same time helping them to change.	Findings suggest increase in treatment retention, reduction in suicidal behavior, decrease in psychiatric hospitalizations, decrease in substance abuse, anger and serious behavior problem behaviors, and reduction in interpersonal difficulties.	Adolescent and family.
Family behavior therapy (FBT)	Targets adolescent substance use and associated behavioral problems; uses community reinforcement approach and techniques such as behavioral contracting, stimulus control, urge control, and communication skills training; flexible in treatment setting.	Findings suggest reduction in frequency of alcohol and drug use, decrease in problem behaviors and depression, improved family relationships, and increase in school attendance.	Adolescent and family.
Multidimensional family therapy (MDFT)	Targets multiple domains of risk, protection, and functioning within the youth, his or her family, and community; interventions concentrate on the individual problems, strengths, and goals of the adolescent, as well as on parent issues, parenting and family relationships, and extrafamilial influences; flexible in treatment setting.	Findings suggest reduction in substance use, decrease in internalizing and externalizing psychiatric symptoms, improvement in school performance, and increase in family functioning.	Adolescent and family.
Multisystemic therapy (MST)	Interventions are developed in conjunction with the family with the explicit goal of structuring the youth's environment to promote healthier, less risky behavior; short term (4–6 months) and administered at home or school.	Findings suggest reduction in alcohol and drug use; decrease in psychiatric symptomatology; improvement in family and peer relations; decrease in out-of-home placements; and decrease in criminal activity, rearrests, and days.	Adolescent and family.

Source: Adapted from Hawkins, 2009; Shipman & Taussig, 2009.

The National Child Traumatic Stress Network is another resource for identifying evidence-based practices in child abuse and neglect. It is "a unique collaboration of academic and community-based centers from all of the United States whose mission is to raise the standard of care and to increase access to evidence-based services to traumatized children and their families" (Shipman & Taussig, 2009, p. 419).

What's the Evidence?

Description of evidence-based practice varies, and some practices are more culturally sensitive than others. Hawkins (2009) describes evidence-based practice as "the integration of the best available research with clinical expertise in the context of patient characteristics, culture, and preferences" (p. 207). At its core, evidence-based practice "holds that treatments of whatever theoretical persuasion need to be based on objective and scientifically credible evidence—evidence that is obtained from randomized clinical trials[—]whenever possible" (Ollendick & King, 2004, p. 4). Research on evidence-based practice and effectiveness for children and youth is ongoing.

There have been efforts funded by the US Office for Victims of Crime and the Kauffman Best Practices Project (see Shipman & Taussig, 2009) that aim to identify the best-practice interventions from among twenty-four interventions that address concerns associated with child physical and sexual abuse and their families. The criteria include strength of empirical support, soundness of theoretical foundation, potential for harm, clinical utility, and acceptance among clinicians. Three interventions were identified as best practices: trauma-focused cognitive-behavioral therapy, parent-child interaction therapy, and abuse-focused cognitive-behavioral therapy (Shipman & Taussig, 2009; see also table 19.1).

Other studies (Ollendick & King, 2004; Weisz, Weiss, Alicke, & Klotz, 1987; Weisz, Weiss, Han, Granger, & Morton, 1995) have found behavioral and cognitive-behavioral treatment to fare better than other interventions. For adolescents who have comorbidity disorders, Hawkins (2009) also reported that cognitive-behavioral therapy in conjunction with motivational enhancement interventions are effective.

Herschell et al. (2004) cited multiple meta-analytic reviews reporting efficacious treatment for general and specific childhood disorders. For example, a meta-analytic review by Lonigan, Elbert, and Johnson (1998) reported that of more than three hundred outcomes studies between 1952 and 1993, involving children between the ages of two and eighteen, "children in the intervention groups scored 76 percent to 81 percent better on outcome measures than did children in the control groups" (Herschell et al., 2004, p. 269). There are also promising treatments for children for anxiety disorders, depression, attention deficit/hyperactivity disorder, conduct and oppositional disorders, and autistic disorder (Chorpita et al., 2002). Further, a combination of psychotherapy and medication has shown to be most effective in treating children with a mental health disorder (US Department of Health and Human Services, 1999).

Assessment and Evaluation

Sound assessment, identification, and evaluation of mental disorders are crucial practice components that can lead to accurate diagnosis and treatment recommendations for children with mental health issues. However, the accuracy of the assessment and evaluation process is often difficult to attain given the confluence of the following: children's dynamic growth, which makes it difficult to differentiate the characteristics of a disorder and normal child development behaviors; lack of scientific research on children and adolescents, given that criteria for diagnosing most mental disorders in children derive from those for diagnosing adults; lack of trained and culturally sensitive clinical professionals, thereby forcing concerned parents or caregivers to rely on pediatricians, family doctors, or school counselors who lack diagnostic expertise (US Department of Health and Human Services, 1999); the possibility of a child having overlapping disorders or comorbidity; the fact that young children often do not have the verbal ability to express their thoughts and feelings; and finally, the fact that clinicians sometimes rely on secondhand (proxy) information for the assessment.

Mental health disorders in children can be caused by various factors such as personal (genetic predisposition), intrapersonal (family and surrounding relationships), and environmental (community) factors, or by an interplay of all three. Each level (personal, intrapersonal, and community) has protective and risk factors. Risk factors are associated with an increased probability of onset, greater severity, and longer duration of major health problems. Protective factors refer to conditions that improve the child's resistance to risk factors and disorders. Examples of risk and protective factors in a child's life include family genetic, biological, and psychological history; prenatal care; stressful life events; child maltreatment and abuse; peer pressure and influence; socioeconomic status; and neighborhood or community location. Information on both risk and protective factors should be part of the assessment process. To achieve an accurate diagnosis, depending on the age and developmental ability of the child, an evaluation may require several hours of direct observation, interviews with a child who is able to read and verbalize his or her thoughts and feelings, and administration of standardized questionnaires (i.e., Children's Depression Inventory; Kovacs, 1985). In addition, interviews with the parents or caregivers and records from schools, hospitals, and other pertinent entities should be obtained and analyzed as a part of the assessment process.

In short, a multidimensional, comprehensive assessment should include information about the mental functioning of a child and a clear delineation of all protective and risk factors involved in the child's life. The final product should be a treatment plan that uses all the preceding information and involves the child's family members, support network, and surrounding environment and community to formulate strategies and goals that can best help the child. It is important to note that the assessment and evaluation process does not end once treatment begins; rather, it should be an ongoing and evolving process until treatment goals are achieved.

Implementation Issues

There are several implementation issues, which can be examined from both the child's perspective and the perspective of professional helpers.

Client Perspective

For clients, cultural factors (e.g., shame, stigma, discrimination, privacy, alternative care, client-therapist racial match, premature termination) and structural factors (e.g., cost of treatment, transportation, inaccessibility of services, language, fragmented service delivery system) can greatly interfere with implementation of treatment. For adolescents who suffer from comorbid disorders, there is a lack of cross-trained mental health professionals who are able to help them (Hawkins, 2009).

Mental Health Professional Perspective

Although there are promising treatments, an issue worth noting is that there is a lack of dissemination and implementation of evidence-based psychological treatments, as well as a lack of adequately trained clinicians to competently administer the treatments (McHugh & Barlow, 2010). Ollendick and King (2004) have addressed concerns that identified evidence-based psychological treatments can lead to the "use of treatment manuals [that can guide] mechanical, inflexible interventions and that such 'manually driven' treatments might stifle creativity and innovation in the therapy process and treatments shown to be effective in randomized clinical trials and based largely in university-based settings might not be generalizable or applicable to 'real-life' clinical practice setting" (p. 9).

Provider Competencies

Competence of providers is extremely important to the therapeutic process and successful outcomes when working with children. A helping professional should have the skills to conduct an in-depth assessment, to suggest and provide client-centered interventions, and to facilitate successful and healthy termination. Specifically, the clinician needs to be competent in several areas of practice, and especially in the various evidence-based treatment methods. For example, a clinician working with an adolescent who has depression as well as substance abuse issues needs to have the skills to deal with both problems. The clinician also needs to be able to work with the family and connect the client to the existing resources in the community. In other words, a competent worker is one who is able to implement an effective holistic and integrative care approach. Further, the worker also needs to be culturally competent when it comes to dealing with children and their families, who may have different backgrounds, values, rituals, and ways of dealing with mental and physical health issues from those of the worker.

Future Directions

Taking into consideration some of the barriers listed in the section on implementation, there are three recommendations for future directions. First, mental health professionals must be able to evaluate intervention appropriateness for diverse populations. Second, there needs to be more research addressing methodological challenges such as sample size. Third, work must be done to develop and evaluate strategies for effective dissemination and implementation of children and youth evidence-based practices in community context (Shipman & Taussig, 2009). In the adolescent co-occurring disorder domain, Hawkins (2009) recommends more research on this population, as the research is still in its infancy. For children who have a comorbid diagnosis, there needs to be greater emphasis on prevention and early intervention for the mental health condition, as research shows that mental health problems often precede substance abuse (Hawkins, 2009). Finally, McHugh and Barlow (2010) have suggested that more evaluation on the competence standards after initiating training of clinicians is needed.

Websites

InCrisis provides Internet-based analysis and screening services for parents and caretakers with children who do not have timely or affordable access to qualified mental health-care services. It uses computer-assisted behavioral analyses for children between the ages of eleven and seventeen to help inform all entities (e.g., parents, school, health care professionals) involved with the child and to screen children privately and quickly to identify clinical and behavioral problems, get help for potentially serious problems, save time and money, and measure the value of medications and therapy—http://www.incrisis.org

National Child Treatment Stress Network—http://www.nctsn.org

National Institute of Mental Health—http://www.nih.gov

Surgeon General's Report—http://www.surgeongeneral.gov/library/mentalhealth/home.html

Glossary

Comorbidity: The presence of one or more disorders.

Diagnostic and Statistical Manual of Mental Disorders (DSM): A manual that contains standard criteria to help clinicians classify mental disorders. It is an evolving manual (currently in its fourth edition), and it can be used in conjunction with other tools to help with diagnosis. It helps guide the assessment and treatment process.

Evidence-based practice: Evidence of effectiveness of treatment via empirical research.

References

American Psychiatric Association. (2000). *Diagnostic and statistical manual of mental disorders* (4th ed., text rev.). Washington, DC: Author.

Chorpita, B. F., Yim, L. M., Donkervoet, J. C., Arensdorf, A., Amundsen, M. J., McGee, C., et al. (2002). Toward large-scale implementation of empirically supported treatments of children: A review and observations by the Hawaii Empirical Basis to Services Task Force. *Clinical Psychology: Science and Practice, 9*(2), 165–190.

Ezpeleta, L., Guillamon, N., Granero, R., de la Osa, N., Domenech, J. M., & Moya, I. (2007). Prevalence of mental disorders in children and adolescents from a Spanish slum. *Social Science and Medicine, 64,* 842–849.

Hawkins, E. H. (2009). A tale of two systems: Co-occurring mental health and substance abuse disorders treatment for adolescents. *Annual Review of Psychology, 60,* 197–227.

Herschell, A. D., McNeil, C. B., & McNeil, D. W. (2004). Clinical child psychology's progress in disseminating empirically supported treatments. *Clinical Psychology: Science and Practice, 11*(3), 267–288.

InCrisis (2007). *The prevalence of mental health and addictive disorder.* Retrieved from http://www.incrisis.org/articles/prevalencemhproblems.htm.

Kazak, A. E., Hoagwood, K., Weisz, J. R., Hood, K., Kratochwill T. R., Vargas, L. A., et al. (2010). A meta-systems approach to evidence-based practice for children and adolescents. *American Psychologist, 65*(2), 85–97.

Kovacs, M. (1985). The Children's Depression Inventory. *Psychopharmacology Bulletin, 21,* 995–998.

Lonigan, C. J., Elbert, J. C., & Johnson, S. B. (1998). Empirically supported psychological interventions for children: An overview. *Journal of Clinical Child Psychology, 27,* 138–145.

McHugh, K. R., & Barlow, D. H. (2010). The dissemination and implementation of evidence-based psychological treatments. *American Psychologist, 65*(2), 73–84.

National Institute of Mental Health. (2007). *US-born children of immigrants may have higher risk for mental disorders than parents.* Retrieved from http://www.nimh.nih.gov/science-news/2007/us-born-children-of-immigrants-may-have-higher-risk-for-mental-disorders-than-parents.shtml.

National Institute of Mental Health. (2011). *Any disorder among children.* Retrieved from http://www.nimh.nih.gov/statistics/1ANYDIS_CHILD.shtml.

Ollendick, T. H., & King, N. J. (2004). Empirically supported treatment for children and adolescents: Advances toward evidence-based practice. In P. M. Barrett & T. H. Ollendick (Eds.), *Handbook of interventions that work with children and adolescents: Prevention and treatment* (pp. 3–25). Hoboken, NJ: Wiley.

Pumariega, A. (2007, May 11). *Responding to the mental health needs of immigrant children and families.* Keynote address at the 45th Annual Child Psychiatry Spring Forum, Virginia Commonwealth University, Richmond, VA.

Shipman, K., & Taussig, H. (2009). Mental health treatment of child abuse and neglect: The promise of evidence-based practice. *Pediatric Clinics of North America, 56,* 417–428.

Substance Abuse and Mental Health Services Administration. (2002). *Report to Congress on the prevention and treatment of co-occurring substance abuse disorders and mental disorders.* Retrieved from http://www.samhsa.gov/reports/congress2002/chap4icacd.htm.

Substance Abuse and Mental Health Services Administration. (2011). *Treatment episode data set (TED): Substance abuse treatment admissions aged 12 to 14.* Retrieved from http://oas.samhsa.gov/2k11/015/015SATreatmentAdmissions.htm.

US Department of Health and Human Services. (1999). *Mental health: A report of the Surgeon General.* Retrieved from http://profiles.nlm.nih.gov/ps/retrieve/ResourceMetadata/NNBBHS.

US Department of Health and Human Services. (2003). *Achieving the promise: Transforming Mental Health Care in America* (Final report). Rockville, MD: New Freedom Commission on Mental Health.

Weisz, J. R., Weiss, B., Alicke, M. D., & Klotz, M. L. (1987). Effectiveness of psychotherapy with children and adolescents: A meta-analysis for clinicians. *Journal of Consulting and Clinical Psychology, 55,* 542–549.

Weisz, J. R., Weiss, B., Han, S. S., Granger, D. G., & Morton, T. (1995). Effects of psychotherapy with children and adolescents revisited: A meta-analysis of treatment outcome studies. *Psychological Bulletin, 117,* 450–468.

Wise, B. K., Cuffe, S. P., & Fischer, T. (2001). Dual diagnosis and successful participation of adolescents in substance abuse treatment. *Journal of Substance Abuse Treatment, 21,* 161–165.

PART VI
Organization-Oriented Best Practices: Pulling It All Together

Organization-oriented best practices are those interventions and strategies that are considered vital to the health and success of any behavioral health organization.

Part 6 provides a single chapter that invites readers to consider the critical role of trauma-informed best practices in the health, welfare, and safety of clients, family members, staff, and administrators of behavioral health organizations. This philosophy emerges from the premise that leaders and the organizations they manage are hampered by an absence of resources and supports, which keeps them from obtaining and adopting the skills and processes that have been identified as most likely to support consumers and workers. These gaps, in turn, can perpetuate organizational environments that induce more trauma than relieve it. So before practitioners and leaders apply any of the best practices identified in this book, it is recommended that entire organizations reexamine their basic assumptions about how the work environment promotes safety and nonviolence across physical, psychological, social, and moral domains. The Sanctuary Model is one such organizational tool for doing so.

In chapter 20, "The Sanctuary Model: A Best-Practices Approach to Organizational Change," Bloom provides a sterling review of the principles and practice model of a trauma-informed organizational approach that guides organizations to develop and model an atmosphere of hope and nonviolence.

20

The Sanctuary Model:
A Best-Practices Approach to
Organizational Change

Sandra Bloom

The Sanctuary Model is an evidence-supported, theory-based, trauma-informed, whole organizational approach that provides a clear and structured methodology for creating trauma-informed systems of care. The model was developed by the Sanctuary Institute, part of Andrus Children's Center in Yonkers, New York. The goal of implementing the model is to enable organizations to more effectively provide a cohesive context in which healing from psychological and social traumatic experience can be addressed. The Sanctuary Model challenges organizations to reexamine their basic assumptions concerning the extent to which social service environments promote safety and nonviolence across physical, psychological, social, and moral domains for everyone involved—clients, family members, staff, and administrators. The Sanctuary Model requires an active process of breaking down institutional, societal, professional, and communication barriers that isolate administrators, staff, family members, and clients from one another. Simultaneously, the rebuilding process involves consciously learning new ways to relate as interdependent community members, creating and modeling healthy and supportive relationships among individuals, and developing an atmosphere of hope and nonviolence. As such, the intervention aims both to strengthen the therapeutic community environment and to empower people to influence their own lives and communities in positive ways. We begin the chapter with a review of a case of organizational change in a psychiatric hospital that implemented the Sanctuary Model (box 20.1).

Box 20.1. Case Study: Using the Sanctuary Model in a Psychiatric Hospital

The administrators of a psychiatric hospital recognize that most of the adults and young people they treat are survivors of trauma and multiple forms of adversity, but they also realize that there are significant barriers to appropriately addressing those problems. Lengths of stay have been shortened, funding for services has been radically decreased, training time has been greatly attenuated, and the staff they hire are often insufficiently trained and supervised for the demands of the job. The result is that there has been a steady rise in staff turnover, staff and patient injuries, workmen's compensation costs, and the use of coercive interventions. A long-term employee who remembers a time when things were very different in this organization brings some information about the Sanctuary model to the attention of the hospital administrators. After conversations among themselves, with the Sanctuary Institute staff, and with other program administrators who have already adopted the Sanctuary model, the hospital leadership decides to commit to a three-year, challenging method of organizational change. A team of key formal and informal leaders attend a five-day training during which this team—the Steering Committee—begins to wrestle with the implications of trauma theory for their patients and for their staff, the ways in which the staff and the organization itself frequently engage in problematic processes that parallel the problems of the patients. When the Steering Committee returns to the organization, they gather a larger core team representing a wider variety of voices from the organization, including, whenever possible, some "people with lived experience" of the mental health system, and they begin working through the Sanctuary model's implementation manual and the direct-care and indirect-care staff training manuals, which guide them through the process of confronting the many-layered interpersonal and systemic problems that pose barriers to delivering trauma-informed services. Technical assistance provided by Sanctuary Institute faculty who have already been through this process supports key change efforts and helps prevent backsliding. The leadership guide the entire staff in adopting the components of the Sanctuary Toolkit including engaging patients in intensive psychoeducational groups around the ways in which trauma and adversity have affected them. Community Meetings, Red Flag Reviews, and the organizing framework of SELF help the administrators, staff, patients, and family members get on the same page about treatment process and goals and while holding one another accountable to the value system encapsulated in the Sanctuary commitments that guide interpersonal and community interactions. Violent episodes rapidly decrease within the hospital, thereby reducing injuries, complaints, staff turnover, critical incidents, and coercive methods. Staff notice that patients are much clearer about the goals of treatment, more motivated toward change, and making more progress in treatment. Clinical staff are now eager to embrace more trauma-specific forms of treatment and are thereby achieving better results. Administrators have to field many fewer complaints that stem from mistreatment of staff or of patients, and so they are able to more successfully address the organizational demands for better methods of adaptive change in a constantly changing environment.

Background

Originally developed from 1985 to 1991 in an acute-care, community-hospital-based psychiatric unit for adults, from 1991 to its closure in 2001, the Sanctuary was an inpatient program designed to treat the complex problems of adults who had been maltreated as children. The first published description of the program came out in 1994, in which I quoted a colleague remarking on the now-often-repeated phrase "It's not what's wrong with you; it's what happened to you" (Bloom, 1994, p. 476). The name itself derived from the first chapter describing the inpatient treatment of trauma survivors, a program for Vietnam veterans, in which I described "sanctuary trauma," the expectation of finding a welcoming and healing environment and finding instead more trauma (Bloom, 1997). In 1997, I published *Creating Sanctuary: Toward the Evolution of Sane Societies*, which described the development of what has since become known as a trauma-informed approach (Bloom, 1997).

After the publication of that book, in the late 1990s, the Jewish Board of Family and Children's Services of New York obtained a grant to study the implementation of the Sanctuary Model in residential treatment programs for children through the National Institute of Mental Health and asked me to collaborate in the development and implementation of that project. The randomized controlled study showed positive findings.

In 2000, together with my colleagues, I began consulting with Andrus Children's Center in Yonkers, New York, and after the Sanctuary program itself closed in 2001, the locus of development shifted to Andrus. In 2005, we created the Sanctuary

Institute, a reeducation methodology and certification program to train mental health and social service organizations in the Sanctuary Model. As of 2011, more than two hundred programs, including a wide variety of mental health, educational, and social service programs for children and adults, nationally and internationally, have been trained in the Sanctuary Model.

The first ten years of development of the Sanctuary were captured in *Creating Sanctuary*, in which the notion of "hurt people, hurt people" was explored (Bloom, 1997, p. 237). The wider public health implications of trauma and its effects were similarly developed in *Bearing Witness: Violence and Collective Responsibility* (Bloom & Reichert, 1998). Most recently, two of the current developers of the Sanctuary Model coauthored a volume describing the impact of organizational stress and the trauma-organized systems that result: *Destroying Sanctuary: The Crisis in Human Service Delivery Systems* (Bloom & Farragher, 2010). Currently in press, the next volume of the series, *Restoring Sanctuary: A New Operating System For Organizations*, will describe in more detail the process of implementing the Sanctuary Model (Bloom & Farragher, in press).

Theoretical Perspective

The Sanctuary Model is structured around a theoretical philosophy of belief and practice informed by the scientific study of attachment and child development and the impact of adversity, toxic stress, and trauma. Attachment between parent and child results in the human operating system, whereas toxic stress disrupts that operating system. Human beings and human organizations are living systems that adapt to changing conditions in complex ways. From these scientific findings new mental models for how we view human problems are beginning to emerge. The notion of parallel processes helps explain how trauma-organized systems develop and provide a framework for helping systems to recover and, in doing so, to become trauma informed.

Principles

In the early years, the practice principles for the Sanctuary Model were grounded in ideas surrounding the eighteenth-century development of moral treatment and the twentieth-century creation of therapeutic communities. Later, the Sanctuary Model evolved as a well-developed philosophical approach grounded in the complex biopsychosocial and existential adaptations that individuals and groups make to cope with overwhelming and repetitive stress. As an organizational approach, the Sanctuary Model views systems as alive and therefore as subject to conscious and unconscious dynamics similar to those of the individuals who work in and are served by those systems.

The phrase "creating sanctuary" refers to the shared experience of creating and maintaining safety in any social environment. In the Sanctuary Model, the notion of safety encompasses physical, psychological, social, and moral safety. The philosophical tenets of the Sanctuary Model are embodied in the Sanctuary Commitments. The seven Sanctuary Commitments are tied directly to trauma-informed treatment goals. The process of creating sanctuary begins with getting everyone on the same page, which means surfacing, sharing, arguing about, and finally agreeing on the basic values, beliefs, guiding principles, and philosophical principles that are to guide decisions, decision-making processes, conflict resolution skills, and behavior.

The Sanctuary Commitments are a core component of the Sanctuary Model. These values structure the organizational norms, determine the organizational culture, and apply to everyone in the organization. The commitments represent the guiding principles for implementation of the Sanctuary Model—the basic structural elements of the Sanctuary "operating system"—and each commitment supports trauma-recovery goals for clients, staff, and the organization as a whole. All seven Sanctuary Commitments (or principles) are complexly interactive and interdependent:

- *Principle of commitment to nonviolence*—Requires a shared definition of safety, the universal development of safety skills, trust, and resilience in the face of stress.

- *Principle of commitment to emotional intelligence*—Fosters emotional management skills, respect for emotional labor, the minimization of the paralyzing effects of fear, and an expanded awareness of problematic cognitive-behavioral patterns and how to change them.

- *Principle of commitment to social learning*—Based on the need to build cognitive skills, to improve learning and decisions, to promote healthy dissent, to restore memory, and ultimately to develop the skills necessary to sustain a learning organization.

- *Principle of commitment to open communication*—Organizations must overcome barriers to healthy communication, discuss the "undiscussables," and thereby undo organizational alexithymia while increasing transparency, improving conflict management skills, and reinforcing healthy boundaries.

- *Principle of commitment to democracy*—Supports the development of the civic skills of participation, self-control, self-discipline, the healthy exercise of authority, and leadership while overcoming learned helplessness.

- *Principle of commitment to social responsibility*—Aims to harness the energy of reciprocity and a yearning for justice by rebuilding restorative social connection skills, establishing healthy and fair attachment relationships, and transforming vengeance into social justice.

- *Principle of commitment to growth and change*—Represents a recognition that all change involves loss and that if people are to cease repeating irrelevant or destructive past patterns of thought, feeling, and behavior, they must be able to envision, be guided by, skillfully plan, and prepare for a different and better future.

Steps for Implementing the Sanctuary Model

The Sanctuary Model offers two approaches to implementing the Sanctuary Commitments: use of the Safety, Emotional Management, Loss, and Future (SELF) Model and the Sanctuary Toolkit.

The SELF acronym represents the four key interdependent aspects of recovery from bad experiences. The SELF Model provides a nonlinear, cognitive-behavioral therapeutic approach for facilitating movement in individuals and organizations, and it is used as a compass to allow for the exploration of four key domains of healing:

1. Safety (attaining safety in self, relationships, and environment)

2. Emotional management (identifying levels of various emotions and modulating emotion in response to memories, persons, and events)

3. Loss (feeling grief and dealing with personal losses and recognizing that all change involves loss)

4. Future (trying out new roles and ways of relating, behaving as a "survivor" to ensure personal safety, and envisioning a different and better future).

The SELF acronym is a simple and effective linguistic tool that enables a wide variety of people to get on the same page about treatment goals, planning, and everyday interactions, without losing the true complexity that is involved in treating very complex problems.

The Sanctuary Toolkit comprises a range of practical skills that enable individuals and organizations to more effectively deal with difficult situations, build community, develop a deeper understanding of the effects of adversity and trauma, and build a common language while remaining consistent in practicing the Sanctuary Commitments. The tool kit guides participants in focusing on six different activities. These activities are listed here along with descriptions of each activity:

1. The safety plan is a list of simple activities that a person can choose when feeling overwhelmed so that the person can avoid engaging in the unsafe, out-of-control, or toxic behavior that he or she is accustomed to resorting to under stress, and instead can engage in an activity that is safe, effective, and self-soothing. In the Sanctuary Model everyone in the organization must develop and use safety plans.

2. Community meetings are deliberate, repetitive transition rituals intended to psychologically move people from some activity that they have been doing into a new group psychological space, thus preparing the way for collective thought and action. In the Sanctuary Model, community meetings are instituted systemwide, from executive meetings to patient interactions.

3. SELF psychoeducational groups help clients shift their understanding of what has happened to them, how they have responded to those events, and the role they must play in their own recovery.

4. Red-flag meetings provide a team with a structured method to respond to any critical incident or concern, to any circumstance that arises that the entire community must respond to as a group so that an existing problem does not escalate to become a bigger problem.

5. SELF team meetings are active, focused meetings in which every member feels comfortable talking and listening, is engaged and contributes, shares insights, and generates new ideas.

6. SELF treatment planning offers a structured, nonhierarchical approach for measuring client progress in treatment while evaluating goals and current

obstacles to improvement, using a language that clients, family members, and all levels of staff can share.

What's the Evidence?

The desired outcomes for the Sanctuary Model are complex; to some extent each organization must decide on them, as the model targets such a wide variety of programs. At a minimum the aim is to eliminate interpersonal violence in all of its forms, as well as all coercive forms of treatment. Early research efforts were both qualitative and quantitative, demonstrating that it was possible to use the Sanctuary Model as a method for reducing violence and coercive forms of intervention in adult psychiatric settings (Bennington-Davis & Murphy, 2005; Bills & Bloom, 1998; Wright, Woo, Muller, Fernandes, & Kraftcheck, 2003). The Sanctuary Model as it is applied to residential child care is considered evidence supported, on the basis of a controlled, randomized study that was funded by the National Institute of Mental Health (Rivard et al., 2004). Subsequent research also demonstrated significant differences in organizational culture in organizations using the Sanctuary Model (McSparren & Motley, 2010).

Assessment and Evaluation

In terms of assessment and evaluation, we look for outcomes that reflect change in measures that the organization has easy access to and that include decreases in workers' compensation claims; in staff and patient injuries; in staff turnover; and in the utilization of coercive measures like seclusion, restraint, and coercion around medications. Less easy to measure are substantial changes in staff attitudes toward patients and toward one another, more clinical sophistication, better assessment and case formulation, and significant increases in the application of complex strategies for change. If all is progressing well, we expect to see an increased clinical commitment to employ trauma-specific forms of treatment by well-trained and supervised staff.

Implementation Issues

Implementation of the Sanctuary Model begins with attendance at the Sanctuary Institute, a five-day intensive training experience. Sanctuary is a registered trademark and the right to use the Sanctuary name is contingent on engagement in the certified training program and an agreement to participate in an ongoing, peer-review certification process. It requires a several-year commitment, and research is under way in the hope of moving the Sanctuary Model from an evidence-supported to an evidence-based approach.

Teams of five to eight people, from various levels of the organization, including executive leadership, come together during the Sanctuary Institute's five-day training to learn from our faculty, who are colleagues from other organizations implementing the Sanctuary Model. These teams become the Sanctuary Steering Committee for their organization. Together they are introduced to the practices of the Sanctuary Model and take home with them the implementation, staff training manuals, and psychoeducational manuals created to assist and structure the implementation process (for steps to implement the Sanctuary Model, see figure 20.1).

Figure 20.1. Implementing the Sanctuary Model of Organizational Change

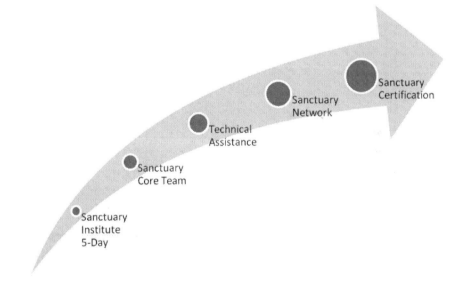

Provider Competencies

Adopting the Sanctuary Model requires a major leadership commitment. Organizational leaders must model the Sanctuary Commitments to nonviolence, emotional intelligence, social learning, open communication, democracy, social responsibility, and growth and change in the way they interact with one another, with staff members, and with clients. The more frequently the other staff members see leaders using the Sanctuary Commitments, SELF, and the Sanctuary Toolkit in everyday interactions, the more rapidly the organizational culture will change.

The first task of the Sanctuary Steering Committee is to go back to their organization and create a core team—a larger, multidisciplinary team that expands its reach into the entire organization. It is this core team that will be the activators of the entire system. The core team is required to have representatives from every level of the organization, to ensure that every "voice" is heard. It is vital that all key organizational leaders become actively involved in the process of change and participate in the core team. In addition to the curricula and manual created to support the implementation process, ongoing consultation and technical assistance from Sanctuary faculty members guide organizations through the process of Sanctuary implementation that extends over three years and leads to Sanctuary certification.

Once an organization has committed to adopting the Sanctuary Model by attending the Sanctuary Institute's five-day training, the organization becomes a part of the Sanctuary Network, a learning community of practice that extends nationally and internationally and that involves many different kinds of mental health and social service organizations, all committed to the development of trauma-informed services.

The Sanctuary implementation manuals systematically guide the process of organizational change over three years. After three years, organizations are encouraged to seek Sanctuary certification, a peer-review process informed by a set of standards that represent the evaluation "We are a Sanctuary organization" at this point in time. Recertification occurs every three years.

Future Directions

Scientific advances in understanding the complex problems associated with exposure to adversity, toxic stress, and trauma across the life span require a radical reformulation of how all of our mental health and social services respond to people who need our help. As a species we are good at responding to acute emergencies like terrorism and hurricanes, but we are less prepared to address the slow-rolling, disastrous impact of chronic stress and trauma on the lives of individuals, families, organizations, and entire societies. Exposure to chronic stress is the greatest public health challenge of the twenty-first century. The publishers and authors of this guidebook hope that in providing these summary accounts, we can promote more rapid dissemination of critical knowledge aimed at positive changes in health, mental health, and social well-being for all of us.

Websites

Andrus Children's Center—http://www.andruschildren.org

Sanctuary—http://sanctuaryweb.com

Sanctuary Institute—http://www.sanctuaryweb.com/institute.php

Glossary

Parallel process: A notion that helps explain how trauma-organized systems develop and provide a framework for helping systems to recover and, in doing so, become trauma informed.

Sanctuary Model: An evidence-supported, theory-based, trauma-informed, whole organizational approach that provides a clear and structured methodology for creating trauma-informed systems of care.

SELF: An acronym for the Safety, Emotional Management, Loss, and Future Model, which represents the four key interdependent aspects of recovery from bad experiences; provides a nonlinear, cognitive-behavioral therapeutic approach for facilitating movement in individuals and organizations.

References

Bennington-Davis, M., & Murphy, T. (2005). *Restraint and seclusion: The model for eliminating their use in healthcare.* Marblehead, MA: HCPro/Opus. (Available from the first author, at maggie.bennington-davis@cascadiabhc.org.)

Bills, L. J., & Bloom, S. L. (1998). From chaos to sanctuary: Trauma-based treatment for women in a state hospital systems. In B. L. Levin, A. K. Blanch, & A. Jennings (Eds.), *Women's health services: A public health perspective.* Thousand Oaks, CA: Sage.

Bloom, S. L. (1994). The Sanctuary Model: Developing generic inpatient programs for the treatment of psychological trauma. In M. B. Williams & J. F. Sommer (Eds.), *Handbook of post-traumatic therapy: A practical guide to intervention, treatment, and research* (pp. 474–491). Westport, CT: Greenwood.

Bloom, S. L. (1997). *Creating sanctuary: Toward the evolution of sane societies.* New York: Routledge.

Bloom, S. L., & Farragher, B. (2010). *Destroying sanctuary: The crisis in human service delivery systems.* New York: Oxford University Press.

Bloom, S. L., & Farragher, B. (In press). *Restoring sanctuary: A new operating system for organizations.* New York: Oxford University Press.

Bloom, S. L., & Reichert, M. (1998). *Bearing witness: Violence and collective responsibility.* Binghamton NY: Haworth Press.

McSparren, W., & Motley, D. (2010). How to improve the process of change. *Non-Profit World, 28*(6), 14–15.

Rivard, J. C., McCorkle, D., Duncan, M. E., Pasquale, L. E., Bloom, S. L., & Abramovitz, R. (2004). Implementing a trauma recovery framework for youths in residential treatment. *Child and Adolescent Social Work Journal, 21*(5), 529–550.

Wright, D. C., Woo, W. L., Muller, R. T., Fernandes, C. B., & Kraftcheck, E. R. (2003). An investigation of trauma-centered in-patient treatment for adult survivors of abuse. *Child Abuse and Neglect, 27*, 393–406.

Concluding Remarks—Are We There Yet? Ensuring Quality Best Practices

Vikki L. Vandiver

In the preface, we opened with dual questions: What are the best practices that I can offer my clients, and where do I go to get them? After reading this book, we hope you have answers to those questions. However, it is fitting to end with another question: How do we ensure that what we offer meets an established standard of quality? What we haven't discussed yet is the *quality* of these mental health best practices. It's one thing for an organization to offer a menu of best practices, but it's altogether different when one begins to ask how to assess the quality of those practices.

Although there is no one perfect standard of what constitutes a best practice in quality mental health care, there are global indicators that administrators, policy makers, and practitioners can look to for guidance in program and organizational self-assessments. Adapting from the seminal work on quality health and mental health care produced by the Institute of Medicine's (2006) Quality Chasm series, let's conclude our pocket guide with a recap of five core aims or indicators for establishing high-quality care in the delivery of best practices in mental health:

1. *Safe*—Avoid primary and/or secondary injury or trauma to clients and staff from the care that is intended to help them.

2. *Effective*—Provide services based on scientific knowledge to all who could benefit and refrain for providing services to those not likely to benefit, avoiding underuse and overuse, respectfully.

3. *Patient-person centered or directed*—Provide care that is respectful and responsive to individual client preferences, needs, and values, ensuring that values guide all clinical decisions.

4. *Timely*—Reduce waits and potentially harmful delays in care for both those who receive care and those who give care.

5. *Equitable*—Provide care that does not vary in quality because of personal characteristics such as gender, ethnicity, geographic locations, and socioeconomic status. (pp. 8, 9)

These five indicators can be a starting point for determining how your organization or community establishes benchmarks or targets to assess the performance and outcomes of the best practices in use.

Last, the goal of this pocket book has been to provide readers with a useful reference guide to some of the most commonly applied best-practice interventions, approaches, and programs used in community mental health settings. As noted throughout this book, best practices are those activities and programs that are in keeping with the best possible evidence about what works. The authors have defined and illustrated many examples of mental health best practices, some reporting findings of randomized, controlled studies, and others reporting practices that are considered proven, promising, and/or emerging. Core themes across all chapters have included choice, wellness, respect, recovery, hope, continuous healing relationships, and customization of services based on client and family needs, staff skill, and community resources.

In closing, the topics covered in this book reflect information about the current evidence to inform decision making about the different elements of care that can ideally exist in each local community mental health system. Descriptions of best practices in many ways resemble descriptions of ideal service delivery systems, although in real-world practice, systems are often far from the ideal. But with an eye for quality and an ear for listening and learning what works, mental health systems, the clients who participate in them, and the staff who care for those clients can all make it a little more ideal—if we can only get there.

Reference

Institute of Medicine. (2006). *Improving the quality of healthcare for mental and substance use conditions: Quality Chasm Series.* Washington, DC: National Academies Press.

Contributors

William Anthony, PhD, professor emeritus, College of Health and Rehabilitation Sciences, Boston University (Boston, Massachusetts)

Kia J. Bentley, PhD, professor, School of Social Work, Virginia Commonwealth University (Richmond, Virginia)

Sandra Bloom, MD, associate professor, Department of Health Management and Policy, School of Public Health, Drexel University, and president, Community Works (Philadelphia, Pennsylvania)

Gary R. Bond, PhD, professor of psychiatry, Dartmouth Psychiatric Research Center, Geisel School of Medicine at Dartmouth (Lebanon, New Hampshire)

David S. Derezotes, PhD, professor and chair, Practice and Mental Health, and director, Bridge Clinic, College of Social Work, University of Utah (Salt Lake City, Utah)

Robert E. Drake, MD, PhD, Andre Thomson Professor of Psychiatry and professor of community medicine, and director, Dartmouth Psychiatric Research Center (Lebanon, New Hampshire)

Rick Forbess, MSSW, associate director of training, Center for Psychiatric Rehabilitation, Boston University (Boston, Massachusetts)

Kathleen Furlong-Norman, MEd, MSW, managing editor, *Psychiatric Rehabilitation Journal*, Boston University (Boston, Massachusetts)

Timothy D. Gearhart, LCSW, Four County Community Mental Health Center (Rochester, Indiana)

Susan Gingerich, MSW, independent trainer and consultant (Philadelphia, Pennsylvania)

Sherilyn Goldstone, PhD, Orygen Youth Health Research Center (Parkville, Victoria, Australia)

Benjamin Henwood, PhD, assistant professor, School of Social Work, University of Southern California (Los Angeles, California)

Marina Kukla, PhD, associated health postdoctoral fellow, Health Services Research and Development Department, Richard L. Roudebush VA Medical Center (Indianapolis, Indiana)

Sungkyu Lee, MSW, PhD, assistant professor, College of Social Work, University of Tennessee (Knoxville, Tennessee)

G. Alan Marlatt, PhD, professor and director, Addictive Behaviors Research Center, Department of Psychology, University of Washington (Seattle, Washington)

Susan E. Mason, PhD, professor of social work and sociology, Wurzweiler School of Social Work, Yeshiva University (New York City, New York)

Patrick McGorry, MD, PhD, FRCP, FRANZCP, professor of youth mental health, University of Melbourne; executive director, Orygen Research Centre; and director of clinical services, Orygen Youth Health (Melbourne, Australia)

Alan B. McGuire, PhD, research health scientist, VA Health Services Research and Development Center of Excellence on Implementing Evidence-Based Practices, Roudebush VA Medical Center, and assistant research scientist, Department of Psychology, Indiana University–Purdue University Indianapolis (Indianapolis, Indiana)

Kim T. Mueser, PhD, executive director, Center for Psychiatric Rehabilitation, and professor of occupational therapy, Boston University (Boston, Massachusetts)

Sara Bressi Nath, PhD, MSW, associate professor, Graduate School of Social Work and Social Research, Bryn Mawr College (Bryn Mawr, Pennsylvania)

Peter V. Nguyen, PhD, LCSW, associate professor, School of Social Work, Virginia Commonwealth University (Richmond, Virginia)

Madeleine S. Rafferty, BA, associate research scientist, Dartmouth Psychiatric Research Center (Lebanon, New Hampshire)

Michelle P. Salyers, PhD, associate professor, Department of Psychology, Indiana University–Purdue University Indianapolis; codirector, ACT of Indiana; research scientist, Center for Health Services Research, Regenstrief Institute Inc., and Center for Health Services and Outcomes Research, Indiana University

Phyllis Solomon, PhD, professor, School of Social Policy and Practice, University of Pennsylvania (Philadelphia, Pennsylvania)

John Spence, PhD, MSW, NW Indian Training Associates (Salem, Oregon), and adjunct assistant professor, School of Social Work, Portland State University (Portland, Oregon)

Victoria Stanhope, PhD, MSW, assistant professor, Silver School of Social Work, New York University (New York City, New York)

Laura Stull, PhD, psychosocial rehabilitation postdoctoral resident, VA San Diego Healthcare System and Department of Psychology, Indiana University–Purdue University Indianapolis (San Diego, California)

Sam Tsemberis, PhD, founder and CEO, Pathways to Housing; faculty member, Department of Psychiatry, Columbia University Medical Center (New York City, New York)

Karen V. Unger, EdD, president, Rehabilitation through Education, and research associate professor, Graduate School of Education, Portland State University (Portland, Oregon)

Vikki L. Vandiver, DrPH, MSW, professor and associate dean, School of Social Work, Portland State University, and affiliate professor, Department of Psychiatry, Oregon Health and Science University (Portland, Oregon)

Joseph Walsh, PhD, professor, School of Social Work, and affiliate professor, Department of Psychology, Virginia Commonwealth University (Richmond, Virginia)

Justin Walthers, BS, research assistant, Center for Alcohol and Addiction Studies, Brown University (Providence, Rhode Island)

Katie Witkiewitz, PhD, associate professor, Department of Psychology, University of New Mexico (Albuquerque, New Mexico)

Yin-Ling Irene Wong, PhD, associate professor, School of Social Policy and Practice, University of Pennsylvania (Philadelphia, Pennsylvania)

Index

About the Editor

Vikki L. Vandiver, DrPH, MSW, is professor and associate dean for academic affairs, School of Social Work, Portland State University, and affiliate professor, Department of Psychiatry, School of Medicine, Oregon Health and Science University. She has worked in the field of community mental health for more than thirty-five years and currently maintains a mental health consulting practice with a specialty in mental health policy and equine-assisted mental health treatment. Her research, publishing, and teaching interests include mental health promotion, evidence-based practices, traumatic brain injury, equine-assisted therapy with vulnerable populations, and health and mental health policy. She previously served on the Institute of Medicine's Study Committee on Traumatic Brain Injury and served for seventeen years as chair or member on the board of directors of a local behavioral-health-care organization. In her spare time, she rides her cranky saddlebred mare, Cindy-Lou, and enjoys every achy minute of it.